Youth and Jobs in Rural Africa

Youth and Jobs in Rural Africa

Beyond Stylized Facts

Edited by

VALERIE MUELLER

and

JAMES THURLOW

INTERNATIONAL
FOOD POLICY
RESEARCH
INSTITUTE

IFPRI

OXFORD
UNIVERSITY PRESS

OXFORD
UNIVERSITY PRESS

Great Clarendon Street, Oxford, OX2 6DP,
United Kingdom

Oxford University Press is a department of the University of Oxford.
It furthers the University's objective of excellence in research, scholarship,
and education by publishing worldwide. Oxford is a registered trade mark of
Oxford University Press in the UK and in certain other countries

© International Food Policy Research Institute 2019

The moral rights of the authors have been asserted

First Edition published in 2019
Impression: 1

Published in the United States of America by Oxford University Press
198 Madison Avenue, New York, NY 10016, United States of America

British Library Cataloguing in Publication Data
Data available

Library of Congress Control Number: 2019952033

ISBN 978-0-19-884805-9

DOI: 10.1093/oso/9780198848059.003.0001

Printed and bound in Great Britain by
Clays Ltd, Elcograf S.p.A.

Links to third party websites are provided by Oxford in good faith and
for information only. Oxford disclaims any responsibility for the materials
contained in any third party website referenced in this work.

Any opinions stated in the book are those of the author(s) and
are not necessarily representative of or endorsed by IFPRI.

Preface

The prospect of widespread youth unemployment in Sub-Saharan Africa (henceforth 'Africa') is a serious concern for governments today, both on the subcontinent and in developed countries. Underlying this is a sense of alarm or urgency, borne out of the view that Africa's 'youth bulge' is an unprecedented global challenge, and that African economies will struggle to absorb enough young job seekers in the coming decades. Concerns are particularly pronounced in *rural* Africa, where most of the world's poor population reside and where farming is still the main livelihood for most households. The conventional view is that African youth do not aspire to work in agriculture, because the sector is characterized by low productivity and is far from the dynamic lifestyles offered by cities. Yet job prospects in Africa's cities and towns are also limited, and so most young Africans will inevitably need to find work somewhere in the rural economy.

While Africa's youth bulge presents a challenge, it can also be viewed as an opportunity for rural development. A young and better-educated workforce might encourage greater use of more sophisticated farm technologies, commercial agricultural practices, and an expansion of rural nonfarm enterprises. These are crucial steps for accelerating agricultural transformation in Africa, and young men and women could be the 'agents of change' that the region so badly needs. The debate around youth employment in Africa is therefore one of contrasts—between urgent concern on the one hand and cautious optimism on the other.

Although African youth receive greater attention today from researchers and policymakers, there are still major gaps in our knowledge. Most reports from international organizations, for example, adopt a regional perspective and identify general trends and constraints. This overlooks differences between African countries. While some studies do consider youth employment within countries, these rarely focus on the specific challenges facing youth in rural areas. As a result, many policies aimed at rural youth in Africa are based on stylized facts drawn from cross-country data and general frameworks.

This book questions some of the stylized facts: Is Africa's youth bulge unprecedented? Are youth more likely than adults to adopt modern farm technologies and practices? Are youth more likely to engage in rural nonfarm activities or migrate to urban centres? Are policymakers adequately responding to the youth employment challenge, and are rural youth themselves mobilizing and demanding policy reforms from their governments?

To answer these questions, this book presents a series of thematic and country case studies that analyse household and firm surveys across a range of country contexts. The book's country focus and use of survey data better reflects the wide variations in trends and constraints observed across and within African countries. The book's focus on rural Africa and the participation of youth in agricultural transformation fills an important gap in our understanding.

This book finds that a balance between alarm and optimism is warranted. Addressing youth employment in Africa is a global challenge, but it is one that was overcome by other developing regions when they underwent similar demographic transitions three decades ago. The pressure to create jobs in rural areas is acute, given that Africa's rural population is growing, and its rural economy is underdeveloped. Yet evidence also suggests that agriculture is transforming in many countries, albeit slowly, and that youth are often participating in this process. Unfortunately, the idea that youth are better positioned than adults to adopt new farm technologies or run successful nonfarm businesses is not borne out in most of the book's case study countries. Even where there is evidence that youth are leading agricultural transformation, the differences between adults and youth are small or the transformation process itself is modest.

More needs to be done by governments to help youth in rural Africa. However, the book finds that, while youth employment is a major policy goal today, policies themselves often fall short of addressing the constraints facing young job seekers. This partly reflects a lack of understanding about country-specific constraints and opportunities—a gap that this book only begins to address. Fortunately, while the policy reforms and actions needed to address Africa's youth bulge are daunting, the book finds that there is increasing alignment between African governments, who have made youth employment a policy priority, and African youth, who are demanding policies to improve their job prospects.

Acknowledgements

We are grateful to four anonymous reviewers who provided comments at different stages of the book. We also appreciate World Development and Journal of Development Studies for granting us permission to reprint the tables in Chapters 7 and 8, respectively. The research in the book was conducted as part of and funded by the CGIAR Research Programme on Policies, Institutions, and Markets (PIM), which is led by the International Food Policy Research Institute (IFPRI) and carried out with support from the CGIAR Trust Fund and through bilateral funding agreements. The United States Agency for International Development (USAID) provided funding for the Ghana chapter via its support for IFPRI's Ghana Strategy Support Programme (grant number: EEM-G-00-04-00013). The United Kingdom's Department for International Development (DFID) provided funding for the Malawi chapter via its support for IFPRI's Malawi Strategy Support Programme (grant number: 203824-106). The International Growth Centre provided funding for the Tanzania chapter (grant number: 1-VCC-VTZA-VXXXX-40414).

Contents

List of Figures

List of Tables

List of Abbreviations and Acronyms

ACLED	Armed Conflict Location and Event Data
ADLI	Agricultural development led industrialization
AfDB	African Development Bank
ANPEJ	National Agency for the Promotion of Youth Employment
ANSD	Senegalese National Agency for Statistics and Demography
ARD	Agricultural research and development
AU	African Union
BRELA	Business Registration and Licensing Agency
CAADP	Comprehensive Africa Agriculture Development Programme
CSA	Central Statistical Agency (of Ethiopia)
CTA	Technical Centre for Agricultural and Rural Cooperation
EA	Enumeration areas
EAP	East Asia and the Pacific
ERSS	Ethiopia Rural Socioeconomic Survey
ESAM	Senegal Household Survey
ESPS	Senegal Poverty Monitoring Survey
ESS	Ethiopia Socioeconomic Survey
FAO	Food and Agriculture Organization
FEES	Formal Employment and Earning Survey
FEP	Food for Education Programme
FEWSNET	Famine Early Warning Systems Network
FISP	Farm Input Subsidy Programme
GDP	Gross domestic product
GGDC	Groningen Growth and Development Centre
GLSS	Ghana Living Standards Survey
GSS	Ghana Statistical Service
Ha	Hectare
HBS	Household Budget Survey
HH	Household
HIES	Household Income and Expenditure Survey
HIPC	Heavily indebted poor countries
HIV	Human immunodeficiency virus
HQ	Headquarters
HR	High-return
IIA	Independent of irrelevant alternatives
ICA	Integrated Country Approach
ID	Identification
IEG	(World Bank) Independent Evaluation Group
IFAD	International Fund for Agricultural Development

IFI	International financial institution
IFPRI	International Food Policy Research Institute
IHPS	Integrated Household Panel Survey
IHS	(Malawi) Integrated Household Survey
ILC	International Labour Conference
ILFS	Integrated Labour Force Survey
ILO	International Labour Organization
ILS	International labour standards
IMF	International Monetary Fund
IOM	International Organization for Migration
IPUMS	Integrated Public Use Microdata Series
IRR	Internal rate of return
ISI	Import substitution industrialization
ISIC	International Standard Industrial Classification
JFFLS	Junior farmer field and life schools
KILM	Key indicators of the labour market
Kg	Kilogram
Km	Kilometre
LAC	Latin America and the Caribbean
LFS	Labour Force Survey
LL	Lower limit
LOASP	Agro-Sylvo-Pastoral Orientation Act
LPI	Lived Poverty Index
LPM	Linear probability model
LR	Low-return
LSMS-ISA	Living Standards Measurement Study—Integrated Surveys on Agriculture
MDG	Millennium Development Goals
MIJARC	International Movement of Catholic Agricultural and Rural Youth
MNL	Multinomial logit
MOE	Ministry of Education
MRHS	Migration and Remittances Household Survey
MSME	Micro, small, and medium enterprises
NBS	National Bureau of Statistics
NEPAD	New Partnership for Africa's Development
NFE	Nonfarm enterprise/economy
NGO	Nongovernmental organization
NLFS	National Labour Force Survey
NSGRP	National Strategy for Growth and Reduction of Poverty
NSO	National Statistics Office
ODA	Official development assistance
OLS	Ordinary least squares
OSH	Occupational safety and health
PNAD	Brazilian National Household Sample Survey
PPEJMR	Politique de Promotion de l'Emploi des Jeunes en Milieu Rural
PPP	Purchasing power parity

PRSP	Poverty reduction strategy papers
PSE	Emerging Senegal Plan
PSU	Primary sampling unit
RIGA	Rural Income Generative Activities
RNFE	Rural nonfarm economy
RRR	Relative risk ratio
SA	South Asia
SAP	Structural adjustment programmes
S.D.	Standard deviation
SE	Standard error
SNNP	Southern nations, nationalities, and peoples
SSA	Sub-Saharan Africa
TZS	Tanzanian shillings
UL	Upper limit
UN	United Nations
UN DESA	United Nations Department of Economic and Social Affairs
UNGA	United Nations General Assembly
US$	United States Dollar
VCD	Value chain development
WB	World Bank
WDI	World Development Indicators
WGI	Worldwide Governance Indicators
YEI	Youth employment inventory

List of Contributors

Bob Baulch is a Senior Research Fellow in the Development Strategy and Governance division at the IFPRI, and the Country Programme Coordinator for IFPRI's Malawi Strategy Support Programme in Lilongwe, Malawi.

Firew Bekele Woldeyes is a Research Fellow in the Macroeconomics and Trade Policy Department at the Policy Studies Institute in Addis Ababa, Ethiopia.

Todd Benson is a Senior Research Fellow in the Development Strategy and Governance division at IFPRI in Washington DC, U.S.A.

Xinshen Diao is a Senior Research Fellow and Deputy Division Director of the Development Strategy and Governance division at IFPRI in Washington DC, U.S.A.

Alvina Erman is an Economist in Disaster Risk Management at the World Bank in Washington DC, U.S.A., and a former Senior Research Assistant Analyst at IFPRI.

Elisenda Estruch is an Economist in the Department of Sectoral Policies at the International Labour Organization in Genève, Switzerland.

Peixun Fang is a Research Analyst in the Development Strategy and Governance division at IFPRI in Washington DC, U.S.A.

Ileana Grandelis is a Rural Employment Officer in the Decent Rural Employment Team at the United Nations Food and Agricultural Organization in Rome, Italy.

Hak Lim Lee is a Senior Research Analyst at the Legal Services Corporation in Washington DC, U.S.A., and a former Research Analyst at IFPRI.

Eduardo Magalhaes (deceased) was an independent consultant and former Research Analyst at IFPRI.

Ian Masias is a Programme Manager in the Development Strategy and Governance division at IFPRI in Washington DC, U.S.A.

Margaret McMillan is a Professor of Economics at Tufts University in Medford MA, U.S.A., and a Senior Research Fellow at IFPRI.

Valerie Mueller is an Assistant Professor in the School of Politics and Global Studies at Arizona State University in Tempe AZ, U.S.A., and a Nonresident Fellow at IFPRI.

Stefan Pahl is a PhD student in the Faculty of Economics and Business at the University of Groningen in the Netherlands.

Josee Randriamamonjy is a Senior Research Analyst in the Development Strategy and Governance division at IFPRI in Washington DC, U.S.A.

Danielle Resnick is a Senior Research Fellow and Governance Theme Leader in the Development Strategy and Governance division at IFPRI in Washington DC, U.S.A.

Gracie Rosenbach is a Research Analyst in the Development Strategy and Governance division at IFPRI in Washington DC, U.S.A.

Emily Schmidt is a Research Fellow in the Development Strategy and Governance division at IFPRI in Washington DC, U.S.A.

David Schwebel is a Community Advisor at Cargill in Amsterdam, Netherlands, and a former Consultant at the United Nations Food and Agricultural Organization in Rome, Italy.

Jed Silver is PhD student in the Department of Agricultural and Resource Economics at the University of California, Berkeley CA, U.S.A., and a former Senior Research Assistant at IFPRI.

James Thurlow is a Senior Research Fellow in the Development Strategy and Governance division at IFPRI in Washington DC, U.S.A.

Lisa Van Dijck is a Consultant in the Decent Rural Employment Team at the United Nations Food and Agricultural Organization in Rome, Italy.

Peter Wobst is a Senior Economist in the Social Policies and Rural Institutions division at the United Nations Food and Agricultural Organization in Rome, Italy.

1

Africa's Rural Youth in the Global Context

Valerie Mueller, James Thurlow, Gracie Rosenbach,
and Ian Masias

1.1 Introduction

Governments in Sub-Saharan Africa are under enormous pressure to create more and better jobs for the region's young and rapidly growing population.[1] Africa is undergoing a 'youth bulge' in which the share of young people in the working age population is peaking due to past declines in mortality coupled with persistently high fertility (Canning, Raja, and Yazbeck 2015). This demographic transition has created a sense of urgency, and even anxiety, within national governments and the international development community (Resnick and Thurlow 2015). With the advent of the Sustainable Development Goals (UNDESA 2016), most policies and strategies in Africa today focus on promoting 'inclusive growth', which means that the population, especially the poor, should not only benefit from, but also participate in, the development process. This has made job creation a major policy objective, alongside the more traditional goals of accelerating economic growth and reducing poverty and hunger.

The successes of other developing countries, especially in Asia, provides African governments with what is sometimes considered a 'blueprint' for inclusive growth. Rapid economic growth in East Asia, for example, was accompanied by a process of 'structural change' in which the share of workers employed in agriculture declined as jobs were created in more productive and remunerative industrial sectors (McMillan, Rodrik, and Verduzco-Gallo 2014). This led to substantial poverty reduction, in large part because poor workers, especially farmers and their families, were able to take advantage of better job opportunities, often by migrating to cities and towns (Ravallion et al. 2007). Urbanization and structural transformation were supported by rising agricultural productivity (Ravallion 2009). This allowed workers to leave farming without raising food prices and urban wages, which might have jeopardized industrialization (Zhang, Yang, and Wang

---

[1] Unless stated otherwise, the terms 'Sub-Saharan Africa' and 'Africa' will be used interchangeably in the book.

Valerie Mueller, James Thurlow, Gracie Rosenbach, and Ian Masias, *Africa's Rural Youth in the Global Context*
In: *Youth and Jobs in Rural Africa: Beyond Stylized Facts*. Edited by: Valerie Mueller and James Thurlow, Oxford University Press (2019). © International Food Policy Research Institute.
DOI: 10.1093/oso/9780198848059.003.0001

2011). Strong agricultural growth meant that rural poverty continued to fall, even as economies reoriented towards urban industry (Christiaensen, Demery, and Kuhl 2011). This stylized model of development, drawn from the East Asian experience, is characterized by rapid economic growth and urbanization, underpinned by agricultural and structural transformation.

Unfortunately, Sub-Saharan Africa does not appear to be emulating the East Asian model. Africa's populations are urbanizing, and its economies are growing, but there has not been a major shift towards high-value manufacturing (Diao, Harttgen, and McMillan 2017). Structural change in Africa is instead driven by workers moving out of agriculture into informal services, particularly small-scale retail trade (de Vries, Timmer, and de Vries 2015; McMillan, Rodrik, and Sepúlveda 2017). This has limited the contribution of structural change to economic growth (Rodrik 2016). Urbanization without industrialization has also given rise to 'consumption cities' rather than engines of national economic growth (Gollin, Jedwab, and Vollrath 2016). Africa's pathway is partly an outcome of today's competitive global economy, which can make it more difficult for late-transforming economies to adopt an export-oriented industrialization strategy (McMillan, Rodrik, and Verduzco-Gallo 2014). It raises doubts about whether Africa can create enough jobs for its growing population (Canning, Raja, and Yazbeck 2015), especially the kinds of jobs that its young men and women aspire to (Sumberg et al. 2012).

Africa has also yet to undergo substantial rural transformation. Agricultural productivity in rural areas remains low, with few farmers using improved technologies (Christiaensen and Demery 2018). Although the agricultural sector is growing, a large part of this growth is driven by extending farmlands, rather than raising productivity (Benin 2016). Africa's rural population continues to expand rapidly, despite urbanization, and this raises further concerns about whether higher rural population density will eventually undermine the traditional role of farming in providing poor Africans with a basic livelihood (Chamberlin, Headey, and Jayne 2014). Indeed, most of the world's poor people today reside in rural Africa, and global projections indicate that this concentration will become more pronounced if current trends continue (Thurlow, Dorosh, and Davies 2019). Projections also indicate that, even with urbanization, about half of Africa's new job seekers will need to find employment in rural areas, at least until 2030 (Filmer and Fox 2014; Thurlow 2015).

Ensuring that Africa's rural youth find decent jobs therefore lies at the heart of the global development agenda. However, it does not necessarily follow that Africa has a 'youth problem'. While there are concerns about Africa's youth bulge, there are also reasons for optimism (Bloom, Canning, and Sevilla 2003). Young Africans may prove to be the 'agents of change' that the region sorely needs (Resnick and Thurlow 2015). African youth, for instance, are better educated than previous generations and so may be better positioned to adopt new technologies and establish new kinds of enterprises. This could help rural households raise and diversify their incomes by adopting modern technologies, operating nonfarm enterprises or migrating to cities and towns in search of work. Concerns about the shortcomings of Africa's development trajectory may also be overstated. While Africa is a late-transforming region, it is not clear whether the economic conditions and challenges it faces today differ significantly from those faced by other developing regions when they underwent their own demographic transitions. Africa's challenge may not lie with its youth bulge per se, but rather in creating better jobs for its entire workforce, both young and old.

The opportunities and challenges of African youth receive greater attention today from researchers, governments, and development partners, but there are still gaps in our knowledge and often an overreliance on stylized facts and general frameworks. Recent reports from international organizations document Africa's demographic transition and the need to create jobs for young men and women (see, for example, AfDB et al. 2012; AfDB 2016; Filmer and Fox 2014). However, while these reports are grounded in cross-country data and have raised the profile of youth, their regional perspective often focuses on general trends, constraints, and policy needs. Recent academic studies address youth employment issues within selected African countries and confirm the importance of understanding country-specific contexts (see, for example, Hino and Ranis 2014; Resnick and Thurlow 2015). However, these studies tend to consider youth employment in general, rather than the specific challenges facing youth in *rural* Africa. Yet it is here where the world's working poor are concentrating and where the challenge of meeting the needs and aspirations of African youth is perhaps most daunting.

This book investigates the role of *rural* youth in Sub-Saharan Africa's development. Are rural youth active participants in the national growth process? What barriers do they face in acquiring more productive jobs, and are there policies in place to help them to overcome those barriers? How are rural youth involved in agricultural technology adoption, rural income diversification, and urban migration, and how do these intersections affect rural transformation? These and other questions are addressed throughout the book, drawing on household surveys rather than cross-country data. Thematic chapters discuss youth dynamics across countries, including migration, political participation, and representation in national policies. Case study chapters analyse selected African countries, focusing on what household surveys tell us about the participation of youth in rural transformation and national development. Together, the authors present a holistic picture of the challenges and opportunities facing youth in rural Africa today and what this means for inclusive growth in the region. The remainder of this chapter revisits the cross-country data and considers whether there is something unique to Africa's youth bulge today. It also highlights the diversity of African countries and the need for country-specific analysis rather than stylized facts.

1.2 Africa's Youth Bulge in Historical Context

Perhaps the most distinguishing feature of Sub-Saharan Africa's demographic transition is that it occurred far later than in other developing regions. Using historical and projected population estimates, we can identify when countries' youth bulges peaked (or will peak).[2] This is defined as the year when the share of youth in the working age population is highest. Africa typically defines 'youth' as people aged 15–34 years, as opposed to the 15–24 years used elsewhere. This reflects the notion that, because of socioeconomic constraints, Africans are living in 'waithood' or a prolonged period before they can support themselves and their families (see Resnick and Thurlow 2015). Africa also uses a more expansive definition of the working age population than, say, the United Nations, which limits the workforce to people aged 15–64 years. For this chapter's global comparison, we will adopt the more restrictive definition of youth (15–24 years), but later chapters will consider both international and African definitions. Figure 1.1 shows the estimated years when developing countries' youth bulges peaked.

Sub-Saharan Africa's youth bulge peaked in 2003, whereas other regions peaked sometime between 1976 and 1985.[3] Despite being decades later, the magnitude of Africa's youth bulge is similar to that of other regions. Regional averages, however, hide wide variation across countries. Within Africa, Mauritius' youth bulge peaked in 1967, but it will only peak in 2027 for the Democratic Republic of the Congo.

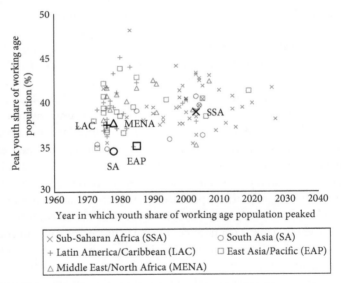

Figure 1.1. National and regional youth bulge peaks, 1960–2030

Notes: Sample includes the 109 countries and dependencies that were, as of 2018, recognized by the United Nations and fall within the low-and middle-income categories and regional groupings defined by the World Bank. Youth bulge is defined as the share of youth (15–25 years) in working age population (15–64 years). Regional averages are weighted by countries' populations.

Source: Authors' calculations using historical and projected population data from UNDESA (2018).

---

[2] Developing countries include all low- and middle-income countries, as classified by the World Bank in 2018. Note that all statistics for Sub-Saharan Africa exclude South Africa.
[3] Sub-Saharan Africa's peak occurs four years later when youth is defined as people aged 15–34 years.

Similarly, South Africa's youth bulge peaked at 35.5 per cent, whereas Cape Verde peaked at 48.1 per cent. This variation underscores the importance of conducting country case studies and avoiding stylized facts about Africa's youth challenge.

Africa's delayed demographic transition means that it will soon become the main source of growth for the world's workforce. Figure 1.2 reports annual changes in the global working age population, with projections until 2100. The largest annual expansion occurred in 2003, when the global working age population increased by 74 million people. This expansion is expected to decline until 2100, at which point the absolute size of the global workforce will have plateaued. However, from 2046 onwards, Africa will be the only region with a growing working age population–a trend that is expected to continue into the next century. The scale of Africa's employment challenge is also evident from the figure. Africa's potential workforce will increase by 21 million people per year during the 2020s, rising to 30 million people during the 2050s, after which it will begin to decline.

The absolute size of Africa's young and growing workforce may be daunting from the perspective of other regions, especially developed countries. However, it is more informative to reflect on the situation that young Africans face within their own economies. Moreover, since we would like to understand if there is something unique about Africa's youth challenge, other than its delayed occurrence, it is useful to compare the economic conditions in Africa today to those of other regions when their youth bulges peaked back in the 1970s and 1980s. Table 1.1 therefore

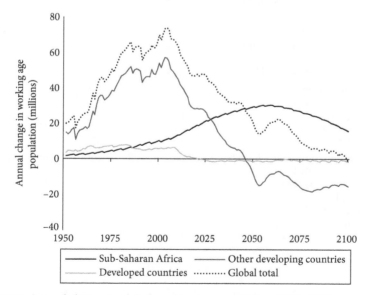

Figure 1.2. Annual change in global working age population, 1950–2100

Notes: Sample includes the 203 countries and dependencies that were, as of 2018, recognized by the United Nations and fall within the low-and middle-income categories and regional groupings defined by the World Bank. Working age population includes all people aged 15–64 years.

Source: Authors' calculations using historical and projected population data from UNDESA (2018).

Table 1.1. Economic conditions over the 15 years following regions' peak youth bulges

Developing country region (year when youth bulge peaked)		EAP (1985)	LAC (1976)	MENA (1978)	SA (1978)	SSA (2003)
Population	Population at peak (millions)	1,475	286	158	858	642
	Rural population share (%)	75.3	40.9	54.1	78.5	70.1
	Annual population growth after peak (%)	1.4	2.2	2.9	2.3	3.0
	Rural areas	0.2	0.3	2.0	1.9	2.2
	Urban areas	4.1	3.3	3.9	3.6	4.7
Gross domestic product	GDP per capita at peak ($)	820	6,498	4,266	457	814
	National GDP share at peak (%)	100	100	100	100	100
	Agriculture	27.9	4.6	6.1	38.9	20.8
	Industry	37.5	47.6	58.7	31.7	38.4
	of which manufacturing	7.1	15.4	4.5	11.0	8.6
	Services	34.6	47.9	35.2	29.4	40.8
	of which trade services	11.7	14.0	6.4	7.8	12.4
	Annual GDP per capita growth after peak (%)	6.0	0.6	−2.1	2.2	3.4
	Agriculture	2.1	0.4	0.4	0.2	3.1
	Industry	7.5	0.1	−2.8	3.0	2.7
	of which manufacturing	6.0	0.2	1.5	2.9	3.4
	Services	6.7	1.0	−1.5	3.5	4.1
	of which trade services	5.2	0.3	0.3	3.1	4.2
Employment	Labour force participation rate after 15 years (%)	79.7	63.2	48.3	61.5	70.1
	Youth (15–24 years old)	64.7	54.4	36.9	49.2	49.8
	Unemployment rate after 15 years (%)	4.4	6.0	13.2	3.9	6.1
	Youth (15–24 years old)	10.4	11.1	26.9	8.6	12.7
	National employment share after 15 years (%)	100	100	100	100	100
	Agriculture	46.1	27.9	30.3	62.4	59.8
	Industry	24.9	21.2	24.6	14.7	10.6
	Services	29.0	50.9	45.1	22.9	29.6
	National employment share after 15 years (%)	100	100	100	100	100
	Self-employed workers	58.0	43.7	44.9	81.9	76.7
	Employers	1.9	5.3	7.3	1.8	2.6
	Family workers	25.7	9.3	11.4	19.7	24.3
	Own-account workers	30.4	29.1	26.1	60.4	49.8
	Wage and salaried workers	42.0	56.3	55.1	18.1	23.3

Education	Primary school enrolment ratio at peak (gross)	115.9	107.2	85.5	76.9	83.9
	Total change over 15 years	−8.5	5.2	7.4	12.1	13.0
	Secondary school enrolment ratio at peak (gross)	34.3	43.2	39.8	25.1	27.1
	Total change over 15 years	24.6	32.5	17.7	17.0	11.2

Notes: GDP data is from UNSD and includes the 109 countries and dependencies that were, as of 2018, recognized by the United Nations and fall within the World Bank's low- and middle-income categories and regional groupings. All other data are regional estimates from the World Bank. EAP is East Asia and Pacific; LAC is Latin American and Caribbean; MENA is Middle East and North Africa; SA is South Asia; and SSA is Sub-Saharan Africa (excluding South Africa). High-income countries are excluded. Growth rates reflect changes over 15 years after the year in which a region's youth bulge peaked. Official urban definitions are used. GDP is measured in constant 2010 US dollars unadjusted for purchasing power parity. Gross enrolment ratios are actual enrolment divided by the population with the correct age for that level of schooling (i.e. higher ratios may indicate late-enrolment or repeated grades).

Source: Authors' calculations using data from the World Bank (2018) and UNSD (2018).

reports key economic and demographic statistics for each region during the year when their youth bulges peaked and over the subsequent 15 years. For example, East Asia's youth bulge peaked in 1985 and so the table reports changes for this region over the 15-year period, 1985–2000.

In some respects, Africa today faces more challenging conditions than other regions did a few decades ago. However, there are also areas where Africa's conditions or trends are no worse, and are sometimes better, than they were elsewhere. For example, Africa is still at an early stage of economic development, but so too were East Asia and South Asia at the time of their youth bulges. This is measured by gross domestic product (GDP) per capita, which was $814 in Sub-Saharan Africa in 2003, but was only $457 in South Asia in 1978 (measured in 2010 prices). In contrast, the Middle East and North Africa had much higher GDP per capita during its demographic transition, but this declined over the next 15 years (−2.2 per cent per year), whereas Africa's has grown relatively fast (3.4 per cent per year). Overall, Africa's economic conditions in 2003 appear to be most like those of East Asia in 1985, both in terms of GDP per capita and the sectoral structure of their regional economies. However, as discussed earlier, East Asia then went on to enjoy a period of far more rapid growth and structural change than Africa has in recent years.

One of Africa's major challenges is its high population growth rate. This means that, despite very rapid urban population growth, Africa's rural population is still growing much faster than it was in East Asia. From a demographic perspective, Africa has far more in common with South Asia. Both regions had high rural population shares and rapid rural population growth during their demographic transitions. Given their similar stages of development, it is not surprising then than a large share of Africa and South Asia's workers continued to be self-employed in rural agriculture 15 years after their youth bulges peaked. It is also in these two regions where most of the world's poor population are concentrated today (Thurlow, Dorosh, and Davies 2019). This underscores the importance of creating jobs and income opportunities in *rural* Africa.

The table also compares education levels across regions. Again, we find that Africa has more in common with South Asia. Both regions had low primary and secondary school enrolment at the peak of their youth bulges, and even though enrolment increased over the next 15 years, much of these gains were achieved by closing primary school enrolment gaps. In contrast, East Asia and Latin America started with much higher school enrolment and were far more successful in closing secondary school enrolment gaps. The quality of education in Africa vis-à-vis other regions three decades ago is difficult to assess. Nevertheless, Africa has moved closer towards achieving universal primary schooling, and this highlights the better educational attainment of young Africans compared to adults. Africa also has much higher labour force participation. This is because more women are part of Africa's workforce today than they were in other regions, except for East Asia. Of course, high participation rates mean that more jobs will be needed as Africa's population grows. However, it also means that a larger share of the African population is participating in, and hopefully benefiting from, the region's growth process.

Finally, we compare the pace of economic growth and structural change during countries' demographic transitions. As mentioned earlier, successful economic development is usually accompanied by a falling share of workers in agriculture, and a shift in employment towards more productive sectors, leading to faster economic growth. Figure 1.3 uses employment data collected from national population censuses and household and labour force surveys around the period when countries' youth bulges peaked. Unfortunately, not all countries have such data, especially those whose youth bulges occurred during the 1960s and 1970s when surveys were conducted less frequently or not at all. It is also not possible to estimate comparable changes in employment patterns for countries that have only recently (or not yet) undergone their peak youth bulge. As a result, the figure only includes information for about half of all developing countries, and so regional averages are not reported.

Despite limited country coverage, it is still possible to discern regional patterns from the figure. East Asian countries, for example, generally experienced strong economic growth (horizontal axis) as well as a rapid decline in agricultural employment shares (vertical axis) (see China and Indonesia). In contrast, Latin American countries experienced more modest, or even negative, economic growth, and a more gradual exit from agricultural employment (see Mexico). Again, there

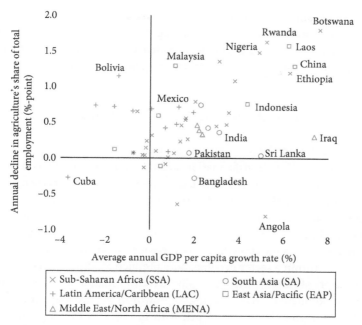

Figure 1.3. Rates of economic growth and structural change during the 15 years following countries' peak youth bulge years

Notes: Sample includes 62 low-and middle-income countries (32 in SSA, 6 in SA, 12 in LAC, 8 in EAP and 4 in MENA). Reported changes are for the 15 years immediately after the year in which a country's youth bulge peaked. GDP is measured in constant 2010 US dollars and not adjusted for purchasing power parity.

Source: Authors' calculations using data from ILO (2018), Timmer et al. (2015), and World Bank (2018).

is especially wide variation across African countries. A few fast-transforming economies experienced rapid growth and structural change similar to East Asia (see Botswana and Rwanda). However, economic growth in most African countries is slow, and workers are only gradually leaving agriculture. This is consistent with projections suggesting that most of the jobs created in rural Africa until 2030 will be in agriculture (Filmer and Fox 2014; Thurlow 2015).

In summary, the lateness and absolute size of Africa's demographic transition is unique. The region will soon become the main driver of growth in the global workforce, and African economies will need to create large numbers of jobs just to keep pace with rapid population growth. Fortunately, African economies are growing, but, except for a few countries, they are not matching East Asia's high rates of economic growth and structural change. Moreover, Africa's rural population continues to expand, despite rapid urbanization. Together, these trends indicate that creating rural employment, including in agriculture, will be crucial in ensuring that African economies can absorb enough job seekers into the workforce and avoid rising unemployment. At the same time, Africa will need to provide better jobs for its adult workforce, who also aspire to improved living standards and working conditions. In that regard, Africa does not necessarily face a *youth* challenge, but rather the broader challenge of promoting inclusive growth and decent employment in today's competitive global economy.

1.3 Framing Agricultural and Rural Transformation

This book focuses on the participation of rural youth in national development. Agricultural and rural transformation are therefore important concepts that help structure the research questions and analysis. As discussed earlier, economic development is strongly associated with structural change, which occurs when workers leave agriculture for more productive jobs in other sectors (Johnston and Kilby 1975; Chenery and Syrquin 1975). However, structural change is not the only driver of economic growth. Economy-wide labour productivity also rises when workers within a sector become more productive without needing to move to other sectors of employment. Agricultural transformation refers to a process in which farm productivity rises, leading to growth in the broader rural economy. Timmer (1988) provides a framework with four stages that are summarized in Figure 1.4.

During the first stage (*subsistence agriculture*), most rural inhabitants are farmers engaged in food production for their own consumption and use rudimentary technologies and farming practices. The focus for policy at this stage is raising farm productivity, such as through greater use of improved seeds, chemical fertilizers, and soil and water management. Land and labour resources at this stage are likely to be underemployed and it may not matter if technological improvements are labour- or land-saving. Since youth in Africa are better educated than adults, many expect that they are more likely to adopt improved farm technologies (see Sheahan and Barret 2017). The country chapters in this book assess the contribution of youth to ongoing changes in the farming sector.

During the second stage, there is an expansion of *farm-nonfarm linkages*, as farm productivity rises and farmers begin to produce marketable surpluses. This leads to growth in goods that are produced in rural areas and primarily sold to other rural households. The rise of rural markets creates nonfarm jobs linked to agriculture, such as traders and transporters. Nonfarm workers may live in rural market centres, where agriculture indirectly supports an even wider range of

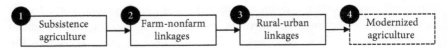

Figure 1.4. Timmer's four stages of agricultural transformation

Source: Authors' interpretation of Timmer (1988).

occupations. New job opportunities encourage farmers to diversify incomes or exit agriculture entirely. However, at this stage of agricultural transformation, farming remains the primary driver of national growth and job creation. Youth are again expected to play a key role during this stage. Better-educated people are more likely to run rural nonfarm businesses (Naglar and Naude 2017), and emerging land constraints may mean that it is youth who are more likely to seek off-farm work (Bezu and Holden 2014). The country chapters examine the links between youth, education, and rural nonfarm employment.

The third stage of agricultural transformation involves a strengthening of *rural-urban linkages*. Nonagricultural sectors, particularly in cities and towns, become drivers of national development. Agriculture increasingly supplies urban consumers and rural inhabitants migrate in search of urban job opportunities. Migrant workers may remit incomes back to their rural families or occasionally return to rural areas to alleviate seasonal labour shortages. Outmigration may require labour-saving technological improvements in agriculture to prevent food prices and urban wages from rising and stalling structural change. At this stage, urban nonagricultural growth drives national development and pulls agriculture behind it. Chapter 2 in this book specifically addresses the role of youth in migration decisions, and the various country chapters examine the links between youth and urbanization.

The final stage is the transition to *modernized agriculture*. This is most relevant for today's developed countries, where high rural-urban inequality and concerns about national food security may prompt governments to subsidize agriculture and protect 'rural lifestyles'. Few, if any, African countries, or even areas within these countries, have reached this late stage of agricultural transformation.

Although Timmer's framework was developed three decades ago and is grounded in the Asian experience, it still provides a useful device for analysing the pace and participation of youth in Africa's agricultural and rural economies. It underpins the view that, despite global developments since the 1980s, agricultural transformation is still essential for economic development in Africa (Diao, Hazell, and Thurlow 2010; Timmer and Akkus 2008). Not only will Africa's youth need to find jobs in agriculture and rural areas, but they could help drive the transformation process. Chapters 3 and 4 in this book examine whether the needs and potential of youth are reflected in national policies, and whether youth are more politically active and demanding of their governments.

1.4 Evidence of Agricultural Transformation in Africa

Most African countries today, or at least most rural populations within African countries, are in the second or third stage of Timmer's transformation framework. Farmers still grow some of the food they consume, but most now sell at least some of their output in local markets (Carletto, Corral, and Guelfi 2017). This marketable surplus is the result of rising farm production levels over the last 15 years. Figure 1.5 reports the growth in agricultural land and labour productivity that occurred after Africa's youth bulge peaked in 2003. The figure shows that both land and labour productivity increased for most African countries, including the region as a whole. However, land productivity growth exceeded labour productivity growth in almost all countries, implying that agricultural labour grew faster than agricultural land. This reflects growing concerns about rising rural population densities and the ability of available lands to support the livelihoods of a rapidly growing rural workforce.

The case study chapters in this book examine the contribution of youth to agricultural transformation in five countries: Ethiopia, Ghana, Malawi, Senegal, and Tanzania. These countries were selected to capture the variation in trends observed across Africa, although data availability was also a consideration. As indicated in the figure, Ethiopian agriculture is transforming rapidly, whereas Malawian and Senegalese agriculture are not. Ghana and Tanzania are close to the African average. The case studies allow us to examine the role of youth in

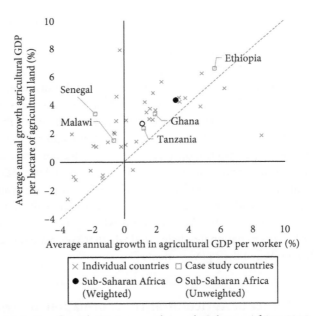

Figure 1.5. Agricultural productivity growth in sub-Saharan Africa, 2003–2016

Notes: Sample includes 42 Sub-Saharan African countries (excluded are Eritrea, Sao Tome and Principe, Seychelles, South Africa, South Sudan, and Sudan). GDP is measured in constant 2010 US dollars unadjusted for purchasing power parity. Agricultural land includes lands used crop cultivation and animal husbandry.

Source: Authors' calculations using data from ILO (2018), FAO (2018), and UNSD (2018).

raising farm productivity–the first stage in Timmer's framework–taking account of how this may vary across African countries.

Although Africa's rural economy is dominated by agriculture, a large share of rural incomes is earned in the rural nonfarm economy (Carletto, Corral, and Guelfi 2017). This is important for the second stage of Timmer's framework, when farm-nonfarm linkages expand. Household surveys suggest that more than a third of rural incomes in Africa are generated through nonfarm employment (Haggblade, Hazell, and Reardon 2007), and that most rural households engage in some form of nonfarm activity (Davis, Di Giuseppe, and Zezza 2017). As mentioned earlier, most of the structural change in Africa in recent years was driven by workers leaving agriculture to work in informal services. Many of these services are agriculture-related, such as the trading and transport of food and agricultural products. While these are not the kinds of high productivity industrial jobs that dominated the East Asian experience, their growth has helped reduce poverty in many parts of Africa (Dorosh and Thurlow 2016).

Figure 1.6 reports changes in urban population shares and nonagricultural employment shares since 2003. For Sub-Saharan Africa as a whole, the decline in the rural population was matched by a decline in agricultural employment (i.e. the

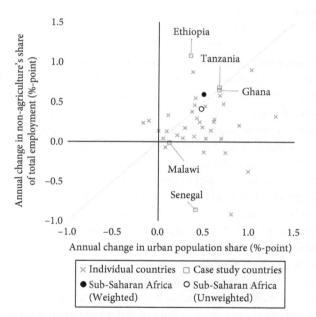

Figure 1.6. Urban population and nonfarm employment shares in sub-Saharan Africa, 2003–2016

Notes: Sample includes 44 Sub-Saharan African countries (excluded are Sao Tome and Principe, Seychelles, South Africa, South Sudan, and Sudan). Official definitions of urban areas are used.

Source: Authors' calculations using data from ILO (2018) and UNDESA (2018).

regional average lies close to the diagonal line in the figure). This suggests that there was no significant change in the share of rural nonfarm employment in the region. Again, we find that regional averages hide wide variation across countries–differences that are captured in our choice of country case studies. The exit from agriculture in Ethiopia, for example, greatly exceeds the pace of urbanization, suggesting that many of the workers that left farming found employment in the rural nonfarm economy. The opposite is true for Senegal, where agricultural employment has risen, despite urbanization. This suggests that some of Senegal's rural nonfarm workers are returning to agriculture. Tanzania and Ghana are again closer to the African average, and there was little agricultural transformation taking place in Malawi. Detailed household surveys allow the country chapters to investigate whether it is youth or adults, or young men or women, who are more actively engaged in the rural nonfarm economy.

The third stage of Timmer's framework is characterized by a strengthening of rural-urban linkages. There is some evidence that Africa's urban consumers are increasingly driving demand for agricultural products (Tshirley et al. 2015). As mentioned earlier, rapid urbanization is a defining feature of African development. Moreover, expanding urban populations and migration within rural areas has meant that many of Africa's rural inhabitants today reside in 'peri-urban areas' adjacent to major urban agglomerations (FAO 2017). It is in peri-urban areas where rural-urban linkages are expected to be strongest and where agricultural transformation should be most advanced (Dorosh and Thurlow 2014).

Cross-country data suggests that young African men may be more likely to migrate than either adults or young women. Figure 1.7 estimates the relative speed of urbanization for youth and adults (horizontal axis) and for young men and women (vertical axis). This is measured by estimating the gap between average annual urban and rural population growth rates for each population subgroup. A large positive number means that the subgroup's urban population is growing much faster than its rural population. The figure reports differences in the speed of urbanization between two population subgroups. For example, the horizontal axis focuses on the differences between youth and adults. The relative speed of urbanization is generally positive, implying that African youth are concentrating in urban areas faster than African adults. This is consistent with findings in other studies (see De Brauw, Mueller, and Lee 2014; Holden and Otsuka 2014), but it hides how most urban migration is to smaller towns, rather than bigger cities (Mueller et al. 2019). The tendency for youth to urbanize faster than adults is most pronounced in Ghana and Malawi, but it is negligible in the other three case study countries. Similarly, there is some evidence that young men are urbanizing faster than young women. Our case studies capture variation across African countries. This variation may reflect differences in education or other factors that influence the decision to migrate. A thematic chapter in this book analyses youth migration decisions using detailed household surveys rather than country-level data.

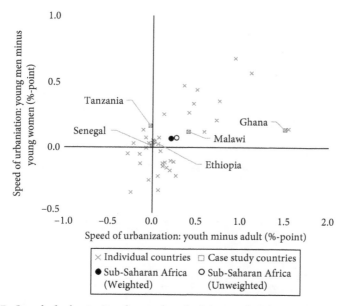

Figure 1.7. Speed of urbanization for youth and adults in sub-Saharan Africa, 2003–2015

Note: Sample includes 44 Sub-Saharan African countries (excluded are Sao Tome and Principe, Seychelles, South Africa, South Sudan, and Sudan). Speed of urbanization is the difference between average annual urban and rural population growth rates, i.e., a number greater than one implies that the urban population share is rising over time). Figure compares the speed of urbanization for different population groups, i.e., a number greater than one means that the first group is urbanizing faster (or deurbanizing slower) than the second group.

Source: Authors' calculations using historical population data from ILO (2018).

In summary, African agriculture is transforming, albeit slowly and with some cause for concern. Agricultural land and labour productivity are growing, but so too are rural population densities. This suggests that agriculture's contribution to future job creation may be constrained as lands become scarce. Africa's rural nonfarm economy is also expanding, although in many countries it is not keeping pace with urbanization. On average, workers are leaving agriculture and moving to urban areas faster than they are finding work in the rural nonfarm economy. As urban centres become congested, more of the population are likely to reside in peri-urban (or peri-rural) areas where rural-urban linkages are often strongest (Thurlow, Dorosh, and Davies 2018). Recent estimates suggest that one third of rural Africans already live within one-hour travel time of cities with populations of 50,000 people or more (SOFA 2017). The nonfarm economy surrounding cities and towns will therefore play an important role in creating work for rural job seekers, including youth. This means that, while agricultural transformation is proceeding in Africa, it is not only uneven across countries, but also across areas within countries. This underscores the need for detailed country case studies and cautions against an overreliance on country-level data.

Table 1.2. Country case studies

Sub-Saharan Africa or Case Study (year when youth bulge peaked)	SSA (2003)	Ethiopia (2014)	Ghana (1987)	Malawi (2010)	Senegal (2000)	Tanzania (2000)
Population						
Population, 2016 (millions)	1,033	102	28	18	15	56
Rural share (%)	61.0	80.1	45.3	83.5	53.7	67.7
Population growth, 2006–16 (%)	2.8	2.6	2.5	3.0	2.9	3.2
Rural areas	1.9	2.2	1.0	2.9	2.2	2.2
Urban areas	4.2	5.0	3.8	3.9	3.9	5.7
GDP						
GDP per capita, 2016 ($)	1,173	426	1,617	448	962	792
Agriculture share (%)	22.3	35.8	23.9	29.9	15.5	25.2
GDP per capita growth, 2006–16 (%)	3.1	7.5	4.4	2.5	1.5	3.3
Agriculture	2.8	3.8	1.2	1.1	1.6	0.3
Employment						
Labour force participation, 2016 (%)	68.2	82.3	76.7	76.8	57.0	83.3
Youth (15–24)	48.6	75.0	53.6	63.0	41.3	72.0
Unemployment rate, 2016 (%)	7.3	5.1	2.3	5.9	4.8	2.2
Youth (15–24)	13.8	7.3	4.7	7.8	5.4	3.8
Agricultural employment, 2016 (%)	57.4	69.0	41.2	84.7	53.6	67.2
Annual change, 2006–16 (%-point)	–0.53	–1.10	–0.38	0.04	1.38	–0.74

Note: GDP is measured in constant 2010 US dollars unadjusted for purchasing power parity.

Source: Authors' calculations using GDP data from UNSD (2018) and other data from the World Bank (2018).

Our country case studies reflect some of the important variations observed across Sub-Saharan Africa. Table 1.2 provides current statistics for the five countries and the region. By design, our cases are either low- or lower-middle-income countries, often with a greater dependence on agriculture and with a larger share of the population in rural areas. Youth unemployment is lower amongst our case study countries than in Africa as a whole, which partly reflects our focus on agrarian economies, which have lower unemployment rates than more mining-based economies like Nigeria or South Africa. Ghana and Ethiopia are two of Africa's fastest transforming countries, but Ghana is at a later stage of development (i.e. GDP per capita is higher and the population is more urbanized). Ghana is also one of the earliest African countries to experience a demographic transition (i.e. its youth bulge peaked in 1987), whereas Ethiopia is one of the last countries. Malawi is at a similar stage of development as Ethiopia, although Malawi, like Senegal, is not experiencing rapid economic growth and the share of employment in agriculture is not falling. Labour force participation in Senegal is one of the lowest in Sub-Saharan Africa, largely because women are less likely to work and because international migration is particularly important for Senegal. Finally, Tanzania provides an intermediate case. The country is transforming, and workers are leaving agriculture, often for urban areas, but the economy, particularly agriculture, is growing much slower than in Ethiopia or Ghana. Our five case studies therefore reflect the diversity of African countries and allow us to gain a more nuanced understanding of youth in rural areas.

1.5 Organization of the Book

There is a large body of research on agricultural transformation and structural change in Africa (see, for example, Diao et al. 2007; McMillan, Rodrik, and Sepúlveda 2016). Few studies, however, examine employment through a *youth lens* and with a focus on *rural* Africa. This book provides new empirical evidence on the participation of rural youth in national development processes. Cross-country evidence is informative, but cannot substitute for detailed case studies that use micro-level data to reveal countries' unique characteristics and challenges. It is only through the collection of robust country-specific evidence that we can move beyond stylized facts and determine to what extent African youth should be a source of optimism or a cause for concern.

The book is separated into two parts. Part I includes three thematic chapters that cover important under-researched areas for youth employment. Rising population densities in rural areas has raised concerns about the future role agriculture in job creation and the prospect of accelerated urbanization. **Chapter 2** uses new household survey data to investigate youth migration patterns in four African countries, paying particular attention to the effect of land scarcity on young people's decision to migrate to urban centres. Despite urbanization, rural job creation is a major policy goal for many African governments. However, it is unclear whether national polices adequately reflect and address the constraints facing young job seekers in agriculture and rural areas. **Chapter 3** reviews national policies in 13 African countries, and uses a novel approach to classify policies according to the employment constraints they address. One reason for the attention given to job creation is the belief that unemployed youth are a potential source of political instability and unrest. **Chapter 4** examines whether African youth are more politically engaged than their older counterparts, and to what extent their demands for political action are motivated by concerns about jobs and unemployment.

Part II includes five country case study chapters that examine youth employment dynamics in Ethiopia, Ghana, Malawi, Senegal, and Tanzania. The chapters address a common set of questions about the roles that youth are playing at different stages of agricultural and rural transformation. How are youth driving the changes that are taking place within the agricultural sector? Are youth more involved in off-farm employment and rural income diversification? And are youth more spatially and occupationally mobile than previous generations? The chapters also address questions that are specific to their respective countries. **Chapter 5** focuses on Ethiopia's land constraints and asks if this is driving youth off the farm and into the rural nonfarm economy. **Chapter 6** addresses Malawi's weak agricultural transformation, and asks if rural households, particularly youth, are engaging in multiple forms of employment that may not be adequately reflected in national data. **Chapter 7** reflects Ghana's later stage of development by focusing on the link between urban development and the livelihoods available to rural youth living close to cities or towns. **Chapter 8** combine household and firm level analysis for Tanzania to examine what determines the success of rural nonfarm enterprises, including the role of young entrepreneurs. Finally, **Chapter 9** on Senegal pays particular attention to international migration and whether young migrants are contributing to rural transformation in their home country. **Chapter 10** concludes by summarizing the major findings and discusses their implications for youth employment and inclusive growth in rural Africa.

References

AfDB. 2016. Jobs for Youth in Africa Strategy for Creating 25 Million Jobs and Equipping 50 Million Youth 2016–2025. Abidjan, Côte d'Ivoire: African Development Bank.

AfDB, OECD, UNDP and UNECSA. 2012. African Economic Outlook 2012: Promoting Youth Employment. Paris, France: African Development Bank, Organization for Economic Cooperation and Development, United Nations Development Program, and United Nations Economic Commission for Africa.

Benin, S. 2016. (ed.) *Agricultural productivity in Africa: Trends, patterns, and determinants.* Washington DC, USA: IFPRI.

Bezu, S., and S. Holden. 2014. Are rural youth in Ethiopia abandoning agriculture? *World Development* 64: 259–72.

Bloom, D.E., D. Canning, and J. Sevilla. 2003. *The demographic dividend: A new perspective on the economic consequences of population change.* Santa Monica, CA, U.S.A.: RAND.

Canning, D., S. Raja, and A.S. Yazbeck. 2015. Africa's demographic transition: Dividend or disaster? Washington DC, USA: The World Bank.

Carletto, C.P. Corral, and A. Guelfi. 2017. Agricultural commercialization and nutrition revisited: Empirical evidence from three African countries. Food Policy 67: 106–18.

Chamberlin, J., D.D. Headey, and T.S. Jayne. 2014. Land pressures, the evolution of farming systems, and development strategies in Africa: A synthesis. *Food Policy* 48(C): 1–17.

Chenery, H.B., and M. Syrquin. 1975. *Patterns of development: 1950–1970.* London, U.K.: Oxford University Press.

Christiaensen, L., and L. Demery. 2018. *Agriculture in Africa: Telling myths from facts.* Washington DC, USA: The World Bank.

Christiaensen, L., L. Demery, and J. Kuhl. 2011. The (evolving) role of agriculture in poverty reduction—An empirical perspective. *Journal of Development Economics* 96(2): 239–54.

Davis, B., S. Di Giuseppe, and A. Zezza. 2017. Are African households (not) leaving agriculture? Patterns of households' income sources in rural Sub-Saharan Africa. *Food Policy* 67: 153–74.

De Brauw, A., V. Mueller, and H.K. Lee. 2014. The role of rural–urban migration in the structural transformation of Sub-Saharan Africa. *World Development* 63: 33–42.

De Vries, G., M. Timmer and K. de Vries. 2015. Structural transformation in Africa: Static gains, dynamic losses. *Journal of Development Studies* 51(6): 674–88.

Diao, X., K. Harttgen, and M. McMillan. 2017. The changing structure of Africa's economies. *World Bank Economic Review* 31(2): 412–33.

Diao, X., P. Hazell, and J. Thurlow. 2010. The role of agriculture in African development. *World Development* 38(1): 1375–83.

Diao, X., P. Hazell, D. Resnick, and J. Thurlow. 2007. The role of agriculture in development: Implications for Sub-Saharan Africa. Research Report 153. Washington DC, USA: International Food Policy Research Institute.

Dorosh, P., and J. Thurlow. 2014. Can cities or towns drive African development? Economywide analysis for Ethiopia and Uganda. *World Development* 63: 113–23.

Dorosh, P., and J. Thurlow. 2016. Beyond agriculture versus non-agriculture: Decomposing sectoral growth–poverty linkages in five African countries. World Development (in press).

FAO. 2017. The state of food and agriculture: Leveraging food systems for inclusive rural transformation. Rome, Italy: Food and Agriculture Organization of the United Nations.

FAO. 2018. FAOSTAT online database. Rome, Italy: The Food and Agriculture Organization of the United Nations.

Filmer, D., and L. Fox. 2014. *Youth employment in Sub-Saharan Africa*. Washington, DC, U.S.A.: The World Bank.

Gollin, D., R. Jedwab, and D. Vollrath. 2016. Urbanization with and without industrialization. *Journal of Economic Growth* 21(1): 35–70.

Haggblade, S., P.B. Hazell, and T. Reardon, eds. 2007. *Transforming the rural nonfarm economy: Opportunities and threats in the developing world*. Baltimore, MD, U.S.A.: The Johns Hopkins University Press.

Hino, H., and G. Ranis. 2014. (eds.). Youth and employment in Sub-Saharan Africa: Working but poor. New York, NY: Routledge.

Holden, S. T., and K. Otsuka. 2014. The roles of land tenure reforms and land markets in the context of population growth and land use intensification in Africa. *Food Policy* 48: 80–97.

ILO. 2018. ILOSTAT online database. Genève, Switzerland: International Labor Organization.

Johnston, B.F., and P. Kilby. 1975. *Agriculture and structural transformation: Economic strategies in late-developing countries*. London, U.K., New York, NY, U.S.A., Toronto, C.A.: Oxford University Press.

McMillan, M., D. Rodrik, and C. Sepúlveda, eds. 2017. *Structural change, fundamentals, and growth: A framework and case studies*. Washington, DC, U.S.A.: International Food Policy Research Institute.

McMillan, M., D. Rodrik, and I. Verduzco-Gallo. 2014. Globalization, structural change, and productivity growth, with an update on Africa. *World Development* 63: 11–32.

Mueller, V., E. Schmidt, N. Lozano-Gracia, and S. Murray. 2019. Implications of migration on employment and occupational transitions in Tanzania. *International Regional Science Review* 42(2): 181–206.

Nagler, P., and W. Naudé. 2017. Non-farm entrepreneurship in rural sub-Saharan Africa: New empirical evidence. *Food Policy* 67: 175–91.

Ravallion, M. 2009. Are there lessons for Africa from China's success against poverty? *World Development* 37(2): 303–13.

Ravallion, M., S. Chen and P. Sangrula. 2007. New evidence on the urbanization of global poverty. *Population and Development Review* 33(4): 667–701.

Resnick, D., and J. Thurlow. (eds). 2015. African youth and the persistence of marginalization: Employment, politics, and prospects for change. New York, NY, USA: Routledge.

Rodrik, D. 2016. Premature deindustrialization. *Journal of Economic Growth* 21(1): 1–33.

Sheahan, M. and C.D. Barret. 2017. Ten striking facts about agricultural input use in Sub-Saharan Africa. *Food Policy* 67: 12–25.

Sumberg, J., N.A. Anyidoho, J. Leavy, D.J.H. te Lintelo, and K. Wellard. 2012. Introduction: The young people and agriculture 'problem' in Africa. IDS Bulletin 43(6): 1–8.

Thurlow, J. 2015. Youth employment prospects in Africa. In Resnick, D., and J. Thurlow (eds). African youth and the persistence of marginalization: Employment, politics, and prospects for change. New York, NY, U.S.A.: Routledge.

Thurlow, J., P. Dorosh, and B. Davies. 2019. Demographic change, agriculture and rural poverty (chapter 3), in Campanhola, Clayton, and Shivaji Pandey (eds.). *Sustainable Food and Agriculture: An Integrated Approach*. London, U.K.: Elsevier and FAO.

Timmer, C.P. 1988. The agricultural transformation. *Handbook of Development Economics* 1: 275–331.

Timmer, C.P., and S. Akkus. 2008. The structural transformation as a pathway out of poverty: Analytics, empirics, and politics. *Center for Global Development Working Paper No. 150.*

Timmer, M.P., G.J. de Vries, and K. de Vries. 2015. Patterns of structural change in developing countries. In J. Weiss and M. Tribe (eds.). *Routledge Handbook of Industry and Development* (pp. 65–83). Routledge.

Tschirley, D., T. Reardon, M. Dolislager, and J. Snyder. 2015. The rise of a middle class in East and Southern Africa: Implications for food system transformation. *Journal of International Development* 27(5): 628–46.

UNDESA. 2018. World Population Prospects, 2018. New York, NY, U.S.A.: United National Department for Economic and Social Affairs, United Nations.

UNDESA. 2016. The Sustainable Development Goals Report 2016. New York, NY, U.S.A.: United Nations Department of Economic and Social Affairs.

World Bank. 2018. World Development Indicators Online Database. Washington DC, U.S.A.: The World Bank.

Zhang, X., J. Yang, and S. Wang. 2011. China has reached the Lewis turning point. *China Economic Review* 22(4): 542–54.

PART I

THEMATIC TRENDS ON YOUTH EMPLOYMENT

2

Can Migration be a Conduit for Transformative Youth Employment?

Valerie Mueller and Hak Lim Lee

2.1 Introduction

Migration has traditionally been considered a necessary component of the transformation process (de Brauw, Mueller, and Lee 2014). Rural workers are attracted to higher earning potential in the manufacturing or rural non-farm sectors (Harris and Todaro 1970). The latter process, which occurred in India, for example, was primarily driven by innovation and shifts in rural worker productivity. Both of these factors allowed for the creation of a rural labour surplus to transfer into the modern sector, as well as generated demand for additional goods and services in rural areas by augmenting the income of farmers (Hazell and Haggblade 1990).

Given demographic trends, African youth will be responsible for spearheading economic growth. Yet, they face more substantive barriers than their predecessors: declines in arable land (Jayne, Mather, and Mghenyi 2010, Muyanga and Jayne 2014), a lack of Green Revolution (Headey, Bezemer, and Hazell 2010, Nin-Pratt and McBride 2014) or government-sponsored industrialization (Jedwab and Vollrath 2015), and competition from the global economy (Headey, Bezemer, and Hazell 2010). In this chapter, we examine whether migration offers youth (ages 15–24, 25–34) access to more transformative forms of employment in four African countries, following the traditional pathways to structural change. While a few seminal youth migration studies have raised awareness of orphanhood in Africa (Beegle, De Weerdt, and Dercon 2006, Beegle et al. 2010), applications which demonstrate whether migration is a conduit for diversification and productive employment among youth are rare.

In what follows, we first establish the knowledge gaps in the literature with respect to the relationship between migration and sector-specific youth employment in Africa. We then focus on addressing a few of the highlighted knowledge gaps using descriptive evidence in four countries. First, we present statistics on the level of engagement in exclusive non-agricultural employment and joint non-agricultural and agricultural employment by youth migration status. Second, we illustrate whether migration allows youth to generate greater returns to

Valerie Mueller and Hak Lim Lee, *Can Migration be a Conduit for Transformative Youth Employment?* In: *Youth and Jobs in Rural Africa: Beyond Stylized Facts.* Edited by: Valerie Mueller and James Thurlow, Oxford University Press (2019). © International Food Policy Research Institute.
DOI: 10.1093/oso/9780198848059.003.0002

production. In particular, we compare the agricultural income per capita of youth migrants and non-migrants over time. We further disentangle whether migrants are more likely to move into high-return versus low-return non-agricultural occupations to supplement the income analysis.

2.2 Literature Review

2.2.1 Youth Engagement in the Agricultural Sector

Recent empirical evidence in Africa suggests declining trends in the size of landholdings of rural households (Jayne, Mather, and Mghenyi 2010, Muyanga and Jayne 2014). In a few concentrated countries, these associations are driven by the underutilization of land due to conflict, forested area, or remoteness and isolation (Chamberlain, Jayne, and Headey 2014). Other African countries, specifically those covered in the LSMS–ISA, suffer from limited surplus of land and high population pressure. In light of the emerging scarcity of arable land, there is a growing research interest to uncover whether diminishing landholdings has been accompanied by increased agricultural intensification to maintain or enhance yields.

Sheahan and Barrett (2014) examine various input practices (use of fertilizer, improved seeds, agro-chemicals, animal traction, and mechanized equipment) among households in the LSMS-ISA countries. Although modern input use is relatively low in aggregate, the application of inorganic fertilizer and agro-chemicals has become more common in Ethiopia, Malawi, and Nigeria than documented in previous work by Minot and Benson (2009). Using alternative data sources, Headey and Jayne (2014) and Muyanga and Jayne (2014) show the application of the aforementioned inputs is positively related to changes in population density. The intersection between input intensification, land size, and labour use is of notable importance for understanding employment trends more broadly and youth employment patterns specifically.

Thus far, multiple studies find negative relationships between farm size and input use (Barrett, Bellemare, and Hou 2010, Bellemare 2013, Carletto, Savastano, and Zezza 2013, Headey, Dereje, and Taffesse 2014, Larson et al. 2014, Sheahan and Barrett 2014), which suggests intensifying farming practices may be used to overcome land constraints to productivity. For the case of Ethiopia, Headey, Dereje, and Taffesse (2014) find a small, positive correlation between farm size and hired labour, but a much stronger negative relationship with family labour and farm size. Their interpretation of the results is that small farms use land more intensively while large farms are labour constrained. Complementary relationships between labour and input use, particularly for small farms, could suggest an increase in the demand for family labour and perhaps youth employment.

Projections of youth employment in agriculture will depend not only on farm size but the substitutive and complementary nature of modern inputs and labour by stage of one's life cycle status.

The existence of agricultural wage labour markets and land rental markets may provide additional forums for youth to continue engaging in agriculture, under sparse opportunities for landownership (for example, as shown in Ethiopia by Bezu and Holden (2014)). With respect to the latter, Deininger, Xia, and Savastano (2015) show land-poor households and households with younger heads are more likely to take advantage of these opportunities to access land in Malawi, Nigeria, Niger, Tanzania, and Uganda. Dillon and Barrett (2014) foreshadow limitations to off-farm employment opportunities in the agricultural sector given existing market failures. First, in most cases, the percentage of households hiring workers for non-harvest types of employment exceeds the percentage of households hiring workers for harvest employment. Second, as the number of acres per household member increases, the hiring of outside workers does not increase proportionally. Economies of scale of labour, or credit market failures possibly explain these patterns.

The above studies imply youth participation in agricultural employment will depend on at least two factors. First, if land-constrained households are driven to intensify their land to overcome productivity constraints, then youth employment on family farms will depend on the complementary nature between those inputs and youth labour. Furthermore, whether youth self-select into on-farm or off-farm agricultural jobs will depend on the factor-bias of the input technology adopted (Bustos, Caprettini, and Ponticelli 2016). Second, increased access to land and opportunities for employment off of the farm may allow youth to continue working in agriculture. Understanding the nature of local land rental and sales markets will be important in measuring the determinants of youth employment in the agricultural sector, as well as the composition of medium and large-scale farms to gauge demand for agricultural wage labour.

2.2.2 Youth Diversification Out of Agriculture

A few stylized facts regarding diversification trends out of agriculture have emerged from the Sub-Saharan Africa employment literature. While diversification out of agriculture is on the rise (Jones and Tarp 2012), agriculture continues to absorb a significant share of the workforce (Jones and Tarp 2012, Page 2012, Davis, Di Giuseppe, and Zezza 2014, McCullough 2017). The nonfarm wage sector (private and public) has grown but participation remains less common (Jones and Tarp 2012, Fox and Sohnesen 2012); instead, the informal sector is the principal locus of new job creation (Jones and Tarp 2012, Fox and Sohnesen 2012, De Vreyer and Roubaud 2013, Nagler and Naudé 2014). Household entrepreneurship has the potential to increase the marginal productivity of labour and enhance welfare (Reardon 1997, Grimm, Knorringa, and Lay 2012, Nagler and Naudé 2014, McCollough 2017).

Earlier household analyses emphasize the importance of household demographic composition and household head's age on diversification out of agriculture. Jones and Tarp (2012) and Nagler and Naudé (2014) find the percentages of adults and young male workers (Jones and Tarp only) are negatively associated with specialization in agriculture in Mozambique. Bezu and Barrett (2012) monitor employment transitions into and between low- and high-return rural nonfarm employment using panel data from Ethiopia (1999, 2004). They find transitions from low-return to high-return rural nonfarm employment are positively correlated with the number of children aged 5 to 14 in 1999. The authors posit that children may not directly engage in rural nonfarm employment, but serve as substitutes for adult household labour. Older heads are also found to be more likely to diversify out of agriculture (Nagler and Naudé 2014), but other studies have shown older heads can also revert back to agriculture after operating an enterprise (Bezu and Barrett 2012).

A logical next question is how will these trends affect youth. Researchers have first focused on educational trends to understand whether youth have different earning potential than previous generations. While education levels have increased, they remain low (Filmer and Fox 2014, Garcia and Fares 2008, Elder and Kone 2014). Rural youth are much less likely to be in school than their urban counterparts (Filmer and Fox 2014, Garcia and Fares 2008). Although labour participation remains high (McCullough 2017, Gracia and Fares 2008, Jones and Tarp 2012), underemployment is rife (Shehu and Nilsson 2014, Jones and Tarp 2012). Opportunities to diversify out of agriculture, particularly into high-return activities, may be low given extant skill deficits (Filmer and Fox 2014).

Elder and Kone (2014) report findings from the ILO's School-to-Work Transition surveys (2012–13) covering 15–29 year old individuals at the national level for eight countries in SSA (Benin, Liberia, Madagascar, Malawi, Tanzania, Togo, Uganda, and Zambia) with an average sample size of 3,300 persons. Forty-six per cent of the unemployed youth indicate employment searches lasting longer than a year, mainly in pursuit of establishing their own business or farm, or finding a job in the public or private sector. The biggest obstacle to finding employment was articulated to be a paucity of jobs, as well as insufficient qualifications for existing jobs. They find working youth tended to engage in skilled agricultural and fishery occupations (35.7 per cent), followed by service (25.7 per cent), shop and market sales work (18.3 per cent), elementary occupations (18.3 per cent), and craft and related trade work (10 per cent).

The aforementioned studies contend relatively high youth participation rates with a concentration in the agricultural sector in rural areas. One open question is to what extent are these rates influenced by the mobility of youth. Youth migration patterns motivated by education (de Brauw, Mueller, and Woldehanna 2013) and orphanhood (Beegle, De Weerdt, and Dercon 2006, Beegle et al. 2010) have been documented in various African contexts. The omission of youth migrants from surveys could influence how labour participation rates and shifts in employment are perceived in the broader literature.

Another discrepancy in the literature arises from the lack of detailed information on agricultural occupations and youth productivity. McCullough (2017) shows that the measure of productivity can affect marginal productivity of labour estimates. For example, when measuring output per person per year, the productivity of workers receiving wages in industry, agriculture, and enterprises are higher than on farms in Malawi, Tanzania, and Uganda. However, when the productivity ratio is based on output per hour, then she finds farm productivity is higher than for all other sectors in Ethiopia and Malawi but not Tanzania and Uganda. The differences are largely due to a higher number of hours supplied to nonfarm work. It is possible for youth to remain in agriculture, but they are positioned to drive a structural transformation in agriculture with respect to being more productive, more likely to work in modern agricultural jobs or jobs at higher stages of the value chain. In this context, migration may still be utilized by youth in order to access land to facilitate entry into more commercialized agricultural self-employment.

2.3 Data

We use the Living Standards Measurement Study-Integrated Surveys on Agriculture (LSMS–ISA) in Ethiopia (2011–12, 2013–14), Malawi (2010–11, 2012–13), Nigeria (2010–11, 2012–13), and Tanzania (2008–19, 2010–11) (World Bank 2016a, b, c, d) to construct an individual dataset of youth ages 15–34 for descriptive statistics on youth migration between baseline and endline per country. Approximately, 5,364 observations in Ethiopia, 4,060 in Malawi, 7,383 in Nigeria, and 4,618 in Tanzania are used to create the migration statistics. Otherwise, when we focus on rural non-migrants, rural–rural migrants, and rural–urban migrants, we have 4,732 observations in Ethiopia, 2,960 in Malawi, 5,179 in Nigeria, and 3,101 in Tanzania, respectively. The analyses using the employment and income outcomes draw from smaller youth samples since we are missing individual responses for those outcomes over time.

We define a person as a migrant if he was a member of the household at baseline and departed the household in the follow-up survey. Different instruments were used to detect migration in the surveys. For the Malawi and Tanzania surveys, the migration definition is based on the diligent tracking of split-off households. In Ethiopia and Nigeria, we rely on information reported by the proxy respondent in the follow-up survey on the whereabouts of each household member from the baseline roster. Since the baseline and follow-up rounds are two years apart, our measure of migration is over a two-year period and therefore considered a permanent move. However, a key limitation in our interpretation of migration across regions will be our inability to disentangle the variation in mobility that stems from differences in contexts across countries from the variation in mobility due to measurement differences associated with the use of different survey instruments and interview times across countries.

We additionally define the migrant by origin and destination using rural and urban classifications established in the surveys: rural–rural, rural–urban, urban–urban, urban–rural. We are unable to compute representative urban–urban and urban–rural migration rates for Ethiopia, because the baseline survey did not sample large towns until the second round and therefore are omitted from the sample. The definition of urban in Ethiopia typically consists of small (population less than 10,000) and large (population greater than 10,000) towns. Thus, the urban–urban and urban–rural migration rates constructed in this chapter reflect migration within and to smaller towns rather than within and to metropolitan areas.

Detailed information on individual employment was extrapolated from the wage, agricultural on–farm labour, and non-agricultural enterprise modules of the surveys. These modules document any engagement in wage or self-employment activities over a 12-month period. We focus on labour participation rather than hours supplied. In our descriptive statistics, a youth is considered to have engaged in a specific activity irrespective of the number of hours reported. This allows us to avoid measurement issues associated with missing hours in the supplied values, but of course fails to account for differences in partial versus full employment. For the purpose of the analysis, we define employment portfolios into four categories: exclusively agriculture, exclusively non-agriculture, mixed agriculture and non-agriculture, and student. For brevity, an individual who was actively a student is automatically placed in the last category, despite evidence of engagement in farm or off-farm activities.

One of the aims of this piece is to evaluate whether relocation offers youth opportunities to diversify employment or improve their agricultural production prospects. This requires knowledge of employment of migrants and non-migrants over time. Since tracking at the individual level was only performed in Malawi and Tanzania, detailed descriptive statistics on employment and income patterns by migration status are only available for these countries.

We compute income by source for each household to illustrate qualitatively whether migration improved the prospects of youths (ages 15–34). The recall period for income dates 12 months prior to the interview for the Tanzania surveys and 12–18 months prior to the interview for the Malawi survey. Incomes are winsorized at the 5 per cent level to remove influences from outliers and measurement error on descriptive statistics.

2.4 Results

2.4.1 Youth Migration

Figure 2.1 provides the youth migration rates by country and gender for two cohorts: 15–24 and 25–34. We focus on those splitting from their household, originating from rural areas given the premise of the book (see Figure 2.2).[1] The percentage of young men in rural areas migrating to other rural areas is as high as 13.6 per cent in Ethiopia and 17.6 per cent in Malawi. Rural–rural migration rates for women in these two countries are slightly greater than the rates of young men at 17.5 per cent and 23.3 per cent. Rural–urban migration rates are considerably lower. The highest migration to cities occurs among Ethiopian young men (9.7 per cent) and women (8.4 per cent). The remaining countries have rural–urban migration rates within the range of 2 to 5 per cent. Young adults (25–34) are less mobile than the younger cohort, particularly in Ethiopia and Malawi.

Figure 2.3 displays the primary motivation for youth migration. Interestingly, the rates of rural youth claiming to move to other rural areas for employment reasons are quite similar across cohorts with the exception of Malawi. For example, 13.7 per cent of 15–24 year old migrants report moving for employment in Nigeria compared to 12.6 per cent of 25–34 year old migrants. The distinctions in reasons for moving are more pronounced among classes of rural–urban migration. The most drastic example takes place in Ethiopia. Approximately, 31.9 per cent of 15–24 year olds state having moved for work, while 55.4 per cent indicate having moved for education. This can be compared to 49.6 per cent of rural–urban young adult migrants reporting having moved for employment and a mere 12.5 per cent for education.

We further compare the distances travelled by migration pattern (not shown here). The median distance that young (15–24) rural–rural male (female) migrants travel is 1.4 (1.4) kilometres in Malawi, and 0.2 (1.6) kilometres in Tanzania. These figures can be compared to those obtained for rural–urban male (female) migrants who undergo median travel distances of 68.1 (59.8) kilometres in Malawi, and 90.3 (54.5) kilometres in Tanzania. These figures are qualitatively comparable for the older youth cohort. For example, the median distance that mature youth (25–34) rural–rural male (female) migrants travel is 1.2 (0.3) kilometres in Malawi, and 0.3 (3.4) kilometres in Tanzania. These figures can be compared to those obtained for rural–urban male (female) migrants who undergo median travel distances of 74.8 (25.2) kilometres in Malawi and 61.9 (37.7) kilometres in Tanzania. Workers

---

[1] Figure 2.2 illustrates youth migration rates for those departing with the entire household. Rates of migration are much lower, although still noteworthy in size for rural populations in Malawi and Tanzania.

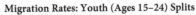

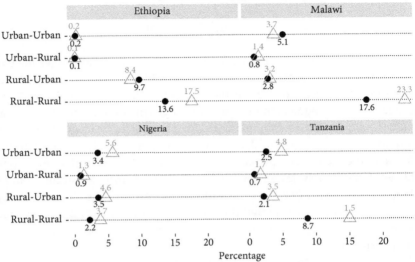

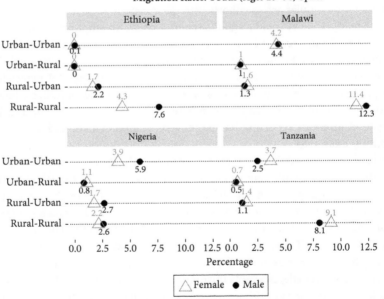

Figure 2.1. Youth migration rates

Note: Sampling weights used to calculate statistics

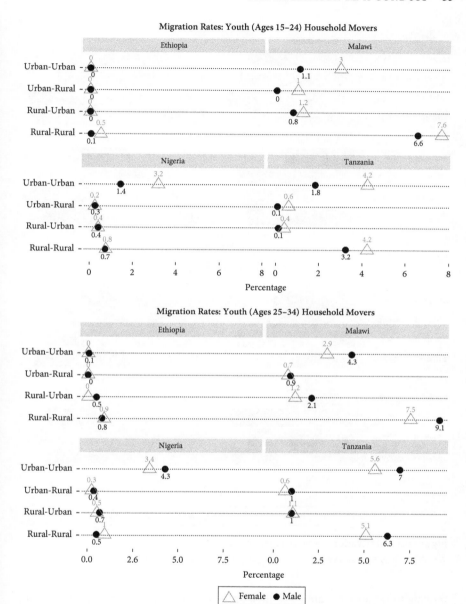

Figure 2.2. Migration rates of youth moving with their entire household

Note: Sampling weights used to calculate statistics

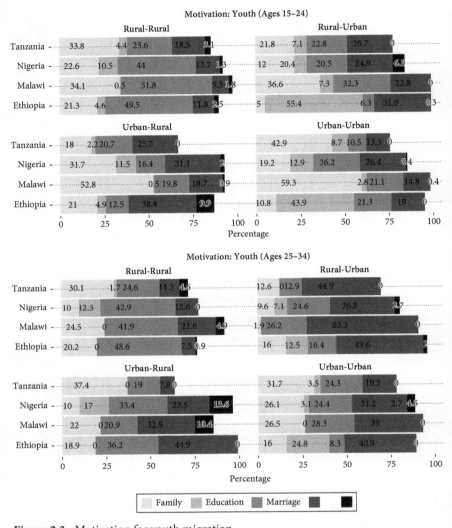

Figure 2.3. Motivation for youth migration

Note: Other motivation category omitted. Sampling weights used to calculate statistics

moving to urban areas are not only more likely to claim that they are moving for employment but they are travelling greater distances to fulfil their objectives.

One might expect differences across cohorts within migration patterns due to variations in life cycle stages. For example, the concept of 'waithood' refers to African youth delaying marriage and other milestones due to unemployment (Honwana 2012). However, what is particularly interesting is that the distribution of employment migrants is quite consistent across cohorts within the rural–rural migrant sample and markedly distinct across cohorts within the rural–urban migrant sample.

A major portion of rural–urban migration may comprise industrious rural youth looking for auxiliary employment opportunities, or, as in Ethiopia, moving to attend secondary and tertiary schools unavailable in their rural locales with the possibility of remaining at their destination for employment upon completion of their degrees.

2.4.2 Evolution of Sectoral Employment among Tracked Migrant and Non-migrant Rural Youth: Malawi and Tanzania Case Studies

As standard panel surveys track the developments of non-migrants, the omission of rural–urban migrants from surveys may be responsible for reporting bias in rural youth employment trends. We next compare the employment patterns of migrants and non-migrants by rural youth cohort starting first with available data in Malawi (Figure 2.4). The majority of rural–urban migrants (aged 15–24) were students at baseline (50.7 per cent). Slightly fewer rural–urban migrants were students following their move (21.7 per cent of migrants compared to 24.9 per cent of non-migrants). All migrants and non-migrants engaged in similar levels of mixed sector employment (9.6 per cent of youth rural–urban migrants and 9.0 per cent of non-migrants) in the follow-up round. While the trend for non-migrants in the youth cohort was an increase of 11.5 per cent working exclusively in the agricultural sector after the baseline, 12.6 per cent of youth migrants left the agricultural sector upon arrival in urban areas. Furthermore, the percentage of rural–urban migrant youth exclusively working in non-agriculture increased from 2.1 per cent to 28.6 per cent.

The young adult cohort employment statistics suggest similar trends as observed for the youth cohort. At baseline, a more substantive portion of rural–urban migrants begin in mixed livelihood strategies (34.5 per cent compared to 19.5 per cent), and much fewer in agriculture (43.4 per cent compared to 75.6 per cent). The rural–urban migrants then shift exclusively to non-agriculture, when only 6.2 per cent of rural–urban migrants were in this category of employment before the move. By the follow up survey, 55.0 per cent of rural–urban migrants worked exclusively in non-agriculture compared to 1.7 per cent of non-migrants within the same age group.

The statistics in Figure 2.4 suggest rural–rural migration enables diversification more than entry into the non-agricultural labour market. For the youngest cohort, exclusive employment in agriculture at baseline is similar among stayers and movers to other rural areas (47.7 and 45.5 per cent, respectively). Yet, the percentage of rural–rural migrants working only in the agricultural sector increases to 60.7 per cent, while for non-migrants the increase is slightly lower (59.2 per cent). Although fewer rural–rural migrants engage in mixed sectoral employment than non-migrants (2.2 per cent compared to 5.4 per cent),

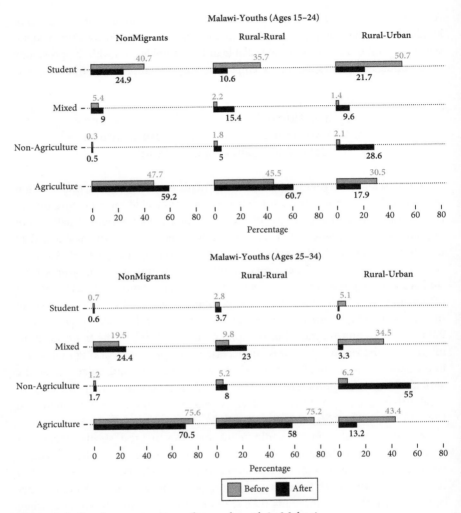

Figure 2.4. Employment patterns for rural youth in Malawi

Note: Unemployment category omitted. Sampling weights used to calculate statistics.

a remarkable percentage of rural–rural migrants diversify in the follow-up round (15.4 per cent compared to 9.0 per cent). The patterns of diversification among the older cohort of rural–rural migrants are quite similar, with the exception that there was an overall decreasing trend in agricultural labour market participation for 25–34 year olds irrespective of mobility in the follow-up round. All rural–rural migrant cohorts are more likely to participate in the non-agricultural sector but at a more modest level than their rural–urban counterparts.

The findings in Malawi offer the hypothesis that migration may facilitate entry into labour markets auxiliary to agricultural wage and self-employment. Young migrants diversify out of agriculture through partial employment in the non-agricultural sector. However, it appears that rural–urban migration in Malawi offers a more significant fraction of youth to gradually progress out of agricultural employment into exclusive non-agricultural employment.

We next turn to the evolution of employment trends for rural youth in Tanzania (Figure 2.5). The youth migrant employment trends are similar but more pronounced than witnessed in Malawi. Fewer rural–urban migrants than non-migrants were employed in the agricultural sector at baseline (36.7 and 46.1 per cent, respectively). By the follow-up round, 28.6 per cent of rural–urban migrants left the agricultural sector when the trend among rural youth was a 10.2 per cent increase in labor participation in the agricultural sector. Although slightly more rural–urban migrants were in the non-agricultural sector at baseline (2.1 per cent compared to 1.3 per cent), their rate of engagement augmented to 34.1 per cent in the follow-up

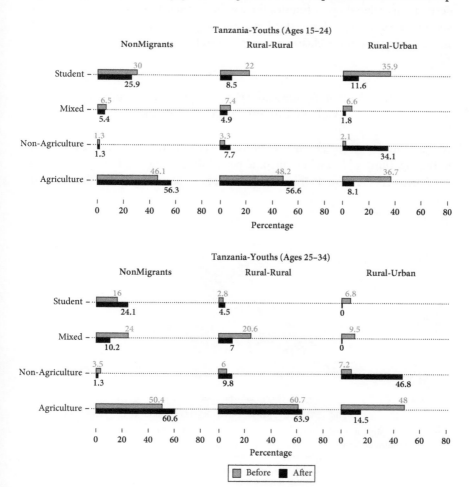

Figure 2.5. Employment patterns for rural youth in Tanzania

Note: Unemployment category omitted. Sampling weights used to calculate statistics.

round compared to a status quo participation of this sector among non-migrants. The trends are quite similar for young adult rural–urban migrants.

In Tanzania, rural–rural migration did not have as much of a prolific impact on labour diversification as in Malawi in the follow-up round. Rather, rural–rural migration encouraged a greater percentage of youth and young adults to participate in exclusive agricultural employment. Similarly, the percentage of youth and young adults working in mixed livelihood strategies diminished from 7.4 per cent to 4.9 per cent and 20.6 per cent to 7.0 per cent, respectively. The growth in participation of exclusive non-agriculture employment almost compensates for the observed loss in mixed sectoral employment for the 15–24 (but not the 25–34) age cohort.

In summary, our case studies show that over the time period covered by the first two rounds of the Malawi and Tanzania panel surveys, migration to urban destinations offered opportunities for youths to enter the non-agricultural market. Rural–rural migration instead guaranteed prospects for diversification with smaller entry into the exclusive non-agricultural sector.

2.4.3 Shifts in Space and More Productive Occupations: Malawi and Tanzania Case Studies

As a first attempt to gauge whether moves are productive, we compare the change in the logarithm of household income per adults among youth originating from rural areas (15–34) and their non-migrant counterparts. Figure 2.6 illustrates the

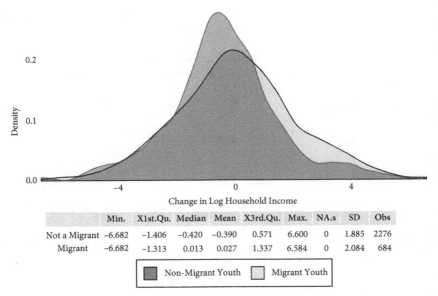

	Min.	X1st.Qu.	Median	Mean	X3rd.Qu.	Max.	NA.s	SD	Obs
Not a Migrant	−6.682	−1.406	−0.420	−0.390	0.571	6.600	0	1.885	2276
Migrant	−6.682	−1.313	0.013	0.027	1.337	6.584	0	2.084	684

Non-Migrant Youth   Migrant Youth

Figure 2.6. Change in income per adults by migration status in Malawi (ages 15–34)

distribution of changes in income which occurred in Malawi, where the dark gray- and light gray-shaded areas reflect the values for the non-migrants and migrants, respectively. On average, the sample of youth experienced losses over this time period. Yet, migrant youth income improved significantly (2.7 per cent) compared to the losses of non-migrant youth (39.0 per cent) according to a simple t statistic (p-value = 0.00). We further reject that the distribution of the change in income is statistically equivalent across the two samples using a Kolmogorov–Smirnov test (p-value = 0.00) (Smirnov 1933).[2]

We perform a similar exercise using information from the Tanzanian youth, leading to quite similar conclusions. In Figure 2.7, we observe that the average change in migrant youth income per adult increased 37.9 per cent relative to an increase of 21.4 per cent experienced by their rural counterparts. We cannot reject that the changes in income per adult on average are statistically different across the two samples (t test p-value = 0.16), but the distributional differences by migration status remain (Kolmogorov–Smirnov p-value = 0.00).

Income measures traditionally suffer from a considerable amount of measurement error, which may influence our ability to affirmatively associate migration with improvements in youth job prospects. To complement the above analysis,

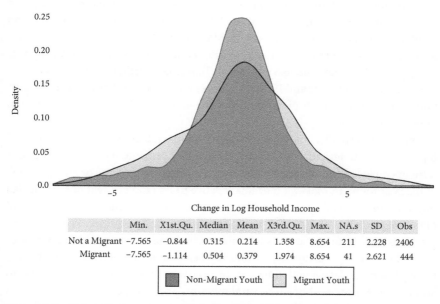

	Min.	X1st.Qu.	Median	Mean	X3rd.Qu.	Max.	NA.s	SD	Obs
Not a Migrant	–7.565	–0.844	0.315	0.214	1.358	8.654	211	2.228	2406
Migrant	–7.565	–1.114	0.504	0.379	1.974	8.654	41	2.621	444

Non-Migrant Youth   Migrant Youth

Figure 2.7. Change in income per adults by migration status in Tanzania (ages 15–34)

[2] We also conduct a sensitivity analysis by reflecting on comparisons of income per individuals (rather than the number of adults) in the household. The patterns are similar as previously observed. The change in income averages and distributions remain different across samples (t test p-value = 0.00; Kolmogorov–Smirnov p-value = 0.00).

we demonstrate whether migrants are more likely to move from presumably low-return agriculture to high-return nonfarm employment. This requires developing a typology similar to Bezu and Barrett (2012), categorizing the occupations of youth into low-return and high-return non-agricultural activities. We then show how the employment transitions between waves 1 and 2 vary by whether youth stayed in their baseline location, moved to a rural destination, or moved to an urban destination in the Malawi and Tanzania surveys.

Table 2.1 displays the employment transitions between waves by migration status in Malawi and Tanzania. In rural areas, 61.7 per cent and 53.6 per cent of the youth non-migrant population remained engaged in agricultural employment throughout the two waves in Malawi and Tanzania, respectively. These figures are comparable to the employment rates of the adult non-migrant population, which we also include in Table 2.1 as a reference but leave out of the discussion hereafter. The figures are only slightly reduced for the rural–rural migrant population (49.5 per cent in Malawi and 40.0 per cent in Tanzania). In short, the majority of the youth population who remains or moves within rural areas stays in the agricultural sector.

In both countries, rural–urban and rural–rural migration offer more possibilities for youth to engage in high-return employment which confers the observed positive income change associated with mobility. A greater percentage of rural–urban migrants (17.3 per cent in Malawi and 15.5 per cent in Tanzania) and rural–rural migrants (13.7 per cent in Malawi and 10.1 in Tanzania) specialize in high-return wage/enterprise activities compared to rural non-migrants (7.6 per cent in Malawi and 6.8 per cent in Tanzania). Further, 22.2 (19.6) per cent of rural–urban migrants and 15.3 (8.4) per cent of rural–rural migrants in Malawi (Tanzania) transition out of agriculture compared to 10.2 (4.8) per cent of rural non-migrants.

Relocation also offers the unemployed additional job opportunities in low- and high-return non-agricultural activities. Less than 1 per cent of rural non-migrants were unemployed and obtained a low-return or high-return wage or enterprise job in the later round in Malawi (Tanzania) relative to 7.5 (7.7) per cent of rural–urban migrants and 2.8 (2.2) per cent of rural–rural migrants. While the probability of obtaining a job in a high-return activity for the unemployed is marked higher for youth moving to urban areas, such movement comes with an additional risk of unemployment. Approximately, 4.6 and 12.7 per cent of rural–urban migrants were unemployed in Malawi and Tanzania, respectively, in both rounds, compared to and 1.7 and 4.0 per cent of rural–rural migrants and 0.8 and 3.3 per cent of rural non-migrants. However, the difference in the proportions of migrant youth that remain unemployed in both rounds (relative to non-migrant rural youth) is only statistically significant when comparing rural–rural migrant employment rates with those of rural non-migrants.

Table 2.1. Employment rates by migration status

Employment Transitions	Malawi				Tanzania			
	Nonmigrant (35–60)	Nonmigrant (15–34)	Rural-urban migrant	Rural-rural migrant	Nonmigrant (35–60)	Nonmigrant (15–34)	Rural-urban migrant	Rural-rural migrant
Agriculture to student	0.000	0.016	0.032*	0.007	0.003	0.015	0.013	0.010
Agriculture to unemployed	0.021	0.031	0.121**	0.055**	0.013	0.037	0.208***	0.120***
Agriculture to agriculture	0.617	0.617	0.172***	0.495***	0.627	0.536	0.097***	0.400***
Agriculture to LR wage or enterprise	0.046	0.056	0.178	0.062***	0.016	0.016	0.129	0.032**
Agriculture to HR wage or enterprise	0.080	0.046	0.044***	0.090	0.031	0.032	0.067	0.052
LR wage or enterprise to student	0.000	0.000	0.000	0.000	0.002	0.001	0.000	0.002*
LR wage or enterprise to unemployed	0.000	0.001	0.000	0.000	0.006	0.005	0.019	0.011
LR wage or enterprise to agriculture	0.030	0.030	0.011*	0.018	0.115	0.075	0.000	0.062***
LR wage or enterprise to LR wage or enterprise	0.026	0.022	0.035**	0.009	0.008	0.010	0.022	0.008
LR wage or enterprise to HR wage or enterprise	0.016	0.004	0.000	0.009***	0.016	0.009	0.031	0.010
HR wage or enterprise to student	0.000	0.000	0.000	0.000	0.001	0.001	0.000	0.000
HR wage or enterprise to unemployed	0.004	0.002	0.029	0.003	0.002	0.002	0.000	0.007**
HR wage or enterprise to agriculture	0.061	0.031	0.000*	0.016***	0.062	0.041	0.000*	0.021***
HR wage or enterprise to LR wage or enterprise	0.008	0.006	0.009	0.008	0.005	0.006	0.000	0.003***

Continued

Table 2.1. Continued

	Malawi				Tanzania			
	Nonmigrant (35–60)	Nonmigrant (15–34)	Rural-urban	Rural-rural	Nonmigrant (35–60)	Nonmigrant (15–34)	Rural-urban	Rural-rural
HR wage or enterprise to HR wage or enterprise	0.070	0.030	0.061	0.024	0.038	0.016	0.011	0.014
Unemployed to student	0.000	0.004	0.000	0.001**	0.000	0.006	0.001***	0.000**
Unemployed to unemployed	0.007	0.008	0.046	0.017*	0.012	0.033	0.127	0.040**
Unemployed to agriculture	0.012	0.029	0.020***	0.079	0.029	0.076	0.066***	0.132
Unemployed to LR wage or enterprise	0.000	0.003	0.023*	0.010	0.001	0.003	0.017	0.005
Unemployed to HR wage or enterprise	0.001	0.004	0.052*	0.018*	0.004	0.008	0.060	0.017*
Student to student	0.000	0.012	0.034**	0.005	0.003	0.025	0.016***	0.001
Student to unemployed	0.000	0.007	0.042	0.005	0.000	0.009	0.070	0.013**
Student to agriculture	0.000	0.043	0.038	0.052	0.004	0.034	0.000	0.028***
Student to LR wage or enterprise	0.000	0.000	0.038**	0.012*	0.000	0.001	0.000	0.003
Student to HR wage or enterprise	0.000	0.002	0.016	0.005	0.001	0.003	0.046	0.008*
Individuals	1353	2276	84	600	1886	2612	96	388

Notes: * $p < 0.1$, ** $p < 0.05$, *** $p < 0.1$. T statistics test the difference between the proportion of migrants and non-migrants in each employment transition category for the consolidated 15–34 youth group. Rural–rural and rural–urban migrants are 15–34 years old.

2.5 Conclusion

The LSMS–ISA surveys are one of the few data collection efforts in Africa that enable researchers to view a more detailed snapshot of youth migration and employment transitions. We find young individuals, ages 15 to 24, are highly mobile in all four countries. The individual tracking protocols performed in the Malawi and Tanzania surveys allowed us to monitor transitions in income and employment between migrant and non-migrant youth samples. This analysis suggests migration is potentially welfare–enhancing both in terms of income improvements and employment prospects particularly for those migrants who were previously unemployed.

One thing to note is that, like any decision, youth face different tradeoffs when contemplating where to relocate. Rural–urban migration facilitates movement out of agriculture with a greater tendency towards high-return activities in Malawi and Tanzania, yet in absolute numbers this affects a small portion of youth. Rural–rural youth migration, in contrast, attracts a greater percentage of youth. It may be the most formative mobility pattern in the transformation process by encouraging youth to diversify from exclusive employment in the agricultural sector.

This chapter focuses exclusively on the migration and employment patterns of youth individuals. However, these patterns likely arise from decision-making behaviour at the household level. Of future interest will be to decipher the extent households spatially allocate young members to access income for agricultural intensification or farm expansion purposes, and further how these household decisions might be beneficial or harmful to youth in the long term. Understanding such household dynamics requires knowledge of whether youth migration patterns are driven by a household wealth effect, for example, from increases in investments (Deininger et al. 2008), or a substitution effect between youth labour and investments. These complementarities are important as the former (not the latter) has the potential to be transformative for youth.

References

Barrett, C., M. F. Bellemare, and J. Y. Hou. 2010. Reconsidering conventional explanations of the inverse productivity-size relationship. *World Development* 38 (1): 88–97.

Beegle, K., J. De Weerdt, and S. Dercon. 2006. Orphanhood and the long-run impact on children. *American Journal of Agricultural Economics* 88 (5): 1266–72.

Beegle, K., D. Filmer, A. Stokes, and L. Tiererova. 2010. Orphanhood and the living arrangements of children in Sub-Saharan Africa. *World Development* 38 (12): 1727–46.

Bellemare, M. F. 2013. The productivity impacts of formal and informal land rights: Evidence from Madagascar. *Land Economics* 89 (2): 272–90.

Bezu, S., and C. Barrett. 2012. Employment dynamics in the rural nonfarm sector in Ethiopia: Do the poor have time on their side? *Journal of Development Studies* 48 (9): 1223–40.

Bezu, S., and S. Holden. 2014. Are rural youth in Ethiopia abandoning agriculture? *World Development* 64: 259–72.

Bustos, P., B, Caprettini, and J. Ponticelli. 2016. Agricultural productivity and structural transformation. Evidence from Brazil. *American Economic Review* 106 (6): 1320–65.

Carletto, C., S. Savastano, and A. Zezza. 2013. Fact or artifact: The impact of measurement errors on the farm size–productivity relationship. *Journal of Development Economics* 103: 254–61.

Davis, B., S. Di Giuseppe, and A. Zezza. 2014. Income diversification patterns in rural Sub-Saharan Africa: Reassessing the evidence. Policy Research Working Paper 7108: Washington, DC, U.S.A.: World Bank.

de Brauw, A., V. Mueller, and H. K. Lee. 2014. The role of rural-urban migration in the structural transformation of Sub-Saharan Africa. *World Development* 10 (63), 33–42.

de Brauw, A., V. Mueller, and T. Woldehanna. 2013. Motives to remit: Evidence from tracked internal migrants in Ethiopia. *World Development* 50: 13–23.

De Vreyer, P., and F. Roubaud. 2013. *Urban labor markets in Sub-Saharan Africa.* Washington, DC, U.S.A.: World Bank.

Deininger, K., D. Ali, S. Holden, and J. Zevenbergen. 2008. Rural land certification in Ethiopia: Process, initial impact, and implications for other African countries. *World Development* 36 (10): 1786–812.

Deininger, K., F. Xia, and S. Savastano. 2015. *Smallholders' land ownership and access in Sub-Saharan Africa: A new landscape?* Policy Research Working Paper 7285. Washington, DC, U.S.A.: World Bank.

Dillon, B., and C. B. Barrett. 2014. Agricultural factor markets in Sub-Saharan Africa An updated view with formal tests for market failure. *Food Policy* 67: 64–77.

Elder, S., and K. S. Kone. 2014. *Labour market transitions of young women and men in Sub-Saharan Africa.* Work4Youth, No. 9. Geneva, Switzerland: International Labour Office.

Filmer, D., and L. Fox. 2014. *Youth employment in Sub-Saharan Africa.* Washington, DC, U.S.A.: World Bank.

Fox, L., and T. P. Sohnesen. 2012. *Household enterprises in Sub-Saharan Africa: Why they matter for growth, jobs, and livelihoods.* Policy Research Working Paper 6184. Washington, DC, U.S.A.: World Bank.

Garcia, M., and J. Fares. 2008. *Youth in Africa's labor market.* Washington, DC, U.S.A.: World Bank.

Grimm, M., P. Knorringa, and J. Lay. 2012. Constrained gazelles: High potentials in West Africa's informal economy. *World Development* 40 (7): 1352–68.

Harris, J. R., and M. Todaro. 1970. Migration, unemployment and development: A two-sector analysis. *American Economic Review* 60 (1), 126–42.

Hazell, P. B. and S. Haggblade. 1990. *Rural–urban growth linkages in India.* Working Paper Series 430. Washington, DC: World Bank.

Headey, D., D. Bezemer, and P. Hazell. 2010. Agricultural employment trends in Asia and Africa: Too fast or too slow? *World Bank Research Observer* 25, 57–89.

Headey, D., and T. S. Jayne. 2014. Adaptation to land constraints: Is Africa different? *Food Policy* 48: 18–33.

Headey, D., M. Dereje, and A. S. Taffesse. 2014. Land constraints and agricultural intensification in Ethiopia: A village-level analysis of high-potential areas. *Food Policy* 48: 129–41.

Honwana, A. M. 2012. *The time of youth: Work, social change, and politics in Africa.* London, U.K.: Kumarian Press.

Jayne, T. S., D. Mather, and E. Mghenyi. 2010. Principal challenges confronting smallholder agriculture in Sub-Saharan Africa. *World Development* 38 (10): 1384–1398.

Jedwab, R., and D. Vollrath. 2015. Urbanization without growth in historical perspective. *Explorations in Economic History* 58, 1–21.

Jones, S., and F. Tarp. 2012. *Jobs and welfare in Mozambique.* WIDER Working Paper 2013/045. Copenhagen, Denmark: UNU-WIDER.

Larson, D. F., K. Otsuka, T. Matsumoto, and T. Kilic. 2014. Should African rural development strategies depend on smallholder farms? An exploration of the inverse-productivity hypothesis. *Agricultural Economics* 45 (3): 355–67.

McCullough, E. B. 2017. Labor productivity and employment gaps in Sub-Saharan Africa. *Food Policy* 67: 133–52.

Minot, N., and T. Benson. 2009. *Fertilizer subsidies in Africa: Are vouchers the answer?* Issue Brief 60. Washington, DC, U.S.A.: International Food Policy Research Institute.

Muyanga, M., and T. S. Jayne. 2014. Effects of rising rural population density on smallholder agriculture in Kenya. *Food Policy* 48: 98–13.

Nagler, P., and W. Naudé. 2014. *Non-farm enterprises in rural Africa: New empirical evidence.* World Bank Policy Research Working Paper 7066: Washington, DC, U.S.A.: World Bank.

Nin-Pratt, A., and L. McBride. 2014. Agricultural intensification in Ghana: Evaluating the optimist's case for a Green Revolution. *Food Policy* 48, 153–167.

Page, J. 2012. *Youth, jobs, and structural change: Confronting Africa's 'employment problem'.* African Development Bank Working Paper 155. Tunis, Tunisia: African Development Bank.

Reardon, T. 1997. Using evidence of household income diversification to inform study of the rural nonfarm labor market in Africa. *World Development* 25 (5): 735–47.

Sheahan, M., and C. B. Barrett. 2014. *Understanding the input landscape in Sub-Saharan Africa: Recent plot, household, and community-level agricultural evidence.* Policy Research Working Paper 7014. Washington, DC, U.S.A.: World Bank.

Shehu, E., and B. Nilsson. 2014. *Informal employment among youth: Evidence from 20 school-to-work transition surveys*. Work4Youth Publication Series 9. Geneva, Switzerland: International Labour Organisation.

Smirnov, N. V. 1933. Estimate of deviation between empirical distribution functions in two independent samples. *Bulletin Moscow University* 2: 3–16.

World Bank. 2016a. Living Standards Measurement Study—Integrated Surveys on Agriculture, Ethiopia. Washington, DC, U.S.A. http://surveys.worldbank.org/lsms/programs/integrated-surveys-agriculture-ISA/ethiopia#bootstrap-panel--4. Accessed October 19, 2017.

World Bank. 2016b. Living Standards Measurement Study—Integrated Surveys on Agriculture, Malawi. Washington, DC, U.S.A. http://surveys.worldbank.org/lsms/programs/integrated-surveys-agriculture-ISA/malawi#bootstrap-panel--4. Accessed October 19, 2017.

World Bank. 2016c. Living Standards Measurement Study—Integrated Surveys on Agriculture, Nigeria. Washington, DC, U.S.A. http://surveys.worldbank.org/lsms/programs/integrated-surveys-agriculture-ISA/nigeria#bootstrap-panel--4. Accessed October 19, 2017.

World Bank. 2016d. Living Standards Measurement Study—Integrated Surveys on Agriculture, Tanzania. Washington, DC, U.S.A. http://surveys.worldbank.org/lsms/programs/integrated-surveys-agriculture-ISA/tanzania#bootstrap-panel--4. Accessed October 19, 2017.

3

Policies for Youth Employment in Sub-Saharan Africa

David Schwebel, Elisenda Estruch,
Peter Wobst, and Ileana Grandelis[1]

3.1 Introduction

The global trend of increased youth unemployment has led many governments and international organizations to develop youth-targeted policies and strategies. The 2030 Agenda for Sustainable Development in its Goal 8 commits to 'promote sustained, inclusive, and sustainable economic growth, full and productive employment, and decent work for all'. Specific targets were incorporated into this goal, including on achieving full employment for young people (8.5); on substantially reducing the proportion of youth not in employment, education, or training (8.6); as well as on developing and operationalizing a global strategy for youth employment by 2020 (8.b) (UNGA 2015).

At the regional level, the African Union (AU) has also a number of initiatives to promote youth employment. In its Agenda 2063, the AU commits to speed up actions to support young people through strategies that combat youth unemployment and underemployment (AU Commission 2015). In its Ouagadougou Declaration, the AU sets an overall regional framework for employment promotion by all AU member states, emphasizing youth and women. The Action Plan of this Declaration underlined the importance of promoting agricultural and rural development. This was followed by the Ouagadougou+10 Declaration on Employment, Poverty Eradicationand Inclusive Development in Africa in January 2015, thus reiterating the importance of placing employment at the centre of development strategies (AU Commission 2015). The Malabo Declaration on Accelerated Agricultural Growth and Transformation for Shared Prosperity and Improved Livelihoods includes a specific target to create job opportunities for at least 30 per cent of the youth in agricultural value chains (AU Summit 2014). Similarly, the Comprehensive Africa Agriculture Development Programme

---

[1] The views expressed in this chapter are the authors' own and do not necessarily reflect the views of the International Labour Organization (ILO) or the Food and Agriculture Organization (FAO).

David Schwebel, Elisenda Estruch, Peter Wobst, and Ileana Grandelis, *Policies for Youth Employment in Sub-Saharan Africa* In: *Youth and Jobs in Rural Africa: Beyond Stylized Facts.* Edited by: Valerie Mueller and James Thurlow, Oxford University Press (2019). © International Food Policy Research Institute.
DOI: 10.1093/oso/9780198848059.003.0003

(CAADP) Results Framework (2015–25) proposes expanding local agro-industry and value chain development (VCD) inclusive of women and youth (NEPAD 2015).

At the national level, many countries of Sub-Saharan Africa (SSA) have included objectives on youth employment promotion in their policies. Yet, much effort is still needed at the policy level to push support on rural youth employment to a scale commensurate with the magnitude of the challenge. In particular, additional efforts are needed to foster policy coherence towards more youth-friendly approaches for agriculture and food systems' development. Policy coherence should especially be encouraged between employment and youth policies, as well as agricultural and rural development policies.

This chapter presents a comparative qualitative policy analysis of national policies in Sub-Saharan Africa (SSA), based on a framework that incorporates the main constraints affecting the quantity and quality of rural youth employment. Whilst youth employment promotion in agriculture and rural areas is high in the regional and national agendas, few policy analytical frameworks and inventories include rural youth as a target group and this prevents analysing in a systematic and structured manner how the issue is being addressed in existing policies. Hence, the chapter builds on existing frameworks, which acknowledge the need for integrated policy approaches to youth employment, and further expands them by adding specific attention to rural youth and to the linkages between employment and rural development. The chapter follows by applying the analytical framework to 47 policies from 13 SSA countries from 1996 to 2016. The analysis follows the policy discourse analysis literature and focuses on the formulation stage of the policymaking process, therefore reviewing if the policy documents address main constraints to rural youth employment. The policies examined include development, agricultural, rural development, youth, and employment policies.

With the analytical framework, this chapter contributes to a more systematic and structured approach to raise awareness among policymakers and the development community about existing gaps in addressing the constraints to rural youth employment at policy level. This framework allows for the first time to systematically assess policies of SSA with a youth employment lens associated to the different pillars of the Decent Work Agenda. The importance of developing such a framework lies in the fact that previous policy reviews showed the prevalence of actions focused on labour supply, and the need to have a stronger focus on interventions addressing the labour demand.

The policy analysis conducted reveals several areas for improvement to create better employment opportunities for rural youth in SSA. In particular, the main findings show that policies focus more on promoting labour supply strategies— such as training programmes on entrepreneurship skills, rather than demand-side ones—such as reducing the constraints to business development and job creation at the sectoral level.

In particular, the unfavourable agribusiness environment for youth in rural areas was the constraint to rural youth employment least addressed by the policies analysed. Also, some constraints related to the quality of employment (labour regulations, social protection, and social dialogue) were insufficiently addressed. Yet, a sound institutional and regulatory framework is crucial to protect workers' rights and vulnerable youth groups. Other relevant aspects often not addressed were access to social protection and youth representation in social and policy dialogue.

3.2 Rural Labour Market Dynamics and Effects on Youth Employment

Employment dynamics in rural labour markets are different from urban areas. They are generally characterized for a sub-optimal allocation of labour and lower income of workers, which leads to limited rural development (Tocco, Davidova, and Bailey 2012). The main employment challenge in rural labour markets is not unemployment, but a higher incidence of underemployment, especially through self-employment and casual wage employment in the informal sector. This is the result of structural constraints in rural labour markets that particularly affect rural youth participation in the labour force. In rural areas of developing countries, the lack of infrastructure, investments, farm inputs, and policy support has led to low levels of human capital, an agricultural sector with low productivity, and limited non-agricultural employment opportunities. It is therefore important to better understand how the conditions affecting labour supply interact with those affecting labour demand across rural labour markets (ILO 2008).

The ILO proposes a comprehensive rural labour market framework (Table 3.1) in terms of supply, demand, and institutions which is useful to analyse its impacts on rural youth in SSA. The supply side is mainly determined by demographics, access to productive assets, education levels, and social norms. The young population in SSA is expected to continue growing in the next decades, leading to approximately 370 million young people joining labour markets in the next 15 years (AfDB et al. 2015). This can produce an oversupply of unskilled labour in rural areas with limited employment opportunities in farm and nonfarm activities. One of the main limiting factors is the low access to productive assets through financial services for rural youth—including credit, savings, and insurance—to start their own business. Another factor is low levels of education and limited skills that curb the productivity of rural youth and hinder their entrepreneurial abilities. Social norms, which define the role that rural youth should play in a community or household, can also impair their ability to find a job or start a business, especially for young women.

The demand side is affected by economic growth, investment levels, and market access. Low public and private investments in rural areas and agriculture causes limited rural enterprise growth and job creation, which contributes to widespread underemployment and offers young school leavers few viable employment

Table 3.1. Main characteristics of rural labour markets

Supply side	Institutions and intermediary structures and processes	Demand side
Conditions influencing supply ■ Population growth and family composition ■ Social norms related to labour supply ■ Migration patterns and intensity ■ Urban growth and associated labour demand ■ Access to land and other productive assets ■ Nutrition and health ■ Education and skills ■ Income transfers Types of work and workers ■ Waged workers, including permanent, fulltime, part-time, casual, temporary, seasonal, and so on ■ Self-employed, including both on-farm (smallholders) and off-farm (service providers and small-scale businesses) ■ Sharecroppers ■ Outgrowers and other rural workers under 'putting out' systems Categories of waged and/or self-employed workers who may be subjected to discrimination include: ■ Young workers ■ Women ■ Migrant workers ■ Landless poor ■ Indigenous people Special consideration needs to be given in rural areas to: ■ Child labour ■ Bonded labour	Government policies, regulations, and services ■ Macroeconomic and financial policies ■ Agricultural and sectoral policies ■ Trade and agricultural policies ■ Public investment (infrastructure, education, health, and so on) ■ Rule of law and property rights ■ Land reform processes ■ Labour codes and regulations, including international labour standards (ILS) ■ Information and marketing systems ■ Employment services ■ Enabling environment for business and investment ■ Donor policy (ODA) Social partners, civil society, and the private sector ■ Trade unions ■ Employers' organizations ■ Farmer/agricultural producer organizations ■ Cooperatives ■ Advocacy and service organizations, including NGOs ■ Private enterprises ■ Value chain and sectoral organizations ■ Marketing intermediaries ■ Financial intermediaries Social and cultural factors and economic institutions ■ Informal networks, family, and kinship ties ■ Cultural norms ■ Sharecropping ■ Contract farming and outgrower associations ■ Non-market-based labour exchanges ■ Debt peonage and bonded labour	Conditions influencing demand ■ General economic growth ■ Growth of agricultural output for the domestic market and for export ■ Market access for agricultural products with trading partners ■ Growth of rural non-farm activities ■ Public and private investment in rural areas ■ Technical progress in agriculture—type and intensity ■ Relative factor prices in agriculture and in relation to other sectors ■ Labour productivity in agriculture ■ Public works ■ Urban growth ■ Farm structure ■ Seasonality ■ Landownership structure

opportunities (ILO 2008). Rural youth also have limited access to land—either to acquire or lease—due to unclear and insecure land rights, inheritance laws, and customs. Young rural entrepreneurs also face difficulties in accessing markets for their products and integrating into value chains.

As can be seen, the rural youth face particular constraints both in the demand and supply side when entering the labour force. Their ability to achieve successful transitions into rural wage and productive self-employment depends on several factors, but most notably on the aggregate labour demand and job opportunities, quality training that meets rural labour market demands, social protection that reaches rural areas, protection of workers' rights, the elimination of youth discrimination, and collective bargaining by including young people in agricultural organizations. To address all these factors, adequate balance should be found between general interventions that favor an enabling environment for decent rural employment promotion and targeted interventions for rural youth.

Rural labour markets have the potential to create quality jobs for the rural youth. Beyond farm jobs, there is also significant potential for job creation in rural nonfarm activities around food value chains linked to sustainable agriculture, agribusiness development, and related support services. In SSA, for instance, the demand for food is increasing due to growing population, urbanization, and rising household income. This creates opportunities for suppliers and suggests that there is a largely untapped reservoir of employment opportunities in agriculture (FAO 2016). However, for the agricultural sector to attract youth, youth-targeted policies and investments are needed to improve the quality of the available jobs. Better working conditions will not only be crucial to sustainably increase agricultural productivity, but also key determinants to attract young people to rural jobs.

3.3 Methodology for Comparative Policy Analysis on Rural Youth Employment

Since the global employment crisis started in 2007, there has been increased attention on generating evidence on the most effective policies and interventions for governments to create jobs, especially for young people. Analytical frameworks increasingly recognize that policies focused only on labour supply (such as skills development) are not enough, and that an equally serious problem is insufficient labour demand (enterprise development and job creation initiatives) as well as poor working conditions (such as social protection programmes). This section provides a short overview of the strengths and gaps of existing frameworks to analyse youth employment, and proposes a new policy framework to better address youth employment focusing on rural areas. It later presents the proposed theoretical framework as well as the used methodology and scoring to analyse the policies.

3.3.1 Existing Frameworks for Employment Policy Analysis

Several frameworks have been recently proposed to analyse labour issues giving importance to different policy areas. The World Bank's MILES framework for employment stresses the importance of placing labour markets at the centre of the structural adjustment policy agenda (WB 2007). This multisectoral framework focuses on five areas: 1) Macroeconomic policies; 2) Investment climate, institutions, and infrastructure; 3) Labour market regulations and institutions; 4) Education and skills; and 5) Social Protection. It is based on the fact that successful policies must concentrate on key constraints to growth and job creation in each area. Its implementation can be examined in the evaluation report of the World Bank's Youth Employment Programmes. The portfolio review found that most youth employment projects focus on interventions in skills development (82 per cent), school-to-work transition (79 per cent), and interventions to foster job creation and work opportunities for youth (54 per cent) (IEG 2012).

Another policy framework focused on youth employment is the one proposed during the 2012 International Labour Conference (ILC), expressing the need for a multi-pronged, coherent, and context-specific approach (ILO 2012a). The policy responses included five policy areas: 1) employment and economic policies for youth employment; 2) employability—education, training, and skills, and the school-to-work transition; 3) labour market policies; 4) youth entrepreneurship and self-employment; and 5) rights for young people. In both the ILO and WB frameworks, there are several overlaps in the focus areas for employment creation.

Other useful tools to identify policies and programmes related to youth employment are the policy inventories and databases. For example, YouthPOL eAnalysis, ILO's database on youth employment policies, includes 65 countries with a total of 486 policy documents as of October 2016 divided into six policy areas: 1) Macroeconomic and sectoral policy; 2) Enterprise development; 3) Education and training; 4) Labour demand; 5) Labour law and legislation; and 6) Labour market policy. The policy area most addressed is education and training, showing a clear focus on labour supply. The database includes policies affecting youth employment in general, without a particular focus on rural youth.

Another relevant database is the Youth Employment Inventory (YEI), which provides comparative information of more than 750 projects to support young workers in over 90 countries. Although it covers some rural development programmes, it does not include a specific category on agriculture and rural development. In contrast, FAO's employment and decent work in rural areas policy database gives a comprehensive overview of agricultural and rural development policy and institutional frameworks. This database is an online inventory of current national, regional, and global policies, programs, and studies that are relevant to the promotion of more and better jobs in the rural areas of developing countries. Although the database does not focus exclusively on rural youth, it is a useful tool to identify and find information on policies that directly affect rural employment and different groups of workers, including rural youth.

The calls to develop policies focused on youth had a positive impact at the national level. According to the report on the State of Youth Policy 2014, from a total of 198 countries, 122 countries (62 per cent) had a national youth policy, a considerable increase from 99 countries in 2013. Another 37 countries (19 per cent) are currently developing or revising their youth policy, 31 countries (16 per cent) have no youth policy, and 8 countries (4 per cent) have unclear or unknown information (youthpolicy.org 2014). The report identified common issues on youth policies across countries including: education, training, employment, labour market access, health, and youth civic involvement. But again, the report does not explicitly assess aspects related specifically to rural youth or agriculture as a source of youth employment.

Few policy frameworks and inventories include rural youth as a target group since policies themselves seldom devote particular objectives to promote rural youth employment. Rural youth rarely participate in the policymaking process and therefore their voices are not heard, causing limited inclusion of their particular needs and constraints to find decent jobs. Policies also often fail to reflect the heterogeneity of young people given the lack of comprehensive data on rural youth as a distinct group (FAO, IFAD, and CTA 2014). As a result, policies are many times not implementable and/or sustainable in rural areas since they are designed by policymakers who are often unaware of the situation of rural youth (MIJARC, IFAD, and FAO 2012). Against this background, the AU has raised awareness in its African Youth Charter on the need to include the African youth in political processes by promoting measures to facilitate youth participation in the design, implementation, monitoring, and evaluation of national development plans, policies, and poverty reduction strategies (AU Commission 2006). It is therefore crucial to develop a comprehensive framework to analyse policies that affect rural employment from a youth perspective, especially in SSA.

3.3.2 Policy Framework for Rural Youth Employment Analysis

The proposed framework for policy analysis integrates the main constraints to rural youth employment into five policy areas: 1) sectoral development; 2) self-employment, employability, and skills development; 3) labour market institutions and regulations; 4) social protection; and 5) social and policy dialogue. The five areas were selected to develop a multipronged framework that covers the main issues that have an impact on youth labour supply and demand as well as on the job quality dimension. Within the policy areas, nine constraints were analysed to achieve productive and decent employment (See Table 3.2). The selection

Table 3.2. Policy framework for rural youth employment analysis

Policy area	Constraint	Importance	Examples of inclusion in policies
Sectoral development (including private sector development)	Low investments in agriculture and rural development	Investments in infrastructure and services, including business development services, make rural markets work better and provide more job opportunities for rural youth. Investments in value chain addition facilitate value chain development (VCD) and job creation.	- Agricultural policy: investments in agricultural diversification, sustainable intensification, micro, small, and medium enterprises (MSMEs), and VCD. - Rural development policy: investments in infrastructure, access to energy and water, quality education, and health.
	Weak labour demand	Innovative mechanisms for youth employment creation in rural areas, including nonfarm and agricultural wage employment. Food systems can be supported through different strategies which might be more or less employment-enhancing.	- Prioritization of employment-intensive sectors/technologies/practices or sectors where most of the rural poor live and work. - Employment-creation among the criteria for value chain/investment selection.
	Unfavourable agribusiness environment for youth	To develop agribusinesses rural youth need access to key productive resources such as land, labour, water, financial services, and infrastructure. Rural youth can also engage in existing agribusiness and agricultural value chains as wage workers, contract farmers, and suppliers.	- Dedicated action to address youth constraints to engage in agribusiness (for example, access to credit, land, markets, and so on). - Specific fora established on youth involvement in specific value chains - Priority on youth intergenerational land and farm transfer. - Youth mainstreaming into agricultural productivity interventions.
Self-employment, employability and skills development	Job-relevant skills constraints and lack of adequate education	Rural skills development, including extension services, and relevant youth training to the needs of rural labour markets can raise youth productivity and employability. Better educated youth are more likely to make good use of resources and adopt agricultural technologies.	- Formal and non-formal agricultural technical and vocation education and training/extension services - Basic education to develop literacy and numeracy skills. - Tertiary agricultural education. - Youth apprenticeship mechanisms. - Skills development programmes. - Certification programmes for rural youth.
	Job search, information, and business start-up constraints	Employment services expanded to rural areas provide job search assistance and information for rural youth. Young farmers need resources and information to start an agribusiness. Partnerships established with the private sector to facilitate school to work transitions.	- Inclusion of youth kits, microfinance mechanisms and saving groups, and so on. - Increase awareness of self-employment and wage employment opportunities, especially for young women. - Introduce agricultural and labour market information systems.

Labour market institutions and regulations	Weak regulations, standards and rights at work	Young rural workers need to improve in the terms and conditions of employment (for example, occupational safety and health (OSH), wages, minimum working age, and so on). ILS should be enforced in rural areas.	- Review regulatory framework to capture youth as a target group. - Ensure enforcement of decent work standards. - Institutional capacity for monitoring OSH standards in enterprises employing youth
	Social constraints	Remove cultural and systematic discrimination (for example, gender, ethnicity, religion, disability, and so on) for vulnerable youth groups to access decent jobs.	- Mainstream gender in all youth development approaches and interventions. - Special attention given to vulnerable rural youth groups, including indigenous, migrant, and poor youth.
Social protection	Limited social protection	Extend social protection coverage to rural areas to protect rural youth, promote their livelihoods and productivity, and overcome socioeconomic exclusion.	- Social support programmes that target youth. - Tax exemptions on agricultural inputs for youth. - Cash transfers include young beneficiaries. - Promote youth-friendly health services.
Social and policy dialogue	Limited social dialogue and youth representation	Facilitate engagement of rural youth in governance mechanisms, including producer associations and cooperatives to defend their interests.	- Promote youth participation in the decision-making processes. - Encourage rural youth to join or form associations and cooperatives.

of the policy areas is based on existing frameworks adapted to the reality of rural labour markets. In particular, they reflect the pillars of the Decent Work Agenda emphasizing the key role that the development of the agricultural sector plays in rural areas as it still occupies the vast majority of the labour force, reaching 75 per cent or above in certain Sahel and East African countries (Losch 2017). Within each of the policy areas, the selected constraints reflect the main bottlenecks that prevent young people from accessing decent jobs in rural areas.

The policy framework was used to analyse the content of 47 policies from 13 countries of SSA (see Table 3.A1 for complete list of policies per country). Its main purpose was to determine whether or not key constraints to rural youth employment were addressed in the policy documents. Depending on availability, four types of policy were taken by country: 1) development policy, vision, or strategy to reduce poverty; 2) employment policy; 3) youth policy; and 4) agricultural or rural development policy. The rationale for selecting these four types was to assess the consistency of interventions across policies and policy coherence towards rural youth employment promotion.

3.3.3 Policy Discourse Analysis

It is important to begin by explaining what is meant by policy analysis as well as the selected theoretical background and methodology. Policy analysis emerged as a technique to better understand the policymaking process and provide decision makers with reliable knowledge and information on pressing economic and social problems (Fischer, Miller, and Sidney 2007). There are multiple quantitative and qualitative methods that can be used to analyse policies depending on the area of interest and purpose of the analysis. The methodology could also vary depending on the stage in the policy cycle being observed: either the formulation, implementation, or evaluation of a policy.[2] As the purpose of the current policy analysis is to examine if the constraints to rural youth employment are addressed in selected policies, we focus on the formulation stage of the policymaking process.

During the policy formulation, the objectives are defined based on the priorities of a government and the development needs of a country. At this stage, it is essential to conduct a thorough analysis of the socioeconomic challenges faced in a country and engage all key stakeholders in order to define the actual priorities and needs (ILO 2012b). There are however vulnerable groups that are sometimes not included in the consultations, as often happens with rural youth. It is therefore crucial to assess if policies are considering rural youth and their employment needs. To carry out an assessment of this type a sound methodology is needed to clearly analyse the content of a policy.

---

[2] Although policies are developed in several standard steps, there is no universal model of the policy cycle and variations might emerge depending on particular contexts and institutional arrangements.

The applied methodology to conduct this comparative policy analysis was based on the discourse theory for policy analysis. A discourse analysis focuses on the use of language in a speech or text (here it will be policies) within a specific context. An important component of policy analysis is the examination of the discourse, in this case policy statements, from a qualitative or quantitative perspective. We therefore consider the discourse as an integral part of the policymaking process. In particular, we focus on the poststructuralist[3] interpretation of the discourse theory that emphasizes the ways in which language materializes in practices (Paul 2009). In other words, we analyse how governmental institutions state in their policy objectives how they will pursue specific actions that will translate into institutional practices. Due to limited availability of information, this analysis focuses on the language throughout the policy design without reaching the point of corroborating if the discourse is actually translated into practice.

The rationale behind selecting discourse theory over other methods for policy analysis is that the main goal of this assessment is to clearly identify if the language being used in the policy statements properly addresses the main constraints to rural youth employment. The main unit of analysis is thus the full text of the policies in which specific words were searched. Then, the linguistic meanings of the policy statements were assessed to see if they appropriately reflected the selected constraints. It is assumed that if the policy statements address the constraints, they will eventually be transformed into a political discourse and consecutively into actions, in this case, to promote rural youth employment. A caveat in the present analysis is that it is confined to the assessment of the explicit wording of the respective policy documents, and thus does not interpret the wording in terms of policy change induced by the policy or overall country performance on rural youth employment. Being a qualitative methodology, policy analysis inevitably entails a certain risk of subjectivity, mainly with regards to the interpretation of words. Hence, in order to mitigate related errors and biases, a methodological approach was applied to the systematic and structured review of the policy documents in relation to how main constraints to rural youth employment are or are not addressed.

3.3.4 Scoring Methodology

A scoring methodology was adopted to conduct desk review of policy documents for all countries and policy areas under consideration. A review of different scoring systems was carried out in order to choose the appropriate method

---

[3] Poststructuralist Discourse Analysis has been instrumental in developing a more dynamic and historically-sensitive mode of critical inquiry claiming that texts are multiply implicated in their social contexts and, thereby, come to shape various forms of knowledge and identity (Chouliaraki 2008).

to assess how rural youth employment is addressed in the policy statements. One system is constructing a discourse quality index based on particular indicators that measure different dimensions of a political discourse (Steenbergen et al. 2003). Another method is using different scales to measure the quality of the discourse, for example a five-point scale ranging from 'very favourable' to 'very unfavourable' for a specific policy issue (Stromer-Galley 2007). A third system is to develop a binary indicator to capture the positive or negative quality of discourse within a policy. In this case it was decided to use the binary measurement system (1 or 0) in order to appreciate in a simple and clear way if the policies did or did not address the main constraints to rural youth employment. The binary criterion to qualify policy statements stems from the fact that general interventions to improve labour market outcomes for rural workers could also contribute to address particular constraints that rural youth face. As they are the predominant cohort facing underemployment, especially in rural areas in SSA, it would be expected that policies addressing employment issues will inadvertently be also covering or targeting the rural youth. However, given the aim of our analysis, our approach gives more weight when rural youth are explicitly mentioned.

The following describes the steps taken to perform the policy discourse analysis. A desk review was first conducted to identify key policies by country. The consulted sources to collect the policies included websites of government ministries, as well as policy inventories and databases. The most recent policies were selected, including the ones that are still under approval in national parliaments. The structure, length, and content of each one varied considerably depending on the country and type of policy. To facilitate comparison, policy statements were selected that expressed the aim or objective of addressing any of the identified constraints. Within the policies, keywords were searched and subsequently assessed consistently. The criterion was assigning 1 on each policy statement if it explicitly mentioned a constraint or 0 if it did not. After scoring the nine constraints per policy, weighted averages were calculated for each policy area per country. It was decided to calculate weighted means to avoid skewness, as some policy areas have one constraint while others have multiple. Since the highest score a country can get is 100, each of the five policy areas has a weight of 20 divided by the number of constraints.

An illustrative example is the analysis of Tanzania's policies. In the case of Tanzania's National Agricultural Policy (2013), looking at the *sectoral development* policy area, specific words were searched linked to the constraint of *unfavourable agribusiness environment for youth*. The related policy statement found was: 'The Government in collaboration with private sector shall create conducive environment for youth to settle in rural areas through improvement of social services, infrastructure, and promote rural development.' As can be seen, it clearly makes reference on how a favourable environment is necessary to attract rural youth to agriculture. Therefore a value of 1 was assigned to this particular constraint.

The same process was followed for Tanzania's four policies, assigning 1 or 0 for each constraint depending on whether they were addressed or not based on the keyword search (see Table 3.3). Once the four policies had binary scores, the weighted averages for each constraint were calculated within each policy area. For example, for the policy area *Sectoral Development* the three constraints were scored in each of the four policies. The constraint *unfavourable agribusiness environment for youth* was addressed in three out of the four policies, its weighted average is therefore 5.00. Once the weighted averages were calculated, they were summed to obtain the overall policy score for Tanzania, which is 73.

The scoring of the policies was not carried out arbitrarily as all policy documents were systematically reviewed based on the proposed framework in order to assess to what extent the main constraints on rural youth employment were being addressed. There are however some limitations in this analysis. First of all, it focuses on the policy design and discourse, and thus not on the implementation of the policies. On the latter, it was only verified that the policy was available online, that it was complemented with an action plan, and that it mentioned specific programmes and projects. However, we did not get to the step of corroborating whether the policies were actually translated into particular actions, nor on their ultimate impacts. The policy analysis was mainly based on a desk review and expert assessment from FAO's Decent Rural Employment Team, as well as building on expertise generated through FAO's field programme on the subject matter. Moreover, we did not look at the interactions and policy coherence among different government ministries and sectors due to limited availability of information. Finally, the policies under consideration covered the period between 1996 and 2016.

3.3.5 Context Indicators for Selected SSA Countries

Before turning into the results of the policy analysis, it is relevant to have a general idea of the socioeconomic and political context in each of the countries. Thirteen countries from SSA were selected based on the availability of data and policies at the national level. The selection captures diversity in terms of social and economic conditions as well as income, geographic area, size, and population. It should be noted that cross-country comparisons can sometimes be misleading as many of the indicators are measured based on national definitions that may vary from country to country. Also, South Africa does not generally follow the trends of other SSA countries due to particular socioeconomic conditions.

Table 3.4 presents eleven key indicators that have an impact on rural labour markets and rural youth employment at the macro level. Due to the lack of available

Table 3.3. Policy scoring example of Tanzania

Policies	Sectoral development			Self-employment capacity, employability, and skills development		Labour market institutions and regulations		Social protection	Social and policy dialogue	
	Unfavourable agribusiness environment for youth	Low investments in ARD	Lack of labour demand	Job-relevant skills, constraints, and lack of education	Job search, info. and business start-up constraints	Weak regulations, standards, and rights at work	Social constraints	Limited social protection	Limited social dialogue and youth rep.	
National Strategy for Growth and Reduction of Poverty II	0	1	1	1	1	0	0	0	1	
National Employment Policy	1	1	1	1	1	1	0	0	0	
National Youth Development Policy	1	1	1	0	1	1	1	1	1	
National Agriculture Policy	1	1	1	1	1	1	1	1	1	
Weighted mean	5.00	6.67	6.67	7.50	10.00	7.50	5.00	10.00	15.00	73.33

Table 3.4. Key indicators of selected countries

Country	GDP per capita, PPP (US$)[1]	Pop. aged 15–34 (%)[2]	Rural pop. (%)[3]	Rural poverty (%)[4]	Agri. emp. (%)[5]	Wage emp. (%)[5]	Self-emp. (%)[5]	Vulner. emp.[5]	Youth unemp. rate (%)[6]	Political stability score[7]	Policy score[8]
Benin	2,272	33.9	53.2	39.7	43.2	8.1	88.9	87.7	5.2	0.05	46
Ethiopia	1,899	36.3	79.7	30.4	68.2	10.0	89.5	88.8	7.4	-1.24	63
Ghana	4,492	34.8	44.6	37.9	40.7	18.2	81.7	76.8	4.9	-0.13	53
Kenya	3,285	36.1	73.4	49.1	38.0	33.4	63.4	77.7	26.2	-1.27	64
Liberia	1,283	33.8	49.3	67.7	43.0	18.1	81.7	78.7	3.3	-0.63	69
Malawi	1,202	35.8	83.3	56.6	84.7	16.1	83.9	83.9	7.8	0.12	52
Nigeria	5,875	32.9	50.5	52.8	36.6	N/A	N/A	N/A	13.4	-2.11	44
Senegal	3,450	34.3	53.3	57.1	53.4	22.3	58.3	58.0	5.5	-0.13	40
South Africa	13,498	35.9	34.2	77.0	5.6	85.9	13.6	9.3	53.5	-0.08	51
Tanzania	2,946	33.2	66.9	33.3	66.7	16.2	75.9	74.0	3.9	-0.54	73
Togo	1,660	34.1	58.8	73.4	37.8	10.9	89.1	89.1	2.8	-0.16	59
Uganda	1,864	34.0	76.8	22.4	69.0	19.6	80.2	78.9	2.9	-0.93	72
Zambia	4,024	35.0	57.0	77.9	53.3	20.4	79.3	79.0	15.94	0.21	55

Sources:

[1] *WB WDI. 2017.* Gross domestic product per capita based on purchasing power parity (PPP).

[2] *UNDESA, World Population Prospects. 2017.* The African Union's definition of youth covers the age range 15–34.

[3] *UN World Urbanization Prospects. 2018.* Rural population refers to people living in rural areas as defined by national statistical offices.

[4] *WB WDI. Latest available year.* Rural poverty headcount ratio is the percentage of the rural population living below the national poverty lines.

[5] *ILOSTAT 2017.* Status in employment distinguishes between two categories of the employed—(a) wage and salaried workers and (b) self-employed workers. The vulnerable employment rate is calculated as the sum of contributing family workers and own-account workers as a percentage of total employment.

[6] *ILOSTAT 2017.* The unemployment rate indicates the proportion of the labour force that does not have a job and is actively looking and available for work covering persons aged 15 to 24.

[7] *WB WGI. 2014.* Political Stability and Absence of Violence/Terrorism measures perceptions of the likelihood of political instability and/or politically-motivated violence, including terrorism. *Units range from –2.5 to 2.5, with higher values corresponding to better governance.*

[8] Own calculations based on rural youth employment policy framework; units range from 0 to 100.

data on rural employment, general employment data was included. The policy score obtained from the discourse analysis was also added to appreciate its relationship with the other indicators. As can be observed in the socioeconomic indicators, the GDP per capita varies between countries: eight are low-income economies, four are lower-middle-income economies, and only South Africa is an upper-middle-income economy. In all countries, young people (aged 15–34) comprise between 30 and 40 per cent of the total population. In 10 out of 13 of the countries more than half of the population lives in rural areas; on the one side Ethiopia has 80 per cent of its population living in rural areas, on the other side South Africa has only 34 per cent (UN DESA 2018). Likewise, rural poverty prevails in many of the countries reflecting low agricultural incomes, with Zambia having around 78 per cent of the rural population living below the poverty line and Uganda with around 22 per cent.

With respect to labour market indicators, agriculture remains the main sector of employment in most countries, employing more than half of the population in 7 out of 13 of the countries. For example, in Ethiopia around 73 per cent of the population works in agriculture against only 4.6 per cent in South Africa. Most of the economically active population is self-employed, including employers, own-account workers, members of producers' cooperatives, and contributing family workers. Also, most of the employment is considered to be vulnerable as the majority of the employed population includes own-account workers and contributing family workers, who are less likely to have formal work arrangements, and are therefore more likely to lack decent working conditions (ILO 2013). Youth unemployment rates also vary considerably between countries; on the one hand Benin has a youth unemployment rate of only 2 per cent, on the other hand 50.7 per cent of South Africa's youth is unemployed.

With regard to the political context, some countries have a low score in political stability and absence of violence/terrorism, which can considerably affect the policy and institutional environment in a country. For example, Nigeria has the lowest score given the current political instability and terrorism in the country, which could hamper the implementation of policies. Finally, the policy score is the result of the analysis carried out with the proposed policy framework reflecting the average of the scored constraints per country. The country that received the highest score is Tanzania with 73, while the one with the lowest is Senegal with 33. As can be seen, the policy scores do not necessarily correspond with the other indicators presented; for example, a low policy score does not translate into a high rural poverty headcount. The reason for this is that the policy assessment only focuses on the policy design without checking whether the policy statements were indeed transformed into concrete actions that have an impact on the economic performance and on rural youth employment in a given country.

3.4 Main Findings of the Comparative Policy Analysis

This section presents the main results of the comparative policy analysis conducted with the rural youth employment policy framework in the selected SSA countries. The implementation of the methodology through the proposed policy framework provided revealing findings which require an in-depth discussion. The results of scoring policy statements within the four types of policies are presented at the policy area, constraint, and country level. The discussion of the findings highlights the issues with lower scores, interprets the results, and proposes strategies to overcome these challenges.

3.4.1 Policy Area Analysis

The scores for the five policy areas let us appreciate the differences between countries in addressing the constraints to rural youth employment within the policies. In Figure 3.1, we can see which policy areas received the highest and the lowest scores on average, and the performance of each country across the five policy areas. In each policy area the scores for the thirteen countries range from 0 to 100, with the average marked with a line. As previously explained, the score for each country within a policy area is the average that resulted in the binary assessment of the nine constraints that were grouped into the five policy areas for each of the analysed policies.

The policy area that received the highest score is self-employment, employability, and skills development (74), supporting the argument that most policies focus on labour supply. Liberia and Benin had the lowest score (33) while South Africa obtained the highest (100). South Africa received the highest possible score because the three analysed policies explicitly addressed the two main constraints on labour supply for rural youth, namely: lack of skills and education, as well as inadequate job matching services, information, and business start-up resources. For example, South Africa's National Youth Policy (2015) states that training young people in skills relevant to agriculture and the agricultural value chain will also help to attract young people to the sector and promote agriculture and agroprocessing.

The second policy area is sectoral development (56), linked with labour demand, which includes ARD investments, rural labour demand, and agribusiness environment for youth. Although many policies include this type of intervention, they do it at a lesser extent than labour supply interventions. Tanzania received the highest score in this policy area (92), while Nigeria and Malawi had the lowest score (33). Kenya has a score in sectoral development on the average (56) given that the three analysed policies addressed only some of the constraints to the labour demand of rural youth. For instance, Kenya's Agricultural

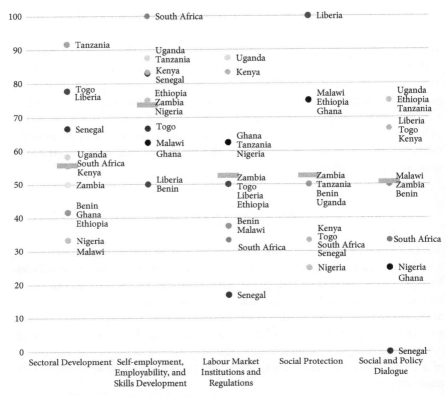

Figure 3.1. Total compliance by policy area

Sector Development Policy (2010) commits to empower the rural youth by sensitizing them on lucrative ventures in the agricultural sector and establishing processing plants for value addition in rural areas to provide employment opportunities for youth.

The third policy area is labour market institutions and regulations (53), indicating that labour standards and social constraints is an issue that needs to be better addressed. Uganda received the highest score (88), while Senegal had the lowest (17). Social constraints are a major challenge for rural youth. Local traditions and social norms prevent young people, and especially young women, from accessing the necessary productive resources. Particularly young women have lower incomes since they are less likely than their male counterparts to own land. Malawi's Youth National Policy (2013) addresses this constraint with the goal of providing access to productive agricultural land in adequate proportion and other factors of production for the youth who fail to access these resources due to culture, gender, and/or other socioeconomic factors.

In third place is also the social protection policy area (53), showing that policies partially cover social security schemes such as cash transfers, minimum wages, tax exemptions, health services, and so on. All of Liberia's policies adequately addressed the access to social protection for rural youth, it thus received the highest score (100). In contrast, only one out of four of Nigeria's policies addressed social protection issues for vulnerable groups, so it received the lowest score (25). One of the policies that explicitly mentioned young people is the National Youth Policy of Ghana (2010) which commits to provide social protection for the vulnerable and excluded youth.

Finally, the least addressed policy area is social and policy dialogue (51) as promoting the organization of rural young workers to increase their bargaining power was only included in around half of the policies. Some policies did commit to promote social dialogue and tripartism, however few explicitly mentioned the importance of engaging rural youth in decision-making processes. For example, the Second National Youth Policy Document of the Federal Republic of Nigeria (2009) declares that governments should always lend support to and be willing to engage in dialogue with youth-led organizations and work with a broad range of the youth population. In contrast, none of Senegal's policies mentioned the importance of involving excluded young people in social dialogue.

As can be seen, the systematic review of policies shows a clear trend to address one policy area, that is, promoting self-employment, employability, and skills development, over the other four policy areas. This finding indicates in turn that policies would focus more on the supply side of the labour market, paying less attention to other constraints that also affect the access of rural youth to decent employment. It is also noteworthy that the other four policy areas had a similar score of just over 50, showing that around half of the policies would be addressing in rather similar ways these policy areas.

3.4.2 Constraint Analysis

The analysis at the constraint level adds further elements to our comparative policy analysis to examine how the policies across 13 SSA countries addressed the main challenges to rural youth employment. Table 3.5 presents the constraints with the lowest scores per country. To capture the binding character of the constraints, countries were bound by the lowest score. As can be seen, the constraint with the lowest score in most countries is unfavourable agribusiness environment for youth within the sectoral development policy area. This shows that most policies do not explicitly focus on creating an enabling environment for youth agribusiness development. Many policies did mention the intention to enhance a conducive business environment to promote private sector growth, but they neither focus on the agricultural sector nor on rural youth.

Table 3.5. Main constraint and score per country

Country	Main binding constraint	Score per constraint
Benin	- Weak regulations, standards and rights at work	0
Ethiopia	- Unfavourable agribusiness environment for youth	0
Ghana	- Unfavourable agribusiness environment for youth	50
Kenya	- Unfavourable agribusiness environment for youth	0
Liberia	- Job search, information, and business start-up constraints - Weak regulations, standards, and rights at work	0
Malawi	- Unfavourable agribusiness environment for youth	0
Nigeria	- Unfavourable agribusiness environment for youth	0
Senegal	- Limited social dialogue and youth representation - Weak regulations, standards, and rights at work	0
South Africa	- Weak regulations, standards, and rights at work	0
Tanzania	- Limited social dialogue and youth representation - Limited social protection	50
Togo	- Social constraints - Limited social protection - Job search, information, and business start-up constraints - Unfavourable agribusiness environment for youth	33
Uganda	- Unfavourable agribusiness environment for youth	0
Zambia	- Unfavourable agribusiness environment for youth	25

3.4.3 Country Analysis

The scores can also be analysed by country to better grasp how national policy documents address issues related to rural youth employment. Such additional level of detail is also useful to compare policy performance on the five policy areas simultaneously within and between the thirteen countries. The disaggregated scores by policy area per country are presented in Table 3.A2. As mentioned before, Senegal received the lowest score (40) and Tanzania the highest (73). Figure 3.2 clearly shows significant differences between these two countries in the scores across the five policy areas. Due to limited space, only the policy context of these two countries will be discussed here. Given the aim of our analysis, it is relevant to look at potential reasons behind these contrasting scores.

The main reason for Senegal's low scores is explained by the lack of mainstreaming youth in the analysed national policies. It is therefore necessary to look further into the content and to discuss main gaps of these policy documents regarding rural youth employment. The Agro-Sylvo-Pastoral Orientation Act (LOASP) adopted in 2004 is Senegal's legal framework for the development of agriculture and the reduction of poverty in rural areas. Its main objectives are to reduce the impact of external shocks to the agricultural sector, increase agricultural exports, improve farmers' social and economic conditions, and establish a system incentivizing private investment in agriculture and rural

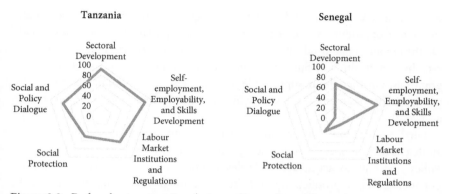

Figure 3.2. Radar chart comparison between Tanzania and Senegal

areas (Seck 2016). The LOASP includes a priority to integrate young people in all activities related to agricultural businesses through access to land and credit, as well as to establish an aid system for young farmers who received agricultural training. It however does not make reference to the particular needs of the rural youth in the areas of labour market institutions and regulations, social protection, and social and policy dialogue.

The Emerging Senegal Plan (PSE) was launched in 2013 as a reference for economic and social policy in the medium and long term, with the aim of making Senegal an emerging economy by 2035. Job creation is a key priority for the PSE and the plan envisages increasing the decent work opportunities (productive and remunerative) at the rate of 100,000 to 150,000 new jobs per year. This policy lacks specific references to the promotion of labour regulations that favour rural youth as well as organizations to encourage their participation in social dialogue. The PSE was supplemented with the Employment and Promotion of Youth Employment Policy. However, at the time of the analysis, the latter document was only a thematic note that delineated the main strategies to promote employment in Senegal and thus would need further development into a more comprehensive employment policy. The main reason for Senegal's low policy scoring was therefore that the available policy documents include objectives with a fairly limited scope with regard to rural youth employment promotion, even though it has to be recognized that more extended policies are under development.[4]

In contrast, Tanzania is well equipped in terms of national pro-poor growth policies, particularly in addressing the challenges to rural youth employment. The National Strategy for Growth and Reduction of Poverty II (NSGRP II) is oriented towards growth and enhancement of productivity, focused on wealth creation as a

[4] Senegal is developing its new National Employment Policy as of 2017, which according to initial information is going to include a strategy component on decent rural youth employment.

way out of poverty. It includes a particular goal on ensuring the creation and sustenance of productive and decent employment, especially for women and youth. On the labour demand side, it addresses underemployment in rural areas through establishing production clusters and promoting nonfarm income generating programmes. On the labour supply side, it promotes the development of skills for productivity enhancing employment and self-employment especially for women and youth.

Furthermore, most of Tanzania's youth or employment related policies and strategies include specific rural and agricultural focus. The National Employment Policy commits to accelerate skills development of the rural labour force for enhancing labour productivity and their income growth giving priority to the youth. Similarly, the National Youth Development Policy promotes the equitable access to land and other resource allocations putting emphasis on rural youth and gender. The National Agriculture Policy is also quite conducive to promote rural youth employment. It has a dedicated section on youth involvement in agriculture with a concrete objective to create an enabling environment to attract youth in agricultural production. One of its goals is to support group cooperation and rural entrepreneurial skills development particularly to women and youths through Junior Farmer Field and Life Schools (JFFLS) and young farmers' associations. As can be seen, Tanzania's policies were the most inclusive from the selected countries with regards to the analysed constraints to rural youth employment. These policies are illustrative of how rural youth can be considered at the policy level in an integrated manner. While beyond the scope of our analysis, it is also acknowledged that bringing these political statements a step forward is equally important, including by complementing them first with an action plan and subsequently with programmes that have the necessary resources to support rural youth, as well as with adequate M&E systems in place to enable measuring their ultimate impacts on rural youth employment.

3.5 Conclusion

The rural youth population in SSA is expected to continue to grow and will gradually join the labour force. This offers both an opportunity and a challenge for rural livelihoods in SSA. Great economic benefits could come from this demographic dividend provided the right policies are developed and implemented. This chapter contributed to achieve this goal by shedding light on the main strengths and weaknesses among policies of SSA from a rural youth employment perspective. It focused on reviewing policy documents based on the proposed policy framework to assess if the main constraints to rural youth employment were being addressed or not at the formulation stage, in order to suggest areas for improvement.

The scores presented in the chapter helped to identify key policy gaps per country across the five policy areas. The policy area that received the lowest scores was *social and policy dialogue*. A likely reason for that is that the interests and needs of rural youth are often not adequately taken into account in policy processes. The lack of participation of rural youth in the policy dialogue leads to an insufficient attention to their needs and to constant difficulties in finding productive and quality jobs in rural areas (Leavy and Smith 2010, Protcor and Lucchesi 2012). Policies should therefore promote the creation of institutionalized channels for the inclusion of rural youth in the decision-making process. Rural youth can create organizations or join existing ones, for example cooperatives, producers' organizations, youth associations, or NGOs. These organizations can provide efficient channels to make their voices heard and facilitate their inclusion in the policy dialogue.

Similarly, social protection as well as labour market institutions and regulations were insufficiently addressed in the policies analysed. Although many policies pledged to expand the *social protection* system, only some explicitly mentioned particular social security schemes that targeted rural youth. Policies should promote social protection interventions that address the particular vulnerabilities and risks faced by rural youth, including education and training, conditional cash transfer programmes, public works programmes, social insurance, and youth employment programmes, among others. Likewise, some policies did not mention the importance of promoting *labour market institutions and regulations* in rural areas. Yet, most of the rural youth are employed in the informal economy and not protected by labour institutions or regulations. The application of International Labour Standards (ILS) in rural areas is essential in improving working conditions, support the transition of the informal economy into formality and progressively improve the quality of jobs undertaken by rural youth.

The second most addressed policy area was *sectoral development*, which is related to labour demand. It is essential to unlock the labour demand in rural areas in order to provide quality jobs for the youth. Policy interventions focused on creating jobs both in agriculture and nonfarm activities can contribute to solve SSA's youth employment challenge. The policies should create a favourable agribusiness environment that attracts rural youth and provides access to credit, technology, skills, land, markets, and infrastructure. It is particularly important to facilitate the engagement of youth across inclusive agrifood value chains by linking youth farms to markets and provide them with the necessary technical support.

Finally, the most addressed policy area was *self-employment, employability, and skills development*, which is linked to labour supply. Most of the policies included actions to improve the skills and education of rural youth as well as measures to improve their access of information and business start-up resources. Further research would still be needed to assess how these actions are being tailored to the skill requirements in rural labour markets, and thus analysis on how these labour supply measures are matching labour demand needs in rural areas would be desirable.

As was observed, policies of SSA still need to integrate additional thematic areas in order to achieve full and productive employment for rural youth. Redesigning policies to stimulate youth employment in both agricultural and non-agricultural sectors is an essential first step to both economic growth and poverty reduction. More evidence is still needed though, especially regarding the translation of policies into concrete actions, as well as to ultimate impact and results of policy interventions on rural youth employment. More integrated policy frameworks with inclusive policies and targeted investments and programmes will create the enabling environment for rural youth to reach their potential.

Appendix

Table 3.A1. List of reviewed policies and scores per country

	Policy	Year	Policy Score
Benin	Stratégie de Croissance pour la Réduction de la Pauvreté (SCRP)	2011–2015	47
	Politique Nationale de l'Emploi	2012–2016	27
	Politique Nationale de la Jeunesse	2002	73
	Plan Stratégique de Relance du Secteur Agricole (PSRSA)	2010–2015	37
Ethiopia	Second Growth and Transformation Plan (GTP II)	2015/16–2019/20	47
	National Employment Policy and Strategy of Ethiopia	2009	93
	National Youth Policy	2004	30
	Rural Development Policies and Strategies	2003	83
Ghana	Ghana Shared Growth and Development Agenda (GSGDA II)	2014–2017	63
	National Employment Policy	2014	63
	National Youth Policy of Ghana	2010	60
	Food and Agriculture Sector Development Policy (FASDEP II)	2007	27
Kenya	Vision 2030	2008–2030	73
	Kenya National Youth Policy	2006	67
	Agricultural Sector Development Policy	2010–2020	53
Liberia	Agenda for Transformation: Steps towards Liberia Rising 2030	2012–2030	80
	Employment Policy	2009	73
	Food Agriculture Policy and Strategy (FAPS)	2009	53

Malawi	Malawi Growth and Development Strategy	2011–2016	67
	National Employment and Labor Policy (Pending approval)	2011	53
	Youth National Policy	2013	67
	National Agricultural Policy	2010	17
Nigeria	Nigeria Vision 20:2020	2009	73
	National Employment Policy	1998	37
	Second National Youth Policy Document of the Federal Republic of Nigeria	2009	50
	The New Nigerian Agricultural Policy	2001	17
Senegal	Plan Sénégal Émergent	2014–2018	63
	Politique de l'Emploi et Promotion de l'Emploi des Jeunes	2014	23
	Loi d'orientation Agro-Sylvo-Pastorale (LOASP)	2004	33
South Africa	National Development Plan 2030: Our future—make it work	2012–2030	63
	National Youth Policy	2015–2020	63
	Integrated Growth and Development Plan (IGDP) for Agriculture, Forestry and Fisheries	2012	27
Tanzania	National Strategy for Growth and Reduction of Poverty II	2010–2015	53
	National Employment Policy	2008	50
	National Youth Development Policy	2007	90
	National Agriculture Policy	2013	100
Togo	Stratégie de Croissance Accélérée et de Promotion de l'Emploi (SCAPE)	2013–2017	47
	Politique Nationale de l'Emploi (PNE)	2013–2017	27
	Plan Stratégique National pour l'Emploi des Jeunes (PSNEJ)	2013–2022	73
Uganda	Second National Development Plan (NDPII)	2015/16–2019/20	37
	The National Employment Policy for Uganda	2011	77
	The National Action Plan for Youth Employment	2015/16–2019/20	73
	National Agricultural Policy	2013	43
Zambia	Zambia Vision 2030	2006–2030	53
	National Employment and Labour Market Policy	2004	93
	2015 Youth National Policy	2015	40
	National Agricultural Policy 2012–2030	2012–2030	33

Table 3.A2. Scores for constraints per country

Country	Sectoral development		Self-employment capacity, employability, and skills development			Labour market institutions and regulations		Social protection	Social and policy dialogue
	Unfavorable agribusiness environment for youth	Low investments in ARD	Lack of labour demand	Job-relevant skills constraints and lack of education	Job search, information, and business start-up constraints	Weak regulations, standards, and rights at work	Social constraints	Limited social protection	Limited social dialogue and youth representation
Benin	25	75	25	75	25	0	75	50	50
Ethiopia	0	75	50	100	50	25	75	75	75
Ghana	0	75	50	25	100	50	75	75	25
Kenya	0	67	100	67	100	67	100	33	67
Liberia	33	100	100	100	0	0	100	100	67
Malawi	0	75	0	75	50	25	50	75	50
Nigeria	0	75	25	100	50	50	75	25	25
Senegal	33	67	100	100	67	0	33	33	0
South Africa	67	33	67	100	100	0	67	33	33
Tanzania	75	100	100	75	100	75	50	50	75
Togo	33	100	100	100	33	67	33	33	67
Uganda	0	100	75	100	75	100	75	50	75
Zambia	25	50	75	100	50	50	50	50	50

References

African Development Bank, OECD, UNDP, and UNECA. 2015. *African economic outlook 2015: Regional development and spatial inclusion.* Paris, France: Organisation for Economic Co-operation and Development.

African Union Commission. 2006. *African youth charter.* Banjul, the Gambia: African Union.

African Union Commission. 2015. *Agenda 2063: The Africa we want.* Addis Ababa, Ethiopia: African Union.

African Union Summit. 2014. *The Malabo declaration on accelerated agricultural growth and transformation for shared prosperity and improved livelihoods.* Malabo, Equatorial Guinea: African Union.

Chouliaraki, L. 2008. Discourse analysis. In *The SAGE handbook of cultural analysis,* ed. T. Bennett, and J. Frow. London, U.K.: SAGE Publications.

FAO. 2016. Incorporating decent rural employment in the strategic planning for agricultural development. *Guidance Material #3.* Rome, Italy: Food and Agriculture Organization of the United Nations.

FAO, IFAD, and CTA. 2014. *Youth and agriculture: Key challenges and concrete solutions.* Rome, Italy: Food and Agriculture Organization of the United Nations.

Fischer, F., G. J. Miller, and M. S. Sidney. 2007. *Handbook of public policy analysis: Theory, politics, and methods.* Boca Raton, FL, U.S.A.: CRC Press.

ILO. 2008. Report IV: Promotion of rural employment for poverty reduction. *International Labor Conference, 97th Session.* Geneva, Switzerland.

ILO. 2012a. The youth employment crisis: A call for action. *Resolution and conclusions of the 101st Session of the International Labor Conference.* Geneva, Switzerland: International Labor Organization.

ILO. 2012b. *Guide for the formulation of national employment policies.* Geneva, Switzerland: International Labor Organization.

ILO. 2013. *The informal economy and decent work: A policy resource guide, supporting transitions to formality.* Geneva, Switzerland: International Labor Organization.

Independent Evaluation Group (IEG). 2012. *Youth employment programs: An evaluation of World Bank and International Finance Corporation support.* Washington, DC, U.S.A.: World Bank.

Leavy, J., Smith, S. 2010. Future farmers? Exploring youth aspirations for African agriculture. *Futures Agricultures Consortium Policy Brief* 037.

Losch, B. 2017. *+789 Million and Counting: the Sub-Saharan African Equation.* Employment Research Brief. Geneva, Switzerland: International Labor Organization.

MIJARC, IFAD, and FAO, 2012. Facilitating access of rural youth to agricultural activities. *Summary of the findings of the project implemented by MIJARC in collaboration with IFAD and FAO.* Rome, Italy: International Fund for Agricultural Development.

New Partnership for Africa's Development (NEPAD). 2015. *The CAADP results framework (2015–2025).* Midrand, South Africa: New Partnership for Africa's Development.

Paul, K. T. 2009. Discourse analysis: An exploration of methodological issues and a call for methodological courage in the field of policy analysis. *Critical Policy Studies* 3 (2): 240–53.

Proctor, F., Lucchesi, V. 2012. *Small-scale farming and youth in an era of rapid rural change.* London/The Hague: IIED/HIVOS.

Seck, A. 2016. Fertilizer subsidy and agricultural productivity in Senegal. *AGRODEP Working Paper 0024.* Washington, DC, U.S.A.: International Food Policy Research Institute.

Steenbergen, M. R., A. Bächtigerb, M. Spörndlib, and J. Steinera. 2003. Measuring political deliberation: A Discourse Quality Index. *Comparative European Politics* 1 (1): 21–48.

Stromer-Galley, J. 2007. Measuring deliberation's content: A coding scheme. *Journal of Public Deliberation.* 2 (1): 1–35.

Tocco, B., S. Davidova, and A. Bailey. 2012. Key issues in agricultural labor markets: A review of major studies and project reports on agriculture and rural labor markets. *Factor Markets Working Paper No. 20.* Brussels, Belgium: Centre for European Policy Studies.

UN Department of Economic and Social Affairs (UN DESA). 2018. *World urbanization prospects: The 2018 revision.* New York, NY, U.S.A.: United Nations.

UN General Assembly (UNGA). 2015. Transforming our world: The 2030 Agenda for Sustainable Development. *Resolution 70/1, 25 September 2015.* New York, NY, U.S.A.: United Nations.

World Bank. 2007. *Miles to go: A quest for an operational labor market paradigm for developing countries.* Washington DC, U.S.A.: World Bank.

Youthpolicy.org. 2014. *The state of youth policy in 2014.* Berlin, Germany: Youth Policy Press.

4

Troublemakers, Bystanders, and Pathbreakers

The Political Participation of African Youth

Danielle Resnick

4.1 Introduction

Creating decent jobs for African youth not only is critical for improving their economic welfare but also has political salience given the historic ability of this constituency to disrupt established governance structures. On the one hand, African youth have been viewed as progressive and pro-democratic. African youth, consisting of secondary school and university students, played a signifi-cant role in the anti-colonial movements of the 1950s and 1960s (Allman 1990, Burgess 2005). Initially motivated by teaching shortages, high food prices, and poor study facilities, they were similarly at the vanguard of protests in the late 1980s and 1990s in more than a dozen African countries, which heralded a wave of transitions from one-party to democratic rule (Bratton and van de Walle 1992). In more recent years, youth groups in countries as diverse as Angola, Burkina Faso, Senegal, South Africa, and Sudan have proved important actors in protest-ing against violations of the constitution and the rule of law by leaders in those countries (Alexander 2010, Hamilton 2010, Wonacott 2012).

On the other hand, there has been concern that unemployed youth are espe-cially prone to radicalization and anti-government behaviour, particularly if they are unemployed. Kaplan (1996) famously suggested that African youth are 'out of school, unemployed, loose molecules in an unstable social fluid that threatened to ignite'. More generally, some research suggests that countries with youth bulges have a higher likelihood of experiencing political violence since high unemploy-ment creates low opportunity costs for this group (Collier 2007, Leahy et al. 2007, Urdal 2006). The role of youth militias at the forefront of some of Africa's civil wars in the 1990s, ranging from Liberia, Rwanda, and Sierra Leone, bolstered this alarmist view. More recently, the enduring presence of youth vigilante groups, such as Nigeria's Bakassi Boys or Côte d'Ivoire's 'microbe' criminal gangs in Abidjan, further creates a sense of urgency about the social implications of youth unemployment.

Danielle Resnick, *Troublemakers, Bystanders, and Pathbreakers: The Political Participation of African Youth*
In: *Youth and Jobs in Rural Africa: Beyond Stylized Facts.* Edited by: Valerie Mueller and James Thurlow,
Oxford University Press (2019). © International Food Policy Research Institute.
DOI: 10.1093/oso/9780198848059.003.0004

Whether peaceful or violent, inspirational or exploitative, these contrasting narratives have played an important role in placing youth and youth employment back on the agenda of African governments, epitomized by the African Union's 2006 Youth Charter (AU 2006) and the more than two dozen African countries that drafted youth policies during the 2000s onwards.[1] Since particularly *urban* youth are seen as potentially more disruptive, and rural youth are perceived as more deprived, practical policy responses have included efforts to improve the attractiveness of agriculture to encourage young people to either stay in rural areas or return to them (Sumberg et al. 2015). Examples include the 'Return to Agriculture' Plan launched by former President Wade of Senegal, and the block farm pro-grammes in countries such as Ghana and Zambia (Benin et al. 2013, Sall 2012).[2]

Yet, do African youth actually mobilize for change through extra-institutional channels, such as protest, more than their older counterparts? Is unemployment their main policy preoccupation, or do other concerns take precedence? Are these behaviours and preferences consistent over time or dependent on the wider economic and political context in which young people are embedded? This chapter addresses these questions in detail by first discussing the literature on youth and protest as well as developments in Africa more recently. In doing so, I look at whether African youth are more likely to protest today than in the past by using the Armed Conflict Location and Event Data (ACLED), which spans the 1997–2015 period and includes all Sub-Saharan African countries. While this analysis pro-vides a macro perspective on trends over time, the chapter subsequently provides a more microanalysis by employing Afrobarometer public opinion data for 16 countries. Focusing on six age cohorts between 2003 and 2014, the analysis probes rural and urban youth's socioeconomic status, policy preferences, political aware-ness and trust in institutions, and their political participation, including in protest activities. This is followed by a multivariate analysis of the micro-level drivers of protest behaviour.

The findings reveal that while slightly higher among the youth, protesting is a form of political participation engaged in by older Africans as well. However, results from surveys conducted in 2014 show that the drivers of youth protest vary from a decade earlier. Specifically, the more recent findings indicate that among the youth, protesters can be characterized as 'frustrated activists' who have higher levels of education and who are more engaged in their communities than non-protesters but who are also unemployed, experience higher levels of deprivation, and have less trust in political institutions. This suggests that for governments intent on minimizing protests, one pathway is to ensure that employment creation projects match young people's skills and aspirations. Moreover, governments

---

[1]   See: http://www.youthpolicy.org/nationalyouthpolicies/.

[2]   OnZambia,see:http://agrf.org/agrf2015/zambia-targets-one-million-hectares-of-farm-block-irrigation-for-youth-led-agriculture-development/.

need to generate greater trust that youth policies and initiatives are aimed at enhancing this constituency's long-term potential rather than simply mobilizing their short-term political support.

4.2 Macro Trends in Protest Activity in Africa

Political participation consists of an array of 'actions by citizens which are aimed at influencing decisions which are, in most cases, ultimately taken by public representatives and officials' (Parry, Moyser, and Day 1992). Globally, young people are associated with certain trends in political participation. On average, younger people are less likely to vote than older ones (Franklin 2004, Wattenberg 2008), but considered more likely to protest. Historically, one reason that they are more likely to protest is because of a lack of career or familial responsibilities (Parry, Moyser, and Day 1992). More recently, others have noted that with the spread of new technologies and shifts in political ideologies, young people are more likely to view themselves as 'self-actualizing' or 'engaged' citizens rather than 'dutiful' citizens (Bennett 2008, Dalton 2008a). While the latter favours conventional forms of participation and the 'politics of loyalties', including voting, the former emphasizes more direct actions and the 'politics of choice' (Norris 2002), which manifests via protests, demonstrations, and boycotts.

Since the late 2000s, and especially from 2011 onwards, Africanists have observed a wave of protests across the continent, particularly in urban areas (Branch and Mampilly 2015). However, the trend is not specific to Africa. Economic crisis and de-alignment with traditional political parties have renewed the salience of protests globally as a major form of political participation (Rüdig and Karyotis 2013). In developing countries, Valenzuela, Arriagada, and Scherman (2012) observe that three key elements have characterized these protests: organization by the masses rather than by political parties, the central role of social media, and the dominant role played by youth.

Consequently, two patterns have been suggested. One is that protests are generally on the rise again and secondly, that protests disproportionately are a modality of participation pursued by the youth. The first idea, but not necessarily the second, appears to be borne out by aggregate data for the African region. Specifically, Figure 4.1 utilizes data on protest events available from ACLED to analyse trends over time.[3] This coding involved first isolating media reports on protest events that mentioned involvement of 'youth', 'young people', 'students', and/or 'teenagers'. Subsequently, I examined the full description of the event to

---

[3] Protest events are not equivalent to outright violence and Raleigh (2015) has found that the locus of violent conflict in Africa has increased considerably over the last 20 years from rural to urban areas.

ensure that it was coding the intended outcome correctly, and I excluded events that mentioned youth being a victim of a crime rather than youth participating in a protest movement. Duplicate events being reported by the same source were removed. However, duplicates were retained if they were referring to events that occurred on the same day but in different locations or if they were the same event dispersed over multiple days (for example, student strike).

Importantly, Figure 4.1 demonstrates that the total number of youth protests has increased dramatically between 1997 and 2015, largely supporting Branch and Mampilly's (2015) observation of a new wave of protest activities in the region. A series of major mobilizing events partially accounts for this trend. For instance, rising costs of electricity, fuel, and schooling motivated Nigeria's Occupy Movement, South Africa's 'Fees Must Fall' campaign, Ghana's Red Friday protests, and Uganda's 'Walk to Work' protests. Electoral malfeasance and attempts to change constitutions were major precipitators in Senegal's Fed Up movement, and in anti-government protests in Burkina Faso and Democratic Republic of Congo.

At the same time, however, as a share of total protests, youth protests tend to wax and wane and have never constituted more than 32 per cent of total protests. Key spikes in activity have occurred in 1999, 2003, 2010, and 2015. This observation suggests that protest is not just a modality of political participation that is intrinsically tied to age; rather, youth protests may simply coincide with broader periods of social and economic discontent. In other words, protest activity may not simply be a life cycle event whereby younger people are more inclined to go into the streets, but a form of political participation that is more (or less) pronounced depending on the broader contextual environment.

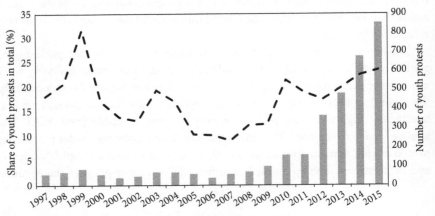

Figure 4.1. Youth protests over time in sub-Saharan Africa

4.3 Identifying Age Cohorts Over Time

The latter observation suggests that three potential effects are relevant for research on youth in Africa and elsewhere: life-cycle, generational, and period effects. Life-cycle, or age, effects imply that individuals' behaviours and characteristics change and mirror those of their older peers as they age (Nie, Verba, and Kim 1974). With the accumulation of more experience, individuals always alter their behaviours over time. Examples of period effects would include if a survey is taken during an election, a food crisis, or a drought (Neundorf and Niemi 2014, Yang and Land 2013). The events affect all age groups at the same time but, the level of impact may differ depending on where one is located in the life-cycle (Neundorf and Niemi 2014). Generational effects imply that period effects disproportionately affect those at a certain stage of life, particularly during late adolescence and early adulthood (Dalton 1988, Markus 1983, Ryder 1965). In other words, while all age groups may be exposed to a civil war, it may leave a deeper impression on younger people that continues to affect their behaviours and outlook as they age. Given the range of political transformations and shifts in economic ideology in Africa since independence, taking all these effects into account is essential for better understanding whether African youth are distinctly different depending on their birth cohort.

The Afrobarometer public opinion data help analyse distinctions between life-cycle, period, and generational effects and their attendant implications for political participation. The Afrobarometer project includes six rounds of data collection.[4] The analysis here employs survey Rounds 2 and 6, which were taken in 2002–4 and 2014–15, respectively. Consequently, the data spans at least a decade. This is necessary since if repeated cross-sectional data is less than 10 years apart, cohort and age effects become increasingly correlated (Smets and Neundorf 2014). The Afrobarometer dataset used here includes sixteen countries with a range of political regimes and economic development: Botswana, Cape Verde, Ghana, Kenya, Lesotho, Malawi, Mali, Mozambique, Namibia, Nigeria, Senegal, South Africa, Tanzania, Uganda, Zambia, and Zimbabwe. Collectively, the data captures 24,301 observations in Round 2 and 29,972 observations in Round 6.

Cohorts refer to a set of individuals who have shared experiences of socialization (Glenn 2005), and they often are operationalized by individuals' birth years (Neundorf and Niemi 2014). In creating cohorts, six age groups were considered. These include three 'youth' groups that span ages 18–24, 25–29, and 30–34. Doing so allows for including both the United Nations' upper youth threshold of 24 and the African Union's more expansive upper threshold of 34. At the same time, 25–29 year olds sandwiched between these two decadal cut-offs may have finished

[4] See http://www.afrobarometer.org/.

school but not yet established families, potentially resulting in distinct priorities and modalities of participation.

Table 4.1 presents the classification of the age cohorts across the two survey rounds, their respective birth years, and the broader political and economic context facing the continent at the time each cohort reached early adulthood, which in this case is symbolized by being 18 years or older. Late adolescence or early adulthood is considered to be a highly impressionable period when behaviours and preferences begin to crystallize and may persist throughout one's life (Jennings 1996, Markus 1983). In this case, 18 years old also is the minimum voting age in most African countries and therefore the time when individuals become most aware of their political environments.

Notwithstanding the diversity of countries in the region, some common trends were occurring as each of these cohorts reached early adulthood. For those born in 1948 or prior to that year, they came of age at a time of transition from colonial

Table 4.1. Description of age cohorts from Afrobarometer

2003 Surveys (Round 2)

Age at survey year	Year of birth	Year turned 18	Political era	Economic era
18–24	1979–1985	1997–2003	Democratic consolidation	HIPC and PRSPs
25–29	1978–1974	1992–1996	Democratic transitions	SAPs
30–34	1969–1973	1987–1991	Democratic liberalization	SAPs
35–44	1959–1968	1977–1986	One party regimes	Stabilization
45–54	1949–1958	1967–1976	One party regimes	ISI
55+	1948 and earlier	1966	Colonial transition	Extractive economies

2014 Surveys (Round 6)

Age at survey year	Year of birth	Year turned 18	Political era	Economic era
18–24	1990–1996	2008–2014	Born frees	Resurgence
25–29	1985–1989	2003–2007	Democratic consolidation	MDGs
30–34	1980–1984	1998–2002	Democratic consolidation	HIPC and PRSPs
35–44	1970–1979	1988–1997	Democratic liberalization and transition	SAPs
45–54	1960–1969	1978–1987	One party states	Stabilization
55+	1959 and earlier	1977	One party states	ISI

Notes: HIPC = Highly Indebted Poor Countries; ISI = Import Substitution Industrialization; MDGs = Millennium Development Goals; PRSPs = Poverty Reduction Strategy Papers; SAPs = Structural Adjustment Programmes. For ease of explication, the Round 2 and Round 6 surveys refer to a base year of 2003 and 2014, respectively since those are the survey years of a majority of the countries in the sample.

Source: Author's compilation

administrations to independent states and from extractive economic policies aimed at benefiting European countries to more inwardly-focused import substitution industrialization (ISI) policies.[5] They were followed by a cohort that, with the exception of a few Southern African countries, largely matured under independent and increasingly autocratic, one-party regimes that sought to solidify their ISI strategies. Those born in the 1960s and early 1970s reached 18 when one-party states were overwhelmingly the norm, but the flaws of ISI were leading to massive debt and macroeconomic contraction. Starting with Ghana in 1982, this period heralded the beginning of stabilization policies under international financial institutions (IFIs). A tumultuous period followed for those born mostly in the 1970s and who reached maturity as IFIs sought not only to stabilize but to actually 'structurally adjust' economies. The resultant austerity measures and privatizations prompted a wave of pro-democracy protests and political liberalization, starting with Benin in 1989 and Zambia in 1991 (Bratton and van de Walle 1992).

The successive cohort, born in the late 1970s to mid-1980s, were often voting in their country's first democratic elections.[6] Around the same time, IFIs and NGOs launched the heavily indebted poor countries (HIPC) initiative and generated a renewed focus on tackling poverty via the poverty reduction strategy papers (PRSPs). Those born in the late 1980s faced similar political circumstances, but matured at the time of major global and regional initiatives, such as the Millennium Development Goals (MDGs) and the Comprehensive African Agriculture Development Program (CAADP), which prompted large investments in education, health, and agriculture. Youth of this generation therefore began seeing a big improvement in educational access compared to youth of prior generations (Resnick and Thurlow 2015).

Finally, those born between 1990–6 are often referred to as the 'born free' generation (Mattes 2012) in that they largely escaped living under purely authoritarian regimes. This cohort matured under a period of relative economic resurgence, bolstered by high commodity prices. This often resulted in dual perspectives, including optimism about Africa's growing middle class (McKinsey 2010, Ncube and Lufumpa 2015) and pessimism that this resurgence did not ameliorate poverty or inequality (World Bank 2016). Beyond political and economic variations, these cohorts obviously have also lived through very different communications, technology, and media environments.

---

[5] See Nugent (2004) for more details on these periodizations, especially prior to 2000.

[6] Within the Afrobarometer sample, there are some important caveats to this characterization. Uganda finally allowed multi-party competition in 2005 and Zimbabwe allowed multi-party competition starting with the 2000 parliamentary and 2002 presidential elections. In both cases, elections have not been deemed 'free and fair', with an uneven playing field for the incumbent presidents.

4.4 Socioeconomic Profiles, Perceptions and Preferences

Taking into account these variations across time, this section presents descriptive trends to analyse whether young people have distinct socioeconomic profiles, perceptions, and policy preferences than their older compatriots.[7] Table 4.2 indicates that one of the trends in education over the last decade has been an improvement in the highest level of schooling achieved. Indeed, among all three youth age groups, there has been an increase in the share of secondary school completion and tertiary schooling. This has been a trend noted in some individual country case studies (Resnick and Thurlow 2016) and a reflection of the emphasis placed on education by both the international donor community as well as national governments. At the same time, when turning to occupations, there is a notable decrease in the share of young people who are employed as professionals compared to the equivalent age groups from a decade ago. A significant share of this shift in employment appears to be into unskilled work. Noticeably, agricultural work has declined significantly among all age groups, with a decrease ranging from approximately 10 to 14 per cent among the youth age groups. While the share of those who have no work but are looking has increased marginally across all age groups between surveys, a more notable increase exists with regards to those who are employed part-time and looking for work. Again, this shift is not necessarily just limited to young people but occurs across all age groups, suggesting the consequences of a general lack of structural transformation rather than one that disproportionately hurts the youth.

While Afrobarometer lacks the refined expenditure data contained in household living standards surveys, it does allow for assessments of economic well-being. One measure is the Lived Poverty Index (LPI), which captures how often an individual had to forego the following five basic needs during the year preceding the survey: food, clean water, medicines or medical treatment, cooking fuel, or cash income. Following Mattes (2008), a composite index integrating all five components was constructed that ranges from 0, indicating that the respondent has never gone without these basic needs, to 4, indicating that the respondent always goes without these basic needs. Table 4.3 below captures the share of each age group that obtains a 2 or higher on the index, suggesting that the respondent had to forego one or more of the five basic needs several or more times in the previous year.

In addition, three measures of subjective deprivation are included. In some ways, this is more directly relevant to understanding linkages with protest behaviour because subjective perceptions of deprivation or marginalization can be more likely

---

[7] Since Afrobarometer samples are designed to be nationally representative, all data is weighted by survey weights The sample design is a clustered, stratified, multi-stage, area probability sample. The sampling frame is stratified by gender. Afrobarometer samples yield a sampling error of +/ −2 percent for samples of 2400 and +/ −2.8 percent of samples of 1200 at a 95 percent confidence error.

Table 4.2. Education and employment (per cent of age groups)

Indicator	2003						2014					
	18–24	25–29	30–34	35–44	45–54	55+	18–24	25–29	30–34	35–44	45–54	55+
Schooling achieved												
No school	6.3	10.1	11.6	15.4	21.9	34.9	4.5	6.9	9.1	12.1	18.2	26.8
Some primary	17.7	19.2	23.3	25.2	29.9	34.8	14.9	15.6	20.6	22.2	28.1	34.6
Primary completed	13.5	18.5	18.9	21.5	19.8	13.9	12.0	13.5	15.7	16.1	17.6	14.2
Some secondary	30.5	21.0	20.2	15.8	12.1	7.9	27.3	21.1	18.2	18.7	14.5	10.7
Secondary completed	23.3	18.5	13.8	11.3	7.5	4.4	27.1	22.6	19.1	16.6	10.9	6.7
Some tertiary	8.1	10.2	9.2	8.1	6.7	3.0	12.4	14.2	11.6	9.9	6.4	4.8
Tertiary completed	0.7	2.5	3.1	2.7	2.2	1.2	1.7	6.2	5.6	4.5	4.3	2.2
Occupations [a]												
Agricultural worker	20.3	28.2	35.4	36.3	43.0	48.5	11.7	16.5	21.1	23.8	28.3	28.6
Hawker	4.5	7.8	7.1	7.3	5.4	4.6	5.1	9.3	9.2	10.6	9.4	6.1
Student	22.4	3.9	0.8	0.1	0.2	0.2	32.0	8.1	2.3	1.3	0.7	0.4
Professional	10.3	21.5	23.2	23.9	20.5	11.8	7.8	16.6	18.3	17.2	15.9	11.3
Skilled work	4.3	6.1	5.8	4.4	3.8	3.3	5.0	8.4	7.5	8.5	7.6	5.9
Unskilled work	3.8	4.2	3.9	3.8	4.0	3.9	8.6	12.2	14.1	13.4	13.3	15.8
Never had a job	22.9	12.9	8.8	7.9	6.8	9.1	19.6	14.5	12.6	10.5	11.1	14.8
Housewife	5.7	7.3	6.6	7.3	6.0	6.0	7.5	9.0	9.3	9.1	8.4	10.7
Other	2.0	4.5	3.9	5.1	6.0	8.9	2.9	5.5	5.7	5.7	5.5	6.3
Employment status												
No work but looking	36.8	31.0	26.1	20.5	20.0	13.6	37.6	32.7	27.1	22.5	18.8	14.0
Part-time and looking	8.2	9.5	9.2	8.3	5.7	3.1	10.1	14.9	15.9	14.8	13.2	9.0
Total observations	5,701	3,926	3,215	4,857	2,912	3,087	6,240	5,059	4,308	6,240	3,773	4,137

Notes: [a] For the occupation categories, a 'professional' refers to someone in retail or clerical work, business, teacher, government worker, a supervisor, doctor, or lawyer. Both skilled and unskilled workers are in textiles, manual work, or are artisans. The 'other category' includes those in security services, clergy people, drivers, and traditional healers. 'Agricultural worker' includes farmers producing for both own consumption and for sale, farm workers, and those involved in fisheries.

Source: Calculated from Afrobarometer, Rounds 2 and 6. All descriptives are weighted by cross-country survey sample weights.

Table 4.3. Perspectives on socioeconomic conditions (per cent of age groups)

Indicator	2003						2014					
	18–24	25–29	30–34	35–44	45–54	55+	18–24	25–29	30–34	35–44	45–54	55+
Moderate to severe deprivation [a]	22.0	24.3	26.7	27.3	28.7	33.7	14.9	18.1	19.3	20.8	21.6	23.7
Present living conditions												
Bad	41.8	47.5	50.7	50.8	55.2	60.7	39.1	45.6	49.3	50.7	53.6	56.3
Neutral	21.5	22.4	21.0	20.1	19.6	15.7	22.4	21.4	19.8	18.9	18.5	16.3
Good	36.7	30.2	28.3	29.2	25.2	23.7	38.6	33.1	30.9	30.4	28.0	27.4
Your living conditions over time												
Worse	33.0	36.7	41.0	36.7	40.9	43.9	31.1	36.4	38.9	40.3	41.6	43.2
Same	30.5	30.0	27.5	29.5	28.2	27.9	33.1	31.2	29.7	28.8	29.9	28.6
Better	36.5	33.3	31.6	33.8	30.9	28.2	35.9	32.4	31.4	30.9	28.5	28.2
Your conditions vs. others												
Worse	36.8	38.6	42.4	40.6	42.6	45.7	31.1	36.4	38.9	40.3	41.6	43.2
Same	12.3	13.2	13.2	12.6	11.5	11.3	33.1	31.2	29.7	28.8	29.9	28.6
Better	50.9	48.2	44.5	46.9	45.8	43.0	35.9	32.4	31.4	30.9	28.5	28.2
Total observations	5,701	3,926	3,215	4,857	2,912	3,087	6,240	5,059	4,308	6,240	3,773	4,137

Note: [a] Moderate deprivation refers to those who receive a 2 or higher on the Lived Poverty Index. See text for details.

Source: Calculated from Afrobarometer, Rounds 2 and 6. All descriptives are weighted by cross-country survey sample weights.

to mobilize action than objective conditions (Klandermans, Van Steklenburg, and Van der Toorn 2008). Sociotropic views capture one's views on the present economic conditions within his/her respective country. Afrobarometer provides five response categories that were collapsed here into three: bad, neutral, and good. Egotropic views reflect one's assessment of individual conditions over time, and the responses were similarly collapsed into categories of worse, same, and better.[8] Relative views capture one's assessment of personal conditions vis-à-vis other citizens in the same country.

Three key observations emerge from the table. First, a larger share of the older age groups experiences moderate or higher levels of deprivation, but this trend seems to have diminished in level over time. Secondly, regardless of time period, younger age groups are marginally more optimistic than their older compatriots regarding sociotropic conditions. This reflects findings from research in developed countries that younger people generally have a more positive outlook on their futures (Pew Research Center 2010). Thirdly, in terms of relative conditions, there is a notable change over the decade encompassed by the surveys. While 50 per cent of 18–24 year olds felt that their own conditions were better than their compatriots in the 2003 survey period, less than one-third of this sample cohort approximately ten years later, which was now in either the 25–29 or 30–34 age group, viewed that they were relatively better off. Encouragingly though, across all age groups, this shift was due more to individuals across all age groups feeling that their conditions were relatively equal to compatriots than to perceptions that personal conditions had worsened.

More leverage can be gained on the specific concerns of different age groups by probing what topic is considered to be the main priority for the government in a respondent's respective country.[9] As seen in Table 4.4, unemployment overwhelmingly was the priority for young people in 2003, especially those in the 18–24 and 25–29 age groups who are the groups that are likeliest to be searching for employment. While also a concern for older age groups, issues of poverty and famine were almost equally important. Ten years later, unemployment was still the top issue but the share of respondents identifying it as a concern had declined. Instead, infrastructure, which encompasses transportation, communications, roads, housing, electricity, and water supply, was increasingly becoming more of an issue across all age groups, reflecting a generational shift. Across time, a generally lacklustre assessment of government performance in creating jobs persisted across all age groups, with one-third or less agreeing that job creation was going well.

---

[8] More specifically, the options for these questions include: very bad (much worse), fairly bad (worse), neither good nor bad (same), fairly good (better), and very good (much better).

[9] Specifically, the Afrobarometer question is worded as follows: 'In your opinion, what are the most important problems facing this country that government should address?' Respondents then can give up to three priorities. The results discussed here though only focus on the first priority identified.

Table 4.4. Identification of priority problem for national government (per cent of age group agreeing)

Most important problem	2003						2014					
	18–24	25–29	30–34	35–44	45–54	55+	18–24	25–29	30–34	35–44	45–54	55+
No problems	0.4	0.1	0.2	0.2	0.1	0.5	0.3	0.2	0.1	0.2	0.1	0.4
Economy	6.8	5.4	7.7	6.4	6.1	5.6	6.7	6.3	7.0	6.9	6.2	5.3
Unemployment, wages, and salaries	37.2	38.7	34.6	32.5	29.5	25.9	30.0	32.2	28.6	26.7	24.9	21.1
Agriculture and farming	4.3	5.4	7.0	7.1	9.1	9.7	3.0	4.0	5.2	6.1	7.1	8.3
Poverty and famine	18.9	19.8	20.8	22.0	21.9	25.3	12.5	13.2	13.6	13.7	15.6	18.4
Infrastructure	9.5	8.6	8.9	9.2	9.4	11.1	16.4	14.9	17.4	16.0	17.3	18.1
Education	5.5	4.5	4.2	4.5	5.6	4.2	7.7	5.8	5.1	6.5	5.7	4.4
Health	5.6	6.2	6.5	7.2	7.4	6.3	6.4	6.1	7.3	7.4	6.9	7.3
Social services	1.5	0.8	0.5	0.9	0.7	0.8	0.8	0.4	0.5	0.6	0.5	1.0
Weather	0.3	0.4	0.2	0.4	0.4	1.0	0.5	0.5	0.7	0.8	0.7	1.2
Land	0.2	0.2	0.3	0.3	0.4	0.5	0.4	0.4	0.5	0.7	0.6	0.9
Financial inputs (loans, taxes, credit)	1.2	1.1	1.4	1.8	1.2	1.3	1.2	1.5	1.5	1.4	1.3	0.9
Crime and security	3.7	3.3	3.3	3.4	3.5	3.6	5.8	6.1	4.1	4.7	4.8	4.7
Corruption	1.9	2.0	1.6	1.4	1.5	1.4	5.1	5.3	4.8	4.6	3.9	3.5
Violence and war	1.1	1.4	1.1	1.2	1.3	1.4	1.1	1.5	1.4	1.8	2.3	2.1
Rights and democracy	0.8	1.0	0.6	0.5	1.1	0.8	0.9	0.7	1.1	1.0	0.9	1.2
Other	1.4	1.2	1.0	0.9	0.9	0.6	1.3	1.0	1.1	1.2	1.4	1.5
Agree that government is handling job creation well	32.2	30.9	31.5	31.9	32.2	33.0	30.7	26.8	26.5	28.1	28.9	30.2
Total observations	5,701	3,926	3,215	4,857	2,912	3,087	6,240	5,059	4,308	6,240	3,773	4,137

Source: Calculated from Afrobarometer, Rounds 2 and 6. All descriptives are weighted by cross-country survey sample weights.

These aggregate averages obscure important variation across and within countries. In 2003, unemployment was seen as a problem by one-third or more young people in the three youth age groups in most of Southern Africa (Botswana, Lesotho, Mozambique, Namibia, South Africa, and Zimbabwe) as well as in Kenya and a handful of West African countries (Cape Verde, Ghana, and Nigeria). A little over a decade later, these patterns mostly persisted, except for unemployment becoming less of a concern in Ghana and Kenya. Youth concerns with unemployment were less pronounced in more agrarian countries, including Malawi, Mali, and Uganda.[10]

Even within countries, there are notable distinctions between rural and urban youth preferences on employment. Figure 4.2 illustrates those identifying unemployment as their primary concern by birth cohort, survey round, and by rural and urban residence. The graphic emphasizes that concerns with unemployment are higher in urban areas than in rural ones. It also illustrates that there are indeed life-cycle effects, such that the 25–29 age group in both survey rounds are most concerned with the lack of jobs and the slopes of the lines generally decrease thereafter, However, urban members of the 1969–73 cohort notably are more concerned with this issue in 2014 than their life-cycle would suggest. As this was the generation that transitioned into young adulthood at the onset of the first round of structural adjustment programmes (SAP) and democratic transitions, this pattern may suggest lasting effects of the disconnect between high expectations

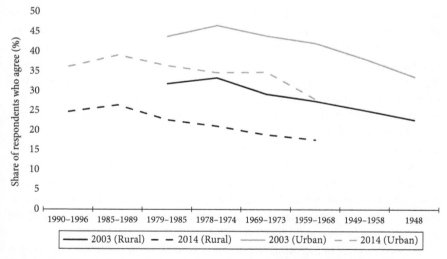

Figure 4.2. Unemployment identified as primary problem by approximate birth cohort and rural–urban

[10] Notably, Zambia was the only country in the whole sample where more than 10 per cent of youth in 2003 identified agriculture as a priority. But this share declined by 2014.

for the future and the reality of far fewer job opportunities as economies contracted under SAP conditions.

4.5 Political Perspectives and Modes of Participation

As noted earlier, today's African youth have not only experienced different eras of economic policy, contraction, and growth but also distinctly different political environments that might condition their modalities of political participation. Two key concepts are probed here. The first reflects respect for the political status quo, which is measured here by both closeness to the incumbent party in government and trust in political institutions. Closeness to the incumbent is captured by first identifying the share of respondents who note that they are close to a political party. Among those who are, Afrobarometer subsequently asks for which specific political party the respondent feels the greatest affinity. If the party chosen was the incumbent party at the time the survey was conducted, then the respondent is coded as being close to the incumbent; otherwise, if any other party is selected instead, the respondent is close to the opposition.

Political trust refers to an orientation towards government based on 'how well the government is operating according to people's normative expectations' (Hetherington 1998). Some argue that the erosion in trust of political institutions can have long term negative consequences for social and political stability (Newton and Norris 2000, Scholz and Lubell 1998). Political trust is operationalized here through an index that encompasses nine different formal political institutions: the president, parliament, electoral commission, local government, ruling party, opposition parties, police, army, and the courts.[11] The index runs from 0, denoting 'not at all', to 3, conveying 'a lot' of trust. Table 4.5 suggests that life-cycle effects are fairly pronounced with a higher share of older age groups across both survey rounds likely to express that they trust institutions a lot and that they feel close to the incumbent party. Notably, though, there is a fairly dramatic increase in trust for institutions *across all age groups in rural areas* between 2003 and 2014, but this is specifically true amongst the youngest age group. This trend suggests important period effects, including that over the decade in question, there was a noticeable reversal of urban bias as African governments try to allocate more distributive goods in rural areas so as to mobilize rural voters for elections (Bates and Block 2013, Boone and Wahman 2015).

The exact source of increased rural trust is difficult to pinpoint but some trends are suggestive from Table 4.6, which disaggregates trust levels by country and

---

[11] Trust in informal institutions, such as religious or traditional authorities, was excluded. In addition, trust in the tax revenue authorities was excluded from the index because the question was omitted from the Round 2 survey.

Table 4.5. Respect for political status quo (per cent of age group)

Variable	2003						2014					
	18–24	25–29	30–34	35–44	45–54	55+	18–24	25–29	30–34	35–44	45–54	55+
Trust institutions a lot												
Total	31.6	33.2	35.7	39.3	41.5	48.1	36.7	34.9	38.1	39.8	43.9	51.1
Rural	34.7	35.1	37.6	43.5	44.6	50.4	42.7	40.1	42.7	45.4	47.8	54.4
Urban	27.8	30.2	32.3	31.3	35.0	42.2	29.5	28.6	31.9	31.7	37.5	44.5
Close to incumbent party												
Total	31.0	34.8	34.9	37.3	39.3	40.1	28.6	30.0	31.4	35.5	37.4	38.4
Rural	35.7	39.5	40.1	41.5	44.0	41.9	32.0	33.0	36.1	38.0	40.1	39.4
Urban	25.1	27.6	25.2	29.0	29.3	35.6	24.5	26.3	25.0	31.9	32.9	36.3
Total observations	5,701	3,926	3,215	4,857	2,912	3,087	6,240	5,059	4,308	6,240	3,773	4,137

Source: Calculated from Afrobarometer, Rounds 2 and 6. All descriptives are weighted by cross-country survey sample weights.

Table 4.6. Trust in government institutions by country and rural youth (per cent trusting a lot)

Country	2003	2014	Difference
	18–34	18–34	
Botswana	29.7	38.9	9.2
Cape Verde	28.2	33.8	5.6
Ghana	33.4	28.1	−5.4
Kenya	25.8	37.1	11.3
Lesotho	28.6	52.0	23.4
Malawi	29.4	41.9	12.5
Mali	61.4	35.9	−25.5
Mozambique	49.4	48.4	−1.0
Namibia	60.4	58.4	−2.0
Nigeria	14.3	12.0	−2.2
Senegal	77.8	60.6	−17.2
South Africa	30.0	32.2	2.2
Tanzania	37.3	51.4	14.1
Uganda	19.6	49.6	30.0
Zambia	31.9	43.1	11.2
Zimbabwe	42.8	44.4	1.6

Sources: Calculated from Afrobarometer, Rounds 2 and 6. All descriptives are weighted by country-specific survey sample weights.

averages across all youth groups (that is, 18–34). For instance, some of the biggest increases in trust over the 2003–14 period were in countries such as Uganda, where many new districts have been purposely created in rural areas (Grossman and Lewis 2014) and in countries that have had sustained targeted input subsidy programmes that began in 2003 or soon thereafter, including in Kenya, Malawi, Tanzania, and Zambia (Jayne and Rashid 2013). By contrast, the large declines in rural trust observed in Mali and Senegal coincide, respectively, with government collapse and the onset of civil war in 2012 (Bleck, Dembele, and Guindo 2016) and to perceptions of growing government corruption (Sall 2015).[12]

Beyond their perspectives on political institutions and parties, the second concept focuses distinctly on political participation, which manifests in a variety of ways. If aligned along a spectrum, the most basic measure is an intrinsic interest in current events and efforts to stay informed of such events. Those who are more informed may be more likely to pursue protest activities as they become aware of perceived injustices or of events that could serve as rallying points for mobilization (Tufekci and Wilson 2012, Valenzuela, Arriagada, and Scherman 2014). To examine these dynamics, I examine young people's degree of interest in public affairs and

---

[12] The Lesotho Round 6 survey occurred in May 2014, prior to the unexpected August 2014 coup, which may partially explain the relatively high trust in government at that time.

how often they access the news. For the former, I focus on those survey respondents who note that they are 'somewhat' or 'very' interested in public affairs. For the latter, an index is created that combines degree of access to the news via various sources, including radio, television, newspaper, internet, and social media. The index runs from 0 to 4 with the former referring to never accessing the news through any media outlet and the latter indicating daily access to the news. For simplicity, Table 4.7 indicates the share of respondents who access the news 'many times a week' or on a daily basis, which is equivalent to 3 and 4 on the index.

In addition to just being informed, there are more proactive modes of engagement. When disgruntled about public policy at either the national or local level, there are various courses of action available. One includes actively contacting the relevant authorities. To capture this, I create an index reflecting whether a respondent has contacted any of the following four authorities either a 'few times' or 'often' over the previous year: local government, member of parliament, an official of a government agency, and/or a political party.[13] Another course of action is to get together with others to raise an issue, and Table 4.7 focuses on the share of those who answered that they have done this at least once during the year preceding the survey. Central to this paper's focus, the most extreme form of political participation is to be involved in a protest march or demonstration during the previous year.[14]

Table 4.7 reveals that interest in public affairs appears to have increased over time among all age groups, with more than 50 per cent of young people in all youth groups expressing their interest. Despite technological advances over the last decade, there is not a massive change in the share of individuals accessing the news on a frequent basis, and access remains relatively low on average. This may reflect that internet and social media in particular continue to have very little penetration across the region due to electricity outages and other infrastructure constraints. There do, however, appear to be some life-cycle dynamics such that regardless of time period, the two oldest age groups are less likely to access the news. In terms of active participation, contacting an authority, or joining others to raise an issue are more common modalities of youth participation than protests. Moreover, while the former two modalities of participation appear to become more pronounced as individuals age, the latter is not especially the reserve of a particular age group, especially in the Round 6 surveys. Indeed, while for example, 21 per cent of all protesters fall into the 18–24 year-old group, only about 9 per cent of that age group claims to have actually participated in a protest.

---

[13] For Malawi, the index does not include contacting local authorities since this option was not included in the country questionnaire.

[14] Whether one voted in the last elections in his/her country is an obvious measure of political participation. Unfortunately, however, this question was not asked in Round 2 of Afrobarometer so temporal comparisons could not be made.

Table 4.7. Level of political engagement and participation by age group (percentages)

Variable	2003						2014					
	18–24	25–29	30–34	35–44	45–54	55+	18–24	25–29	30–34	35–44	45–54	55+
Interest in public affairs	42.0	39.4	40.1	42.0	43.7	43.5	55.9	59.4	59.7	62.2	62.0	59.3
Access news many times a week or everyday	29.3	18.4	13.9	20.0	10.8	7.8	30.5	24.4	16.6	18.3	6.8	3.5
Contact authority (once or few times)	31.5	38.3	40.8	42.6	43.4	41.3	22.0	31.1	35.6	38.9	39.9	39.4
Join others to raise an issue	46.5	51.2	53.0	55.1	54.8	54.3	33.4	39.4	42.9	46.8	49.8	49.3
Protest	16.6	15.7	14.6	14.2	12.4	9.4	8.7	9.8	9.5	9.4	8.6	6.3
Total observations	5,701	3,926	3,215	4,857	2,912	3,087	6,240	5,059	4,308	6,240	3,773	4,137

Source: Calculated from Afrobarometer, Rounds 2 and 6. All descriptives are weighted by cross-country survey sample weights.

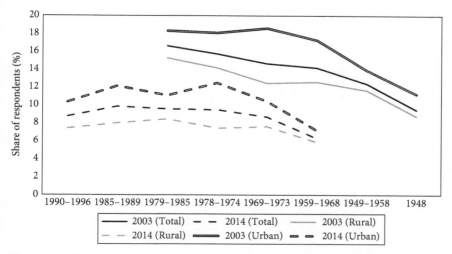

Figure 4.3. Participation in protest or demonstration by approximate birth cohort

Figure 4.3 further disaggregates these protest trends with a specific focus on rural and urban respondents and their corresponding birth cohorts. Protest is an activity that a higher share of urban than rural respondents claim to engage in, which is true across all age groups. In addition, the figure suggests that while older birth cohorts no longer protest as much as they did in the past, their levels of protest are not necessarily significantly below those of today's younger age groups. This implies that some lingering generational effects persist, especially for urban members of the 1974–8 generation, which came of age during the onset of 'third wave' democratic transitions in the early to mid-1990s, often due to protests.

Although protest remains relatively low on average among the various age groups in the Round 6 surveys, Table 4.8 examines country-specific dynamics with a focus on urban areas where protest is generally higher. Malian youth between 18–24 were particularly mobilized, followed by their counterparts in Senegal. While South Africa also has relatively high levels of youth protest, it was concentrated more among 25–34 year olds. In Nigeria, protest activity was actually highest among older age groups, perhaps reflecting the concerns with civil service salaries and fuel subsidies that were more specific to those older age groups.

4.6 Drivers of Youth Protest

In order to determine in a more rigorous manner what individual-level characteristics are associated with protest activity and whether these have changed over time, I employ separate logit, country-level fixed effects models to both the Round 2 and

Table 4.8. Protest by age groups in urban areas from Round 6 Afrobarometer (percentages)

Country	Age groups						Total	Total urban observations
	18–24	25–29	30–34	35–44	45–54	55+		
Botswana	10.34	7.77	8.03	13.11	11.31	6.46	9.54	760
Cape Verde	10.23	18.7	11.01	14.24	19.63	11.92	13.86	776
Ghana	9.28	7.83	8.14	8.84	4.84	4.82	7.54	1,304
Kenya	9.59	10.18	9.47	12.37	1.02	1.84	8.96	872
Lesotho	7.07	7.2	6.09	4.55	0.0	4.87	5.13	360
Malawi	8.56	16.34	9.35	10.57	0.0	5.11	9.46	448
Mali	34.26	20.36	27.54	23.2	18.84	7.88	23.48	304
Mozambique	9.68	9.51	7.79	12.26	4.24	9.4	9.33	840
Namibia	8.79	12.77	14.72	14.36	13.49	14.98	12.56	584
Nigeria	11.75	11.71	16.09	16.78	22.79	19.02	14.68	1,048
Senegal	19.36	16.98	20.85	19.23	11.79	2.72	15.63	592
South Africa	13.27	20.63	19.78	19.14	14.59	11.15	16.61	1,627
Tanzania	1.23	5.65	2.71	7.1	6.73	4.53	4.83	836
Uganda	6.46	13.78	9.6	4.21	7.11	3.06	7.72	448
Zambia	5.87	11.36	1.51	2.72	6.71	3.4	5.31	520
Zimbabwe	2.65	1.83	2.54	4.07	3.53	1.22	2.76	888

Round 6 data to estimate whether one has engaged in a protest or demonstration. Three basic demographic control variables are included, which are age, gender, and whether one lives in a rural area. In addition, consideration is given to testing four alternative hypotheses that may underlie one's propensity to protest.

First, relative deprivation is considered a strong incentive to protest. Grievance theories of protest long ago stressed that poverty, unemployment, and inequality were likely to provide the substantive incentive to engage in non-formal modes of political participation (Gurr 1970). The primary driver is the psychological and emotional stress created by economic deprivation, which prompts individuals to challenge the prevailing political order (Buechler 2004, Opp 1988). More recent studies of the relationship between economic crises and protests in Greece (Rüdig and Karyotis 2013) and Iceland (Bernburg 2015) have again uncovered that perceived economic deprivation is an important predicator of who goes to the streets. Key variables to test this hypothesis include the LPI, relative perceptions of socioeconomic status vis-à-vis other compatriots, and those who are not employed but looking.

Secondly, and in contrast to the deprivation hypothesis, the resource mobilization school has placed greater emphasis on the need for resources in order to organize protests, including skilled and educated protest leaders (McCarthy and Zald 1977, McVeigh and Smith 1999). Furthermore, individuals with a broad social network, who are well-informed with the capacity to process complex political information and recognize its consequences, and who have a greater sense of civic responsibility may be more likely to protest (Dalton 2008b, Rosenstone and Hansen 1993).[15] Relevant variables to test this hypothesis include respondents' education levels, access to the news, interest in public affairs, contacting an authority, and joining with others to raise an issue.

Thirdly, partisanship and trust in government may mitigate how one views his/her economic circumstances. Those who are close to a party, and particularly those who are close to the ruling party, may be less critical of the party and avoid pursuing activities that question the government's legitimacy. Relatedly, those with higher levels of trust in the government are less likely to resort to extra-institutional modalities, such as protest, in order to convey their preferences. By contrast, those with lower levels of trust are more likely to view the status quo as unresponsive and unrepresentative and to challenge political elites (Gamson 1968, Inglehart and Catterberg 2002). Labelled 'disaffected radicalism' by Norris, Walgrave, and

---

[15] In addition, some argue that those who are more involved in civic associations or who are embedded in social networks, such as those found through trade unions or religious organizations, have a greater propensity to be mobilized for protest activities (Putnam 1993, Verba, Schlozman, and Brady 1995). While Afrobarometer does ask about membership in such associations, the associations included varied substantially across the two rounds. In addition, the question was not asked in Zimbabwe. As such, the variable is not included in the analyses here.

Aelst (2005), this view has more recently been challenged by those who argue that protest behaviour may actually be driven more by trust in government if protesters believe their voices will be heard by politicians and their concerns will be addressed accordingly (Dubrow, Slomczynski, and Tomescu-Dubrow 2008). Including the measure of incumbent closeness and trust in political institutions allows for testing these arguments.

Finally, positions on policy could very likely be the proximate driver of protest activities. Indeed, individuals are not likely to go into the streets to protest if there is not a policy lever that they intend to change. Bermeo and Bartels (2014) stress this point in their work on developed countries recently facing economic crisis whereby protesters were more likely to oppose austerity policies rather than to feel economically deprived per se. Consequently, the analysis here draws on Table 4.4 and includes a dummy variable capturing whether a respondent feels that unemployment is the most important policy priority for their country and whether s/he believes that that the government is handling job creation well.

The findings in Table 4.9 show the results for the full sample for both the Round 2 and Round 6 surveys (models 1 and 4) as well as for sub-groups of the sample. For ease of explication and presentation, the three separate youth and non-youth groups were collapsed into one youth group (models 2 and 5) and one non-youth group (models 3 and 6). The results suggest that there are common profiles of protesters across age groups and survey rounds as well as important period and cohort effects.

In terms of demographics, age demonstrates a strong effect in general, indicating that the likelihood of protest is lower as one becomes older, and this is even true among those in the non-youth group. In other words, there are indeed some strong life-cycle effects to protest. By contrast, there is no clear pattern to other demographic variables. Despite the patterns from the descriptive statistics, rural youth are not more likely to protest than their urban counterparts over time at a statistically significant level. However, today's older rural residents are significantly less likely to protest. Similarly, young women may have been more likely to stay away from protest ten years ago but this pattern is insignificant at the time of the Round 6 surveys. These findings counter the perception that protests in Africa are purely the reserve of young men.

More broadly, the findings suggest that the deprivation and resource mobilization hypotheses are equally relevant in the African context. Particularly, protest likelihood is highest among those who are worse off on the LPI, and this trend persists across the two rounds of surveys. At the same time, those with higher levels of education, who are intrinsically interested in public affairs, who frequently access the news, and who engage in other forms of participation, such as contacting a government authority or joining others to raise an issue, demonstrate a correlation

Table 4.9. Logit analysis of protest likelihood across survey rounds and youth/non-youth age groups

Independent variables	Round 2 survey (2003)			Round 6 survey (2014)		
	Full sample	18–34	35 and older	Full sample	18–34	35 and older
	(1)	(2)	(3)	(4)	(5)	(6)
Age	0.0177***	−0.0283***	−0.0139***	0.00917***	−0.0177*	−0.0105**
	(0.00199)	(0.00660)	(0.00370)	(0.00193)	(0.00711)	(0.00346)
Rural	0.123*	−0.0915	−0.151	0.162**	−0.0809	−0.231**
	(0.0552)	(0.0710)	(0.0888)	(0.0535)	(0.0720)	(0.0805)
Female	0.121*	−0.133*	−0.104	0.00420	−0.0611	0.0544
	(0.0483)	(0.0613)	(0.0794)	(0.0486)	(0.0648)	(0.0739)
Lived poverty index	0.167***	0.158***	0.190***	0.210***	0.231***	0.199***
	(0.0300)	(0.0394)	(0.0466)	(0.0302)	(0.0408)	(0.0452)
Relative living conditions	0.0411	−0.0356	−0.0462	0.0722*	−0.0733	−0.0679
	(0.0296)	(0.0378)	(0.0481)	(0.0306)	(0.0412)	(0.0460)
Not employed and looking	−0.0606	−0.0750	−0.0236	0.223***	0.338***	0.0835
	(0.0547)	(0.0660)	(0.0987)	(0.0632)	(0.0834)	(0.0987)
Education level	0.0738***	0.118***	0.0334	0.0891***	0.0825***	0.0962***
	(0.0184)	(0.0250)	(0.0280)	(0.0190)	(0.0271)	(0.0273)
News access index	0.138***	0.136***	0.154***	0.135***	0.174***	0.0909*
	(0.0272)	(0.0357)	(0.0427)	(0.0285)	(0.0370)	(0.0457)
Interest in public affairs	0.178***	0.216***	0.116	0.289***	0.290***	0.298***
	(0.0490)	(0.0628)	(0.0789)	(0.0534)	(0.0709)	(0.0821)
Contacted government authority	0.338***	0.426***	0.243***	0.722***	0.772***	0.676***
	(0.0342)	(0.0453)	(0.0526)	(0.0339)	(0.0470)	(0.0497)
Joined others to raise an issue	0.536***	0.528***	0.558***	0.242***	0.250***	0.239***
	(0.0207)	(0.0265)	(0.0339)	(0.0214)	(0.0295)	(0.0314)
Close to incumbent party	0.0688	0.114	−0.00934	0.0543	0.0156	0.0811
	(0.0545)	(0.0699)	(0.0882)	(0.0560)	(0.0780)	(0.0816)

Continued

Table 4.9. Continued

Independent variables	Round 2 survey (2003)			Round 6 survey (2014)		
	Full sample	18–34	35 and older	Full sample	18–34	35 and older
	(1)	(2)	(3)	(4)	(5)	(6)
Trust index	-0.0652	-0.0922	-0.0253	0.0950**	-0.151**	-0.0391
	(0.0424)	(0.0554)	(0.0668)	(0.0360)	(0.0490)	(0.0538)
Identify employment as top priority	0.238***	0.151*	0.386***	0.0824	0.0324	0.154
	(0.0507)	(0.0641)	(0.0835)	(0.0539)	(0.0718)	(0.0817)
Believe government has handled job creation poorly	-0.0509	-0.0699	-0.0216	0.103	-0.111	-0.0719
	(0.0536)	(0.0688)	(0.0861)	(0.0538)	(0.0730)	(0.0805)
N	15,612	8776	6836	23,960	12,773	11,187

Note: * $p < 0.05$, ** $p < 0.01$, *** $p < 0.001$; Standard errors in parentheses.

Source: Logit fixed effects estimation across 16 countries based on Afrobarometer surveys.

with protest activity. This suggests that protesters are most likely among those with frustrated aspirations but who are proactive in pursuing other forms of mobilization to register discontent. Across surveys, education has become important for not only the youth groups but also the non-youth groups, which reflects that education has expanded over time, often facilitated by government programmes aimed at subsidizing education (Stasavage 2005).

These effects become even more pronounced by looking at the youth and non-youth cohorts. In the Round 6 survey, young people who are unemployed are significantly more likely to protest while their older, unemployed counterparts are not. This is particularly notable given that the same dynamic is not apparent ten years earlier, suggesting strong period and generational effects. At the same time, however, those who felt that unemployment was their country's most important policy priority were more likely to protest in the 2002 survey period, in both age groups, with the effects greatest among the older age groups. As seen in Figure 4.2, this had been a more pressing issue in that period than ten years later, especially in urban areas. For the more recent period, the employment policy variables demonstrate little significant association with protest activity.[16] This may not mean that employment is less substantively significant but that the distance in policy priorities between employment and other issues, such as infrastructure, has shrunk over time.

While partisan affinity with the ruling incumbent party appears insignificant over time and age group, a lack of trust in formal political institutions has become more significantly associated with protest among young people in the more recent survey period. In other words, even though today's younger generations are not necessarily more distrustful of political institutions than their historical counterparts and even though rural youth are even more trustful, those who are disenchanted with their institutions are likely to uphold the expectations of the disaffected radicalism hypothesis. As many of Africa's leaders, including those in the sample, are sexagenarians or older, the sense that political leaders do not genuinely understand or care about youth issues could quite conceivably underlie some of this distrust.

In sum, the results reveal that rather than there being a dichotomy between protesters driven by grievances and desperation on the one hand and by resources and networks on the other, these two dynamics can be mutually reinforcing. This results in a set of 'frustrated activists', who do not let their circumstances result in a sense of apathy and detachment. At the same time, they are not necessarily opportunistic troublemakers; rather, their protest activities are a natural extension of their generally higher levels of political participation in less dramatic contexts, such as contacting an authority or joining others to raise an issue.

---

[16] Although the results are not shown, this pattern is also true if variables are included for other policy issues, such as infrastructure, health, agriculture, and education.

In addition, while some variables appear relatively time invariant and important regardless of cohort (for example, age, LPI, contacting authorities, joining others to raise issues), others are much more sensitive to the period in which the surveys occurred. This is particularly true for employment status, perspectives on employment policies, and trust in political institutions.

4.7 Conclusions

One of the key reasons for tackling youth unemployment is because it is both the overarching policy priority for the young and historically, young people have effectively mobilized against sitting governments over jobs, as well as social services and the cost of living. By taking into account temporal and spatial dynamics, this chapter has examined whether and how the preferences and behaviours of young Africans have shifted over the last decade and whether they vary significantly from their older compatriots. Following much of the recent literature on youth participation and socialization (Grasso 2014, Smets and Neundorf 2014), efforts were made to interrogate both macro- and micro-level data and to specifically take into account life-cycle, generational, and period effects. Although there are clear life-cycle effects underlying protest behaviour such that younger individuals are more likely to protest than older ones, protest activity is a form of mobilization used by all age groups. For both young and old, being better educated and informed as well as engaging in other forms of activism are strong predictors of protest regardless of time period. Similarly, deprivation of basic goods is a strong motivator for protest. More recently, however, young people in particular are also more likely to protest if they are unemployed and if they lack trust in political institutions.

These findings have parallels in the conflict literature. For instance, Watts (2009) finds that youth violence in the Niger Delta of Nigeria is linked to perceptions of relative deprivation and frustration with a perceived gerontocratic and authoritarian local political setting. More generally, Raleigh (2015) uncovers support for the 'fragile city' thesis in Africa, which is that especially in urban areas, poor conditions motivate violence, including by the youth, in states viewed as incapable of providing adequate public goods and opportunities.

At least one caveat of the present research is, however, worth noting. Due to the data availability, the analysis only examined street protests rather than online protests. In some ways then, the levels of protest by the youth are therefore probably understated in the analysis here. However, given that street protests are much more visible, the results are probably more substantively meaningful since they identify the characteristics of a smaller group of youth who would risk revealing their discontent in public.

Notwithstanding this caveat, this chapter clearly highlights the linkages between demographics, employment, and political participation. Although not all protests are tied to employment or economic issues, the fact that more recent protests have a significant association with those who are unemployed and dismissive of their political institutions is revealing. Identifying and implementing employment initiatives that match the aspirations of today's better-educated and informed youth is pivotal and may require reconsideration of whether explicitly youth-focused policies, and those that attempt to re-locate youth into rural areas or farming careers, are the most effective way forward.

References

African Union Commission (AU). 2006. *African Youth Charter.* Banjul, The Gambia: African Union.

Alexander, P. 2010. Rebellion of the poor: South Africa's service delivery protests—a preliminary analysis. *Review of African Political Economy* 37 (123): 25–40.

Allman, J. 1990. The young men and the porcupine: Class, nationalism and Asante's struggle for self-determination, 1954–1957. *Journal of African History* 31 (2): 263–79.

Bates, R., and S. Block. 2013. Revisiting African agriculture: Institutional change and productivity growth. *Journal of Politics* 75 (2): 372–84.

Benin, S., M. Johnson, E. Abokyi, G. Ahorbo, K. Jimah, G. Nasser, V. Owusu, J. Taabazuing, and A. Tenga. 2013. Revisiting agricultural input and farm support subsidies in Africa: The case of Ghana's mechanization, fertilizer, block farms, and marketing programs. *IFPRI Discussion Paper 01300.* Washington, DC, U.S.A.: International Food Policy Research Institute.

Bennett, W. L. 2008. Changing citizenship in the digital age. In *Civic life online: Learning how digital media can engage youth,* ed. W. L. Bennett. Cambridge, MA, U.S.A.: The MIT Press.

Bermeo, N., and L. Bartels. 2014. Mass politics in tough times. In *Mass politics in tough times: Opinions, votes and protest in the Great Recession,* ed. N. Bermeo, and L. Bartels. Oxford, U.K.: Oxford University Press.

Bernburg, J. G. 2015. Economic crisis and popular protest in Iceland, January 2009: The role of perceived economic loss and political attitudes in protest participation and support. *Mobilization: An International Quarterly* 20 (2): 231–52.

Bleck, J., A. Dembele, and S. Guindo. 2016. Malian crisis and the lingering problem of good governance. *Stability: International Journal of Security and Development* 5 (1): 1–18.

Boone, C., and M. Wahman. 2015. Rural bias in African electoral systems: Legacies of unequal representation in African democracies. *Electoral Systems* 40: 335–46.

Branch, A., and Z. Mampilly. 2015. *Africa uprising: Popular protest and political change.* London, U.K.: Zed Books.

Bratton, M., and N. van de Walle. 1992. Popular protest and political reform in Africa. *Comparative Politics* 24 (4): 419–42.

Buechler, S. M. 2004. The strange career of strain and breakdown theories of collective action. In *The Blackwell companion to social movements*, ed. D. A. Snow, S. A. Soule, and H. Kriesi. Malden, MA, U.S.A.: Blackwell.

Buechler, S. M. 2005. Introduction to youth and citizenship in East Africa. *Africa Today* 51 (3): vi–xxiv.

Burgess, Thomas. 2005. Introduction to Youth and Citizenship in East Africa. *Africa Today*, (3): vii–xxiv.

Collier, P. 2007. *The bottom billion: Why the poorest countries are failing and what can be done about it.* Oxford, U.K.: Oxford University Press.

Dalton, R. 1988. *Citizen politics in Western democracies.* New Jersey, U.S.A.: Chatham House.

Dalton, R. 2008a. Citizenship norms and the expansion of political participation. *Political Studies* 56 (1): 76–98.

Dalton, R. 2008b. *Citizen politics: Public opinion and political parties in advanced industrial democracies.* Washington, DC, U.S.A.: CQ Press.

Dubrow, J. K., K. M. Slomczynski, and I. Tomescu-Dubrow. 2008. Effects of democracy and inequality on soft political protest in Europe. *International Journal of Sociology* 38 (3): 36–51.

Franklin, M. 2004. *Voter turnout and the dynamics of electoral competition in established democracies since 1945.* Cambridge, U.K.: Cambridge University Press.

Gamson, W. A. 1968. *Power and discontent.* Homewood, IL, U.S.A.: Dorsey Press.

Glenn, N. 2005. *Cohort analysis (2nd Edition).* Thousand Oaks, CA, U.S.A.: Sage.

Grasso, M. 2014. Age, period, and cohort analysis in a comparative context: Political generations and political participation repertoires in Western Europe. *Electoral Studies* 33: 63–76.

Grossman, G., and J. Lewis. 2014. Administrative unit proliferation. *American Political Science Review* 108 (1): 196–217.

Gurr, T. 1970. *Why men rebel.* Princeton, NJ, U.S.A.: Princeton University Press.

Hamilton, R. 2010. Young standing up for democracy in Sudan: Movement forged in run-up to April elections encourages citizens to know and demand their rights. *The Washington Post* 14 August: A7.

Hetherington, M. J. 1998. The political relevance of political trust. *American Political Science Review* 92: 791–808.

Inglehart, R., and G. Catterberg. 2002. Trends in political action: The developmental trend and the post-honeymoon decline. *International Journal of Comparative Sociology* 43 (3–5): 300–16.

Jayne, T. and S. Rashid. 2013. Input subsidy programs in Sub-Saharan Africa: A synthesis of recent evidence. *Agricultural Economics* 44 (6): 547–62.

Jennings, M. K. 1996. Political knowledge over time and across generations. *Public Opinion Quarterly* 60 (2): 228–52.

Kaplan, R. 1996. *The ends of the Earth: From Togo to Turkmenistan, from Iran to Cambodia, a journey to the frontiers of anarchy.* New York, NY, U.S.A.: Random House.

Klandermans, B., J. Van Steklenburg, and J. Van der Toorn. 2008. Embeddedness and identity: How immigrants turn grievances into action. *American Sociological Review* 73 (6): 992–1012.

Leahy, E., R. Engelman, C. Vogel, S. Haddock, and T. Preston. 2007. *The shape of things to come: Why age structure matters to a safer, more equitable world.* Washington, DC, U.S.A.: Population Action Council.

Markus, G. B. 1983. Dynamic modeling of cohort change: The case of political partisanship. *American Journal of Political Science* 27 (4): 717–39.

Mattes, R. 2008. The material and political bases of lived poverty in Africa: Insights from the Afrobarometer. In *Barometers of quality of life around the globe: How are we doing?,* ed. V. Moller, D. Huschka, and A. Michalos. Netherlands: Springer.

Mattes, R. 2012. The 'born frees': The prospects for generational change in post-apartheid South Africa. *Australian Journal of Political Science* 47 (1): 133–53.

McCarthy, J., and M. Zald. 1977. Resource mobilization and social movements: A partial theory. *American Journal of Sociology* 82 (6): 1212–41.

McKinsey Global Institute. 2010. *Lions on the move: The progress and potential of African economies.* Washington, DC, U.S.A.: McKinsey Global Institute.

McVeigh, R., and C. Smith. 1999. Who protests in America: An analysis of three alternatives—Inaction, institutionalized politics, or protest. *Sociological Forum* 14 (4): 685–702.

Ncube, M., and C. L. Lufumpa. 2015. *The emerging middle class in Africa.* New York, N.Y, U.S.A.: Routledge, and Abidjan, Ivory Coast: African Development Bank.

Neundorf, A., and R. Niemi. 2014. Beyond political socialization: New approaches to age, period, and cohort analysis. *Electoral Studies* 33 (1): 1–6.

Newton, K., and P. Norris. 2000. Confidence in public institutions: Faith, culture, or performance? In *Disaffected democracies: What's troubling the trilateral countries,* ed. S. Pharr, and R. Putnam. Princeton, NJ, U.S.A.: Princeton University Press.

Nie, N., S. Verba, and J. Kim. 1974. Political participation and the life cycle. *Comparative Politics* 6 (3): 319–40.

Norris, P. 2002. *Democratic phoenix: Reinventing political activism.* Cambridge, U.K.: Cambridge University Press.

Norris, P., S. Walgrave, and P. Aelst. 2005. Who demonstrates? Disaffected rebels, conventional participants, or everyone? *Comparative Politics* 37 (2): 189–205.

Nugent, P. 2004. *Africa since independence.* New York, NY, U.S.A.: Palgrave Macmillan.

Opp, K. D. 1988. Grievances and participation in social movements. *American Sociological Review* 53: 853–64.

Parry, G., G. Moyser, and N. Day. 1992. *Political participation and democracy in Britain.* New York, NY, U.S.A.: Cambridge University Press.

Pew Research Center. 2010. *Millennials: Confident. Connected. Open to change.* Washington, DC, U.S.A.: Pew Research Center.

Putnam, R. 1993. *Making democracy work: Civic traditions in modern Italy.* Princeton, NJ, U.S.A.: Princeton University Press.

Raleigh, C. 2015. Urban violence patterns across African states. *International Studies Review* 17: 90–106.

Resnick, D., and J. Thurlow. 2015. Introduction: African youth at a crossroads. In *African youth and the persistence of marginalization: Employment, politics, and prospects for change*, ed. D. Resnick, and J. Thurlow. New York, N.Y, U.S.A.: Routledge.

Resnick, D., and J. Thurlow. 2016. The political economy of Zambia's recovery: Structural change without transformation? In *Structural change, fundamentals, and growth*, ed. M. McMillan, D. Rodrik, and C. Sepúlveda. Washington, DC, U.S.A.: IFPRI.

Rosenstone, S. J., and J. M. Hansen. 1993. *Mobilization, participation, and democracy in America.* New York, N.Y, U.S.A.: Palgrave Macmillan.

Rüdig, W., and G. Karyotis. 2013. Who protests in Greece? Mass opposition to austerity. *British Journal of Political Science* 44 (3): 487–513.

Ryder, N. B. 1965. The cohort as a concept in the study of social change. *American Sociological Review* 30 (6): 843–61.

Sall, I. 2015. Trust in political institutions in Senegal: Why did it drop? *Afrobarometer Policy Paper No. 24.* http://afrobarometer.org/sites/default/files/publications/Policy%20 papers/ab_r6_policypaperno24_trust_in_political_institutions.pdf.

Sall, M. 2012. The REVA Plan in Senegal: Does modern farming change minds of young people about agriculture? Presented at the Young People, Farming and Food Conference, March 19–21, Accra, Ghana.

Scholz, J., and M. Lubell. 1998. Trust and taxpaying: Testing the heuristic approach to collective action. *American Journal of Political Science* 42 (2): 398–417.

Smets, K., and A. Neundorf. 2014. The hierarchies of age-period-cohort research: Political context and the development of generational turnout patterns. *Electoral Studies* 33: 41–51.

Stasavage, D. 2005. Democracy and education spending in Africa. *American Journal of Political Science* 49 (2): 343–58.

Sumberg, J., N. A. Anyidoho, M. Chasukwa, B. Chinsinga, J. Leavy, G. Tadele, S. Whitfield, and J. Yaro. 2015. Young people, agriculture and employment in rural Africa. In *African youth and the persistence of marginalization: Employment, politics, and prospects for change*, ed. D. Resnick, and J. Thurlow. London, U.K.: Routledge.

Tufekci, Z., and C. Wilson. 2012. Social media and the decision to participate in political protest: Observations from Tahrir Square. *Journal of Communication* 62 (2): 363–79.

Urdal, H. 2006. A clash of generations? Youth bulges and political violence. *International Studies Quarterly* 50 (3): 607–29.

Valenzuela, S., A. Arriagada, and A. Scherman. 2012. The social media basis of youth protest behavior: The case of Chile. *Journal of Communication* 62 (2): 299–314.

Valenzuela, S., A. Arriagada, and A. Scherman. 2014. Facebook, twitter, and youth engagement: A quasi-experimental study of social media use and protest behavior using propensity score matching. *International Journal of Communication* 8: 2046–70.

Verba, S., K. L. Schlozman, and H. Brady. 1995. *Voice and equality: Civic voluntarism in American politics.* Cambridge, MA, U.S.A.: Harvard University Press.

Wattenberg, M. 2008. *Is voting for young people?* New York, N.Y, U.S.A.: Pearson Longman.

Watts, M. 2009. Oil, development, and the politics of the bottom billion. *Macalester International* 24 (1): 1.

Wonacott, P. 2012. Youth protests shake politics across Africa—Angola's long-serving president, though seen as secure in re-election, is one of many facing pressure in Arab Spring's wake. *Wall Street Journal* 30 August: A16.

World Bank. 2016. *Africa's pulse: An analysis of issues shaping Africa's economic future.* Washington, DC, U.S.A.: World Bank.

Yang, Y., and K. C. Land. 2013. *Age—period—cohort analysis: New models, methods, and empirical applications.* Boca Raton, FL, U.S.A.: CRC Press, Taylor & Francis Group.

PART II

CASE STUDIES ON THE ROLE OF YOUTH EMPLOYMENT IN STRUCTURAL TRANSFORMATION

5

Rural Youth and Employment in Ethiopia

Emily Schmidt and Firew Bekele Woldeyes

5.1 Introduction

The economic growth literature argues that as an economy grows, the location and structure of labour transitions from primarily rural, agriculture-focused activities to more urbanized activities in the industry and service sectors. This structural transformation improves the livelihood of those who earn higher wages outside of agriculture, as well as increases land to labour ratios of those who remain in agriculture. Increases in household income (via diversified labour portfolios) often provide capital to spur innovation and agricultural productivity growth in rural areas. Over the last few decades, Ethiopia's economic development strategy, the Agricultural Development Led Industrialization (ADLI) strategy, aimed to increase agricultural productivity, and in doing so, encouraged labour diversification via the development of rural nonfarm activities. This mode of development is supported by a large body of research literature which suggests that growth in the rural nonfarm sector is driven by agricultural productivity growth (Haggblade, Hazell, and Reardon 2002, Haggblade, Hazell, and Dorosh 2006, Mellor 1976).

Given Ethiopia's focus on ADLI, agricultural production has increased substantially and the country has experienced impressive economic growth over the last decade of approximately 11 per cent per year. However, macroeconomic trends suggest that Ethiopia's economy remains at a very early stage in its structural transformation. A puzzle presents itself as to how such growth can be maintained given that Ethiopia is one of the least urbanized countries in Africa south of the Sahara (84 per cent of the total population lives in rural areas) with approximately three quarters of the population engaged in agricultural activities (FDRE Population Census Commission 2008, Central Statistical Agency 2013). From a policy point of view, understanding how youth can take advantage of employment opportunities, both in the agriculture and non-agriculture sectors, will inform future economic growth potential in years to come.

Slow urbanization paired with vibrant economic growth suggests that rural youth will remain an important component of the agricultural labour force, while

Emily Schmidt and Firew Bekele Woldeyes, *Rural Youth and Employment in Ethiopia* In: *Youth and Jobs in Rural Africa: Beyond Stylized Facts*. Edited by: Valerie Mueller and James Thurlow, Oxford University Press (2019).
© International Food Policy Research Institute.
DOI: 10.1093/oso/9780198848059.003.0005

also seeking to diversify into non-agricultural, higher-value labour opportunities. Within the agricultural sector, transformation includes moving from low-value cereal production, which is characteristic of current Ethiopian agricultural production patterns, to high-value crops, such as fruit and vegetables. Rural youth may seek to modernize agricultural practices and utilize new technologies to enhance agricultural growth in the medium term. Regarding the overall economic landscape, as structural transformation progresses in Ethiopia, youth may drive labour diversification trends from predominantly rural agricultural activities to more urban focused manufacturing and service sector activities.

This chapter examines current trends in labour diversification in Ethiopia, focusing on youth employment activities, and explores the structure of livelihood decisions given underlying agricultural endowments. Although the majority of rural youth work exclusively on their own family farm, it is not clear that focusing on agriculture is a strategy that will provide a sufficient livelihood for future generations. Recent data collected by the Ethiopia Socioeconomic Survey (ESS) suggest that youth in particular may have less access to important agricultural assets than do their elders. In response to these constraints, one might expect youth to implement more intensive farming. However, the same data show that households headed by youth are not more likely to use agricultural production enhancing technologies than are mature-headed farming households.

Given that youth face constraints in the agricultural sector, we examine youth nonfarm labour engagement in rural and small town areas. We find that youth (those aged 25 to 34 years) have a greater probability of working in nonfarm enterprises (NFE) compared to mature individuals (ages 35–64). The majority of individuals working in nonfarm employment are engaged in small-scale trade activities, such as street and market vending, while there exists limited demand for more skilled labour in the construction and manufacturing sectors. Our analysis suggests that push factors are at play with regards to nonfarm diversification, whereby those that live in areas with less favourable agricultural potential, who possess few assets, like livestock, and have less access to agricultural credit are more likely to seek off-farm work.

This chapter provides evidence that youth are currently driving the limited structural changes observed in employment patterns in Ethiopia's economy via employment diversification into nonfarm enterprises. However, low demand for higher-skilled labour, including in the rural nonfarm sector, remains a major obstacle to achieving structural transformation in the near to medium term. The remainder of the chapter is organized as follows: the second section reports employment trends in Ethiopia with a focus on youth activities in rural, small town, and urban areas. The third explores the difference in agricultural production practices between mature-headed households and youth-headed households. The fourth section focuses on youth nonfarm activities using a multinomial logit model to explore correlates of youth decisions to work in the nonfarm sector. The fifth discusses results of the multinomial logit, and then the chapter concludes.

5.2 Employment in Ethiopia

5.2.1 Employment Trends

We utilize two nationally representative survey datasets to explore overall labour activity in Ethiopia: the National Labour Force Surveys (NLFS) of Ethiopia and the Ethiopia Socioeconomic Survey (ESS). Although the NLFS data provide nationally representative data on labour trends in the country, it restricts data collection to 'main occupation'. Thus, we are unable to assess the portfolio of economic activities individuals pursue, in particular rural nonfarm work by members of farming households. In order to provide a more comprehensive analysis of labour participation, we complement the NLFS evaluation with a detailed labour decomposition in rural, small town, and large cities using the ESS. The ESS requests that each individual household records the amount of time worked on agriculture (own-farm), wage, and nonfarm enterprises over a 12-month period. Given that 82 per cent of Ethiopia's population reside in rural areas, where a majority of individuals define their primary occupation as agriculture, the ESS supports a more diversified analysis of individual work portfolios.

5.2.2 National Labour Force Surveys, 2005 and 2013

When analysing the NLFS data, we adopt the Central Statistical Agency (CSA) definition of the active labour force. Labour force participants include individuals who are at least 10 years old (Ethiopia does not limit the labour force to retirement at 64 years old). Within the working age population, individuals who are not engaged in work and would not be available to take up work if it was offered, as well as individuals who are students, handicapped, or have long-term illnesses, are not considered a part of the active labour force.[1]

Although we follow CSA definitions for active labour force, we adjust the 2013 definition of economically active to provide a more accurate comparison with the 2005 NLFS data. In 2005, data collected on occupation and industry concentrated on individuals who worked at least four hours per day, while in 2013, individuals

---

[1] The CSA does not include 'seeking work' as a criterion for being considered economically active. This is due to local conditions of inadequate labour absorption, a large share of labour force being self-employed, and inconsistencies in time accounting of individuals who work in the informal labour market.

who reported working at least one hour were provided an industry classification. This modification in the questionnaire resulted in a large share of household unpaid family labour (firewood and water collectors) being classified as working in the household services sector in 2013. We adjust for this discrepancy by reclassifying individuals who stated their main occupation as 'wood and water collection' into 'not in the labour force' in order to provide comparable estimates of employment shares within sectors between the two survey years. We report labour shares using NLFS 2013 official definitions (including wood and water collectors in the economically active population) as well as our adjusted 2013 statistics.[2]

Between 2005 and 2013, while official definitions suggest a greater transition out of agriculture from 80 to 73 per cent of economically active population, we find that, after adjusting the data for water and firewood collectors, the share of people working in agriculture decreased by only 3 percentage points from 80 to 77 per cent over this period (Table 5.1). Overall employment shares in the services sector also reflect the reallocation of water and firewood collectors. Official statistics reported the overall services sector to encompass 20 per cent of the economically active population in 2013, of which private household work increased from 6 to 36 per cent of service employment. Adjusting for the discrepancies between the 2005 and 2013 surveys in the definition of those employed, we find that the service sector employed 16 per cent of the economically active population in 2013. Finally, the industry sector has not experienced significant growth over the last decade in terms of job creation, with employment shares increasing by only about one percentage point between 2005 and 2013.

Although the government of Ethiopia has made significant investments in education with an emphasis on increasing access to secondary education

Table 5.1. Employment shares by industry of the economically active population (ages 10 years and older), per cent

Industry	2005	2013 unadjusted	2013 adjusted
Agriculture	80.2	72.7	76.6
Industry	6.7	7.3	7.7
Services	13.2	20.0	15.7
Private households	6.0	36.4	10.2

Source: National Labour Force Survey (2005, 2013). '2013 unadjusted' represents the national CSA-based definition of sectors. '2013 adjusted' reclassifies water and firewood collectors as 'not economically active'—this sort of work is not taken into account in the figures in this column.

[2] In 2013, 88 per cent of individuals who reported water and wood collecting as their primary occupation reported that this activity was classified as unpaid family worker. The majority of these workers were female (89 per cent) and rural (94 per cent). This category was not present or accounted for in 2005. For more information on these individuals see Appendix 5.A1.

Table 5.2. Share of non-agricultural employment in Ethiopia by occupational group, 2013, present

Occupational group	Share of non-agricultural employment
Sales workers	30.2
Street and market salespersons	*43.6*
Shop salespersons	*22.1*
Alcohol sales	*20.6*
Other sales	*13.7*
Construction and mining	10.6
Food processing, wood and garment craft	7.6
Refuse workers	7.0
Teacher	6.5
Personal service worker	5.9
Other	32.2

Source: National Labour Force Survey (2013).

opportunities, non-agricultural workers are predominantly engaged in low-skill sectors. Sales workers make up 29 per cent of non-agricultural work, of which street and local market vendors comprise 42 per cent (Table 5.2). Formal shop-keepers and informal home-brewed alcohol sellers comprise almost equivalent shares of 22 and 21 per cent of sales workers, respectively. These employment trends suggest a mode of development that is moving, albeit slowly, towards a service sector focused economy. However, the specific service activities that individuals are engaged in reflect a low level of development with limited labour demand.

In order to better understand employment activities within the Ethiopian economy, we disaggregate employment numbers by geographic area (rural, small town, and urban areas) and by age group. Focusing on youth, the data suggest that rural youth are primarily engaged in agriculture, while a greater share of youth living in 'other urban' locations and in large cities are engaged in non-agricultural work. As per the CSA definition of 'other urban', we can assume that these centres represent secondary cities that are urban centres with populations of less than 100,000 people and are not considered regional capitals. When comparing the percentage share of individuals working in agriculture between rural areas and these secondary cities, diversification is primarily occurring in the secondary cities whereby 22 and 12 per cent of youth aged 15 to 24 years and 25 to 34 years, respectively, report their primary occupation is in agriculture (Table 5.3). However, it is important to note that 'other urban' represents only 12 per cent of the economically active population, both overall and for youth.

Evaluating employment transitions between 2005 and 2013 disaggregated by age and spatial domain, the NLFS results presented in Table 5.3 suggest very little

Table 5.3. Per cent of employed population whose primary occupation is in agriculture, 2005 and 2013, by age cohort and spatial domain

Spatial domain	Age 10–14	Age 15–24	Age 25–34	Age over 35	Total
Ethiopia					
2005	92.0	77.6	74.8	80.7	80.2
2013*	93.4	75.4	66.3	77.3	76.6
Rural					
2005	94.2	85.8	85.6	89.7	88.5
2013*	95.3	86.9	83.9	90.1	88.9
Other urban[1]					
2005	48.5	21.6	11.5	18.5	19.9
2013*	54.1	19.1	14.5	23.0	21.0
Major urban[2]					
2005	17.9	3.6	2.1	4.3	3.8
2013*	22.9	3.6	2.5	5.4	4.2

Notes: * 2013 data are based on reclassification of individuals that reported their primary occupation as 'wood and water collectors' into 'not in the labour force'.
[1] Other urban centres are urban centres with populations of less than 100,000 people in 2007 and which are not considered regional capitals.
[2] Major urban centres include all regional capitals and the 15 other major urban centres that had a population size of 100,000 or more in 2007.
Source: Ethiopia National Labour Force Surveys (2005, 2013).

movement out of agriculture. Almost equivalent shares of youth aged 15–24 and youth aged 25–34 worked in agriculture in 2013 as there were in 2005. The share of youth working in agriculture in secondary cities shifted slightly down by 3 percentage points (from 22 to 19 per cent) for those aged 15–24. However, individuals in secondary cities aged 25–34 and over 35 years experienced slight increases in the overall share of the economically active engaged in agriculture. As expected, individuals living in major urban cities, who represent 10 per cent of the economically active population, predominantly work in the non-agriculture sector. Given that the NLFS restricts data collection to the main occupation of individuals, we now turn to the ESS, which comprises a comprehensive account of time spent on specific activities in order to evaluate the portfolio of rural youth activities.

5.2.3 Ethiopia Socioeconomic Survey

The Ethiopia Socioeconomic Survey (ESS) 2013/14 was implemented in 433 enumeration areas and comprises 5,262 sample households.[3] Sampling of rural, small town (population with less than 10,000 people) and urban areas

---

[3] ESS began as the Ethiopia Rural Socioeconomic Survey (ERSS) in 2011/12. The first wave of data collected in 2011/12 included only rural and small town areas. The 2013/14 ESS (wave 2), which we use in this chapter, was expanded to include all urban areas.

(greater than 10,000 people) was implemented to allow representative sampling of the population in order to estimate regional and national level data.[4]

The ESS requested information on the amount of time worked on specific activities for each individual in the household. The post-planting and post-harvesting modules of the questionnaire recorded the activity and number of hours, days, and weeks enumerated individuals worked on the household farm during the last 12 months. Similarly, the time use and labour module recorded the occupation and industry of wage employment of the respondent, as well as the number of days and weeks worked during the last 12 months for primary and secondary occupations. Finally, a nonfarm enterprise module asked the household to report any nonfarm enterprise that was operating in the last 12 months, its primary activity, the number of months (and days in the month) that the enterprise was active, and finally the household members that worked in the nonfarm enterprise. We use data from these four modules to create a portfolio of individuals' labour activities based on time worked in a specific sector.

Based on the ESS data, Ethiopia comprises 93.5 million people, of which 51 per cent are aged between 15 and 64 years (inclusive). Within this age group, approximately 76 per cent (36.4 million) reported that they worked on their own farm, for wages, or within a nonfarm enterprise. Of this working population, the majority of individuals (78 per cent) are engaged solely in own-family farm activities, while only 12 per cent report having a secondary job outside of their own farm. Similar results were found by Bachewe et al. (2016) using a large-scale household survey dataset in high potential agricultural areas (Agricultural Growth Programme survey). They report that total off-farm income comprised 18 per cent of total rural income. Although the ESS data are instructive in understanding labour portfolios, they do not allow an accurate estimation of unemployment. Rather, the 'not working' population are those who do not report working in any labour activity and are not currently students. Under these definitions, approximately 19 per cent of the working age population is not working.[5]

5.2.4 Labour Diversification Can Be Viewed from Two Levels

At the household level, diversification is used as a way to augment overall income and/or increase income during the slack agricultural season. Given that Ethiopia is characterized by rainfed agriculture, households may also diversify their income to smooth consumption when the household is faced with exogenous shocks. At the individual level, there is a division of labour within the household of who is asked to diversify. For example, some members of the household may be

---

[4] Regional strata include: Addis Ababa; Amhara; Oromiya; Southern Nations, Nationalities, and Peoples (SNNP); Tigray; and 'Other regions'.
[5] According to the CSA (2013), approximately 20 per cent of age eligible (10–64 years) individuals were considered to be not economically active, and 4.5 per cent of the economically active population was unemployed.

better students or more entrepreneurial, while others are more equipped, meaning, physically or in terms of skills, to remain working on the farm. In addition, cultural norms characterize specific individual activities. For example, women in Ethiopia are discouraged to plow agricultural land and engage in other specific agricultural activities. We assess both household- and individual-level labour diversification in order to assess how youth are taking advantage of employment opportunities outside of their own-family farm work. We first evaluate labour portfolios at the household-level to understand how diversification of income differs by the age of the household head. Then, we investigate individual-level labour activities to understand who diversifies within the household.

5.2.5 Household-level Labour Diversification

In order to evaluate labour diversification within households, we split the sample by youth and mature households based on the age of the household head. We compare mature-headed households to three youth categories (overall youth ages 15–34 years; young youth ages 15–24; and experienced youth ages 25–34). The data suggest that a significantly lower proportion of workers in youth-headed households, in all youth age cohorts, work exclusively on their own agricultural land (Table 5.4). Whereas 84 per cent of mature-headed households dedicate all of their household labour to their own agricultural production, approximately 8 percentage points less, 76 per cent, of youth-headed households focus their available labour solely on own family farm agricultural activities (Table 5.4).

More youth-headed households have diversified labour portfolios compared to mature-headed households. A greater share (16 per cent) of youth-headed households between the ages of 25 and 34 years have a mix of own family farm and nonfarm labour compared to mature households (13 per cent), while younger households (age 15–24) show less diversification compared to mature households (Table 5.4). This may be because older youth (age 25–34) have gained the necessary experience and have expanded their social network to search out nonfarm opportunities, while the younger households are still reliant on parental support, have fewer household members, and lack the necessary resources to diversify their household labour portfolio. Finally, a greater share of youth-headed households in all age cohorts are engaged exclusively in the nonfarm sector. Within the nonfarm category, most individuals are working in the non-agricultural sector. This follows agricultural practices in Ethiopia, where limited labour demand for agricultural work exists due to labour–sharing customs in rural areas (*debbo* and *wonfel* systems).[6]

---

[6] For more information on *debbo* and *wonfel* systems, see Krishnan and Sciubba (2009).

Table 5.4. Allocation of household labour to own farm, other farms, or off-farm, by age cohort of household head, 2013–14, per cent of households

	Mature-headed HHs (aged 35–64)	Youth-headed HHs (aged 15–34)	Young youth-headed HHs (aged 15–24)	Experienced youth-headed HHs (aged 25–34)
Own family farm	83.8	75.5 ***	74.9 ***	75.6 ***
Mixed own farm and nonfarm	12.9	16.3 ***	11.4	16.9 ***
Off own-farm (agriculture)	*9.1*	*10.3*	*12.6*	*10.1*
Off own-farm (non-agriculture)	*90.9*	*89.7*	*87.4*	*89.9*
Off-farm	3.4	8.1 ***	13.7 ***	7.5 ***
Off own-farm (agriculture)	*7.5*	*7.0*	*7.9*	*6.9*
Off own-farm (non-agriculture)	*92.5*	*93.0*	*92.1*	*93.1*

Note: t-tests are relative to mature households; *** $p < 0.01$, ** $p < 0.05$, * $p < 0.1$.

Source: Ethiopia Socioeconomic Survey (2013/14).

5.2.6 Individual-level Labour Diversification

Given that the majority of agricultural production in Ethiopia involves a single harvest annually, on-farm work is a highly seasonal activity. Individuals may seek out other income-earning opportunities off the farm during the slack agricultural season. In order to compare individual engagement in nonfarm labour opportunities, we split the sample of individual workers between youth aged 15 to 34 years and mature individuals aged 35 to 64 years. In addition, we disaggregate individuals over geographic space to explore the supply of nonfarm labour opportunities in rural, small town (centres with a population of less than 10,000 people), and urban areas (centres with more than 10,000 people).

Focusing on rural areas, and taking into account only those individuals who report working on at least one activity (on-farm or off-farm) approximately the same amount of youth work exclusively on own-farm activities (83 per cent) compared to mature rural individuals (85 per cent). The data suggest that there is little demand for nonfarm work in rural Ethiopia, with only 11 per cent of youth and mature individuals having a mixed on-farm and nonfarm work portfolio (Table 5.5). When splitting the youth cohort between young youth (those aged 15–24) and experienced youth (aged 25–34), data suggests that a greater share of the young youth (87 per cent) in rural areas are engaged exclusively in own-farm activities while 77 per cent of experienced youth are exclusively working on their own farm. Almost one-fifth (19 per cent) of experienced youth in rural areas have a mix of on-farm and off-farm employment (Appendix 5.A2).

Table 5.5. Labour type, by location and age cohort, 2013

	Percentage share of youth (age 15–34)			Percentage share of mature (age 35–64)		
	Rural	Small town	Urban	Rural	Small town	Urban
Own farm only	83.0	24.2	6.3	84.7	23.0	5.7
Own farm and off-farm	13.6	16.7	4.0	13.3	25.5	5.8
Own farm & NFE	11.2	12.6	2.6	10.5	15.3	3.6
Own farm & wage	2.2	3.3	1.4	2.4	8.4	1.9
Own farm & NFE & wage	0.3	0.7	0.0	0.4	1.8	0.3
Off-farm[1]	3.4	59.1	89.7	2.0	51.5	88.6
NFE	2.3	37.5	34.7	1.3	36.1	35.6
Wage	1.0	17.8	52.6	0.6	9.9	49.2
NFE & wage	0.1	3.7	2.4	0.2	5.5	3.8
Working population (thousands)	19,791.0	135.1	2,241.1	12,840.4	98.8	1,331.1

Notes: [1] Off-farm work comprises individuals who work in off-farm enterprise and/or wage work.
[2] Students are defined as those who do not report time working in own-farm, wage, or off-farm enterprise activities and report activity as 'student'.
Source: Ethiopia Socioeconomic Survey (2013/14).

Given the limited nonfarm activity reported in rural areas, one would expect that small towns play an important role in providing light manufacturing, trade, and other services. Small towns do provide greater opportunities for nonfarm labour compared to rural Ethiopia. Almost 60 per cent of youth in small towns report working exclusively in off-farm activities, while 52 per cent of mature individuals work in off-farm activities. A greater share of mature individuals in small towns (26 per cent) work in a mix of own- and off-farm work, while 17 per cent of youth work in a mix of own- and off-farm work. Among the youth population, small towns are important hubs for education (approximately 17 per cent of youth in small towns are students). However, it is unclear how potential higher educational attainment is translated into higher paying nonfarm wage employment (Table 5.5). Nonfarm enterprise work is the predominant nonfarm labour opportunity for youth in small towns, encompassing more than double the number of youth engaged exclusively in wage work.

Finally, working individuals living in urban areas (cities of 10,000 people or more) are predominantly engaged in nonfarm work. Wage labour is the primary income earning activity in urban areas, encompassing 53 per cent of youth and 49 per cent of mature individuals' activities. Nonfarm enterprise work remains an important share of nonfarm work in urban areas—35 per cent of youth and mature individuals (Table 5.5).

The youth workforce that focuses solely on own-farm activities reports working for only 21 weeks of the year on average (Table 5.6). Mature workers

Table 5.6. Average time worked per year by type of work, by age cohort, weeks

Working youth (15–34 years)	All workers	Exclusive farmers	Exclusive off-farmers	Mixed farm and off-farm workers
Average time worked per year	27.7	21.6	45.7	45.7
Farming own-farm	18.1	21.6	–	15.3
Off-farm work[1]	9.5	–	45.7	30.4
Wage	3.9	–	25.5	5.9
Nonfarm enterprise[2]	5.6	–	20.2	24.4
Working mature (35–64 years)				
Average time worked per year	32.2	27.2	48.2	49.1
Farming own-farm	23.2	27.2	–	18.2
Off-farm work[1]	8.9	–	48.2	30.9
Wage	3.7	–	26.8	7.4
Nonfarm enterprise[2]	5.2	–	21.4	23.5

Notes: [1] Off-farm work consists of off-farm enterprise and wage work.
[2] Individual time worked in a nonfarm enterprise was not collected, thus we allocate the full amount of time that the nonfarm enterprise was in operation (total weeks) to each person that is reported working in the nonfarm enterprise.

Source: Ethiopia Socioeconomic Survey (2013/14).

engaged exclusively in farming report working for 27 weeks of the year. These data suggest that the majority of the workforce in Ethiopia (68 per cent of rural workers and 58 per cent of the overall workforce) are not economically active for more than half of the year. Individuals who have a mixed portfolio of own-farm and nonfarm labour are engaged in work for more than double the time—46 and 49 weeks for youth and mature workers, respectively—spent at work by those who work exclusively on their own farm (Table 5.6). However, workers who mix farm and nonfarm work make up only about 10 per cent of the total workforce regardless of age. Similarly, youth and older workers exclusively engaged in wage or nonfarm enterprise activities report working for 46 and 48 weeks, respectively, but these also represent a small share of the overall workforce. We find similar results when splitting the youth sample into young youth (15–24) and experienced youth (25–34) (Appendix 5.A3).

5.3 Youth and Agricultural Productivity

The labour trends discussed above suggest that agriculture remains an important livelihood for the majority of rural youth (63 per cent) and the overall population. However, limited nonfarm labour opportunities are constraining a large share of individuals from reaching their full working potential. Those who are solely engaged in own-farm activities, 78 per cent of the overall working population, report being economically active for only about half of the year. Given limited nonfarm labour demand, as well as the large share of rural youth that work exclusively in agriculture, we now assess to what degree youth are leading any agricultural transformation processes in Ethiopia, particularly those that involve specialization in high-value crops or the utilization of modern technologies.

The goal of education policy in Ethiopia has been, in part, to produce educated farmers who would then be able to effectively adopt new agricultural technologies (MOE 2005). These objectives continue to underpin the national education policy. This would suggest that as rural youth create their own, independent households and acquire their own agricultural land, they may seek solutions to increase agricultural productivity and overall welfare via agricultural intensification, diversification, and modernization.

Table 5.7 compares the characteristics of agricultural households located in rural and small towns (less than 10,000 people), disaggregated by the age of the household head.[7] Several differences stand out. First, youth-headed households have access to significantly less agricultural land compared to mature-headed households. Youth-headed households own and operate approximately 0.8 and 1.4 hectares, respectively, compared to mature-headed households that own and operate 1.5 and 1.7 hectares, respectively. Limited data suggest that the young youth-headed households (aged 15–24 years) have greater difficulty accessing land than the experienced youth-headed households (between the ages of 25 and 34 years), however this result should be read with caution given the small sample size of young youth-headed households.

Landlessness is also greater among youth-headed households. For example, 7 per cent of mature-headed households living in rural and small town areas are landless, compared to 14 per cent of youth-headed households. Similarly, the share of landlessness among the youngest households (15–24 years old) reaches 21 per cent, while 13 per cent of experienced youth-headed households are landless (Table 5.7). This follows recent research by Bezu and Holden (2014) who found that youth in the rural south of Ethiopia have limited access to agricultural land due to land scarcity and land market restrictions. Headey, Dereje, and Taffesse (2014) also report declining farm sizes over time, with younger rural households facing larger constraints in obtaining agricultural land.

Finally, youth are not more likely to implement agricultural enhancing technologies (improved seed, cash crop production, and row planting) compared to

[7] Research shows that a variety of factors affect household uptake of agricultural technologies. Extensive literature has analysed specific issues including: physical and human capital endowments (Pender and Fafchamps 2006); access to agricultural extension (Abrar, Morrissey, and Rayner 2004); supply of seeds (Dercon and Hill 2009); heterogeneity of fertilizer success (Suri 2011); risks of negative shocks (Dercon and Christiaensen 2011); and access to credit (Duflo, Kremer, and Robinson 2011).

Table 5.7. Agricultural household-level characteristics in rural and small town areas, by age cohort of household head, means

	Mature-headed HHs (35–64)	Youth-headed HHs (15–34)	Young youth-headed HHs (15–24)	Experienced youth-headed HHs (25–34)
Land characteristics				
Operated area, ha	1.74	1.38 *	0.75 **	1.46
Owned area, ha	1.49	0.82 ***	0.59 *	0.85 ***
Landless, %	7.2	14.0 ***	20.6 ***	13.2 ***
Good agricultural potential, %	26.4	24.1	16.5 **	25.0
Agricultural inputs				
Inorganic fertilizer, %	59.9	57.7	44.5 ***	59.3
Organic fertilizer, %	67.7	59.8 ***	53.0 ***	60.7 ***
Irrigation, %	09.8	10.8	14.5	10.4
Herbicide, %	33.9	39.3 ***	33.9	40.0 ***
Tractor, %	4.2	6.6 ***	08.9 **	06.3 **
Improved seed, %	30.1	29.0	26.5	29.3
Row planting, %	50.0	45.1 ***	51.2	44.4 ***
Grow cash crop, % [a]	82.3	78.3 ***	75.6 **	78.7 **
Receive agricultural credit, %	23.8	20.5 **	08.4 ***	21.9
Receive agricultural extension, %	45.8	40.2 ***	26.2 ***	41.8 **
Household characteristics				
Household size, number	6.18	4.85 ***	3.82 ***	4.97 ***
Number of observations	*2,752*	*1,024*	*135*	*889*

Note: t-tests are relative to mature households; *** p < 0.01, ** p < 0.05, * p < 0.1.

[a] Cash crops include beans, nuts, sesame and other seeds, spices, fruit, vegetables, coffee, chat, cotton, sugar cane, and tobacco.

Source: Ethiopia Socioeconomic Survey (2013/14).

mature-headed households. However, compared to mature households, youth use more technologies that are labour-reducing, such as herbicides and tractors. This is in line with recent work by Bachewe et al. (2015) and Minten et al. (2013) who found that substitution of labour with labour-saving modern inputs, in particular herbicides, is increasing in lieu of time spent on weeding. This may be due to the smaller household size of youth-headed households which creates a labour-constrained environment in which such households will seek technologies to decrease labour demands in agricultural work. Overall, these figures suggest that agriculture may not be the optimal or first choice of employment among youth-headed households, given the current environment.

5.4 Correlates of Youth Engagement in Nonfarm Employment

A rich literature has evaluated the determinants of nonfarm labour engagement including disaggregated analysis of individuals' decisions to seek out skilled versus unskilled nonfarm labour opportunities (Reardon, Berdegue, and Escobar 2001, Winters et al. 2009, Mduma and Wobst 2005, Bezu, Holden, and Barrett 2009); market access and nonfarm participation (Fujita, Krugman, and Venables 1999, Renkow 2006, Henderson, Shalizi, and Venables 2001, Fafchamps and Shilpi 2003, Deichmann, Shilpi, and Vakis 2009); and effects of income or wealth on nonfarm labour choices (Bezu, Barrett, and Holden 2012, de Janvry and Sadoulet 2001, Woldehanna and Oskam 2001, Dercon and Krishnan 1996). However, largely missing from the literature on Ethiopia is an in-depth evaluation of the transition of youth from employment on-farm into the nonfarm sectors. A recent report by the World Bank outlines the opportunities and challenges for youth employment in Africa and provides a comprehensive overview of potential growth sectors, including agriculture. However, the discussion in this overview is limited to country and regional levels (Filmer and Fox 2014). Bezu and Holden (2014) evaluated the determinants of youth aspirations to pursue nonfarm employment in Ethiopia. However, they did not examine the experience of youth that already are in the nonfarm work force. This section addresses some of these knowledge gaps by evaluating the determinants of youth employment in the nonfarm sector.

Appendix 5.A4 provides the average values for key variables used in the empirical analysis. The profiles of rural and small town workers in Ethiopia differ in terms of individual, household, and location characteristics. Youth between the ages of 25 and 34 years are generally more active in the nonfarm sector (wage or nonfarm enterprise), while youth between the ages of 15 and 24 tend to work more on own-farm labour. Those that diversify into wage labour activities have completed more schooling (36 per cent completed primary school). Primary school completion rates of about 10 per cent are approximately the same for individuals that diversify into a nonfarm enterprise activity and those that work solely on own-farm activities, suggesting that nonfarm enterprise activities do not require a significantly different skill set or greater experience level than does own-farm work. Compared to own-farm workers, wage and nonfarm enterprise workers report higher annual expenditure per capita, which may be associated with higher potential profitability of off-farm work.

In this analysis, nonfarm labour activities refer to any labour that is conducted off the own-family farm. We limit our sample to individuals living in rural or small town areas. We are interested in assessing workers that choose to diversify into nonfarm labour activities, meaning wage or nonfarm enterprise activities, in addition to working on their own-family farm in either planting or harvesting.

The sample is split into three categories: individuals who work solely on their own family farm (omitted); individuals who report working in a mix of own-family farm and NFE; and individuals who report working in a mix of own-family farm and wage work.[8] Correlates with diversification are estimated using a multinomial logit model:

$$\log\left(\frac{\pi_{wi}}{\pi_{ni}}\right) = \alpha_{wr} + \beta_w X_i,$$

where π_{wi} is the odds of seeking off-farm work w, π_{ni} is the odds of remaining on the family farm and working solely in agriculture, and parameter α_{wr} is the baseline hazard of work in region r for the specific work type w. β_w is a vector of parameter estimates. X is a vector that denotes the factors that influence labour choice. In order to take into account unobserved variables within districts that affect employment, such as access to infrastructure, information, or agroecological zone, standard errors are clustered at woreda level. Finally, the coefficients in a multinomial logit model are calculated in relation to a base outcome and thus are difficult to interpret directly. However, average marginal effects can be predicted, so we focus the discussion on the reported marginal effects. We set our base outcome as individuals who work exclusively on their own-farm.

We estimate three models to assess correlations between youth and livelihood choice. The first model pools the rural and small town working samples ages 15 to 64 years old to test if youth (aged 15–34) are more likely to enter off-farm labour opportunities compared to mature individuals (aged 35–64). The second model is limited to youth aged 15–24 to evaluate how individual, household and location variables are correlated with nonfarm labour. The third model is limited to youth aged 25–34 and follows the same methodology of the second model to evaluate how more established youth are engaged in the labour market. We split youth categories assuming that young youth and experienced youth differ by the amount of work experience they have attained and the social network they have built, which may affect an individual's ability to secure off-farm work.

5.4.1 Potential Determinants of Engaging in Off-farm Employment in Rural Ethiopia

Diversification into nonfarm employment is shaped by a variety of conditioning factors. Individuals may be *pushed* from agricultural work into nonfarm activities

---

[8] Estimation of the multinomial logit model assumes that probabilities of alternative choices are independent of each other, referred to as the Independence of Irrelevant Alternatives (IIA). In order to test for this independence, we use the Small-Hsiao test, and find we are unable to reject the IIA assumption for the multinomial logit model presented in this analysis (Small and Hsiao 1985).

in order to seek out sufficient sources of income, alternatively individuals may be *pulled* into nonfarm activities given higher returns to labour and capital compared to agriculture. [9] Lucas (2015) focuses on rural–urban migration issues and argues that these decisions are driven by differentials in opportunities across locations. Focusing specifically on the choice of diversifying labour portfolios, individuals differ in their ability to take advantage of nonfarm opportunities based on their human, physical, and financial capital. For example, some individuals are more educated, with better access to savings for start-up capital and greater options for nonfarm work due to proximity to a market or transportation network.

We include a variety of explanatory variables in our multinomial logit analysis in order to account for differences across individuals and households. At the individual level, we include a variable that disaggregates odds of employment by age in the regression that pools all age groups: youth aged 15–24, youth aged 25–34, and mature aged 35–64 (omitted category). Including these variables in a multi-variation regression allows us to adjust for inherent differences across age groups which may mask the interpretation of the descriptive statistics discussed above. These age variables attempt to capture experience level and potential life-cycle effects, as well as to explicitly evaluate youth participation in nonfarm activities. We also include whether or not the individual is a household head, female, or married. If an individual is the household head, she or he may be more inclined to stay working on the farm in order to insure sufficient agricultural output. In addition, Ethiopia's land tenure system requires residency on the farm to maintain usufruct rights to farmland which may create greater disincentives for household heads to seek alternative employment. Education—measured by whether an individual completed primary school—is also an important factor, given that it improves the value of labour, raises the opportunity costs for an educated individual to stay at home and engage in lower paying agricultural work, and potentially enhances the individual's social network to facilitate access to nonfarm jobs.

At the household level, we include a variety of variables that take into account household assets. For example, owning a relatively large agricultural land area may indicate better farming potential and food self-sufficiency, which may incentivize individuals to remain in agriculture. Alternatively, larger land holdings may be associated with higher crop incomes, which could provide start-up capital for work in the nonfarm sector.[10] Due to restrictions on land ownership in Ethiopia, land rental markets are very active, thus we include both *total agricultural land owned* and *total agricultural land operated* to account for these factors. Given that

---

[9] Moretti (2004) and Ciccone and Peri (2006) examine pull factors of migration and their links to agglomeration economies.

[10] See Reardon et al. (2007) and Bezu and Barrett (2012) for a greater discussion on land holdings and nonfarm labour diversification.

we are limited to cross-sectional data, it is possible that we introduce simultaneity bias in our regression framework by including household assets. For example, not only does land holding size potentially affect diversification but diversification could affect land holding size. This is particularly accute when using contemporraneous explanatory variables. Thus, we discuss the results in terms of correlates of diversification rather than addressing causation.

We also include livestock ownership in the form of Tropical Livestock Units owned by the household, per capita expenditure of the household, and whether a household is located in an area with good agricultural potential. We hypothesize that youth who have access to land with good agricultural potential are less likely to seek nonfarm employment. In addition, we include whether a household has experienced a flood or drought during the last year in order to take into account potential fluctuations in agricultural productivity. Such fluctuations may incentivize individuals to seek other forms of employment as a means of insurance against agricultural uncertainty.

In addition to physical endowments at the household level, individuals coming from larger households with greater potential labour resources may exhibit a greater probability of working in the nonfarm sector because their labour would not be as critical for agricultural production within such households. In order to account for differences in female and male labour roles in rural Ethiopia (for example, it is rare for females to cultivate land in Ethiopia—see Deininger, Ali, and Tekie 2008), we include the number of working age (ages 15–64) females and the number working age males within the household, as well as total household size.

Household variables are included to differentiate between households that have received agricultural credit or agricultural extension. These variables represent incentive factors to stay working on-farm because they are targeted to augment agricultural productivity.[11] Finally, distance to a market or trafficked road captures a household's locational potential for nonfarm labour opportunities, as well as assessing the effect on transaction costs, and thus, an individual's willingness to seek nonfarm labour. Job search costs would be lower for those that live closer to markets or key transportation corridors, while at the same time they may be better informed of potential job opportunities.

---

[11] Recent work evaluated credit via microfinance programmes aimed at nonfarm activities and found mixed results with regards to such credit inducing greater engagement in non-agricultural income earning opportunities. Hagos (2003) found a positive effect of microfinance credit programmes on income level changes derived from self-employment. However, no effect was found on participation in wage employment. Bezu and Holden (2014) reported that access to savings and credit are significant factors for transitioning into high-return rural nonfarm activities. Tarozzi, Desai, and Johnson (2015) evaluated access to microfinance credit in Amhara and Oromiya on a variety of outcomes and found no significant effects on nonfarm enterprise creation.

5.4.2 Results and Discussion

The coefficients in a multinomial logit model are calculated in relation to a base outcome and are difficult to interpret directly. However, average marginal effects can be predicted, so we focus the discussion on the reported marginal effects. Model 1 evaluates whether youth are more likely to diversify into wage or non-farm enterprise opportunities in addition to working on own-family farm, by testing whether the coefficients on the age indicators are statistically different than zero. Analysis suggests that older youth (age 25–34) have a greater probability of diversifying into nonfarm enterprise activities compared to mature individuals, however this does not hold true for youth ages 15–24 (Table 5.8). It may be that the younger cohort of youth have not built up sufficient work experience or developed an appropriate social network to successfully engage in a nonfarm enterprise. Although older youth are more engaged in nonfarm enterprise labour, wage labour is less accessible to Ethiopia's youth. According to Model 1, youth (regardless of their age) are no more active in the wage labour market than are mature individuals (aged 35–64).

Focusing specifically on youth (Models 2 and 3), those who are located in areas with good agricultural potential have a greater probability of diversifying into nonfarm enterprises, especially older youth aged 25–34 years old (Table 5.8, Model 3). This supports the findings of previous research that contended that local nonfarm income is greater in better agroclimatic areas, whereas migration is a more common strategy in unfavourable climatic areas (Reardon 1997, Reardon et al. 2007). Woldehanna and Oskam (2001) reported that households in Tigray during good production seasons prefer nonfarm enterprise work over wage employment, suggesting that a good production season gives farmers the financial capacity to start a nonfarm enterprise. Youth aged 15–24 that are located in good agricultural productivity areas are also more likely to mix farm and non-farm enterprise work (Table 5.8, Model 2). Research conducted by Bezu and Holden (2014) found that a lack of access to land was driving youth migration from agriculture. Our analysis suggests that youth (age 25–34) with greater land ownership have a 3 per cent lower probability of diversifying into wage labour compared to working exclusively on their own family farm. Overall, assets and capital are associated with mature youth employment decisions. Greater ownership of land, livestock, and access to agricultural credit decrease the probability that mature youth diversify out of farming into wage labour activities (Table 5.8, Model 3). We do not witness the effects of asset ownership in the young youth sample due to lack of variation among variables; young youth have less asset accumulation across all categories.

Similar to agricultural endowments, agricultural shocks can have an effect on an individual's choice to seek alternative income sources outside of agriculture.

Table 5.8. Multinomial models of determinants of type of labour engagement for rural workers in Ethiopia, by age cohort

Explanatory variables	Model 1		Model 2		Model 3	
	Working population: age 15–64		Young youth working population: age 15–24		Experienced youth working population: age 25–34	
	Mix of own-farm and wage work	Mix of own-farm and nonfarm enterprise	Mix of own-farm and wage work	Mix of own-farm and nonfarm enterprise	Mix of own-farm and wage work	Mix of own-farm and nonfarm enterprise
Age 15–24, 0/1	−0.016 (0.010)	0.013 (0.019)	–	–	–	–
Age 25–34, 0/1	0.000 (0.006)	0.049 *** (0.015)	–	–	–	–
Household head, 0/1	0.002 (0.009)	0.037 ** (0.017)	0.019 ** (0.009)	0.030 (0.035)	−0.014 (0.016)	0.049 (0.033)
Female, 0/1	−0.036 *** (0.011)	0.037 ** (0.016)	−0.004 (0.009)	0.034 (0.021)	−0.061 ** (0.025)	0.079 *** (0.028)
Married, 0/1	0.005 (0.007)	0.011 (0.016)	−0.001 (0.010)	0.039 (0.024)	−0.006 (0.012)	0.016 (0.034)
Completed primary school, 0/1	0.045 *** (0.008)	0.001 (0.018)	0.030 *** (0.010)	0.018 (0.020)	0.055 *** (0.011)	−0.032 (0.035)
Adult (age 15 to 64) males in household, number	−0.006 ** (0.003)	−0.022 *** (0.007)	0.000 (0.004)	−0.009 (0.010)	−0.015 (0.008)	−0.003 (0.021)
Adult (age 15 to 64) females in household, number	0.004 (0.003)	0.002 (0.008)	0.002 (0.004)	0.001 (0.011)	0.008 (0.005)	0.018 (0.019)
Expenditure, '000 birr/capita/year	0.005 *** (0.001)	0.025 *** (0.005)	0.003 *** (0.001)	0.016 *** (0.006)	0.006 *** (0.002)	0.031 *** (0.011)
Agricultural area owned, ha	−0.002 (0.002)	−0.006 (0.006)	0.007 (0.011)	−0.003 (0.009)	−0.026 ** (0.011)	0.001 (0.022)
Agricultural area operated, ha	0.002 (0.002)	0.004 (0.007)	−0.017 (0.014)	0.006 (0.009)	0.004 (0.002)	−0.010 (0.014)
Receive agricultural extension, 0/1	−0.016 ** (0.006)	−0.003 (0.017)	−0.007 (0.010)	−0.012 (0.025)	−0.018 (0.011)	0.013 (0.030)
Receive agricultural credit, 0/1	−0.006 (0.009)	−0.021 (0.019)	0.001 (0.009)	−0.004 (0.024)	−0.068 ** (0.027)	−0.051 (0.033)

Continued

Table 5.8. Continued

Explanatory variables	Model 1		Model 2		Model 3	
	Working population: age 15–64		Young youth working population: age 15–24		Experienced youth working population: age 25–34	
	Mix of own-farm and wage work	Mix of own-farm and nonfarm enterprise	Mix of own-farm and wage work	Mix of own-farm and nonfarm enterprise	Mix of own-farm and wage work	Mix of own-farm and nonfarm enterprise
Livestock ownership, Tropical Livestock Units	−0.002 * (0.001)	−0.004 (0.003)	0.000 (0.000)	−0.005 (0.003)	−0.006 * (0.003)	0.000 (0.006)
Experienced drought, 0/1	0.005 ** (0.007)	−0.079 ** (0.036)	0.005 (0.009)	−0.054 * (0.050)	0.013 (0.017)	−0.095 (0.070)
Experienced flood, 0/1	−0.031 (0.020)	−0.005 (0.050)	−0.007 (0.012)	0.028 (0.044)	−0.366 *** (0.069)	−0.028 (0.102)
Good agricultural potential land, 0/1	−0.010 (0.009)	0.052 * (0.020)	−0.020 * (0.011)	0.042 * (0.025)	−0.011 (0.017)	0.086 *** (0.031)
Distance to nearest market, km	−0.001 (0.001)	0.001 (0.002)	−0.001 (0.001)	−0.001 (0.003)	−0.003 (0.002)	0.002 (0.003)
Distance to nearest major road, km	0.001 (0.003)	0.002 (0.006)	−0.004 (0.005)	0.005 (0.007)	0.004 (0.003)	0.000 (0.010)
Observations	*7,567*		*2,526*		*1,754*	

Note: The base outcome for all three models are individuals that work exclusively on their own-farm. Standard errors in parentheses; *** $p < 0.01$, ** $p < 0.05$, * $p < 0.1$.

Source: Ethiopia Socioeconomic Survey (2013/14).

We find this particularly true for youth aged 25–34 years. In this case, those who experienced a flood during the last year had a 37 per cent less probability of expanding into a wage labour job, however this effect may be temporary and reflect a post-shock necessity of rehabilitating own agricultural land rather than an overall trend of off-farm labour activity. Alternatively, this analysis does not capture wage or nonfarm employment at alternative locations, thus a reduction in wage labour may coincide with an increase in wage labour outside of the sample woreda. Research on the impact of shocks on labour diversification suggests a greater propensity to diversify. Bezu and Barrett (2012) assessed employment transitions out of agriculture between 2004 and 2009 and found that shocks that reduced agricultural income motivated individuals to seek out high-return rural nonfarm employment. Similar results of agricultural shocks increasing longer term non-agricultural earnings were reported by Porter (2012) using data from 1994–2004.

While good agricultural potential and greater access to capital and assets (agricultural credit and livestock) decrease the likelihood of diversifying into nonfarm labour, distance to a market or road does not affect the probability of youth finding nonfarm employment. This may be due to several reasons. First, a large share of the rural population in this sample live relatively far from a market (on average about 55 km). Second, thin labour markets in small towns and rural areas may limit youth's ability to take advantage of off-farm wage opportunities simply because there is not enough off-farm labour demand. These relationships suggest that in Ethiopia the rural and small town nonfarm sector is influenced primarily by push factors (lack of land, agricultural services, and assets) rather than driven by urban or small town labour demand.

When comparing youth labour decisions to diversify into nonfarm employment, it becomes apparent that experienced youth (ages 25–34) have a greater likelihood of engaging in nonfarm work (in addition to own-family farm labour) compared to mature individuals (age 35–64). Although difficult to determine from cross-sectional data, the analysis presented in this chapter suggests that youth—in particular, experienced youth—may be driving the small share of labour diversification in rural and small towns. Moving forward, understanding if labour diversification occurs step-wise—meaning, individuals move from working exclusively on their own-farm activities to diversifying into nonfarm in addition to own-farm activities, and then finally transitioning fully into nonfarm labour activities—will provide greater insight into Ethiopia's likely economic trajectory over the next few decades. If this is the mode of labour transition within Ethiopia, we may be witnessing the initial transition of an economy moving towards greater structural transformation.

5.5 Conclusion

Over the last several decades, Ethiopia has focused its public investments in economic growth according to its ADLI strategy. This led to large increases in agricultural output. Simultaneously, the country has experienced impressive economic growth at approximately 11 per cent per year during the last decade. Although these trends point to structural transformation as a major driver of economic growth, labour force survey data suggest that Ethiopia remains at a very early stage in its structural transformation. Whereas one would expect to see a transition out of agriculture into higher value nonfarm employment, we find that the share of economically active people working in agriculture only decreased by approximately 3.6 percentage points (from 80.2 to 76.6 per cent) between 2005 and 2013.

Focusing on youth employment, the data suggest that few rural and small town youth (13 per cent) engage in nonfarm economic activities. However, individuals who are exclusively engaged in own-farm activities are underemployed, working approximately for half of the year given the seasonality inherent to crop agriculture in Ethiopia. Given the large share of rural youth that have remained working exclusively in agriculture, we assess if youth are taking a lead role in agricultural transformation processes in Ethiopia. Comparing youth- versus mature-headed households, we find that on average youth-headed households have less agricultural land, less access to services (credit and extension) and are less likely to implement agricultural enhancing technologies (inorganic fertilizer, improved seeds, row planting, and so on) compared to mature-headed households. Although, compared to more established households headed by older adults, youth-headed households face greater constraints in the agricultural sector, the analyses do not show that youth are leading the adoption of agricultural enhancing technologies, such as improved seed, cash crop production, or row planting. However, we do see a greater share of youth using technologies that are labour-reducing, such as herbicides and tractors.

Given the constraints faced by Ethiopian youth to access land and agricultural services, we evaluate whether youth are turning towards nonfarm employment as an alternative livelihood strategy. The econometric results suggest that youth aged 25–34 have a higher probability of engaging in nonfarm enterprise activities. However, neither youth age cohort is more likely to work in wage labour compared to exclusively working on own-farm activities. The analysis suggests that wage labour opportunities are few, and those who obtain wage employment tend to be male, with a higher education, and have fewer agricultural resources than those who do not engage in wage labour. This last factor suggests that push factors have a large influence on youth nonfarm employment decisions.

Although diversification out of agriculture reaps potentially higher wage opportunities in the nonfarm sector, our analysis suggests that employment opportunities outside of agriculture are limited in rural Ethiopia. This finding parallels that of recent research by Diao and McMillan (2015) in which they suggest from their results that proactive policies or foreign investment may be needed to spark structural transformation. Given that the majority of Ethiopia's population lives in rural areas and works in agriculture, investments in agriculture-enhancing technology and services remains important to increase productivity, and ultimately to spark greater nonfarm demand for goods and services. Continuing to evaluate constraints and ameliorate conditions for youth to be productively employed in agriculture and in the nonfarm sector as the economy continues to grow is crucial to ensuring healthy, sustainable economic growth moving forward.

Appendix

Table 5.A1. Water and wood collectors, numbers (in thousands) and percentage of the economically active population, by age cohort, sex, and rural/urban, 2013

Age category	Male	Female	Urban	Rural
10 to 14 years	311.7	1,072.7	89.1	1,295.3
	(22.5)	(77.5)	(6.4)	(93.6)
15 to 24	178.6	1,254.6	88.9	1,344.3
	(12.5)	(87.5)	(6.2)	(93.8)
25 to 35	30.3	933.3	42.2	921.3
	(3.1)	(96.9)	(4.4)	(95.6)
36 to 55	22.8	842.8	38.2	827.4
	(2.6)	(97.4)	(4.4)	(95.6)
Over 55	12.3	208.1	12.1	208.3
	(5.6)	(94.4)	(5.5)	(94.5)
Total	555.7	4,311.5	270.5	4,596.7
	(11.4)	(88.6)	(5.6)	(94.4)

Note: Percentage shares are reported in parentheses.

Source: National Labour Force Survey (2013).

Table 5.A2. Youth labour type, by location and age cohort, 2013, present

	Percentage share of young youth (age 15–24)			Percentage share experienced youth (age 25–34)		
	Rural	Small town	Urban	Rural	Small town	Urban
Own-farm only	87.1	32.9	10.3	77.4	15.6	3.3
Own-farm and off-farm	9.9	12.2	3.3	18.7	21.2	4.5
Own-farm & nonfarm enterprise	8.2	9.4	2.3	15.3	15.8	2.8
Own-farm & wage	1.5	2.8	1.0	3.1	3.8	1.7
Own-farm & nonfarm enterprise & wage	0.2	0.0	0.0	0.4	1.5	0.0
Off-farm[1]	3.0	54.8	86.3	3.9	63.3	92.2
Nonfarm enterprise	2.3	42.3	36.5	2.3	32.7	33.3
Wage	0.6	10.2	47.7	1.5	25.5	56.2
Nonfarm enterprise & wage	0.1	2.4	2.1	0.1	5.1	2.7
Working population (thousands)	11,367.6	67.4	959.4	8,423.4	67.6	1,281.7

Notes: [1] Off-farm work comprises individuals who work in off-farm enterprise and/or wage work.
[2] Students are defined as those who do not report time working in own-farm, wage, or off-farm enterprise activities and report activity as 'student'.

Source: Ethiopia Socioeconomic Survey (2013/14).

Table 5.A3. Average time worked per year by type of work, by youth age cohort, weeks

Working young youth (age 15–24)	All workers	Exclusive farmers	Exclusive off-farmers	Mixed farm and off-farm workers
Average time worked per year	24.7	20.2	43.5	44.2
Farming own farm	17.6	20.2	0	13.9
Off-farm work[1]	7.1	0	43.5	30.3
Wage	*2.7*	*0*	*21.9*	*5.8*
Off-farm enterprise[2]	*4.4*	*0*	*21.7*	*24.6*
Working experienced youth (age 25–34)				
Average time worked per year	31.4	23.8	47.4	46.7
Farming own farm	18.8	23.8	0	16.3
Off-farm work[1]	12.6	0	47.4	30.4
Wage	*5.5*	*0*	*28.3*	*6.1*
Off-farm enterprise[2]	*7.1*	*0*	*19.1*	*24.4*

Notes: [1] Off-farm work consists of off-farm enterprise and wage work.
[2] Individual time worked in a nonfarm enterprise was not collected, thus we allocate the full amount of time that the nonfarm enterprise was in operation (total weeks) to each person that is reported working in the nonfarm enterprise.

Source: Ethiopia Socioeconomic Survey (2013/14).

Table 5.A4. Profile of rural and small town workers (ages 15–64) by employment type, mean characteristics

	Own-farm	Wage	Nonfarm enterprise
Age 15–24, proportion	0.36	0.24 ***	0.29 ***
Age 25–34, proportion	0.24	0.35 ***	0.35 ***
Age 35–64, proportion	0.40	0.41	0.37
Household head, proportion	0.33	0.60 ***	0.39 ***
Female, proportion	0.49	0.20 ***	0.54 **
Married, proportion	0.59	0.69 **	0.67 ***
Completed primary school, proportion	0.10	0.36 ***	0.10
Student, proportion	0.13	0.05 ***	0.09 ***
Household size, number	6.64	5.89 ***	6.50
Adult males (age 15 to 64 years), number in household	1.82	1.52 ***	1.55 ***
Adult females (age 15 to 64 years), number in household	1.71	1.56 *	1.69
Expenditure, '000 birr/capita/year	1.38	2.95 ***	2.25 ***
Agricultural area owned, ha	1.62	1.24	1.22 *
Agricultural area operated, ha	1.94	2.23	1.60
Receive agricultural extension, proportion	0.52	0.34 ***	0.48
Receive agricultural credit, proportion	0.27	0.18 ***	0.22 ***
Livestock ownership, Tropical Livestock Units	4.24	2.87 ***	3.64 ***

Experienced drought, proportion	0.08	0.09	0.04 ***
Experienced flood, proportion	0.03	0.01 ***	0.03
Land with good agricultural potential, proportion	0.26	0.19 *	0.35 ***
Distance to nearest major market centre, km *	62.2	55.9 *	64.3
Distance to nearest major road, km	13.8	15.2	14.4
Observations	*5,737*	*337*	*1,493*

Note: t-tests are relative to own-farm workers; *** p < 0.01, ** p < 0.05, * p < 0.1. * Major market centres
are defined by FEWSNET and do not include weekly markets

Source: Ethiopia Socioeconomic Survey (2013/14).

References

Abrar, S., O. Morrissey, and T. Rayner. 2004. Crop-level supply response by agro-climatic region in Ethiopia. *Journal of Agricultural Economics* 55: 289–311.

Bachewe, F., G. Berhane, B. Minten, and A. S. Taffesse. 2015. *Agricultural growth in Ethiopia (2004–2014): Evidence and drivers.* ESSP Working Paper 81. Addis Ababa: IFPRI-Ethiopia Strategy Support Program.

Bachewe, F., G. Berhane, B. Minten, and A. S. Taffesse. 2016. *Nonfarm income and labor markets in rural Ethiopia.* ESSP Working Paper 90. Addis Ababa: IFPRI-Ethiopia Strategy Support Program.

Bezu, S., and C. B. Barrett. 2012. Employment dynamics in the rural nonfarm sector in Ethiopia: Do the poor have time on their side?. *Journal of Development Studies* 48 (9): 1223–40.

Bezu, S., S. Holden, and C. B. Barrett. 2009. *Activity choice in rural nonfarm employment: Survival versus accumulation strategy.* Centre for Land Tenure Studies Working Paper 11/14. Ås, Norway: Centre for Land Tenure Studies, Norwegian University of Life Sciences.

Bezu, S., C. B. Barrett, and S. Holden. 2012. Does the nonfarm economy offer pathways for upward mobility? Evidence from a panel data study in Ethiopia. *World Development* 40 (8): 1634–46.

Bezu, S., and S. Holden. 2014. Are rural youth in Ethiopia abandoning agriculture? *World Development* 64: 259–72.

Central Statistical Agency of Ethiopia (CSA). 2013. Ethiopia National Labour Force Survey 2013 (2005 E.C.). Addis Ababa, Ethiopia: Federal Democratic Republic of Ethiopia.

Ciccone, A., and G. Peri. 2006. Identifying human capital externalities: Theory with applications. *Review of Economic Studies* 73 (2): 381–412.

de Janvry, A., and E. Sadoulet. 2001. Income strategies among rural households in Mexico: The role of off-farm activities. *World Development* 29 (3): 467–80.

Deichmann, U., F. Shilpi, and R. Vakis. 2009. Urban proximity, agricultural potential and rural nonfarm employment: Evidence from Bangladesh. *World Development* 37 (3): 645–60.

Deininger, K., D. A. Ali, and A. Tekie. 2008. *Impacts of land certification on tenure security, investment, and land markets: Evidence from Ethiopia.* World Bank Policy Research Working Paper 4764. Washington, DC, U.S.A.: World Bank.

Dercon, S., and L. Christiaensen. 2011. Consumption risk, technology adoption and poverty traps: Evidence from Ethiopia. *Journal of Development Economics* 96: 159–73.

Dercon, S., and R. Hill. 2009. *Growth from agriculture in Ethiopia: Identifying key constraints.* Working Paper prepared for a Study on Agriculture and Growth in Ethiopia, Department for International Development. Oxford, U.K.: Centre for the Study of African Economies, University of Oxford.

Dercon, S., and P. Krishnan. 1996. Income portfolios in rural Ethiopia and Tanzania: Choices and constraints. *Journal of Development Studies* 32 (6): 850–75.

Diao, X., and M. McMillan. 2015. *Toward an understanding of economic growth in Africa: A re-interpretation of the Lewis model.* NBER Working Paper No. 21018. Cambridge, MA, U.S.A.: National Bureau of Economic Research.

Duflo, E., M. Kremer, and J. Robinson. 2011. Nudging farmers to use fertilizer: Theory and experimental evidence from Kenya. *American Economic Review* 101: 2350–90.

Fafchamps, M., and F. Shilpi. 2003. Spatial division of labor in Nepal. *Journal of Development Studies* 39 (3): 23–66.

Federal Democratic Republic of Ethiopia (FDRE) Population Census Commission. 2008. *Summary and statistical report of the 2007 population and housing census: Population size by age and sex.* Addis Ababa, Ethiopia: Central Statistical Agency, Federal Democratic Republic of Ethiopia.

Filmer, D., and L. Fox. 2014. *Youth employment in Sub-Saharan Africa.* Africa Development Series. Washington, DC, U.S.A.: World Bank.

Fujita, M., P. Krugman, and A. J. Venables. 1999. *The spatial economy: Cities, regions and international trade.* Cambridge, MA, U.S.A.: MIT Press.

Haggblade, S., P. Hazell, and T. Reardon. 2002. *Strategies for stimulating poverty-alleviating growth in the rural nonfarm economy in developing countries.* EPTD Discussion Paper 92. Washington, DC, U.S.A.: International Food Policy Institute.

Haggblade, S., P. Hazell, and P. Dorosh. 2006. Sectoral growth linkages between agriculture and the rural nonfarm economy. In *Transforming the rural nonfarm economy: Opportunities and threats in the developing world,* ed. S. Haggblade, P. B. R. Hazell, and T. Reardon. Baltimore, MD, U.S.A.: Johns Hopkins University Press.

Hagos, F. 2003. *Poverty, institutions, peasant behavior, and conservation investments in northern Ethiopia.* PhD diss., Department of Economics and Social Sciences, Agricultural University of Norway.

Headey, D., M. Dereje, and A. S. Taffesse. 2014. Land constraints and agricultural intensification in Ethiopia: A village-level analysis of high-potential areas. *Food Policy* 48: 129–41.

Henderson, J. V., Z. Shalizi, and A. J. Venables. 2001. Geography and development. *Journal of Economic Geography* 1 (1): 81–105.

Krishnan, P., and E. Sciubba. 2009. Links and architecture in village networks. *The Economic Journal* 119: 917–49.

Lucas, R. E. B. 2015. Internal migration in developing economies: An overview of recent working evidence. Geopolitics, History, and International Relations, 8 (2), 159–91.

Mduma, J., and P. Wobst. 2005. Determinants of rural labour market participation in Tanzania. *African Studies Quarterly* 8 (2): 32–47.

Mellor, J. 1976. *The new economics of growth: A strategy for india and the developing world.* Ithaca, NY, U.S.A.: Cornell University Press.

Ministry of Education (MOE). 2005. *Education sector development Program III* (ESDP-III) 2005/2006–2010/2011. Addis Ababa, Ethiopia: Government of Ethiopia.

Minten, B., S. Tamru, E. Engida, and T. Kuma 2013. *Ethiopia's value chains on the move: The case of Teff.* ESSP Working Paper 52. Addis Ababa, Ethiopia: IFPRI-Ethiopia Strategy Support Program.

Moretti, E. 2004. Estimating the social return to higher education: Evidence from longitudinal and repeated cross-sectional data. *Journal of Econometrics* 121 (1): 175–212.

Pender, J., and M. Fafchamps. 2006. Land lease markets and agricultural efficiency in Ethiopia. *Journal of African Economies* 15 (2): 251–84.

Porter, C. 2012. Shocks, consumption and income diversification in rural Ethiopia. *Journal of Development Studies* 48 (9): 1209–22.

Reardon, T., J. Berdegue, and G. Escobar. 2001. Rural nonfarm employment and incomes in Latin America: Overview and policy implications. *World Development* 29 (3): 395–409.

Reardon, T. 1997. Using evidence of household income diversification to inform study of the rural nonfarm labour market in Africa. *World Development* 25: 735–47.

Reardon, T., J. Berdegue, C. Barrett, and K. Stamoulis. 2007. Household income diversification into rural nonfarm activities. In *Transforming the rural nonfarm economy: Opportunities and threats in the developing world,* ed. S. Haggblade, P. B. R. Hazell, and T. Reardon. Baltimore, MD, U.S.A.: Johns Hopkins University Press.

Renkow, M. 2006. Cities, towns and the rural nonfarm economy. In *Transforming the rural nonfarm economy: Opportunities and threats in the developing world,* ed. S. Haggblade, P. B. R. Hazell, and T. Reardon. Baltimore, MD, U.S.A.: Johns Hopkins University Press.

Small, K. A., and C. Hsiao. 1985. Multinomial logit specification tests. *International Economic Review* 26 (3): 619–27.

Suri, T. 2011. Selection and comparative advantage in technology adoption. *Econometrica* 79: 159–209.

Tarozzi, A., J. Desai, and K. Johnson. 2015. The impacts of microcredit: Evidence from Ethiopia. *American Economic Journal: Applied Economics* 7 (1): 54–89.

Winters, P., B. Davis, G. Carletto, K. Covarrubias, E. J. Quiñones, A. Zezza, C. Azzarri, and K. Stamoulis. 2009. Assets, activities and rural income generation: Evidence from a multicountry analysis. *World Development* 37 (9): 1435–52.

Woldehanna, T., and A. Oskam. 2001. Income diversification and entry barriers: Evidence from the Tigray region of northern Ethiopia. *Food Policy* 26 (4): 351–65.

6

Change and Rigidity in Youth Employment Patterns in Malawi

Todd Benson, Alvina Erman, and Bob Baulch

6.1 Introduction

In the over fifty years since attaining independence, Malawi's population has continued to grow strongly, increasing from just over 4 million in 1966 to 17.6 million in 2018. Yet, most of the population continues to reside in rural areas pursuing agricultural livelihoods—at the last census in 2018, only 16 per cent of the population lived in cities or towns. Due to high fertility rates, Malawi has one of the youngest age structures in the world with 43.9 per cent of its population being under the age of 15, and 34.3 per cent being between 15 and 34 years of age (NSO 2018). In 2017, the agriculture sector contributed 26 per cent of the total Gross Domestic Product (GDP) of Malawi's economy (World Bank 2019). While the significance of agriculture has dropped from 50 years ago when the sector provided one-half of total economic output, Malawi's economy remains among the 15 national economies globally that are most dependent upon agriculture. Although the service sector has grown significantly over the past 20 years, with a small manufacturing sector and limited non-agricultural natural resources to exploit economically, agricultural production remains at the centre of most economic production and household livelihoods. This is most evident in how the workforce of the country is allocated across sectors. Estimates from the 2013 Malawi Integrated Household Panel Survey (IHPS) are that 87.0 per cent of those of working age (15 to 64 years) are employed in agriculture.[1]

The factors that might push Malawians out of agriculture and into employment in other sectors have only intensified with time. Although dropping fertility rates may result in the population growth rate starting to decline soon, the annual population growth rate has been above 2.8 per cent for the last two decades. The 2008 to 2018 intercensal annual growth rate was 2.9 per cent (NSO 2018). With

---

[1] Estimate based on author analysis of 2013 IHPS. Using a stricter definition of employment—those engaged exclusively in subsistence agricultural production for less than 48 hours a week were not considered employed, an employed individual could work only in a single sector, and a strict one week recall period was used—estimates from the 2013 Malawi Labour Force Survey are that 64.1 per cent of those who are of working age and are employed worked in agriculture (NSO 2014).

Todd Benson, Alvina Erman, and Bob Baulch, *Change and Rigidity in Youth Employment Patterns in Malawi* In: *Youth and Jobs in Rural Africa: Beyond Stylized Facts*. Edited by: Valerie Mueller and James Thurlow, Oxford University Press (2019). © International Food Policy Research Institute. DOI: 10.1093/oso/9780198848059.003.0006

this continued significant growth in the population and a large share of the population remaining in agriculture, there is increasing land pressure: the average farm size in Malawi now is around 1.0 ha per household, with a median value close to 0.8 ha (Ricker-Gilbert, Jumbe, and Chamberlin 2014, NSO 2010). The low-input, low-output smallholder farming systems that dominate agriculture in Malawi result in many observers today echoing concerns expressed by observers since the colonial period as to whether most Malawians will be able to obtain sustainable livelihoods primarily from agriculture for much longer.

In parallel, some factors that might attract Malawians in the labour force to seek employment outside of agriculture have also intensified. Growth in the economy of Malawi since 2000 has been slowly positive overall, if erratic from year to year. Average annual growth in GDP between 2000 and 2017 was 4.3 per cent. The services sector has expanded significantly over this period rising from a 43 per cent share of the economy in 2000 to 52 per cent in 2017, while the industrial sector has remained relatively stable to declining slightly, contributing 14 per cent of Malawi's economic output in 2017 (World Bank 2019). At the same time, stocks of human capital have improved since the introduction of free primary education in 1994. While problems related to the quality of instruction and of available facilities continue to plague education in Malawi, the improved access to schooling since has resulted in sharp increases in educational attainment among younger youth (ages 15 to 24 years), particularly for females (World Bank 2010).

The government of Malawi has also invested significant resources to enhance agricultural productivity over the past 10 years, particularly through the Farm Input Subsidy Programme (FISP). The increased maize production resulting from FISP has contributed to agricultural sector growth. There is also evidence that reasonably significant second-round benefits have been achieved through FISP that are linked to the increased economic activity, lower food prices, and increased demand for labour the programme fostered (Arndt, Pauw, and Thurlow 2016). Although all independent assessments conclude that the programme could be implemented more efficiently and achieve significantly broader impact, particularly at farm level (Lunduka, Ricker-Gilbert, and Fisher 2013), FISP has the potential to propel the sector towards sustained improvements in agricultural productivity. This in turn should allow for increased investment in other areas of the economy and release considerable labour, including that of youth, from farming households to work elsewhere other than in agriculture.

In this chapter, we seek to better understand how the changes in and interplay of these factors affect the employment choices of Malawians in the workforce. Might we now see some movement of labour out of agriculture into other sectors, particularly services, even if slight and in its earliest stages? We also seek to determine whether the youth of Malawi are central to any changes occurring in employment patterns in the country, possibly drawing upon their increased levels of training, benefitting from higher agricultural production levels overall linked to FISP, and responding to increased pressures to obtain a livelihood elsewhere than on increasingly small agriculture landholdings. Are Malawi's youth entering the workforce in a different manner than previous generations?

Through analysis primarily of data from the Malawi Integrated Household Survey (IHS) series, in this chapter we examine changes in employment among those of working age in Malawi. First, using data from three IHS surveys—2004, 2010, and 2013—we examine how strong are movements of labour, if any, out of agriculture and into industry and services. In making this assessment, we disaggregate our analysis by whether the workers are younger youth (ages 15 to 24 years), older youth (25 to 34 years), or non-youth (35 to 64 years); resident in rural or urban areas; and female or male. This first analysis is based on categorizing each working age individual in our analytical data sets into a single employment category in the manner that the National Statistical Office of Malawi uses to analyse the data it collects on labour force participation.

We then extend this analysis to investigate the factors associated with the type of employment an individual has using the 2010 IHS-3 survey data. The analysis, based on an econometric multinomial logit model, permits a multivariate assessment of the factors associated with an individual choosing a particular pattern of employment, including working in several sectors simultaneously, for example, working in both farming and petty trading (services). Here too, the analysis considers the age of the individual to determine whether the correlates of youth engagement in the workforce are comparable to those of their elders.

To summarize the results of our analysis, we find little evidence of any significant processes of transformation in the structure of Malawi's economy or of youth being in the vanguard of any changes in cross-sectoral patterns of employment. While there has been some increase in employment in the services sector between 2004 and 2013, it is older youth and non-youth, particularly males, who are engaging in such work. In contrast, younger youth are extending the length of their schooling. Although we find that higher educational attainment is strongly associated with nonfarm employment, agriculture remains the sector into which most youth first obtain employment. There are still few high-quality jobs in Malawi in which well-trained Malawians can use their skills productively.

6.2 Economic, Demographic, and Educational Trends in Malawi

Malawi has experienced moderate, if erratic economic growth over the past 15 years. While between 2000 and 2015 the economy contracted only in one year (2001), economic growth was lower than population growth in six years (Figure 6.1). Given the significance of agriculture in the economy, overall annual economic growth broadly tracks the annual growth of the agriculture sector—the correlation

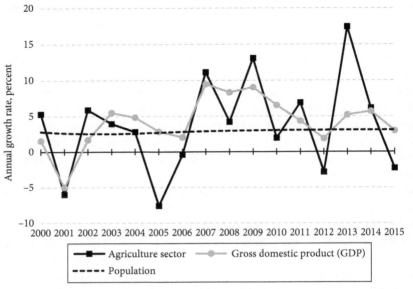

Figure 6.1. Malawi's agriculture sector, economy, and population, annual growth, 2000 to 2015

Source: World Bank, 2019.

coefficient between the two time series over this period is 0.63. Growth trends in the agricultural sector are more volatile than those of the economy as a whole, reflecting the exposure of the sector to adverse weather-related production shocks. Total value added in the agriculture sector fell from year to year five times between 2000 and 2015, primarily because of droughts or erratic rainfall, exacerbated in 2012 by weak economic conditions in Malawi's economy more broadly.

Greater economic growth is needed. Malawi has one of the fastest growing populations in the world, with a population of 17.6 million in 2018, a more than four-fold increase in fifty years from just over 4 million when Malawi conducted its first post-independence Census in 1966. Projections from the 2008 Census estimate that the population will be about 45 million by 2050. Although population growth rates should begin declining in coming decades, nonetheless the share of the population that is made up by youth aged 15 to 34 years will increase slightly from 34.2 per cent at the last census in 2018 to a peak of just over 35 per cent in around 2043, before beginning to decline. However, the youth population of Malawi will continue to grow for many decades thereafter. Currently, the number of youth is growing by about 170,000 persons per year. Projection estimates are that by 2050 this number will rise to 370,000 (NSO 2011a).

The principal investments that the government of Malawi have made to enable youth to obtain good jobs so that they are able to meet the needs of their households are through providing free primary education. While politically it has proven extremely popular, the programme has been subject to continual criticism since its launch for the poor quality of education provided using existing facilities to teach the large numbers of new students enrolling. The government and its development partners have invested heavily in teacher training and in building classrooms over the past 20 years. However, due to large numbers of primary students repeating classes or dropping out, it was found that in 2007 the system provided 23 student-years of instruction for every student successfully completing the eight years of primary education (World Bank 2010).

Despite the inefficiencies in implementation, the free primary education programme has resulted in improved educational outcomes. The years of education successfully completed for the 15 to 24 years age-cohort increased by 1.2 years between the 1998 and 2008 Censuses from 5.0 to 6.2 years (analysis by authors). Tracer studies done as part of the World Bank 2010 study demonstrated strong social returns (for example, improvements in social behaviours and health outcomes), particularly for primary education. Private financial returns to education in Malawi obtained through the labour market also were found to be significant at all levels of education, but being especially large at higher levels of educational attainment (World Bank 2010). As has been recognized for many generations, education remains a powerful means to achieving economic well-being in Malawi.

However, despite continuing public investment to improve the education system, coupled with significant resources allocated to efforts to increase the productivity of the agriculture sector, and in context of fair, although not stellar, economic growth over the past 15 years, there is as yet little evidence to show that there has been any growth in employment in higher productivity jobs. We now examine more closely the evolution in the structure of employment over this period and how Malawi's youth choose to engage in the workforce using three rounds of data from the Malawi IHS series for individuals of working age—ages 15 to 64 years.

6.3 Structure of and Trends in Employment in Malawi, 2004 to 2013

6.3.1 Data

We rely on the last three IHS surveys for our analysis—2004, 2010, and 2013.[2] These three multitopic household surveys have very similar questionnaires so

---

[2] Malawi has several nationally representative data sets that include information on employment. These include the 1998 and 2008 Malawi Population and Housing Censuses, the 2013 Labour Force Survey, and four rounds of the IHS survey series, starting in 1998 with the IHS-1 and continuing with the IHS-2 in 2004, IHS-3 in 2010, and the Integrated Household Panel Survey (IHPS) in 2013, the last involving a repeat enumeration of a large sub-set of the IHS-3 sample. These data sets were created by the National Statistical Office (NSO) of the government of Malawi.

that we were able to categorize individuals of working age in the survey samples into comparable employment categories. Moreover, the fact that the third round of the IHPS in 2013 was a panel survey of a subset of the sample for the second round in 2010 allowed us to trace changes in how individuals enumerated in both surveys engaged in the workforce over time.

The IHS surveys are the principal living standard measurement surveys for Malawi. The nationally representative samples for the surveys are selected using a two-stage cluster sampling approach. Using the districts of Malawi and the four major urban centers as strata, enumeration areas (EA) within each stratum are randomly selected with the probability of selection being proportional to the population of the EA. Either 16 or 20 households, depending on the survey round, were then randomly selected in each selected EA to make up a survey sample. The IHS-2 and IHS-3 surveys were administered over 12 to 13 months to capture annual seasonal variation in household consumption and expenditures, while the IHPS was administered over a nine-month period. Table 6.1 provides selected descriptive statistics on the three IHS surveys.

The employment categorization scheme used in our analysis is that of the International Labour Organization, which was used for the analysis by NSO of the 2013 Malawi Labour Force Survey. The *working age population* is defined as those aged 15 to 64 years. Within the working age population, we further distinguish *younger youth* aged 15 to 24 years, *older youth* aged 25 to 34 years, and *non-youth* aged 35 to 64 years. These individuals are categorized as being either *economically active* or *not economically active* depending on whether they are

Table 6.1. Sample size and period of administration of Malawi Integrated Household Surveys used

	IHS-2	IHS-3	IHPS
Sample size, households	11,280	12,271	4,000
Working age (15 to 64 years of age) sample size, individuals	25,144	27,842	10,349
Survey administration period	March 2004 to March 2005	March 2010 to March 2011	April 2013 to December 2013

Source: Analysis by authors of IHS-2, IHS-3, and IHPS.

To characterize the structure of employment in Malawi, given their universal coverage, our prefer-ence was to use the censuses, together with the Labour Force Survey. However, the questionnaires for the two censuses were sufficiently different that we were unable to categorize the working age popula-tion enumerated in each into similarly defined employment groups. Similar problems were observed in trying to combine either census with the 2013 Labour Force Survey to further assess trends in employment. The 1998 IHS-1 questionnaire differs significantly from those of the other IHS survey rounds, so it also was excluded from our analysis.

engaged in economic activities or actively seeking employment in such activities. The economically active are further disaggregated into *employed* and *unemployed*, depending upon whether they are working or not working, but actively seeking work, respectively. The employed can be further disaggregated into the economic sector of employment—*agriculture, industry,* or *services*. Similarly, the not economically active can be further disaggregated into students, homemakers, retired or ill individuals, or otherwise not economically active. In the analysis here, for the not economically active category we focus on *students* and all *other not economically active*.

As the IHS surveys are not specifically designed to examine questions of employment, the specific criteria used to assign an individual to one category or another differed from those used in the analysis of the 2013 Labour Force Survey. Information was used from both the household and the agricultural questionnaires of the IHS surveys. In doing so, we privileged certain information in assigning an individual to an employment category. Individuals who had stated that they were students; were not working, but actively seeking work; or were formally employed (primarily for a wage) were assigned to the student, unemployed, and employed categories, respectively, even if the individual also reported that they had also engaged, most commonly, in agricultural production. Similarly, individuals who worked on a non-agricultural household enterprise, even if also engaged in farming, were considered to be employed in either the industrial or services sector, depending on the nature of the household enterprise. However, in our analytical data set, we compiled information on individuals who reported working in more than one sector, as this information on employment in multiple sectors is among the information used to create the dependent variable for the multinomial logit analysis discussed later.

In addition, employment surveys typically involve strict recall periods of the previous one week to determine the employment status of survey respondents. The data used from the IHS surveys for our analysis, however, involved varying recall periods—for farming activities, this typically was for the previous twelve months. As working age individuals are much more likely to report having worked sometime over the past year than over the past week, our approach results in a larger share of individuals being categorized as employed, rather than 'not economically active' (if not students), than is found in employment surveys. Given these differences, we emphasize that the results of our employment categorization should not be considered comparable to, for example, seemingly similar results from the 2013 Labour Force Survey or the most recent population censuses for Malawi. However, we are confident that our approach to assigning working age members of the IHS survey samples to employment categories allows for valid comparisons to be made over the three rounds of the IHS examined.

6.3.2 Results

6.3.2.1 Structure of Employment in Malawi in 2013

The share of the population by working age population age group (younger youth, older youth, and non-youth) assigned to each employment category estimated from a weighted analysis of the 2013 IHPS data is presented in Figure 6.2 as a 100 per cent bar chart. The continued dominance of agricultural employment in Malawi is apparent. Among the older youth and non-youth, over 70 per cent of all individuals are working in agriculture, and 87 per cent of those who are employed work in agriculture. Even among the younger youth, while students are the largest employment category for this age group, most younger youth who are not students work in agriculture. Across all age groups, females are more likely than men to work on the farm. Given the customary land tenure system that provides access to land for almost all Malawians, agriculture is observed to be the default employment category for all, including for many individuals residing in urban centres.

The shares of each population group employed in industry and services are relatively small compared to agriculture. In urban areas, shares of those employed in the nonfarm sectors are higher, particularly for services.[3] Moreover, of those employed, the share of older youth and non-youth working in industry and services is somewhat higher than it is for the younger youth. This suggests that younger youth immediately upon entering the workforce are unable to readily obtain work outside of agriculture.

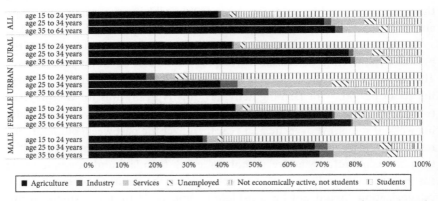

Figure 6.2. Malawi 2013, size of employment categories by age cohort, disaggregated by rural and urban and by male and female, percentage share of population

Source: Analysis by authors of 2013 Malawi Integrated Household Panel Survey. Weighted analysis.

---

[3] Urban areas include the four major cities of Malawi, district headquarters (*boma*s), and other gazetted towns. In the 2008 Census, 15.3 per cent of the population were enumerated as residents of urban areas, of which 78 per cent lived in the four major cities– Lilongwe, Blantyre, Zomba, and Mzuzu.

Unemployment is not common in Malawi. Following the statistical definition of unemployment used in the analysis of the 2013 Labour Force Survey for Malawi, any individual of working age in the survey sample who reported not having worked over the past four weeks, but who was actively looking for work, was categorized as unemployed. Such individuals in the sample were categorized as unemployed for the analysis here regardless of whether they indicated elsewhere in the survey that they had worked in some capacity before the four-week recall period used to assess unemployment. However, few individuals were categorized as such.

In the report on the 2013 Labour Force Survey, it is asserted that this strict definition of unemployment is not useful in the Malawi context, since the country's underdeveloped labour markets make it quite difficult to actively seek work (NSO 2014). More importantly, with broad access to small plots of agricultural land through the dominant customary land tenure system, most individuals can engage in farming to provide for some of their basic subsistence. However, given the small agricultural landholdings and the strongly seasonal pattern of rainfed agricultural production, they are unable to farm fulltime at a scale sufficient to meet all their welfare needs. In consequence, there is significant underemployment. Many working Malawians are unable to use their abilities sufficiently productively to meet their own needs or those of their households, or to expand Malawi's economy. The low unemployment figure obtained in our analysis masks this deficiency in the quantity and quality of employment available for both youth and older workers.

Over a quarter of Malawi's working age population are economically inactive. However, there are strong age-specific patterns to those who fall into this category. More than half of younger youth are economically inactive, given that so many are students. However, most students end their education by age 20, so the proportion of students in older age categories is very small. For older youth and non-youth, the share of the not economically active is relatively small, reflecting in part the long recall period used to flexibly define employment in this analysis. Nonetheless, in these age groups, women are more likely than men to be not economically active, as are those residing in urban areas relative to those in rural areas. For women, this may reflect maternal responsibilities, particularly for older youth. For urban dwellers, the higher rates of individuals not being economically active relative to rural residents likely reflects the greater barriers to employment in towns and cities, where opportunities for obtaining work, particularly formal employment, remain quite restricted, particularly in industry.

Many younger youth are continuing their education. This results in significant differences in cross-sectional employment patterns between younger and older youth. However, comparing older youth to non-youth, the patterns of employment in Figure 6.2 do not show that older youth participate in the workforce in Malawi in any qualitatively different manner than do non-youth. The only exception to this is for women, in that, relative to non-youth women, those in the older youth age category are more likely to be not economically active, likely due to their increased maternal responsibilities at this point in their life-cycle.

6.3.2.2 Evidence of Structural Shifts in Employment in Malawi, 2004 to 2013

While Figure 6.2 provides a static, cross-sectoral overview of employment among the working age in Malawi in 2013, the details presented in Table 6.2 sketch out what changes, if any, have occurred in employment patterns between 2004, 2010, and 2013. While information is presented for the three years for which we have data from the IHS series, our examination here primarily focuses on differences in the compound annual growth rate between 2004 and 2013 in the number of individuals who fall in each employment category reported.

Growth in the number of employed is less than growth in the working age population for all age groups. This is primarily due to higher growth over this period in the share of the population that is not economically active and, within this category, particularly due to growth in the number of students among young adults.

For those employed, the share working in the agriculture sector, by far the largest sector of employment, is relatively stable across the three points in time overall and when disaggregated by sex—around 94 per cent of all women employed consistently worked in agriculture over this period, while around 80 per cent of men did so. There is little evidence in these data sets that any movement of labour out of agriculture is occurring in Malawi. While we can point to small changes that might encourage one to see the start of such a process, particularly with the modest growth of employment in services, these changes are not sufficiently large as yet to convince any observer that a process of structural change in Malawi's economy is now gaining momentum.

This tabular analysis does not provide evidence that the substantial public investment in agricultural productivity in Malawi since 2005 through the Farm Input Subsidy Programme has resulted in any obvious changes in how people allocate their labour, whether into or out of agriculture. While more detailed, multivariate econometric analyses may more clearly link FISP impacts on farm household productivity with employment choices, particularly among working age members, these links are unlikely to be especially strong.

The sector in which growth in employment is seen is in services, and this growth is primarily among the older youth and the non-youth. For the younger youth, there has been a reduction in employment across all sectors, as increasing numbers maintain their student status. Growth rates for all sectors of employment for younger youth are lower than the rate of growth in the working age population for this age group, reflecting increasing delays in their entering the workforce. Nationally, agriculture is the dominant sector for those younger youth who enter into employment. Two factors likely account for this. First, many of the

Table 6.2. Malawi, change in size of employment categories by age cohort, disaggregated by rural and urban and by male and female

	Ages 15 to 64 years				Younger youth, ages 15 to 24				Older youth, ages 25 to 34				Non-youth, ages 35 to 64			
	2004	2010	2013	Annual growth, 2004–13, %	2004	2010	2013	Annual growth, 2004–13, %	2004	2010	2013	Annual growth, 2004–13, %	2004	2010	2013	Annual growth, 2004–13, %
NATIONAL Working age population, '000s	5,975	6,871	7,207	2.1	2,338	2,556	2,771	1.9	1,603	1,980	2,024	2.6	2,034	2,335	2,412	1.9
Employed, % share of working age population	76.7	72.8	69.2	0.9	53.7	46.6	43.0	−0.6	90.0	85.6	83.4	1.8	92.7	90.6	87.5	1.2
Agriculture, % share of employed	85.3	87.1	87.0	1.0	89.8	93.1	92.4	−0.3	82.0	83.8	85.6	2.1	84.7	86.3	85.0	1.1
Industry, % share of employed	5.8	3.2	2.4	−8.6	4.0	1.6	1.8	−9.1	7.3	4.3	2.6	−9.5	5.9	3.4	2.6	−7.6
Services, % share of employed	8.9	9.7	10.6	2.8	6.1	5.3	5.8	−1.2	10.7	11.9	11.9	2.8	9.4	10.3	12.4	4.2
Unemployed, % share of working age pop.	0.7	1.3	2.6	18.1	0.9	1.4	2.0	11.0	0.9	2.0	3.5	19.9	0.4	0.8	2.6	27.2
Not economically active, % share of working age pop.	22.6	25.9	28.2	4.7	45.4	52.0	55.1	4.1	9.1	12.4	13.1	6.8	6.9	8.6	9.9	6.1
Students, % share of not economically active	13.9	15.7	17.6	4.8	34.9	40.7	43.9	4.5	1.0	1.8	1.9	10.8	0.1	0.3	0.5	27.5

Continued

Table 6.2. Continued

	Ages 15 to 64 years				Younger youth, ages 15 to 24				Older youth, ages 25 to 34				Non-youth, ages 35 to 64			
	2004	2010	2013	Annual growth, 2004–13, %	2004	2010	2013	Annual growth, 2004–13, %	2004	2010	2013	Annual growth, 2004–13, %	2004	2010	2013	Annual growth, 2004–13, %
RURAL Working age population, '000s	4,804	5,683	5,925	2.4	1,855	2,118	2,316	2.5	1,249	1,570	1,587	2.7	1,700	1,995	2,022	1.9
Employed, % share of working age population	80.4	75.9	70.6	0.9	58.8	50.4	45.6	−0.4	93.4	89.6	85.2	1.6	94.3	92.4	87.8	1.1
Agriculture, % share of employed	89.9	92.3	91.8	1.1	93.3	96.3	95.0	−0.2	88.1	90.3	91.9	2.1	89.0	91.4	89.7	1.2
Industry, % share of employed	5.1	2.3	1.5	−12.2	3.4	1.0	0.9	−13.6	6.4	3.1	1.7	−12.6	5.2	2.3	1.6	−11.4
Services, % share of employed	5.0	5.5	6.8	4.3	3.3	2.7	4.0	1.8	5.5	6.7	6.4	3.3	5.8	6.2	8.7	5.7
Not economically active, % share of working age pop.	19.4	23.2	27.0	6.2	40.9	48.9	52.8	5.5	6.4	9.3	11.6	9.7	5.5	6.9	9.5	8.4
Students, % share of not economically active	13.2	15.3	17.1	5.4	33.5	40.0	42.4	5.2	0.9	1.3	1.6	10.0	0.0	0.2	0.3	30.8
URBAN Working age population, '000s	1,171	1,187	1,282	1.0	483	438	455	−0.7	354	410	436	2.4	334	339	390	1.7
Employed, % share of working age	61.8	57.8	62.7	1.2	34.1	28.6	29.5	−2.2	77.8	70.4	76.8	2.2	84.6	80.2	85.8	1.9

Agriculture, % share of employed	57.0	49.1	57.1	0.6	63.7	61.7	67.4	−2.1	51.2	46.6	54.5	2.6	58.4	45.9	55.6	0.4
Industry, % share of employed	10.2	10.5	8.3	−1.7	8.7	7.0	9.9	−1.2	11.8	11.2	7.0	−3.8	9.8	11.4	9.0	0.0
Services, % share of employed	32.8	40.4	34.5	1.2	27.6	31.3	22.7	−4.8	37.1	42.2	38.6	2.4	31.8	42.7	35.4	2.1
Not economically active, % share of working age pop.	35.6	38.5	33.8	0.4	62.8	66.9	66.8	0.0	18.9	24.5	18.7	2.2	14.1	18.8	12.1	0.1
Students, % share of not economically active	17.1	17.8	19.8	2.6	40.4	44.3	51.4	2.0	1.4	3.5	3.2	12.4	0.2	1.0	1.4	24.6
FEMALE Working age population, '000s	3,039	3,550	3,688	2.2	1,221	1,349	1,379	1.4	785	1,039	1,101	3.8	1,033	1,162	1,208	1.8
Employed, % share of working age population	75.4	71.7	69.2	1.2	57.8	50.8	46.8	−1.0	84.9	81.2	79.7	3.1	89.1	87.6	85.1	1.2
Agriculture, % share of employed	93.3	94.6	93.6	1.0	93.8	96.4	95.6	−0.9	91.5	92.7	92.8	3.0	94.0	95.0	92.9	0.9
Services, % share of employed	4.7	4.6	5.8	3.3	4.7	3.3	3.9	−3.1	5.8	6.0	6.3	3.8	4.0	4.3	6.5	6.8
Not economically active, % share of working age pop.	24.0	27.0	28.2	4.0	41.5	48.0	50.9	3.7	14.4	16.8	16.7	5.5	10.7	11.8	12.7	3.7
Students, % share of not economically active	10.6	13.3	14.4	5.7	26.0	33.8	37.0	5.4	0.5	1.3	1.3	15.6	0.1	0.2	0.4	27.5

Continued

Table 6.2. Continued

	Ages 15 to 64 years				Younger youth, ages 15 to 24				Older youth, ages 25 to 34				Non-youth, ages 35 to 64			
	2004	2010	2013	Annual growth, 2004–13, %	2004	2010	2013	Annual growth, 2004–13, %	2004	2010	2013	Annual growth, 2004–13, %	2004	2010	2013	Annual growth, 2004–13, %
MALE Working age population, '000s	2,936	3,321	3,519	2.0	1,117	1,206	1,392	2.5	818	942	922	1.3	1,001	1,173	1,204	2.1
Employed, % share of working age population	78.1	74.0	69.2	0.7	49.2	42.0	39.2	-0.1	94.9	90.4	87.8	0.5	96.5	93.6	89.8	1.3
Agriculture, % share of employed	77.2	79.2	80.1	1.1	84.6	88.6	88.6	0.5	73.6	74.9	77.8	1.1	75.8	78.2	77.5	1.3
Services, % share of employed	13.2	15.0	15.7	2.6	8.1	8.1	8.0	0.0	15.1	17.8	17.8	2.4	14.7	15.9	17.9	3.4
Not economically active, % share of working age pop.	21.0	24.7	28.2	5.4	49.6	56.6	59.2	4.5	4.1	7.6	8.8	10.4	3.0	5.5	7.2	12.4
Students, % share of not economically active	17.4	18.3	20.9	4.2	44.6	48.4	50.7	3.9	1.4	2.2	2.6	8.6	0.1	0.4	0.5	27.5
Observations (national)	25,144	27,842	10,349	–	9,844	10,427	4,214	–	6,772	8,026	2,847	–	8,528	9,389	3,288	–

Note: Weighted analysis. 'Annual growth' is the compound annual growth rate in the number of individuals who fall in the employment category in question between 2004 and 2013. Sample design corrected standard errors are not reported here, but are available upon request.

Source: Analysis by authors of data from the Malawi Integrated Household Survey (IHS) series for 2004 (IHS-2), 2010 (IHS-3), and 2013 (IHPS).

younger youth, particularly males, are still dependents in their households—analysis of the IHS-3 shows that 56 per cent of females and 80 per cent of males in this age category are dependents, meaning, not household head or spouse of the household head. These dependent household members will be obligated to provide farm labour to the household. Secondly, most younger youth will not have sufficient capital to engage in petty trading, in particular, in the service sector. For younger youth in Malawi, the nonfarm employment sectors are not absorbing their labour. If they are not students, most younger youth work in agriculture.

It is among the older youth that one observes growth in employment in services, even if the absolute numbers involved remain dwarfed by those working in agriculture. The national growth rate for employment of older youth in services, but not agriculture and industry, is higher than the rate of population growth for this age group. Older youth tend to live independently—87 per cent are either a household head or the spouse of a household head—and many will have achieved higher educational levels than did their elders in the non-youth age cohort, providing them with skills that can be used effectively in employment in the services sector. Growth in employment in services for older youth is most notable in rural areas and among men.

Nonetheless, the largest growth in employment in the services sector is among the non-youth. This higher growth in employment in services applies across the board to rural and urban and male and female non-youth, suggesting that broad capital accumulation over time may be a more important factor than education in enabling individuals to find employment in the services sector.

In contrast to growing employment in services and a relatively constant large share of the employed in agriculture, employment in the industrial sector in Malawi declined between 2004 and 2013. This is particularly the case in rural areas, though urban employment in industry has also declined. Malawi's national accounts indicate that the recent performance of the industrial sector has been positive but erratic, with a mean annual growth rate between 2000 and 2014 of 4.0 per cent. However, we may be seeing a reduction in labour-intensive operations in manufacturing being replaced by more capital-intensive operations.

Outside of the employed categories, younger youth in both rural and urban areas increasingly are delaying their entry into employment by extending their education. This is an outcome of the increased access to education for all offered by the free primary education programme. The positive trends in educational attainment between 2004 and 2013 for all working age individuals and by age group are detailed in Table 6.3.

Over this period, the share of younger youth who are students rose from 35 to 44 per cent (Table 6.2). The highest growth rates are seen among women and in rural areas. Although males in the younger youth age category remain more likely to be students, the number of females in this age category who are students is growing faster than for their males counterparts. However, educational attainment

Table 6.3. Changes in educational attainment among working age individuals in Malawi, 2004 to 2013

	Ages 15 to 64 years			Younger youth, ages 15 to 24			Older youth, ages 25 to 34			Non-youth, ages 35 to 64		
	2004	2010	2013	2004	2010	2013	2004	2010	2013	2004	2010	2013
NATIONAL—Years schooling completed, avg.	5.0	5.8	6.1	6.1	6.7	6.9	5.2	6.3	6.6	3.7	4.5	4.7
Completed primary school, per cent	*23.2*	*27.3*	*29.1*	*27.1*	*30.4*	*32.2*	*26.3*	*32.7*	*33.5*	*16.3*	*19.5*	*21.8*
Completed secondary school, per cent	*4.4*	*7.1*	*7.8*	*3.1*	*4.9*	*5.8*	*6.8*	*10.5*	*10.9*	*4.1*	*6.8*	*7.3*
Rural—Years schooling completed, avg.	4.4	5.3	5.5	5.6	6.3	6.5	4.5	5.7	5.9	3.2	3.9	4.1
Urban—Years schooling completed, avg.	7.5	8.6	8.7	8.0	8.9	9.2	7.9	8.8	8.8	6.4	8.0	7.9
Female—Years schooling completed, avg.	4.1	5.1	5.4	5.6	6.5	6.7	4.0	5.4	5.9	2.5	3.2	3.5
Male—Years schooling completed, avg.	6.0	6.6	6.8	6.6	6.9	7.1	6.4	7.3	7.4	5.0	5.8	5.9
Observations (national)	*25,098*	*27,736*	*10,296*	*9,839*	*10,370*	*4,193*	*6,762*	*7,998*	*2,835*	*8,497*	*9,368*	*3,268*

Note: Weighted analysis. Sample design corrected standard errors are not reported here, but are available upon request.

Source: Analysis by authors of data from the Malawi Integrated Household Survey (IHS) series for 2004 (IHS-2), 2010 (IHS-3), and 2013 (IHPS).

levels differ between rural and urban younger youth. In rural areas, two-thirds of younger youth students are still in primary school, albeit at upper levels. Only one-third of rural younger youth students attend secondary school and almost none attend university or training colleges. In contrast, for urban younger youth who are students, one-third attend primary school, 60 per cent attend secondary school, and 7 per cent are in university or training colleges.

The highest growth rates for the student category are seen among older youth and non-youth. However, note that the number of students in these older groups remains very small. The increase in student numbers in these categories likely reflects the recent expansion in tertiary education opportunities from about 8,400 places nationally in 2008 to 11,600 in 2011 (Mambo et al. 2016). Nonetheless, the student category is unlikely to ever be a significant employment category among these older workers.

We also see high growth rates in the share of the working age population that is unemployed. However, as discussed earlier, the absolute numbers of individuals in this category are few, and the category as narrowly defined here does not reflect the widespread nature of underemployment in Malawi.

Finally, the growth rates computed for the base working population pose a few puzzles. Overall the working age population is growing at 2.1 per cent per year, about one per cent lower than the growth of the population as a whole over the period examined. Emigration out of Malawi may be a factor in this, as emigration for wage labour, whether temporary or permanent, has been an important economic strategy for many Malawians since the colonial period (Coleman 1979, Vail 1983). In the 2008 census, heads of household were asked about household members who had left Malawi in the past ten years. Of the almost 130,000 emigrants enumerated, 61 per cent were men aged 20 to 39 years of age (NSO 2011b). This pattern of age-specific male emigration is consonant with the pattern of working age population growth seen in Table 6.2, which shows that male older youth have the second lowest rate of growth in population among the groups examined. The lowest rate of population growth is among younger youth in urban areas, which shows an absolute decline in numbers between 2004 and 2010. While this may reflect increased educational choices in rural areas, given significant public investment in rural education since 1994, reducing the traditional flow of secondary and post-secondary students of rural origin to urban schools, the determinants of population growth among younger youth in urban centres of Malawi requires additional study.

6.3.2.3 Change Over Time in Employment Categories for Individuals of Working Age

The panel nature of the IHS-3 of 2010 and the IHPS of 2013 allow the tracing of changes in employment category for individuals enumerated in both surveys. The results of this analysis are presented in Table 6.4. The dominance of agriculture in employment choice is the principal pattern seen in this table. For any working age

Table 6.4. Change in category of employment between 2010 and 2013 for working age individuals in Malawi, row totals in per cent

Category of employment in 2010	Working age, 15 to 64 years in 2010						Younger youth, 15 to 24 years in 2010					
	Category of employment in 2013											
	Agric	Ind	Serv	Un-empl	Not actv	Stdnt	Agric	Ind	Serv	Un-empl	Not actv	Stdnt
Agriculture	75	1	3	3	11	6	68	0	2	2	13	15
Industry	46	27	13	2	9	2	59	5	30	0	0	6
Services	32	4	52	3	4	5	43	7	31	3	4	12
Unemployed	55	2	6	3	27	8	38	6	3	3	36	14
Not economically active, not student	57	1	6	4	21	11	46	0	4	3	25	21
Student	24	1	4	2	11	59	25	1	2	1	11	60
Total	61	2	7	3	12	15	47	1	3	2	14	33
observations	5,887						2,228					

Category of employment in 2010	Older youth, 25 to 34 years in 2010						Non- youth, 35 to 64 years in 2010					
	Agric	Ind	Serv	Un-empl	Not actv	Stdnt	Agric	Ind	Serv	Un-empl	Not actv	Stdnt
Agriculture	76	2	4	4	10	5	79	1	3	3	11	2
Industry	39	33	7	0	19	2	49	27	14	5	3	2
Services	28	3	52	5	5	7	32	4	57	1	4	2
Unemployed	52	0	10	4	27	7	86	0	0	0	14	0
Not economically active, not student	62	0	8	5	19	7	66	1	6	3	20	4
Student	20	9	26	8	2	36	5	0	88	0	0	7
Total	66	3	10	4	11	6	71	2	10	3	11	2
observations	1,643						2,016					

Note: Age ranges based on age at the time of enumeration in 2010 for the earlier IHS-3 survey. Table presents row totals, for example, upper left cell in top-left sub-table indicates that 75 per cent of all working age individuals who were employed in agriculture in 2010 were still employed in agriculture in 2013, while the upper right cell in the same sub-table indicates that 6 per cent of those who were employed in agriculture in 2010 were reported in 2013 to be students.

Source: Analysis by authors of data from the Malawi Integrated Household Survey (IHS) series for working age individuals that can be identified in both the 2010 (IHS-3) and 2013 (IHPS). Weighted estimates.

individual who changed their category of employment between 2010 and 2013, employment in the agriculture sector is the most common employment category destination. The only exceptions to this pattern are for older youth and non-youth students, who were more likely to have obtained employment in the services sector than in agriculture in 2013. However, the numbers of individuals involved in these exceptional categories are few.

Moreover, there is considerable stability in the sector of employment for those employed in agriculture or in the services sector—75 per cent of those in agriculture in 2010 were still in agriculture three years later, and 52 per cent of those in services were still in services. The proportion of those still working in the same sector for agriculture and services goes up with age—non-youth are more likely than older youth to be in the same employment sector and, in turn, older youth are more likely than younger youth to remain in the same sector of employment over the three years. Stability in employment, however, is not seen in the industrial sector, where almost three-quarters of those who were working in the sector in 2010 were no longer doing so in 2013. However, note that the changes for the industrial sector are based on very small numbers overall.

Quite a bit of movement out of the 'not economically active, not student' category is seen, primarily into agriculture, reflecting the insight repeatedly observed earlier in this analysis of agricultural employment being the dominant employment choice for most working age Malawians. Two-thirds of those who move into or out of the 'not economically active, not student' category are female, suggesting that membership in this category may be driven primarily by life cycle stage considerations, notably pregnancy and child care.[4]

The key finding from this analysis is that there is no evidence of a substantial movement of labour out of the agricultural sector of Malawi's economy and into the industry or services sectors between 2004 and 2013. The share of those of working age who are employed who are working in agriculture has remained quite stable over this period at around 87 per cent. However, there has been some growth in employment in the services sector, particularly among older youth and the non-youth. Younger youth aged 15 to 24 years are seen to be extending their period of schooling, but, nonetheless, generally enter into employment in the agriculture sector after they complete their schooling. That older workers are more likely to be employed in the services sector suggests that broad capital accumulation, work experience, or the development of personal social and economic networks over time may be more important factors than education in enabling individuals to find employment outside of agriculture.

---

[4] Seasonal factors related to agriculture could also account for some of the movement of individuals between employment categories. However, an analysis was done of the IHS-3 data to determine if there was any association between younger youth reporting that they are students and the month in which their household was interviewed. Only those interviewed in April and August showed a significantly higher propensity to be categorized as students, a finding that would appear unrelated to seasonal cropping cycles.

6.4 Analysis of the Determinants of Category of Employment

In this section, a multivariate analysis is used to identify factors potentially associated with the decision by an individual to participate in a specific pattern of employment. We use a multinomial logit (MNL) regression model (Amemiya 1985, Greene 2012) with data for sample members of working age from the 2010 IHS-3 survey.

This analysis involves splitting our sample of working age individuals into six employment categories, including those who are not economically active, and then estimating relative risk ratios for a particular characteristic of a working age individual being associated with that individual being a member of a specific employment category. To gain insights through this analysis into how youth engage in employment in Malawi, we include age range dummy variables in our MNL model.

6.4.1 Data

We use the IHS-3 data from 2010–11 for this analysis. Although this dataset is not as recent as the 2013 IHPS, it has a much larger sample. As our MNL analysis involves examining six categories of working age individuals, some of which are quite small, it is important to have sufficient observations to draw inferences from the covariates of employment choice made by individuals in the smaller categories.

The employment categories that we use as the dependent variable for the MNL model are different from those which were used in the analyses presented earlier. The statistical employment categories used for the earlier analysis, based on definitions of the International Labour Organization, rely upon a relatively restricted understanding of the economic engagements individuals of working age in Malawi might pursue. In particular, that categorization scheme does not allow for individuals to work in more than a single sector, for example, working in both agriculture and services. Such diversification of livelihoods within households and by individuals is relatively common in Malawi. In consequence, for the MNL analysis to identify factors associated with the employment choice of an individual, we developed six broad employment categories consisting of individuals who are

  i. employed in agricultural sector only, which is our reference category in the MNL analysis;
  ii. employed both in agricultural sector and in household enterprise(s) in the industry or services sectors;
  iii. employed both in agricultural sector and in wage employment in the industry or services sectors;

iv. only employed in household enterprise(s) in the industry or services sectors;

v. only employed for wages in the industry or services sector; or

vi. not economically active.

In this employment categorization scheme, we maintain a distinction between informal (categories ii and iv above) and formal (iii and v) employment in the industry and services sectors (see, e.g. Hart 1973, Fox, Senbet, and Simbanegavi 2016). Informal employment is centred on the operations of generally small-scale, minimally-capitalized enterprises within the household that make use primarily of household labour. In contrast, formal employment generally involves an individual having some type of working agreement with an employer with salary and benefits, a specific work location outside the household residence, and regular hours, with payroll taxes and social security payments being made to government agencies as part of the formal working arrangement. Obtaining informal employment is generally easier than obtaining formal wage employment, but the nature of informal employment is less stable. The returns to informal employment are also generally lower than what can be obtained from formal employment. In most developing countries, including Malawi, youth have the greatest opportunities for entering the non-agricultural workforce through informal employment, something they do generally with ambitions to obtain formal employment as soon as possible (ILO 2015).

Note that we exclude from the categorization scheme for our analysis the small number of formally unemployed. Moreover, sample size considerations dictate that we cannot differentiate employment in the industrial sector from employment in the services sector, or single out students from others who are not economically active.

The Venn diagrams in Figure 6.3 provide a graphical representation of how these categories are organized for the working age sample of the IHS-3 as a whole and by youth and non-youth sub-samples. The diagrams, however, do not differentiate those who are employed for wages in the industry or services sectors (formal employment) from those employed in household enterprises (informal employment) in these sectors. The dominance of exclusive agricultural sector employment is apparent in the diagrams, as is the large share of younger youth who are not economically active.

The potential factors associated with an individual being a member of a particular employment category that we consider include demographic characteristics, educational attainment, household assets, physical access to markets, and recent experiences of economic shocks.[5] These are described in Table 6.5 for the entire working age sample.

---

[5] This analysis is based on a cross-sectional data set and involves at least one choice variable (that on FISP) among the explanatory variables. Consequently, while the analysis enables the identification

Working age sample   Younger youth sub-sample Older youth sub-sample Non-youth sub-sample

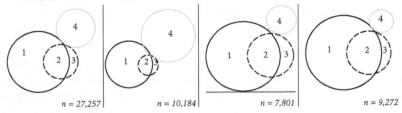

1 - Employed in agricultural sector only;
2 - Employed in agricultural sector and in the industry or services sectors (not differentiated between
    employment in household enterprise or for wages);
3 -Employed only in the industry or services sectors (not differentiated between employment in household
    enterprise or for wages);
4 - Not economically active.

Figure 6.3. Venn diagrams of the relative sizes of the employment categories, for full working age sample and age-based sub-samples

The explanatory variables included in the model have been selected based on research literature assessing determinants of participation in non-agricultural activities, including being not economically active in rural areas in developing countries. Broadly, individuals may choose to engage in nonfarm activities because of the potential benefits, such as high returns or to diversify risk (Lucas and Stark 1985). External shocks and risks associated with agricultural production may also lead to individuals being forced to move away from agriculture and into other sectors. Factors associated with these two distinct scenarios are referred to as 'pull' and 'push' factors. In both scenarios, an individual's labour allocation (both in amount and across sectors) is a function of variables related to incentives—the returns to labour and the relative risks to attaining those returns; and to capacity—human, social, financial, and other assets that make possible one's engagement in a particular type of employment (Reardon et al. 2007). The explanatory variables used in the analysis here are primarily related to capacity, reflecting various assets upon which individuals might draw in pursuing particular forms of employment. Although the distinction is not exact, only the access to markets and the shock-related explanatory variables reflect incentives in any significant manner.

Specifically, the demographic variables included in the MNL model are linked to the broader question of how youth in Malawi enter the workforce. However, we also include two factors that may be associated with an individual not being economically active: whether an individual is a dependent within the household or is a woman who gave birth in the past two years. As gender plays a key role in employment status, being an important determinant of access to land, labour,

of associations between specific factors and the nature of one's employment, it does not permit one to claim any cause-and-effect relationships.

Table 6.5. Dependent and explanatory variables for multinomial logit analysis of determinants of an individual being a member of a particular employment category, working age sample

	Variable	Variable definition	Mean (s.e.)
Dependent categorical variable components:			
	farm_only	Employed in agricultural sector only, 0/1	0.526 (0.0080)
	farm_NFent	Employed both in agricultural sector and in household enterprise(s) in the industry or services sectors, 0/1	0.077 (0.0026)
	farm_NFwage	Employed both in agricultural sector and in wage employment in the industry or services sectors, 0/1	0.084 (0.0036)
	NFent_only	Only employed in household enterprise(s) in the industry or services sectors, 0/1	0.016 (0.0014)
	NFwage_only	Only employed for wages in the industry or services sector, 0/1	0.033 (0.0022)
	not_econ_active	Not economically active, 0/1	0.264 (0.0049)
Explanatory variables:			
Demographic	male	male, 0/1	0.482 (0.0024)
	youth15_19	age 15 to 19 years, 0/1	0.206 (0.0030)
	youth20_24	age 20 to 24 years, 0/1	0.165 (0.0031)
	youth25_29	age 25 to 29 years, 0/1	0.158 (0.0029)
	youth30_34	age 30 to 34 years, 0/1	0.128 (0.0031)
	dependent	Individual is a dependent within household (not head or spouse of head), 0/1	0.297 (0.0045)
	recent_birth	Individual gave birth in past two years, 0/1	0.135 (0.0027)
Ethnicity	Chewa_Nyanja	Chewa or Nyanja ethnicity, 0/1	0.632 (0.0089)
	Yao_Lomwe	Yao or Lomwe ethnicity, 0/1	0.157 (0.0075)
	Tmbka_Ngoni_Tnga	Tumbuka, Ngoni, or Tonga ethnicity, 0/1	0.149 (0.0067)
	Other_north	Other northern ethnic groups, 0/1	0.017 (0.0023)
	Other_ethnicity	Other ethnic groups, 0/1	0.045 (0.0033)
Education	ed_not_fin_prmry	Did not complete primary school, 0/1	0.730 (0.0070)
	ed_prmry_cmplt	Completed primary school, 0/1	0.201 (0.0050)

Continued

Table 6.5. Continued

Variable		Variable definition	Mean (s.e.)
Dependent categorical variable components:			
	ed_scndry_cmplt	Completed secondary school, 0/1	0.053 (0.0025)
	ed_tertiary	Received tertiary level education— university or vocational, 0/1	0.016 (0.0020)
Household wealth	house_perm_mtrl	Individual lives in house constructed with some permanent materials, for example, metal roofing sheets, cement, or tile, 0/1	0.572 (0.0091)
Agriculture	land_cap_ha	Household landholding per capita, ha	0.179 (0.0302)
	FISP_hh	Member of Farm Input Subsidy Programme beneficiary household, 0/1	0.431 (0.0083)
	mid_alt_plt	Resident in Mid-altitude Plateau and Highlands agroecological zone, 0/1	0.757 (0.0122)
	Lower_Shire_Valley	Resident in Lower Shire Valley agroecological zone, 0/1	0.045 (0.0040)
	Lakeshore	Resident in Lakeshore and Upper Shire Valley agroecological zone, 0/1	0.198 (0.0123)
Access to markets	trvl_5k_town_hr	Travel time to nearest urban centre with population above 5,000, hours	0.970 (0.025)
	trvl_50k_town_hr	Travel time to nearest urban centre with population above 50,000, hrs	1.790 (0.031)
Shocks	shock_idiosync	Household experienced idiosyncratic shock in past 12 months, 0/1	0.273 (0.0060)
	drought	Drought in community in past five years, 0/1	0.228 (0.0145)
Observations			27,257

Source: Analysis by authors of IHS-3 data. Weighted estimates. Standard errors corrected to reflect clustered design of survey sample reported in parentheses.

technology, and other productive assets that will affect the propensity of an individual to obtain employment within a specific category (Andersson Djurfeldt, Djurfeldt, and Bergman Lodin 2013), the model's covariates include the sex of the individual.

We include several dummy variables on ethnicity (based on language spoken in the household). Ethnicity tends to overlap and therefore be highly correlated with other economic and social disadvantages that impact on the employment choices that an individual might exercise. As has been shown in other countries, ethnic disadvantage tends to be both a multidimensional factor and to increase cumulatively over the life course because of the complex interplay of several over-lapping layers of disadvantage, which start from conception and continue through adult life (Hall and Patrinos 2014).

We include a range of educational attainment variables to assess the importance of human capital accumulation by an individual on the type of employment obtained. Education is expressed in terms of education levels, as credentialism plays an important role in screening for formal wage jobs in Malawi and many other African countries (Lewin 2009). To capture the effect of household capital stocks on employment choice, we include a dummy variable of whether the individual lived in a house that was at least partly constructed of modern, permanent building materials as a proxy identifier of households that are likely to be able to offer a member financial resources to establish a business. Several dimensions of agricultural production that might affect employment choice are also included, such as agricultural landholding size and whether an individual was a member of a FISP beneficiary household, as well as the broad agroecological potential of the area in which an individual was resident.

Physical access to markets may be expected to influence the extent to which individuals work outside of agriculture (Jonasson and Helfand 2010, Deichmann, Shilpi, and Vakis 2009). We include travel time to the nearest populated area with greater than 5,000 persons and greater than 50,000 persons respectively, as proxies for access to markets at different ends of the market size distribution.

Important factors affecting incentives to diversify away from agriculture include volatile variables such as exogenous shocks (Ellis 2000). We include variables indicating if the household of which the individual is a member experienced an idiosyncratic shock (illness, child birth, death, and so on) in the last year and whether the community in which an individual resides has experienced drought over the past five years.

6.4.2 Multinomial logit results

The results of the MNL model for the six employment categories with the full working age population in the IHS-3 sample are presented in Table 6.6. The results are presented as relative risk ratios (RRRs), which show how a one unit change in an explanatory variable will change the relative probability of an individual being in one employment category relative to the base category. RRRs are analogous to odds-ratios used in bivariate logit models (Long and Freese 2014), with an RRR>1.0 showing an increase in the relative probability of being in a particular employment category and a RRR<1.0 indicating the reverse. The base or reference category for the MNL model is being employed in the agriculture sector only, so all the relative risk ratios are expressed relative to this. For example, in the first row of Table 6.6, an individual being male increases their probability of being employed in both agriculture and a nonfarm enterprise (column 3) by 55.1 per cent, that is, 1.551—1.000, and in a wage job in industry or services by a factor of over three (3.192). In contrast, being a youth aged between 15 and 19 years (row 2) decreases the relative probability of being employed in all categories except for the not economically active one.

It should be noted that, although the MNL is regarded as the 'work horse' of categorical variable models, it is predicated on the assumption of the independence of irrelevant alternatives (IIA). The IIA assumption states that the odds ratios in the MNL model are independent of the other states (Greene 2012). The validity of the IIA assumption is often questionable in the application of an MNL model to discrete choice issues as in the analysis of employment category choice here. However, we are unable to reject the IIA assumption for our preferred MNL model in Table 6.6, using the Small-Hsaio post-estimation test (Small and Hsaio 1985).

Examining the results of our MNL analysis, we find that the sex of the individual is an important component of employment choice. Males dominate employment outside of agriculture. Women are remaining in agriculture to a much greater extent than men, while also experiencing periods of not being economically active more commonly than men.

While the MNL analysis permits a clearer interpretation of employment patterns across age groups than does the earlier tabular analysis, examining the youth components of our model, our MNL results simply confirm the findings from our tabular analysis that younger youth, ages 15 to 24, are either in agriculture or are not economically active. This is seen by the relative risk ratios for individuals of these ages all being significantly less than 1.0 for any employment categories that include nonfarm work. In contrast, the statistically insignificant relative risk ratios across all categories for those aged 25 to 29 years suggest that these somewhat older youth are in something of a transitional period in terms of the nature of their employment, with a clearer pattern being established in the following five years, ages 30 to 35, during which we find these oldest youth more likely to be employed both in agriculture and in the nonfarm sectors, whether informally in household enterprises (more strongly) or formally in wage employment (to a lesser extent). Across all youth age ranges, however, none have a significant probability of obtaining work exclusively in the nonfarm sectors. The youth are not in the vanguard of those Malawians taking up employment, whether informal or formal, in the services and industrial sectors and abandoning agriculture.

The hypothesis from our tabular analysis that women likely move into the category of not being economically active due to recurring maternal responsibilities is not confirmed by the MNL results—having given birth in the last two years is not positively associated with being in this category. We see, however, that women who have recently given birth are also not likely to engage in nonfarm employment of any sort—all relative risk ratios are below 1.0 for this explanatory variable. In contrast, infant care seemingly does not draw a mother away from engaging in farm work, our base employment category for the MNL. However, our expectation that household members, primary youth, who are dependents within a household

Continued

Table 6.6. Determinants of employment category for working individuals in Malawi, multinomial logit results presented as relative risk ratios

Explanatory variable category	Explanatory variable (potential determinant)	Employment in agriculture and in household enterprise in industry or services sectors	Employment in agriculture and in wage employ-ment in industry or services sectors	Only employment in household enterprise in industry or services sectors	Only wage employment in industry or services sectors	Not economically active
Demographic	male	1.551*** (0.1010)	4.865*** (0.4143)	2.327*** (0.3061)	3.192*** (0.3477)	0.727*** (0.0384)
	youth15_19	0.498** (0.1271)	0.597* (0.1282)	0.193* (0.0984)	0.815 (0.2728)	8.342*** (0.7989)
	youth20_24	0.788* (0.0770)	0.682** (0.0848)	0.522* (0.1172)	0.789 (0.1527)	1.718*** (0.1527)
	youth25_29	1.139 (0.0928)	0.924 (0.0843)	0.890 (0.1506)	1.213 (0.1663)	1.127 (0.1062)
	youth30_34	1.433*** (0.1121)	1.208* (0.0999)	1.092 (0.1874)	1.205 (0.1532)	1.310* (0.1439)
	dependent	0.250*** (0.0645)	0.369*** (0.0584)	0.173** (0.0541)	0.665* (0.1143)	4.240*** (0.313)
	recent_birth	0.788 (0.0726)	0.435*** (0.0712)	0.720 (0.1787)	0.369** (0.097)	0.654*** (0.055)
Ethnicity	Yao_Lomwe	0.726** (0.0803)	0.784* (0.0865)	0.868 (0.2076)	0.673 (0.1469)	0.884 (0.0788)
	Tmbka_Ngoni_Tnga	0.841 (0.0885)	0.623*** (0.0729)	0.412** (0.102)	0.515** (0.0898)	0.971 (0.0968)
	Other_north	1.781* (0.4061)	1.194 (0.3058)	2.655 (1.6851)	0.512 (0.2803)	2.615*** (0.4833)
	Other_ethnicity	1.170 (0.1749)	0.804 (0.1606)	1.324 (0.5004)	1.212 (0.3073)	1.524 (0.2733)
Education	ed_prmry_cmplt	1.607*** (0.1232)	2.302*** (0.1771)	2.119*** (0.3025)	3.156*** (0.488)	2.232*** (0.1433)
	ed_scndry_cmplt	1.909*** (0.3205)	8.413*** (1.0385)	3.808*** (0.9809)	14.104*** (2.4966)	2.857*** (0.3941)
	ed_tertiary	7.716*** (2.6866)	76.257*** (26.7075)	26.987*** (13.277)	200.232*** (79.1474)	24.251*** (9.3287)
Household wealth	house_perm_mtrl	1.402*** (0.1011)	1.479*** (0.1674)	2.433*** (0.5836)	2.970*** (0.5276)	1.634*** (0.1163)
Agriculture	land_cap_ha	0.883 (0.1049)	0.230*** (0.0895)	0.000*** (0.0000)	0.000*** (0.0000)	1.055* (0.0275)
	FISP_hh	0.955 (0.0649)	0.603*** (0.0489)	0.000*** (0.0000)	0.170*** (0.0376)	0.616*** (0.0400)
	Lower_Shire_Valley	0.728 (0.1302)	0.704 (0.2832)	0.415 (0.2400)	0.610 (0.2190)	0.582* (0.1014)
	Lakeshore	1.120 (0.0990)	0.874 (0.0962)	0.908 (0.2971)	0.822 (0.1861)	0.955 (0.0872)
Access to markets	trvl_5k_town_hr	0.854 (0.0750)	0.825 (0.0824)	0.975 (0.1825)	0.817 (0.1401)	1.021 (0.0771)
	trvl_50k_town_hr	0.946 (0.0596)	0.877 (0.0680)	0.643** (0.0979)	0.683** (0.0755)	0.690*** (0.0353)

Table 6.6. Continued

Explanatory variable category	Explanatory variable (potential determinant)	Employment in agriculture and in household enterprise in industry or services sectors	Employment in agriculture and in wage employ-ment in industry or services sectors	Only employment in household enterprise in industry or services sectors	Only wage employment in industry or services sectors	Not economically active
Shocks	shock_idiosync	1.111 (0.0927)	1.223 (0.1551)	1.082 (0.3611)	0.712 (0.1268)	0.840* (0.0726)
	drought	1.561** (0.1154)	1.364** (0.1522)	1.751** (0.3393)	1.392* (0.2019)	0.920 (0.0638)
	Constant	0.125* (0.0166)	0.101* (0.0143)	0.184* (0.0056)	0.090* (0.0252)	0.231* (0.0287)
Employment category observations		2,175	2,297	465	984	7,434

Total observations in analytical data set: 27,257; Employed in agricultural sector only (base category): 13,902, pseudo R^2: 0.3110; $F_{(115,623)} = 334.50$, Prob > F = 0.0000

Note: The reference employment category is 'Agricultural sector employment only'. For the categorical explanatory variables, the base case for ethnicity is 'Chewa or Nyanja'; for educational attainment, 'Did not complete primary school'; and for agroecological zones, 'Mid-altitude Plateau and Highlands'. Statistical significance of relative risk ratios denoted by * for $p < .05$, ** for $p < .01$, and *** for $p < .001$.

Source: Analysis by authors of IHS-3 data. Weighted estimates. Standard errors corrected to reflect clustered design of survey sample reported in parentheses.

are likely not to be economically active is seen in the model results. Dependent household members of working age are also shown to be unlikely to engage in employment outside of the agricultural sector.

With regards to employment patterns and ethnicity, the Yao and Lomwe, primarily found in the south of the country, and the Tumbuka, Ngoni, and Tonga, primarily in the north (and centre for the Ngoni), are less likely than the Chewa and Nyanja, our base category for ethnicity, to engage in nonfarm activities, whether informal or formal or in combination with farming or not. Identifying the constraints that restrict individuals in these ethnic groups from engagement in work outside of agriculture merits further investigation. These constraints may include lower demand for nonfarm workers in the north and lower educational attainment among the Yao and Lomwe relative to the Chewa and Nyanja.

The important role for education in moving people out of farming and into the nonfarm sectors is consistently and strongly seen in the association between educational attainment and the employment category of an individual—greater educational attainment results in much higher probabilities of working outside of agriculture and in formal, wage-based employment.[6]

There is a strong association between the level of household wealth, as proxied by the quality of housing for an individual, and engagement in any nonfarm employment, with somewhat stronger associations for purely nonfarm employment. This suggests that there are capital or other financial hurdles that may restrict working age individuals from poorer households engaging in nonfarm employment.

Turning to the results for the agriculture-related determinants, larger landholdings are associated with a lower propensity to be in nonfarm wage employment.[7] The significant relative risk ratio in the third column of results in Table 6.6 shows that wage employment is quite strongly associated with smaller landholdings. The results from separate MNL models for the age-defined sub-samples (not presented here) show that this is particularly the case for older youth and non-youth workers, rather than for younger youth, many of whom are dependents within their households. This is evidence that declining landholding size, driven in large part by population pressure, potentially is a significant push factor propelling heads of farming households and their spouses to seek a portion of the livelihoods for their households in wage labour off-farm.

---

[6] We also find that higher educational attainment is associated with a greater likelihood of not being economically active. However, this result primarily reflects current students at higher grade levels in the IHS-3 sample.

[7] The results on the landholding size variable for the two exclusively nonfarm employment categories (columns 5 and 6 in Table 6.6) should be disregarded, as these individuals principally will come from non-agricultural households.

Our MNL results provide no evidence that the receipt of Farm Input Subsidy Programme (FISP) benefits by a household in the cropping season prior to the IHS-3 survey resulted in individuals in that household being more likely to obtain work outside of agriculture. The significant association between a household having received FISP benefits and working age individuals in such households being unlikely to be employed both in agriculture and in nonfarm wage labour (column 4 in Table 6.6) can be interpreted in two ways: first, as the receipt of FISP benefits forestalling the need for an individual to engage in wage labour off-farm or, secondly, as simply reflecting the targeting of FISP, the eligibility criteria for which include the requirement that beneficiary households be fulltime farmers with no formal employment off-farm.

We do not find any effect of broad agroecological potential on employment choice. The base category is the relatively productive Mid-altitude Plateau and Highland agroecological zone. However, residence in the Lower Shire Valley zone or the Lakeshore (which here includes the Upper Shire Valley) zones, both of which experience more erratic or lower rainfall and are subject to more weather-related shocks than is seen in the Mid-altitude Plateau and Highland zone, does not result in a significantly different pattern of employment choice among those of working age.

The variables on market access (travel time) to small (5,000 population and up) and large (over 50,000 population) urban centres provide contrasting results. While the overall pattern for small population centres is that the longer it takes for an individual to travel to a small centre, the less likely they are to engage in nonfarm activities, this relationship is weak, with the relative risk ratios for most categories not being statistically significant. In contrast, poor access to large urban centres is strongly negatively associated with nonfarm employment. Given that larger urban centres are where most formal nonfarm employment opportunities are concentrated, this result is not surprising—improved access to a greater number of nonfarm employment opportunities will pull people out of exclusive agricultural employment. However, the limited impact of smaller population centres in rural areas on the employment choices of individuals located close to them calls into question whether these smaller towns have much of a role to play in changing labour patterns in Malawi and contributing to a structural transformation of the economy.

Finally, with regards to an individual experiencing a recent economic shock, we find that idiosyncratic shocks are not strongly associated with a propensity to engage in nonfarm employment, but are negatively associated with being not economically active. This may be a result of important variability in the economic significance of the shocks households reported experiencing, with this variability not being captured in the dummy variable used in the model, or through social community and kin networks effectively assisting households to cope with such shocks, minimizing the need for any workers in the household to seek out new employment. In contrast, individuals residing in communities that experienced drought are shown to be much more likely to engage in nonfarm employment either exclusively or in combination with farming. The shocks to agriculture-based livelihoods brought about by droughts provide incentives for individuals and households to diversify their economic activities beyond agriculture alone. As such, this result implies that if droughts in Malawi increase either in frequency or severity under climate change, they are likely to constitute an important push factor that encourages people to diversify their employment beyond agriculture.

To summarize the findings from our multinomial logit modelling of employment choice in Malawi, we find further confirmation that younger youth are not implicated in any shift in the sectoral composition of employment in Malawi. Older youth and non-youth, particularly males, are more central to such shifts. Educational attainment is strongly associated with employment outside of agriculture. This suggests that there are incentives associated with employment in the industry services and sectors operating to 'pull' people out of agriculture. However, the model results also show that small agricultural landholdings and experience of drought are factors 'pushing' people out of agriculture to seek nonfarm employment, whether on a part-time or exclusive basis or under formal (wage-labour) or informal (household enterprise) arrangements.

6.5 Discussion

This close analysis of patterns and trends in employment in Malawi does not provide evidence that the youth of Malawi are central to the slight shift in employment into the services sector observed over the period 2004 to 2013. The largest increase in share of those employed working in the services sector is among the non-youth group aged 35 to 64 years. Over this period, younger youth aged 15 to 24 are seen to increasingly choose to stay out of employment and extend their period of education. Those younger youth who are in the labour force, meaning, no longer in education, are much more likely to be working in agriculture than in the nonfarm sectors. This employment pattern reflects the fact that most of these younger youth remain dependents within their households and, for those coming from farming households, are expected to contribute their labour to family farm operations. Youth that are increasingly engaging in nonfarm employment are older males, those between 30 and 34 years of age. However, the sectoral share of employment of older youth is very similar to the share of the non-youth. In consequence, we find little evidence that there has been much change in how youth enter the workforce in Malawi.

The historical pattern of agriculture being the principal sector of engagement for those entering the workforce remains in place. Although we see some small movements of labour into the services sector, particularly by older workers, there is scant evidence of structural transformation in Malawi's economy. The share of those employed who work in agriculture remained relatively stable from 2004 to 2013, while a significant decline in the share of those who work in the industrial sector is observed. This decline balances to a large degree any increase in the share of workers in services, leaving the share in the agricultural sector comparatively fixed. Our analysis of employment in Malawi dampens hopeful thoughts that we might be seeing the start of a transformation in the structure of Malawi's economy. The structure remains dominated by agriculture, as it has been for generations.

Working in the nonfarm sectors is a step that increasing numbers of workers, but still relatively few, will take later in their work lives after they have built the financial capital, experience, and social networks needed to succeed outside of agriculture. The factors that push Malawians out of agriculture, some of which we have identified in our analysis, will continue to intensify due to rapid population growth. The government should take actions and undertake public investments that increasingly will pull people out of farming.

These include continued investments in education to improve access and quality. The strong association between educational attainment and engagement in remunerative formal nonfarm employment is clear and has been recognized for generations. In consequence, the free primary education programme of government over the past 20 years has played a role in the increasing share of older youth employed outside of agriculture. Maintaining high levels of investment in education is likely to be a factor in turning the small trickle of older youth seeking employment in the nonfarm sectors into a much more substantial flow.

However, while we see that younger youth are delaying their entry into employment in order to study further and higher educational attainment is strongly associated with improved chances for young people to find non-agricultural sector jobs, still agriculture remains the entry point for most Malawians entering employment. While better training may equip young farmers to adopt improved agricultural technologies and be more productive, we find mixed, if somewhat encouraging evidence in analysis of the IHS-3 of this being the case. Thirteen per cent of farming households headed by younger youth (ages 15 to 24 years) received a visit from an agricultural extension agent in the previous year and 21 per cent used inorganic fertilizer, compared to 17 and 29 per cent, respectively, of farming households headed by those aged 25 to 64 years of age. However, when the youth category is expanded to include those up to age 34 years, the pattern is reversed—households headed by youth ages 15 to 34 years are more likely than households headed by non-youth to receive visits from extension agents (20 per cent for youth-headed households, as against 15 per cent for non-youth headed households) and to use inorganic fertilizer (33 per cent, as against 25 per cent). This pattern is consistent with younger youth engaged in agricultural employment, as they become heads of their own households, having a greater propensity than their parents' generation to seek out and use improved farming techniques.

But for those Malawian youth who seek work outside of farming, it remains the case that for most education alone is not sufficient to enable them to obtain non-farm employment. There are relatively few high-quality jobs in Malawi in which well-trained Malawians can use their skills productively. Designing programmes and incentives to supply such jobs should be as pressing a public policy concern for the government of Malawi as improving the skills of the population through improved education services. Many of the jobs which are being created in the non-farm sectors today are relatively low productivity and offer little more in terms of economic output than can be achieved in smallholder farming. There is a foreign direct investment element to creating higher productivity jobs, as investors can provide the technology and access to markets upon which such jobs often will be based. Government can facilitate such increased investment from outside of Malawi. Government will also need to continue its efforts to upgrade energy and transport infrastructure and significantly increase its investments in urban development, as most of these new jobs will be located in the cities of Malawi and will require reliable power and better connections to regional and global markets.

Finally, while government needs to act in a manner that puts in place adequate incentives for all Malawians to find and engage in sufficiently remunerative work in any of the three sectors of the economy, agriculture will remain the sector in which most Malawians are employed for the foreseeable future. Consequently, it is important that public investments made to support growth and to promote change in the structure of the economy of Malawi do not neglect agriculture, particularly investments that strengthen its linkages with the industry and services sectors. Increased value-addition activities on agricultural products that involve more complex processing techniques and an expansion in the range of commodities used and products manufactured are likely to be central components in any structural transformation of the economy that results in significant expansion in employment in both the industry and services sectors. In consequence, we should expect that any growth in employment in the nonfarm sectors will primarily find its origins in a more vibrant, diverse, and productive agriculture sector. While balancing public investments across the three economic sectors is necessary, the level of effort being made to improve the productivity, linkages, and commercial prospects of Malawian agriculture should be increased.

References

Amemiya, T. 1985. *Advanced econometrics*. Cambridge, MA, U.S.A.: Harvard University Press.

Andersson Djurfeldt, A., G. Djurfeldt, and J. Bergman Lodin. 2013. Geography of gender gaps: Regional patterns of income and farm–nonfarm interaction among male- and female-headed households in eight African countries. *World Development* 48 (c): 32–47.

Arndt, C., K. Pauw, and J. Thurlow. 2016. The economy-wide impacts and risks of Malawi's Farm Input Subsidy Program. *American Journal of Agricultural Economics* 98 (3): 962–80.

Coleman, G. 1979. *International labour migration from Malawi.* Development Studies Occasional Paper No. 1. Norwich, U.K.: University of East Anglia, School of Development Studies.

Deichmann, U., F. Shilpi, and R. Vakis. 2009. Urban proximity, agricultural potential and rural nonfarm employment: Evidence from Bangladesh. *World Development* 37 (3): 645–60.

Ellis, F. 2000. *Rural livelihoods and diversity in developing countries.* Oxford, U.K.: Oxford University Press.

Fox, L., L. W. Senbet, and W. Simbanegavi. 2016. Youth employment in Sub-Saharan Africa: Challenges, constraints and opportunities. *Journal of African Economies* 25 (suppl. 1): i3–i15.

Greene, W. 2012. *Econometric analysis.* 7th ed. Upper Saddle River, NJ, U.S.A.: Prentice Hall.

Hall, G., and H. Patrinos (eds.). 2014. *Indigenous peoples, poverty and development.* Cambridge, U.K.: Cambridge University Press

Hart, K. 1973. Informal income opportunities and urban employment in Ghana. *The Journal of Modern African Studies* 11 (1): 61–89.

ILO (International Labour Organization). 2015. *Global employment trends for youth 2015: Scaling up investments in decent jobs for youth.* Geneva, Switzerland: ILO.

Jonasson, E., and S. M. Helfand. 2010. How important are locational characteristics for rural non-agricultural employment? Lessons from Brazil. *World Development* 38 (5): 727–41.

Lewin, K. M. 2009. Access to education in sub-Saharan Africa: Patterns, problems and possibilities. *Comparative Education* 45 (2): 151–74.

Long, J. S., and J. Freese. 2014. *Regression models for categorical dependent variables using Stata.* 3rd ed. College Station, TX, U.S.A.: Stata Press.

Lucas, R., and O. Stark. 1985. Motivations to remit: Evidence from Botswana. *Journal of Political Economy* 93 (5): 901–18.

Lunduka, R., J. Ricker-Gilbert, and M. Fisher. 2013. What are the farm-level impacts of Malawi's Farm Input Subsidy Program? A critical review. *Agricultural Economics* 44: 563–79.

Mambo, M. M., M. S. Meky, N. Tanaka, and J. Salmi. 2016. *Improving higher education in Malawi for competitiveness in the global economy.* A World Bank Study. Washington, DC, U.S.A.: World Bank.

NSO (National Statistical Office). 2010. *The 2006/07 Malawi National Census of Agriculture and Livestock.* Zomba, Malawi: NSO.

NSO (National Statistical Office). 2011a. *The 2008 Malawi Population and Housing Census—Population Projections Report.* Zomba, Malawi: NSO.

NSO (National Statistical Office). 2011b. *The 2008 Malawi Population and Housing Census—Migration Report*. Zomba, Malawi: NSO.

NSO (National Statistical Office). 2014. *Malawi Labour Force Survey 2013*. Report. Zomba, Malawi: NSO.

NSO (National Statistical Office). 2018. *Malawi Population and Housing Census—Preliminary Report*. Zomba, Malawi: NSO.

Reardon, T., J. Berdegue, C. B. Barrett, and K. Stamoulis. 2007. Household income diversification into rural nonfarm activities. In *Transforming the rural nonfarm economy: Opportunities and threats in the developing world*, ed. S. Haggblade, P. B. R. Hazell, and T. Reardon. Baltimore, MD, U.S.A.: Johns Hopkins University Press.

Ricker-Gilbert, J., C. Jumbe, and J. Chamberlin. 2014. How does population density influence agricultural intensification and productivity? Evidence from Malawi. *Food Policy* 48: 114–28.

Small, K., and C. Hsaio. 1985. Multinomial logit specification tests. *International Economic Review* 26: 619–28.

Vail, L. 1983. The state and the creation of colonial Malawi's agricultural economy. In *Imperialism, colonialism, and hunger: East and Central Africa*, ed. R. I. Rotberg. Lexington, MA, U.S.A.: Lexington Books.

World Bank. 2010. *The education system in Malawi*. World Bank Working Paper no. 182. Washington, DC, U.S.A.: World Bank.

World Bank. 2019. *World development indicators*. Washington, DC, U.S.A.: World Bank. http://wdi.worldbank.org/tables. Accessed 3 February 2019.

7

Cities and Rural Transformation

A Spatial Analysis of Rural Youth Livelihoods in Ghana

Xinshen Diao, Peixun Fang, Eduardo Magalhaes,
Stefan Pahl, and Jed Silver

7.1 Introduction

Ghana has been rapidly urbanizing in the past two decades. The 2010 Population and Housing Census revealed that for the first time more than half of the population lived in the country's urban areas. However, urbanization and economic structural change in Ghana has not followed the normal historical pathway for the economic transformation of an agrarian country (Osei and Jedwab 2016). In China, and much of Asia, urbanization typically followed a period of substantial growth in agricultural productivity (the Green Revolution) that, amongst other things, freed up labour to move into the urban sectors. At the same time, rapid growth in labour-intensive industries, especially export manufacturing, offered productive jobs to workers leaving agriculture (Timmer 1988, Mellor 1976, Rosegrant and Hazell 2000). The pattern of transformation in Ghana is quite different. Ghana has neither undergone a Green Revolution (Nin-Pratt and McBride 2014) nor an industrial revolution (Jedwab 2013), yet urbanization has nonetheless been rapid without industrialization, which typically leads to the rise of 'consumption cities' dominated by employment in nontradable services (Gollin, Jedwab, and Vollrath 2013). A similar phenomenon has been observed for many African countries (Headey, Bezemer and Hazell 2010, McMillan and Rodrik 2011, Diao, McMillan, and Rodrik 2017).

Ghana is one of the many African countries that have experienced recent youth bulges coupled with increasing concerns from policymakers about youth employment. With manufacturing share of GDP falling from 15 per cent in the early 1980s to less than 5 per cent in recent years (The World Bank 2018), the slow creation of manufacturing jobs has particularly strong implications for youth entering the

Authors of this chapter would like to dedicate the chapter to the memory of Eduardo Magalhaes who sadly and prematurely passed away in August 2017.

Xinshen Diao, Peixun Fang, Eduardo Magalhaes, Stefan Pahl, and Jed Silver, *Cities and Rural Transformation: A Spatial Analysis of Rural Youth Livelihoods in Ghana* In: *Youth and Jobs in Rural Africa: Beyond Stylized Facts*. Edited by: Valerie Mueller and James Thurlow, Oxford University Press (2019). © International Food Policy Research Institute. DOI: 10.1093/oso/9780198848059.003.0007

labour force. Moreover, youth are entering the workforce with higher educational attainment, leading them to demand a different type of job. As is the case throughout the world, the aspirations of most youth in Ghana lie in urban areas and away from rural lifestyles, especially farming (Anyidoho, Leavy, and Asenso-Okyere 2012). However, not only are jobs scarce, but even many highly educated youth lack the necessary skills for them (Aryeetey and Baah-Boateng 2015). Rapid urbanization has also raised concerns among policymakers about the potential effects of the exit of youth from agriculture and an aging agricultural labour force on production and productivity. As youth leave farming and rural areas with rapid urbanization as a backdrop, this chapter assesses the level of the exit from agricultural employment, to what extent youth are leading this process, and if it is true, what are the effects on the structure of rural economy and livelihoods.

It is important to situate the youth employment discussion within the broader context of urbanization. Much of the literature surrounding urbanization and its effects on the rural nonfarm economy (RNFE) builds off the classic Harris and Todaro (1970) framework, in which higher potential returns encourage labour to move from less productive rural agriculture to more productive urban sectors. According to this theory, increases in agricultural productivity also create a push effect that complements the pull of urban manufacturing in influencing rural–urban migration. The RNFE also develops as a result of agriculture–consumption linkages driven by rising farm incomes—particularly through increases in informal trade and local food processing (Haggblade, Hazell, and Brown 1989). Such linkages may contribute to urbanization by releasing labour from agriculture or result from it as urban sectors absorb excess rural employment and open up land for the remaining farmers. As all of these changes take place, the induced technical change theory developed by Hayami and Ruttan (1970, 1985) predicts that farmers would shift their production practices towards more intensive technologies such as fertilizers, hired labour, and other modern inputs to meet rising market demand while also adopting labour-saving technologies such as mechanization as labour becomes more scarce. Through all these factors working together, it can be expected that urbanization would lead to poverty reduction and a more vibrant economy in rural areas. Ravallion, Chen, and Sangraula (2007) show that this has occurred on aggregate in all regions except for Sub-Saharan Africa, where there is no evidence of a strong association between urbanization and rural poverty reduction overall. However, such trends may have recently developed in many African countries, potentially those with strong economic growth performance and at relatively more advanced stages of economic transformation, including Ghana (Kolavalli et al. 2012).

Ghana has always been relatively urbanized compared to other African countries. This is partially due to the post-independence expansion of the cocoa sector (Jedwab, 2013) and the promotion of state-owned industry in the later 1960s and early 1970s (Ackah, Adjasi, and Turkson 2014). By 2010, Ghana's urban population—defined as people living in settlements of more than 5,000 people—surpassed 50 per cent of total population for the first time (GSS 2013). While Accra and Kumasi, Ghana's two megacities, continue to attract migrants, the growth of secondary cities and rural towns has also contributed to Ghana's urbanization in recent years.

Although Ghana has become a low middle-income country and has been considered an African success story, urbanization in Ghana appears not to be associated with the development of labour-intensive manufacturing as observed in much of Asia. Cocoa, gold, and oil accounted for about 80 per cent of Ghana's exports in 2013, while manufacturing growth has been minimal (Aryeetey and Baah-Boateng 2015). Such a case of urbanization without industrialization typically leads to the rise of 'consumption cities' dominated by employment in nontradable services (Gollin, Jedwab, and Vollrath 2016). Therefore, urbanization in Ghana may not be able to generate sufficient manufacturing jobs although engaging in urban informal economy could still be an alternative to the rural poor. As such, development of the RNFE, which can also be driven by urbanization, may be especially important for growth and poverty reduction in Ghana. In a previous study in Northern Ghana, Owusu, Abdulai, and Abdul-Rahman (2011) show that diversification of farm households into nonfarm work is associated with higher income and greater food security.

Therefore, rather than focusing on the rural to urban migration in understanding the impact of urbanization on Ghana's economic transformation, we focus on the proximity of rural areas to different sizes of cities to assess the linkages between urbanization and rural economic structural change. Similar to Berdegue et al. (2015) in Latin America, we group districts in Ghana by the size of their largest city into four categories; those with no city, small (3rd tier) cities, medium (2nd tier) cities, and metropolises (big cities). This is because other studies have found a population threshold below which cities do not have a major impact on the RNFE while large metropolises exert much larger impacts (Berdegue et al. 2015, Deichmann, Shilpi, and Vakis 2008). An alternative method of capturing the effect of proximity to cities on rural areas would be to measure urban gravity by the light intensity emanating from urban areas reaching rural villages as Binswanger et al. (2016) do for Kenya; however, the required panel data is not available for Ghana.

Ghana has a well-defined south–north divide, which, amongst other things, reflects spatial differences in agroecological conditions, population density, rural infrastructure, and levels of urbanization. We therefore need to take this south–north divide into consideration when analysing spatial heterogeneity associated with cities of different sizes. Focusing on the geographical divide and spatial heterogeneity associated with cities of different sizes, we analyze recent trends in rural household livelihoods in Ghana with a focus on youth. We use data from the two rounds of Ghana's Population and Housing Census in 2000 and 2010 (GSS 2003, 2013) and the two rounds of Ghana Living

Standards Surveys conducted in 2005–6 and 2012–13 [GLSS5 (GSS 2008) and GLSS6 (GSS 2014)] in our analysis.

We focus on four broad questions in the analysis. First, are patterns of rural employment changing with urbanization and do these changes have any spatial patterns that are associated with proximity to cities of different sizes? Secondly, what are the impacts of rural transformation on the youth in rural areas? Thirdly, what are the impacts of urbanization on agricultural intensification for youth and non-youth? Finally, what are the welfare or income implications of the rural transformation that has created heterogeneous livelihood opportunities? In the next section we address the first two questions together. The third section turns to the third question and analyses the relationship of urbanization and agricultural intensification. The following section addresses the fourth question and discusses the heterogeneous outcomes of poverty reduction and rising middle-class associated with patterns of rural livelihoods. The final section concludes with a few key policy implications.

7.2 Changing Patterns of Rural Employment and Economic Activities with Urbanization

In Ghana, a steady rise in the share of urban population has been accompanied by a rapid exit from agriculture. As shown in Figure 7.1a, the urban population growth rate is consistently more than triple the rural population growth rate, except during the period of poor economic growth under the import substitution strategy between 1970 and 1984. Meanwhile, the share of agriculture in total employment also drops, down to 41.6 per cent in 2010 according to the 2010 census. In 2000–10, the growth rate of agricultural employment falls to below 1 per cent, or about half the rural population growth rate, while the growth rate of non-agricultural employment rises from 3 per cent to above 5 per cent in the same period (Figure 7.1b). This indicates that a rapid expansion of RNFE in the recent years could be a reason for the larger discrepancy between growth rates in agricultural and non-agricultural employment than that between growth rates in rural and urban population.

We classify rural households into three types based on members' reported primary occupations in both the Census and GLSS data: (1) rural households whose members' primary employment is in agriculture and no family members primarily engaged in non-agriculture, for which we call 'agriculture only' households; (2) rural households of which all members' primary employment is in non-agriculture, which are called 'non-agriculture only' households; and (3) households that have members with primary employment in both agriculture and non-agriculture, called 'mixed' households. There is also a small percentage of rural households that do not report any primary employment (classified as 'no-job' households) that are not covered in the analysis.

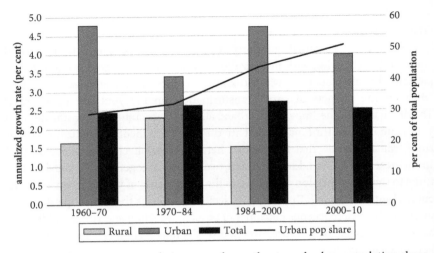

Figure 7.1a. Inter-census population annual growth rate and urban population share in census years

Note: Urban population share is for the census years, which is the ending year of each period in x-axis.

Source: Authors' calculation using data from the five rounds of censuses (GSS 2013).

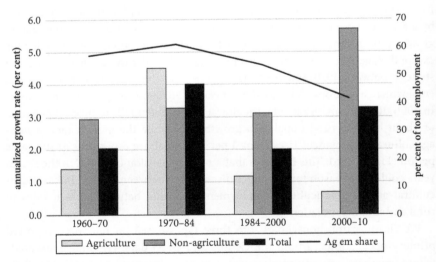

Figure 7.1b. Inter-census employment annual growth rate and agricultural share of total employment in census years

Note: Urban population share is for the census years, which is the ending year of each period in x-axis.

Source: Authors' calculation using data from the five rounds of censuses (GSS 2013).

The groups of households are based on household members' primary employment, which does not imply that agricultural or non-agricultural households do not have incomes created outside their primary jobs. In fact, it is common that some agricultural households have nonfarm income from secondary employment or household enterprises while many rural non-agricultural households also farm. The secondary employment in rural nonfarm activities and nonfarm household enterprises are highly seasonal and unlikely to be households' main income sources. 70 per cent of non-agricultural households who farm have cultivated land less than 2ha, indicating that farming is a part-time activity for most of them. Based on the two rounds of the Census and two rounds of GLSS, Table 7.1 provides the distribution of agricultural and non-agricultural households in the four different survey years. Using data from GLSS5 and GLSS6, the last two columns of Table 7.1 also provide percentages of agricultural and non-agricultural households that have income outside their primary jobs.

Table 7.1 shows the increases in the proportion of non-agricultural households in total rural households alongside a declining share of agricultural households over time according to both the census and GLSS. Somewhat surprisingly, the share of mixed households increased modestly between the GLSS survey years and declined modestly between the two rounds of the census. Compared with the percentage of agriculture-only households in total rural households, shares of agricultural households with nonfarm enterprises are small and declined over time (14.6 per cent versus 11.6 per cent of total rural households in GLSS5 and GLSS6, respectively, see column (5) of Table 7.1). On the other hand, the share of non-agricultural households with cultivated farmland is significant in 2005–6, that is, 9.6 percentage points out of the 19.7 per cent of rural households classified as non-agricultural households do farm. However, in 2012–13, when the share of non-agricultural households increased to 24.8 per cent, the percentage of such households with farmland actually fell (to 8.6 per cent, column (6) of Table 7.1). Table 7.1 seems to suggest a trend in which rural households in Ghana tend to be exiting agriculture altogether rather than diversifying within households. This finding is somewhat puzzling given the extensive literature on intra-household diversification (Owusu, Abdulai, and Abdul-Rahman 2013).

7.2.1 Spatial heterogeneity of rural employment patterns

We now turn to the spatial heterogeneity of rural employment patterns. Ghana has a well-defined south–north divide, which, amongst other things, reflects spatial differences in agroecological conditions, population density, rural infrastructure, and levels of urbanization. We therefore first differentiate between two major regions based on both the north–south divide and agroecological conditions. We define the agriculturally dominant north, which comprises the regions of Brong

Table 7.1. Distribution of rural households by members' primary employment in Ghana (Columns (1)–(4) sum to 100 in each survey year)

Survey	Survey year	Agriculture only	Non-agriculture only	Agriculture and non-agriculture mixed	No job	Agricultural with nonfarm enterprise	Non-agricultural with cultivated farmland
		(1)	(2)	(3)	(4)	(5)	(6)
Census	2000	56.9	15.9	18.3	8.9		
GLSS5	2005/06	58.3	19.7	15.7	6.3	14.6	9.6
Census	2010	51.1	25.0	17.2	6.7		
GLSS6	2012/13	54.2	24.8	16.6	4.5	11.6	8.6

Notes: The type of households is defined according to the household members' primary employment status; column (5) is part of column (1) and column (6) is part of column (2).

Sources: Authors calculation using data of Census 2000 and Census 2010 (GSS 2003, 2013) and GLSS5 and GLSS6 (GSS 2008, 2014).

Ahafo, Northern, Upper East, and Upper West, as the 'North'. The North has a low population density, is relatively far from large cities, and most of its rural households are predominantly engaged in farming. The North also corresponds closely to the Savanna and Transition agroecological zones. The remaining six regions: Ashanti, Central, Eastern, Greater Accra, Volta, and Western, are then grouped into the 'South', which is less reliant on agriculture, is more urbanized, has a higher population density, and has a more developed RNFE. The South corresponds closely to the Forest and Coastal agroecological zones.

Like cities, most rural non-agricultural households are also concentrated in the six southern regions of Ghana. For the South as a whole, 30 per cent of rural households are non-agricultural in 2010, increasing from 18 per cent in 2000. While the North is much more agriculture dominant, the share of non-agricultural households also increases, but more slowly, from a lower base of 10 per cent in 2000 to 13 per cent in 2010.

Combining the north–south divide with the proximity to different sized cities that are considered at district level, we further define types of districts in both regions: (a) 'big city districts' that contain cities of more than 500,000 people; these districts correspond to the cities of Accra and Kumasi and are therefore all located in the South; (b) '2nd-tier city districts' whose largest cities have populations between 100,000 and 500,000; (c) '3rd-tier city districts' whose largest cities have populations between 40,000 and 100,000; and (d) 'no city districts' groups in which there are no cities or towns with populations over 40,000. In summary, there are three district groups in the North (in which there are no big city districts) and four in the South.

Figure 7.2 combines 2010 Census data and spatial data for cities to display the geographic locations of these seven groups of districts.

Although the South covers a much smaller land area than the North, the 2010 census shows that 73 per cent of the total population and 63 per cent of the rural population lives in the South. Moreover, the majority of the total population lives in districts with cities of at least 40,000 people in both types of regions, while about 40 per cent of the rural population lives in such districts. Table 7.2 displays the distribution of rural households by the three groups among the seven types of districts for all households versus youth-headed households. We ignore the small 'no-job' group in the table.

Comparing with the employment patterns for all rural households, the patterns for the youth-headed households in the North are similar but quite different in the South in 2000. This is particularly true for the proportion of rural households engaging in agriculture. In 2000, 60.9 per cent northern rural households could be defined as agriculture only, and the share is even higher, at 62.2 per cent, for the youth-headed in the region. In the same year on the other hand, 55.3 per cent southern rural households are agricultural only, and the share for the youth-headed households in the South is 51.1 per cent. Between the rural total and youth-headed households, the differences in the proportion engaging in

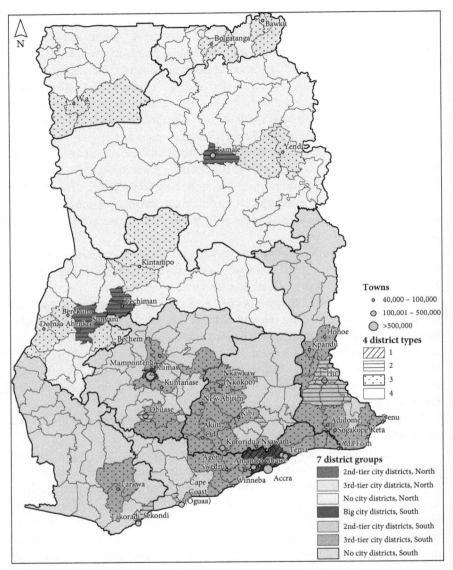

Figure 7.2. Ghana map showing the different types of districts

Source: This map was created by Mekamu Kedir Jemal (IFPRI), combining 2010 Census data with other spatial data including cities and road networks. Spatial data of cities, towns and road network are from University of Ghana—Remote Sensing and Geographic InfoSystems website (accessed on 25 March 2016 and retrieved from http://www.ug.edu.gh/rsgislab/rs-gis-geonode-app.html).

non-agriculture are larger than that engaging in agriculture. In 2000, only 9.7 per cent northern rural households engaged in non-agriculture, while the share was 12.7 per cent for youth-headed in the North. In the South, the discrepancy in this share is as high as 7.5 percentage points for all rural households (18.4 per cent) and for youth-headed (25.9 per cent).

Table 7.2. Distribution of rural households by agricultural, non-agricultural, and mixed occupations across district groups—rural total versus youth-headed households

	North			South		
	Ag only	Nonag only	Ag&nonag mixed	Ag only	Nonag only	Ag&nonag mixed
Rural all households						
2000						
Big city districts				27.7	50.3	12.3
2nd tier city districts	53.8	18.2	20.3	38.3	32.4	14.9
3rd tier city districts	58.2	11.2	19.1	50.1	21.1	18.8
No city districts	62.6	8.2	19.0	61.5	13.9	17.9
Total	60.9	9.7	19.1	55.3	18.4	18.0
2010						
Big city districts				9.0	74.1	6.6
2nd tier city districts	37.7	34.9	20.4	14.9	59.7	10.2
3rd tier city districts	63.7	14.5	17.8	39.4	34.1	17.4
No city districts	67.5	10.5	18.6	53.4	23.0	17.0
Regional total	64.7	13.0	18.5	45.6	29.7	16.7
Rural youth-headed households						
2000						
Big city districts				25.1	53.9	9.5
2nd tier city districts	55.4	22.5	12.1	30.4	38.2	11.3
3rd tier city districts	58.5	14.9	14.7	45.2	30.0	14.4
No city districts	64.3	10.7	15.3	58.1	20.4	13.7
Total	62.2	12.7	14.9	51.1	25.9	13.7
2010						
Big city districts				6.3	76.5	4.3
2nd tier city districts	30.6	45.4	9.5	9.1	64.1	4.3
3rd tier city districts	57.0	23.1	12.2	28.8	48.9	11.0
No city districts	64.9	15.9	14.8	45.4	34.3	11.6
Regional total	60.3	20.0	13.7	36.4	42.5	10.9

Note: the households that did not report any primary job are not reported in the table; therefore, the sum of the three groups of households does not equal 100.

Source: *Understanding the Role of Rural Non-Farm Enterprises in Africa's Economic Transformation: Evidence from Tanzania*, Xinshen Diao, Eduardo Magalhaes, et al, Journal of Development Studies, May 4 2018, Taylor and Francis, reprinted by permission of the publisher (Taylor & Francis Ltd, http://www.tandfonline.com).

Between 2000 and 2010, the share of 'non-agriculture only' rural households increased in all district groups in both South and North for all households as well as for youth-headed, though most rapidly in the South and especially in the big city and 2nd tier city district groups, and more so among youth-headed households. This was mirrored by an almost equivalent pattern of decline in the shares of 'agriculture only' rural households in the South and in the district group with 2nd tier cities in the North for all households, while for youth-headed households, it happened almost everywhere. For the North as a whole or in its districts that either have small cities or no cities, the shares of agriculture only households increased in this period for all households but declined for youth-headed (and only in the no-city district group did it keep almost constant). Thus, there has been a sizeable shift from agriculture to RNFE in the South for all rural households but mainly for youth-headed households in the North. In both South and North, the agriculture exits of rural households including youth-headed ones are highly correlated with proximity to cities. Despite this exit, the share of 'agriculture only' youth-headed households remains high in the North mainly in its districts without cities. On the other hand, 'non-agriculture only' households constitute the majority of southern youth-headed households in 2010 even in the district group without cities.

There has been a modest but surprising decline in the shares of mixed employment rural households across district groups in both North and South both for youth-headed and all households (Table 7.2). These are households where some members have diversified into primary non-agricultural occupations while other members continue to work primarily in agriculture. Thus, while many rural households have switched their primary occupation entirely from agriculture to non-agriculture, a declining share of rural households are straddling the two sectors through their primary occupations. However, Table 7.2 is based on the census data, which does not capture secondary or part time occupations. So it is possible that many more rural households have mixed livelihoods than shown in Table 7.2, although on a part time basis.

7.2.2 Factors Determining the Patterns of Rural Livelihoods

We next try to understand factors associated with the determinants of being a non-agricultural household in the rural areas as well as the changes that have taken place between two rounds of surveys. We pool the two most recent rounds of GLSS together for the analysis. Given the binary nature of the employment outcomes, we estimate a series of probit regressions to investigate the effects of covariates of interest on the probability of household being a non-agricultural household.

Equation (1) provides a general specification of the probit models used throughout this chapter:

$$y = \alpha + \sum_{k=1}^{K} \beta_k x_k + \varepsilon \tag{1}$$

where y takes the value of 1 if the household is non-agricultural, and zero otherwise. The estimation of y is conditional on observables. In equation (1), α is a constant, x_k and β_k refer to each covariate of interest and its corresponding parameter, and ε is an identically identified and distributed error term assumed to be distributed normally with mean zero and variance Ω.

We consider individual (household), spatial and community characteristics in the analysis. For the individual characteristic variables, the covariates are as follows: whether the household is headed by a young member (15 to 34 years old), by female, and the three levels of education of the household head. The spatial factors are a set of dummies for the seven district types representing the levels of urbanization, while the community factors are a set of public-good variables including accesses to electricity, public transport, and market. Since we have pooled two years of survey data, we also include a year dummy (2012–13) for GLSS6 and two interaction terms: a year dummy interacted with whether the household head is young, and a year dummy interacted with whether the household head is female. We also stratify regressions by the sample of i) youth-headed rural households, and ii) other adult households separately. In all the regressions for the three types of household (all, youth-headed, other-adult-headed), we compare non-agriculture-only households with the rest of rural households (Table 7.3, columns (a)–(c)) as well as with agriculture/non-agriculture mixed households (Table 7.3, columns (d)–(f)). The similar exercise was done also for pooling two rounds of census data for 2000 and 2010, of which the results are provided in the (see Tables 7.A1 and 7.A2).

Starting with Columns (a)–(c) of Table 7.3, we observe an increase in the probability of being a non-agricultural household over time. Yet, mainly youth-headed rural households lead the transition from agricultural to non-agricultural-dominated activities in 2005–12. The finding that youth households have left agriculture more than other adult households is consistent with the descriptive analysis in the previous section.

Being a female-headed rural household also increases the probability of being a non-agricultural household. However, the interaction between the year and gender dummies is negative, implying that, over time, gender becomes a less important factor in the explanation of being a non-agricultural household.

The sign and magnitude of the marginal effects of education on the probabilities of being a non-agricultural household are expected, that is, the more educated a head of household is, the higher the probability for this household to be non-agricultural, regardless of whether the head is young.

The estimation results for district group dummies are more consistent across districts in the South than in the North, that is, the marginal effect on the probability of being a non-agricultural household (relative to northern rural areas without city) is 27.2 per cent in the southern district group with big cities, while the probability is 7.75 per cent and 7.40 per cent, respectively, in the southern districts groups with 2nd tier or 3rd tier cities, and it reduces further to 2.55 per cent for the group of southern districts without a city. On the other hand, in the North, the coefficient is not significant for the 2nd tier city district group and is only weakly significant for the 3rd tier city district group, indicating that proximity to

Table 7.3. Marginal effects of probit model regressions on factors affecting being a non-agricultural household, pooled data of GLSS5 and GLSS6

Independent variable	Comparing with the rest of households (agricultural households and mixed households)			Comparing with mixed households only		
	All households	Youth-headed households	Other-adult-headed households	All households	Youth-headed households	Other-adult-headed households
	(a)	(b)	(c)	(d)	(e)	(f)
Year dummy for 2012–13	0.0232**	0.0677***	0.00870	0.0205	0.0628**	0.000740
	(0.00921)	(0.0186)	(0.0102)	(0.0175)	(0.0250)	(0.0228)
Youth-headed households	0.123***			0.216***		
	(0.00908)			(0.0166)		
Female-headed households	0.150***	0.232***	0.132***	0.291***	0.349***	0.296***
	(0.00984)	(0.0215)	(0.0111)	(0.0182)	(0.0326)	(0.0231)
Year dummy * Youth	0.0487*			0.0552		
	(0.0209)			(0.0552)		
Year dummy * Gender	-0.0548***			-0.1038***		
	(0.0232)			(0.0355)		
Education level ('no education' omitted)						
Primary completed	0.0802***	0.0720***	0.0780***	0.0545***	0.00719	0.0704***
	(0.0102)	(0.0204)	(0.0115)	(0.0196)	(0.0284)	(0.0256)
Secondary completed	0.213***	0.198***	0.214***	0.154***	0.0303	0.215***
	(0.0156)	(0.0283)	(0.0187)	(0.0287)	(0.0395)	(0.0371)
University and above	0.411***	0.560***	0.353***	0.385***	0.455***	0.396***
	(0.0445)	(0.125)	(0.0490)	(0.0677)	(0.105)	(0.0842)

Type of district group (base is no-city district, North)

	(1)	(2)	(3)	(4)	(5)	(6)
2nd-tier-city districts, North	0.0205 (0.0417)	−0.0241 (0.0733)	0.0382 (0.0458)	0.0637 (0.0763)	0.0845 (0.117)	0.0308 (0.0929)
3rd-tier-city districts, North	0.0290* (0.0161)	0.0398 (0.0347)	0.0194 (0.0170)	0.0649** (0.0329)	0.0373 (0.0509)	0.0790** (0.0389)
Big-city districts, South	0.272*** (0.0428)	0.470*** (0.0855)	0.176*** (0.0494)	0.261*** (0.0815)	0.396*** (0.0928)	0.180* (0.108)
2nd-tier-city districts, South	0.0775* (0.0409)	0.254*** (0.0772)	0.0145 (0.0482)	−0.0353 (0.0729)	0.130 (0.101)	−0.116 (0.0980)
3rd-tier-city districts, South	0.0740*** (0.0129)	0.143*** (0.0262)	0.0462*** (0.0140)	0.0367 (0.0248)	0.0901*** (0.0344)	0.0108 (0.0310)
No-city districts, South	0.0255** (0.0117)	0.0954*** (0.0232)	−0.00721 (0.0130)	0.00189 (0.0235)	0.111*** (0.0326)	−0.0577* (0.0297)
Community variable						
Access to markets	0.0675*** (0.0107)	0.0745*** (0.0218)	0.0603*** (0.0119)	0.0837*** (0.0198)	0.0576** (0.0291)	0.0949*** (0.0255)
Access to public transportation	0.0556*** (0.0106)	0.0799*** (0.0219)	0.0461*** (0.0116)	0.0407* (0.0217)	0.0398 (0.0314)	0.0482* (0.0278)
Access to electricity	0.0665*** (0.0101)	0.112*** (0.0196)	0.0434*** (0.0113)	0.0538*** (0.0199)	0.0687** (0.0284)	0.0403 (0.0260)
Observations	11,245	3,255	7,990	4,202	1,357	2,845

Notes: Only rural households are included in the regressions. Number of the pooled sample obs. is 12,515. * $p < 0.1$, ** $p < 0.05$, *** $p < 0.01$.
The regressions include only rural households. Number of the pooled sample obs. is 12,515. * $p < 0.1$, ** $p < 0.05$, *** $p < 0.01$.

Source: Authors' own estimation using GLSS5 and GLSS6.

cities seems to be less important for determining northern rural households to be non-agricultural. In the South, the consistent patterns persist among youth-headed households, with the magnitude of the marginal effect being even larger, but only hold for the big city districts and 3rd tier city districts for the other adult households. Again, in the North, the coefficients of district group dummies for youth or other adult-headed households are all insignificant. The estimation results for district group dummies seem to indicate that it is the combination of north–south divide and proximity to different sized cities that determines the likelihood of being non-agricultural households in the rural areas. Only in the more urbanized South that proximity to larger sized cities could further increase the likelihood of being non-agricultural households.

The sign and magnitude of the marginal effects for a set of variables representing the infrastructural conditions at the rural community level are also as expected. Better access to market, public transportation or electricity seems to positively contribute to the likelihood of a rural household to be non-agricultural, regardless of whether the household head is young.

In the second panel of Table 7.3 (columns (d)–(f)), non-agricultural households are compared with the mixed group instead of the rest of the households. The purpose for this comparison is that households in the mixed group have also had nonfarm activities. Since some non-agricultural households also farm (not as primary employment), this comparison can help us to see whether these two groups are indeed different or just a way households report their primary employment. The marginal effects of some of the selected variables change in this comparison (in columns (d)–(f)) from those in columns (a)–(c). First, the significance of the coefficients on the year dummy and its interaction with the youth dummy disappear. Second, there are only a few cases in which the signs for the district group dummies are fully consistent. However, the likelihood of being a rural non-agricultural household still increases in southern districts with proximity to cities when it is compared with a mixed household, at least in the big-city and third-tier-city district groups (but not in the second-tier-city districts in the South).

7.2.3 Structure of the RNFE

With rural youth increasingly being engaged in the RNFE, it is important to further examine the patterns of rural non-agricultural employment. It is well known that recent non-agricultural employment growth in many African countries has occurred predominantly in the informal economy (McMillan and Rodrik 2011). This is also the case for Ghana, both in its rural and urban areas, in which 76 per cent and 69 per cent of employment was informal according to the 2010 Census. We define the formal economy as the combination of public sector (including international organizations and NGOs) and the formal private sector (including foreign companies) and is characterized by formal wage earnings. We define the informal economy as those working on their own businesses or as self-employed. The growth of nonfarm employment in rural areas may support the theory that as the influence of cities spreads to rural areas, their employment structures begin to more closely resemble those of urban areas. As in urban areas, formal employment could also provide better and more reliable livelihood opportunities for rural workers, especially youth.

We consider non-agricultural only household in this sub-section (that is, do not include the mixed group), and classify these households into different non-agricultural employment categories according to all household members' engagement in the formal and informal economies. We classify a rural household as 'formal only' if all the employed household members are in the formal non-agricultural economy. For a household with family members working in both the formal and informal nonfarm economies, we classify it as 'formal/informal combined'. Households with all employed members working in the informal nonfarm economy are classified as 'informal only', which is further grouped as 'informal manufacturing' and 'informal trade' (see Table 7.4).

We focus on a comparison between youth and all rural households first. As can be seen from Table 7.4, while the rural nonfarm sector is largely informal, youth-headed households seem to have fewer chances to be either in the formal only category or in the formal/informal combined category than other adults. This holds in both years, at the national level, as well as in the North and the South. With few exceptions, this is also true across district groups in both years. This is an alarming finding, indicating that while youth are more likely to leave agriculture than other adults, they have much fewer opportunities than other adults to get formal employment jobs. The fact that a majority of youth who exit from agriculture are engaging in the informal sector seems to call a different type of policy emphasizing the improvement of labour productivity and hence income generation for youth in the informal sector rather than focusing on job creation in the formal sector.

For the rural non-agricultural households that engage in the rural informal economy, it seems that the majority of them engage in only one type of informal activity—either informal manufacturing or trade. This is also true for youth-headed households. For rural non-agricultural households as a whole, informal trade is more prevalent than informal manufacturing at the national level, particularly in the South, and more so in 2010 than in 2000. For youth-headed non-agricultural households, there seems to be little difference between these two types of activities at the national level and in the South, while for the northern young households, they are actually engaging more in manufacturing. Essentially, rural manufacturing seems to be dominant in areas that are less urbanized and thus more isolated from the national market, likely because rural informal manufacturing primarily consists of food processing for the local

Table 7.4. Types of different non-agricultural households according to family members' employment

	Rural households, all				Rural youth-headed households			
	Formal only	Inf. mfg only	Inf. trade only	Formal/informal combined	Formal only	Inf. mfg only	Inf. trade only	Formal/informal combined
2000								
North								
2nd tier city districts	30.1	10.5	21.6	23.7	28.1	15.7	23.3	16.7
3rd tier city districts	16.1	27.5	14.0	19.3	11.7	31.7	19.7	7.8
No city districts	21.7	25.6	18.7	15.7	20.8	30.0	23.5	5.5
North total	21.0	24.4	17.6	17.8	19.4	28.3	22.4	7.8
South								
Big city districts	27.7	6.3	15.5	34.5	30.7	10.6	21.2	19.8
2nd tier city districts	24.8	10.1	22.7	27.1	22.8	15.1	28.8	14.2
3rd tier city districts	19.4	16.2	23.6	22.1	16.2	24.0	26.4	9.2
No city districts	23.6	16.8	22.1	20.9	21.1	24.6	25.7	9.9
South total	22.1	15.3	22.2	22.9	19.7	23.1	26.0	10.3
National total	21.9	16.9	21.4	22.0	19.6	24.0	25.4	9.9
2010								
North								
2nd tier city districts	29.2	5.4	20.8	30.0	30.1	17.9	23.6	9.8
3rd tier city districts	24.0	14.7	21.2	21.5	12.5	30.0	22.9	5.4
No city districts	22.9	19.0	22.0	20.4	19.3	29.8	23.3	3.8
North total	24.3	15.6	21.6	22.3	19.0	28.1	23.2	5.1
South								
Big city districts	24.0	6.0	19.5	36.6	26.4	11.3	25.8	17.0
2nd tier city districts	25.4	8.8	20.0	31.9	22.3	16.7	31.7	10.1
3rd tier city districts	20.5	14.5	24.1	24.5	16.0	25.5	24.6	7.4
No city districts	23.6	13.3	25.3	22.4	20.6	26.2	25.8	7.3
South total	22.3	13.2	24.1	24.8	19.2	24.7	25.7	7.9
National total	22.6	13.5	23.7	24.4	19.1	25.3	25.3	7.4

Note: We skip the households that report both manufacturing and trade informal employments or any other informal employment (without formal employment) from the table; therefore, the sum of the four groups of households does not equal 100.

market, which can take place at the household level. For example, in the northern district group with small cities or without a city, 30 per cent or more youth-headed non-agricultural households fall into 'informal manufacturing only' category in both 2000 and 2010. Meanwhile informal trade may signify the opposite, given that trade activities are associated with both agricultural and non-agricultural commodities to meet local demand in rural areas, reflecting greater connectivity with the broader economy. This pattern of non-agricultural activities can be found in the more urbanized South and is particularly true in southern district groups with big and secondary cities both for youth-headed households and rural non-agricultural households in general. This reflects the findings of Haggblade, Hazell, and Brown (1989) and the literature on urban–rural linkages in general.

7.3 Urbanization and Agricultural Intensification

Drawing on the Boserup (1965)–Ruthenberg (1980) theories of farming systems evolution, impact of urbanization on technology adoption in agriculture is mainly through increases in population density and market access, which is expected to lead to more intensive farming practices and adoption of modern technology for improving land and labour productivity (Binswanger and Ruttan 1978, Ruttan 2002, Diao et al. 2014). We examine these relationships in this section.

We use a probit model to test how the probability of using different types of modern inputs is associated with urbanization, while controlling for a number of household and locational characteristics. These characteristics include farm size thresholds, household head characteristics (youth, gender, level of education), the degree of urbanization of the districts in which the households live (using our district typology), and a set of infrastructure variables such as access to markets, public transportation, and electricity at the rural community level. In the regression, we only include the rural households of which agriculture is the primary occupation for all or some family members, since for most households defined as 'non-agriculture only' in the section above, agricultural activity, if there is any, appears to be part-time.

As in the second section, we have pooled data together from the two rounds of surveys—GLSS5 and GLSS6 in the regression, and hence we also include a dummy for 2012–13 (GLSS6), as well as the interaction terms for year and youth, and year and gender in the regression. In spite of the limitations of using repeated cross-sections for this analysis, for example, omitted variable bias, the regressions reveal some interesting associations.

In Table 7.5, the regression estimates illustrate that urbanization, as captured through our typology, has significant yet complex links with agricultural intensification. Rural households in all the three district groups in the agriculturally

Table 7.5. Marginal effect of probit model regressions on factors affecting agricultural input use, pooled data of GLSS5 and GLSS6

Independent variable	(1)	(2)	(3)	(4)
	Fertilizer	Herbicides/ Insecticides	Hiring labour	Mechanization
Farm size				
Less than 2 ha	−0.278***	−0.147***	−0.223***	−0.286***
	(0.0461)	(0.0449)	(0.0501)	(0.0389)
2–5 ha	−0.140***	−0.0236	−0.116**	−0.187***
	(0.0463)	(0.0447)	(0.0503)	(0.0388)
5–20 ha	−0.0842*	0.0709	−0.00961	−0.0869**
	(0.0475)	(0.0462)	(0.0519)	(0.0399)
Base is > 20 ha				
Types of district groups				
2nd tier city districts, North	0.250***	0.174***	0.177***	0.0803**
	(0.0452)	(0.0522)	(0.0508)	(0.0383)
3rd tier city districts, North	0.187***	−0.172***	−0.0150	−0.000881
	(0.0184)	(0.0181)	(0.0205)	(0.0172)
No city districts, North	0.139***	−0.0827***	0.0103	−0.00338
	(0.0138)	(0.0137)	(0.0154)	(0.0128)
Big city districts, South	0.0217	−0.0730	0.180*	0.175**
	(0.107)	(0.109)	(0.103)	(0.0857)
2nd tier city districts, South	−0.00633	−0.159***	0.0604	−0.0807
	(0.0621)	(0.0587)	(0.0669)	(0.0630)
3rd tier city districts, South	−0.0693***	−0.0404***	−0.0254	−0.00712
	(0.0156)	(0.0150)	(0.0166)	(0.0140)
Base is no city districts, South				
Year dummy for 2013	0.156***	0.346***	−0.0743***	0.149***
	(0.0108)	(0.00876)	(0.0124)	(0.00993)
Youth headed household	0.00104	0.0234*	−0.0433***	0.00602
	(0.0134)	(0.0134)	(0.0147)	(0.0123)
Female headed household	−0.0695***	−0.0842***	0.0612***	−0.0385***
	(0.0159)	(0.0155)	(0.0168)	(0.0144)
Year dummy * Youth	0.0596**	−0.0663**	−0.0200	0.0295
	(0.0266)	(0.0269)	(0.02904)	(0.0245)
Year dummy * Female	−0.00362	−0.0440	−0.0184	−0.0773**
	0.02845	(0.0286)	(0.0303)	(0.0261)
Education level				
Primary completed	0.0265**	0.0647***	0.0609***	0.0601***
	(0.0134)	(0.0131)	(0.0144)	(0.0121)
Secondary completed	0.0828***	0.0961***	0.0833***	0.0863***
	(0.0267)	(0.0276)	(0.0303)	(0.0241)
University and above	0.0130	0.352**	0.184	0.136
	(0.0894)	(0.148)	(0.142)	(0.143)
Base is no education				
Access to markets	−0.0335**	−0.0276*	0.0314*	−0.0278**
	(0.0145)	(0.0143)	(0.0161)	(0.0126)

Access to public transportation	0.0418***	0.103***	0.0769***	0.0904***
	(0.0125)	(0.0124)	(0.0138)	(0.0116)
Access to electricity	−0.00848	−0.0381***	0.0284**	−0.00746
	(0.0124)	(0.0122)	(0.0134)	(0.0116)
Observations	13,388	13,340	13,340	13,340

Notes: Farm size is based on cultivated area. Rural households defined as agricultural only or agricultural and non-agricultural mixed households in GLSS5 are included in the regressions. Number of pooled sample obs. is 9,877. * $p<0.1$, ** $p<0.05$, *** $p<0.01$.

Agricultural only or agricultural and non-agricultural mixed rural households in GLSS5 are included in the regressions. Number of pooled sample obs. is 9,877. * $p<0.1$, ** $p<0.05$, *** $p<0.01$.

Source: Authors own estimation using GLSS5 and GLSS6 data.

important North have a higher predicted probability of using fertilizers than households in the South, which may be driven by poorer soil fertility in the North (Houssou et al. 2016). However, besides this agroecological factor for the North, the probit estimation shows that in the North, the higher the urbanization level (measured by the size of cities in different district groups), the higher the predicted probability of using fertilizer. For example, compared with households in the Southern districts without cities, the predicted probability of using fertilizer increases by 25 per cent in the Northern districts with secondary cities, while the marginal effects are smaller in Northern districts with 3rd tier cities or without cities, at 18.7 per cent and 13.9 per cent, respectively. There is no such systematical relationship between the use of fertilizer and proximity to different sized cities in the South.

The marginal effect of urbanization on the use of other inputs is not always consistent with that for fertilizer use. Compared with no city districts in the South, only in the districts with 2nd tier cities in the North or with big cities in the South, the marginal effect of using other inputs is mostly positive and significant. The sign of marginal effect tends to be negative, if significant, for the other types of district groups in both North and South.

In terms of education, the probit analysis shows that for the farm households whose heads are more educated, particularly for those completing secondary education, the probability of use fertilizer increases compared with the less educated ones. On the other hand, the dummy variable for youth headed households only significantly affects the probability of fertilizer use through its interaction with the year dummy; this suggests that youth headed households only started having a higher probability of using fertilizer in recent years. The sign of the marginal effect for the youth dummy is not consistent and often insignificant in the other regressions. This result is somewhat surprising, since younger farmers might be expected to be more open to new technologies and knowledge than older adults.

Among the three variables related to market access or public infrastructure, the marginal effect of input use is positive only for the access to public transportation variable. The probability for any modern input use or labour hiring increases by 4.18–10.3 per cent in the communities with easy access to public transportation, while market access seems to be only positively associated with hiring labour and the sign is negative for the use of other inputs. Market access is measured by whether a rural community has a daily or periodic market. It is also possible that better access to public transportation allows farmers to get access to market through traders who can come to villages directly.

In summary for the focus of youth, while the regression results are unexpected, they at least seem to indicate that the constraints against modern input adoption could be binding for all farmers including youth, and farmers in more urbanized locations. Moreover, the results support the patterns of agricultural productivity growth observed from the macro data. As shown in Figure 7.3, Ghana's agricultural labour productivity has grown much faster than its land productivity. This tells us that recent agricultural growth in Ghana has been accompanied by more efficient use of labour without significant increases in land intensification. The continuous

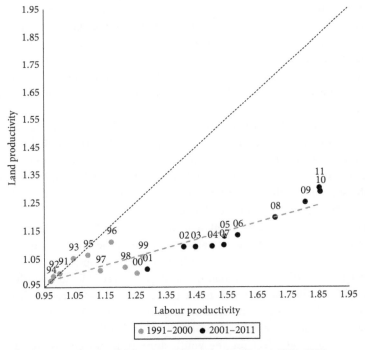

Figure 7.3. Trends in land and labour productivity in Ghana, 1991–2011

Note: In index form with 1991 = 1.0. Each dot in the chart represents an individual year, blue dots are for 1991–2000 and red dots for 2001–2012.

Source: Authors' calculation using data from GGDC for agricultural value added and agricultural employment (Timmer et al. 2015) and data from FAO (2016) for cultivated agricultural land.

exit of youth from agriculture could further enhance this trend, indicating the importance of labour saving technologies for agricultural intensification in Ghana.

7.4 Welfare Outcomes of Changing Rural Livelihoods

Structural change in the rural economy often leads to rural poverty reduction. Indeed, the data shows that rural youth households appear to be in a better position to benefit from proximity to cities with more engagement in the non-agricultural economy. While the development of a vibrant RNFE can serve as an alternative to migration to major cities, it depends on whether the changes in rural livelihoods can provide positive welfare outcomes. We therefore focus on the effects of the exit from agriculture associated with the proximity to cities and rural nonfarm employment on the level of and change in poverty reduction. We analyse welfare outcomes using both poverty and middle-class measures calculated from the two rounds of GLSS.

Measured by the national poverty line of US$1.90 per day, the data shows that the rural poverty rate is generally higher among agricultural households than non-agricultural households. This holds for the country as a whole and for both the North and South. While the poverty rate is much higher in the North than in the South, within the North the difference in poverty rate between these two groups of rural households is still considerably visible (Figure 7.4).

The national poverty rate for rural agricultural households is 48 per cent in 2005, compared to 26 per cent for rural non-agricultural households. While the poverty rate falls between 2005 and 2012 for both rural agricultural and non-agricultural households, the gap between them seems to be stable in the South but even wider in the North (Figure 7.4). This result displays the important role of the RNFE, particularly in the North, has played in reducing rural poverty. Moreover, the number of rural non-agricultural households increased while the number of rural agricultural households fell between the two rounds of GLSS, which seems to further confirm this important role of RNFE in reducing rural poverty in 2005–12.

We also want to examine whether rural non-agricultural households are ascending to the middle-class at a faster rate than their agricultural counterparts. For this purpose, we calculated the proportion of rural households whose income (proxied by expenditures) is above US$3.10 day, a level of income that is often used to define middle-class in Africa (Banerjee and Duflo 2008, Ncube and Shimeles 2013[1]). Figure 7.5 presents the result. The difference in the share of

---

[1] The definition of middle-class is for individuals earning between 2$ and 10$ per day. 2$ is based on 2005 international prices, and has been adjusted by the World Bank to 3.1$ based on 2011 international prices (World Bank 2016). In this chapter, given that we focus only on rural households, we did not limit middle-class by an upper income threshold.

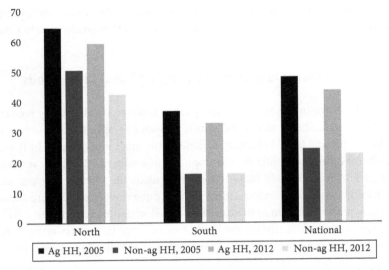

Figure 7.4. Rural poverty rates for agricultural and non-agricultural households
Source: Authors' calculation using data of GLSS5 and GLSS6 (GSS 2015).

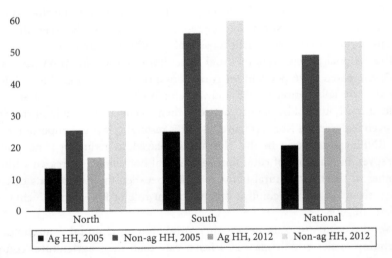

Figure 7.5. Shares of middle-class population (with per capita income more than US$3.10 per day) in total population for rural agricultural and non-agricultural household groups
Source: Authors' calculation using data of GLSS5 and GLSS6 (GSS 2015).

middle-class households between agricultural and non-agricultural households is large throughout Ghana but more so in the South than in the North. In the North, fewer rural households belong to middle-class both for agricultural and non-agricultural households, which is expected given that the North is less developed and generally poorer than the South. However, as seen from Figure 7.4, the proportion of Northern non-agricultural households' population that belongs to middle-class is similar to the proportion for Southern agricultural households. This share rapidly increases from a low base for Northern non-agricultural households, from 17 per cent in 2005 to almost one-third in 2012, while the share for Southern non-agricultural households increases slowly from a relatively high base (from 55.5 per cent to 59.4 per cent).

However, the absolute population of rural middle-class agricultural households is still more than the population of rural non-agricultural households in both the North and South, even in 2012. This is because agricultural households are still prevalent in rural Ghana, although the middle-class population is disproportionately higher among non-agricultural households than among agricultural households.

Both Figure 7.4 and Figure 7.5 can only display bivariate relationships between nonfarm engagements and level of poverty rate or proportion of middle-class at the regional level. Again, further insights can be obtained by using regression techniques to unravel more complex multivariate relationships. Similarly, as in the third section, a probit model is used to test how the probability of being a nonpoor or a middle-class household is associated with being a non-agricultural household and some other factors. In addition to use being a non-agricultural household as a dummy, in the regression we include dummies for youth as head of households, female-headed household, level of education, the degree of urbanization of the districts in which the households live (using our district typology), and a set of infrastructural variables such as access to markets, public transportation, or electricity at the rural community level as a set of independent variables, which are all similar to those in the probit model applied in the third section. Again, we pool together GLSS5 and GLSS6 and hence a year dummy for 2012–13 and interactions of the year dummy with being a non-agricultural household, headed by youth and by female are included in the regression. The nonpoor is defined as a household whose per capita expenditure is more than the national poverty line of US$1.90 per day, while a middle-class household is the one whose per capita expenditure is US$3.10 and more per day. We focus only on the marginal effect of the regression and Table 7.6 reports the result of the regression.

We first need to note that the data used in the regression for identifying factors of being a middle-class household is a subset of the full sample, containing data for nonpoor rural households only. By excluding poor households from the regression, the data in the second regression should be more homogenous than the full dataset; hence, we may expect the magnitude of the marginal effects of many variables affecting being a middle-class household to be smaller than those

Table 7.6. Marginal effects of probit model regressions on factors affecting being a nonpoor or a middle-class household in rural Ghana, pooled data of GLSS5 and GLSS6

Variable	Nonpoor vs. poor (1a)	Middle-class vs. other nonpoor (2a)	Variable	Nonpoor vs. poor (1b)	Middle-class vs. other nonpoor (2b)
Non-agriculture only household	0.0681*** (0.0134)	0.118*** (0.0167)	*Education level*		
Year dummy for 2013	0.0163* (0.00925)	0.0525*** (0.0134)	Primary completed	0.0671*** (0.0105)	0.0351** (0.0149)
Youth headed household	0.102*** (0.0102)	0.0608*** (0.0139)	Secondary completed	0.206*** (0.0219)	0.167*** (0.0244)
Female-headed households	0.0612*** (0.0118)	0.0694*** (0.0160)	University and above	0.424*** (0.0638)	0.337*** (0.0798)
			Base is no education		
Year dummy × youth	-0.0353* (0.1914)	-0.0356 (0.02758)	*Community level variable*		
Year dummy × gender	-0.0577*** (0.0217)	-0.02413 (0.0302)	Access to markets	-0.0109 (0.0118)	-0.00991 (0.0168)
Year dummy × non-agricultural household	-0.0530** (0.02447)	0.02474 (0.03140)	Access to public transportation	0.0782*** (0.0101)	0.0455*** (0.0160)
			Access to electricity	0.0660*** (0.0101)	0.0298** (0.0101)
Types of district groups (base is non city districts, North)					
2nd tier city districts, North	0.115*** (0.0378)	0.0671 (0.0509)	Access to markets	-0.0109 (0.0118)	-0.00991 (0.0168)
3rd tier city districts, North	0.0236 (0.0149)	0.00773 (0.0278)	Number of observation	11,245	7,030
Big city districts, South	0.209*** (0.0565)	0.0473 (0.0741)	F	78.82	35.98
2nd tier city districts, South	0.169*** (0.0538)	0.0666 (0.0662)			
3rd tier city districts, South	0.175*** (0.0127)	0.0459** (0.0199)			
No city districts, South	0.168*** (0.0108)	0.0498*** (0.0182)			

Notes: The regressions include only rural households. Number of the pooled sample obs. is 12,515. *$p<0.1$, ** $p<0.05$, *** $p<0.01$.

affecting being a nonpoor household. Keeping this in mind, we actually find that the marginal effect of the probability of being a non-agriculture only household on being a middle-class household is considerably stronger (11.8 per cent) than that of being a nonpoor household (6.55 per cent), suggesting that not only is nonfarm employment important in reducing rural poverty, but it also is important in ascending to the middle-class. However, the sign of the coefficient is negative when the variable of being non-agricultural interacted with the year dummy in comparison of nonpoor versus poor and not significant in the case of middle-class versus other nonpoor, indicating that the positive strong relationship of being a non-agricultural household and being nonpoor is possibly weakened over time and being non-agricultural is less time relevant for belonging to the middle-class when more rural households become non-agricultural.

We already saw from Table 7.3 that the marginal effect of youth or female household head is positive for the probability of being a non-agricultural household. Table 7.6 further tells us that this effect is also positive on the probability of being nonpoor and middle-class. However, in both cases and similar as being non-agricultural, the sign of the coefficient is negative when these two variables are interacted with the year dummy in the comparison of nonpoor versus poor and not significant in the case of middle-class versus other nonpoor, which again seems to imply that the youth or gender factor is less time relevant, or at least not further strengthened over time.

The findings that female-headed households are positively associated with the probability of being nonpoor or middle-class requires more attention, since this contradicts conventional perceptions that female-headed households are more susceptible to poverty. Since our regressions control for variables such as livelihood source, education levels, and proximity to cities, this result may be driven by other factors not captured in our regressions. While identifying these factors is beyond the scope of this chapter, more research is important for fully understanding these factors.

We now turn to the location factor. As expected, the location factor matters in the probability of being a nonpoor household. Compared with the no-city district group in the North, the marginal effect of the probability of being nonpoor increases in the 2nd tier city Northern districts and everywhere in the South; the coefficient is largest for the big city district group in the South. However, the difference in probability of being nonpoor is insignificant between being in no-city or small city districts in Northern Ghana. For being a middle-class household, we only see significance for the coefficient of 3rd tier city and no city district groups in the South, while for all other district groups, the coefficients are not significant. It is possible that among the nonpoor households in these districts, the nonpoor households are more homogenous when their number (sample size) is small. Therefore, there is less variation among the households in such district groups, which leads to a lower level of significance.

The significant positive marginal effect for the level of education on the probability of being nonpoor or becoming middle-class is also expected, as well as the order of the magnitude of the marginal effect. Moreover, it is seen as an exponential increase in the value of the marginal effect when the level of education moves from primary to secondary and then to university. Compared with no education, having primary education only increases the probability of being non-poor by 6.73 per cent and 3.49 per cent for being middle-class, while the probability of being nonpoor increases by 20.6 per cent and 42.2 per cent for secondary and college education, respectively. The probability of being middle-class increases by 16.7 per cent and 33.7 per cent for these two levels of education, respectively.

Community-level infrastructure (but not market access) also plays a role in increasing the probability of being nonpoor and becoming middle-class. The marginal effect of access to public transportation and electricity on the probability of being nonpoor is similar, 7.78 per cent versus 6.53 per cent, and the magnitude of these marginal effects is smaller but still similar for being middle-class, which is possibly due to a more homogenous sample set in the latter case, as we explained before.

In summary, urbanization and city expansion seem to have important effects not only on poverty reduction but also for further moving up the income ladder for rural households that remain in the rural areas and enter the rural nonfarm sector. These effects are stronger in the more urbanized South, for the youth-headed households and especially for households whose heads have higher levels of education.

7.5 Conclusions

This chapter examines the impact of urbanization—measured by a typology of districts according to proximity to cities—on rural livelihoods in Ghana. We classify the country's districts into seven spatial groups according to the size of the largest city in each district in Southern and Northern Ghana. The chapter does not address rural–urban migration but instead focuses on the livelihoods of rural households in each of these seven district groups. We find that proximity to cities affects the patterns of rural livelihoods. Many rural households have shifted from solely agricultural to solely non-agricultural. While these trends are observed across Ghana, they appear to be much stronger among the youth and in the more urbanized South that already had relatively higher shares of non-agricultural households than in the poorer, more agrarian North. Proximity to cities has a strong effect on the exit of rural households from agriculture, and this trend is stronger with increases in the size of the city. This trend holds for both youth-headed and other type of households but more so for the youth. Essentially, diversification in rural livelihood among youth and other adult headed households appears predominantly inter-household, rather than intra-household in which some members are primarily employed in agriculture and others in non-agriculture. The proportion of this latter type of household in both total and youth-headed rural households has changed little (between the two rounds of GLSS) or fallen (between the two rounds of Census).

While the non-agricultural economy is becoming increasingly important for rural households, informality dominates the rural non-agricultural economy as it does in urban areas. This is alarmingly true particularly among rural youth households. Informal trade and informal manufacturing (mainly agro-processing) are the two most important sectors for rural nonfarm activities. Only in the rural areas close to Accra and Kumasi as well as the mining boom areas in Western Region, do more employment opportunities in the formal non-agricultural sector exist to the rural households. Still, in these areas, youth headed rural households have fewer opportunities of working in the formal sector than other type of households. These results provide a number of policy implications. First, informal non-agricultural activities often have a closer tie with agriculture than the formal ones, and their products and services are also mainly for satisfying local rural demand. In addition to rural–urban linkages that will create opportunities for agricultural growth and for rural employment through migration, it would be worthwhile to further explore agricultural growth opportunities through agricultural and non-agricultural geographic linkages in the areas dominated by rural. Second, given the fact that youth are more likely to exit from agriculture but less likely to engage in the formal sector than other adults, it is important for policies to focus on the improvement of labour productivity and hence income generation for youth in the informal sector (including the RNFE) rather than focusing too much on an unrealistic target of job creation in the formal sector.

While more youth appear to be exiting agriculture, the majority of youth in the North without big and second tier cities still work in agriculture. However contrary to expectations, the results of the probit model did not show greater agricultural technology adoption among the youth particularly in the more urbanized locations. Making agriculture attractive to the youth requires increasing its profitability, which depends on modern technology adoption and agricultural intensification and commercialization. With more rural youth becoming more educated, and more rural households being expected to switch from agriculture to the RNFE in the near future, a different range of technologies would be required from what has been done in the past. Additionally, deepening urbanization means that labour, land, and other capital markets are likely to become more integrated between rural and urban areas. Many non-agricultural policies that would indirectly affect agricultural performance could directly affect the attractiveness of agriculture to the youth. A territorial approach and related policies that integrate secondary cities and small towns with the rural economy deserve more attention such that the diversification of rural livelihoods can become a viable alternative or complement to rural–urban migration for the youth.

Table 7.A1. Marginal effects in the probit estimations on the determinants of being a non-agricultural household, pooled data of Census 2000 and 2010

Independent variable	Comparing with the rest HH			Comparing with mixed HH		
	All households	Youth-headed households	Other adult households	All households	Youth-headed households	Other adult households
Year dummy for 2010	0.0123	0.0243	0.00867	0.0154	0.0310**	0.0114
	-0.0144	-0.0151	-0.0144	-0.0172	-0.0146	-0.0194
Youth-headed households	0.0746***			0.170***		
	-0.00489			-0.0064		
Female-headed households	0.126***	0.151***	0.107***	0.196***	0.224***	0.194***
	-0.00747	-0.00796	-0.00665	-0.00894	-0.00873	-0.0104
Year dummy * Youth	0.0250***			0.0418***		
	-0.0057743			-0.00557		
Year dummy * Gender	0.0353***			0.0435***		
	-0.00736			-0.00897		
Types of district groups (base is no city district, North)						
2nd tier city districts, North	0.0933**	0.0867***	0.0901*	0.120***	0.124***	0.110***
	-0.0472	-0.0305	-0.0465	-0.0366	-0.0231	-0.0414
3rd tier city districts, North	0.0375	0.0431	0.0358	0.0726	0.0700*	0.0678
	-0.0419	-0.0438	-0.0401	-0.0567	-0.0405	-0.0623
Big city districts, South	0.279***	0.230***	0.234***	0.286***	0.223***	0.341***
	-0.0424	-0.037	-0.0331	-0.0343	-0.026	-0.0408
2nd tier city districts, South	0.137***	0.0958***	0.143***	0.199***	0.159***	0.219***
	-0.038	-0.0325	-0.0436	-0.0469	-0.0354	-0.0571
3rd tier city districts, South	0.0698**	0.107***	0.0518*	0.0866**	0.0977***	0.0780*
	-0.0276	-0.0261	-0.0283	-0.0355	-0.0226	-0.0403
No city districts, South	0.0144	0.0475**	0.000859	0.0335	0.0603***	0.0177
	-0.0182	-0.0211	-0.0196	-0.027	-0.0203	-0.0297

Education level (no education omitted)						
Primary completed	0.112***	0.137***	0.0988***	0.109***	0.0895***	0.109***
	-0.00548	-0.00575	-0.00541	-0.00745	-0.00715	-0.00788
Secondary completed	0.318***	0.267***	0.268***	0.250***	0.197***	0.270***
	-0.00918	-0.0105	-0.00699	-0.00883	-0.00966	-0.0091
Tertiary and above	0.470***	0.386***	0.350***	0.293***	0.210***	0.330***
	-0.0122	-0.0151	-0.0114	-0.0122	-0.0185	-0.0153
Community variable						
Electricity	0.267***	0.333***	0.239***	0.335***	0.328***	0.334***
	-0.0529	-0.0526	-0.0547	-0.0632	-0.0482	-0.0751
Observations	374,568	116,965	257,603	150,066	50,514	99,552

Notes: The regressions include only rural households. Number of the pooled sample obs. is 403,938. $^{*}p < 0.1$, $^{**}p < 0.05$, $^{***}p < 0.01$

Source: Authors' own estimation using Census 2000 and Census 2010 data.

References

Ackah, C., C. Adjasi, and F. Turkson. 2014. *Scoping study on the evolution of industry in Ghana*. Washington, DC, U.S.A.: Learning to Compete Working Paper No. 18 Africa Growth Initiative (AGI) at Brookings.

Anyidoho, N., J. Leavy, and K. Asenso-Okyere. 2012. Perceptions and aspirations: A case study of young people in Ghana's cocoa sector. *IDS Bulletin* 43 (6).

Aryeetey, E., and W. Baah-Boateng. 2015. *Understanding Ghana's growth success story and job creation challenges*. WIDER Working Paper 2015/140.

Banerjee, A., and E. Duflo. 2008. What is middle class about the middle class around the world? *Journal of Economic Perspectives* 22 (2): 3–28.

Berdegue, J., F. Carriazo, B. Jara, F. Modrego, and I. Soloaga. 2015. Cities, territories and inclusive growth: Unraveling urban–rural linkages in Chile, Colombia and Mexico. *World Development* 73: 56–71.

Binswanger-Mkhize, H., T. Johnson, P. Samboko, and L. You. 2016. *The impact of urban growth on agricultural and rural nonfarm growth in Kenya*. International Fund for Agricultural Development.

Binswanger, H., and V. W. Ruttan. 1978. *Induced innovation*. Baltimore, U.S.A. and London, U.K.: The Johns Hopkins University Press.

Boserup, E. 1965. *The conditions of agricultural growth: The economics of agrarian change under population pressure*. London, U.K.: George Allen and Unwin.

Deichmann, U., F. Shilpi, and R. Vakis. 2008. Urban proximity, agricultural potential and rural nonfarm employment: Evidence from Bangladesh. *World Development* 37 (3): 645–60.

Diao, X., M. McMillan, and D. Rodrik. 2017. The recent growth boom in developing economies: A structural change perspective. NBER Working Paper No. 23132. Cambridge, MA: National Bureau of Economic Research.

Diao, X., F. Cossar, N. Houssou, and S. Kolavalli. 2014. Mechanization in Ghana: Emerging demand, and the search for alternative supply models. *Food Policy* 48 (October): 168–81.

Gollin, D., R. Jedwab, and D. Vollrath. 2016. Urbanization with and without industrialization. Journal of Economic Growth 21 (1): 35–70.

GSS (Ghana Statistical Service). 2003. Population and Housing Census 2000. Census data. Accra, Ghana.

GSS (Ghana Statistical Service). 2008. Ghana Living Standards Survey Round 5 (GLSS 5). Survey Data. Accra, Ghana.

GSS (Ghana Statistical Service). 2013. Population and Housing Census 2010. Accra, Ghana.

GSS (Ghana Statistical Service). 2014. Ghana Living Standards Survey Round 6 (GLSS 6). Survey data. Accra, Ghana.

Haggblade, S., P. Hazell, and J. Brown. 1989. Farm-nonfarm linkages in rural Sub-Saharan Africa. *World Development* 17 (8): 1173–201.

Harris, J. R., and M. P. Todaro. 1970. Migration, unemployment and development: A two-sector analysis. *American Economic Review* 60 (1): 126–42.

Hayami, Y., and V. Ruttan. 1970. Factor prices and technical change in agricultural development: The United States and Japan. *Journal of Political Economy* 78 (5): 1115–41.

Hayami, Y., and V. Ruttan. 1985. *Agricultural development: An international perspective.* Baltimore, MD, U.S.A.: Johns Hopkins University Press.

Headey, D., D. Bezemer, and P. Hazell. 2010. Agricultural employment trends in Asia and Africa. Too fast or too slow? *World Bank Research Observer* 25 (1): 57–89.

Houssou, N., M. Johnson, S. Kolavalli, and C. Asante-Addo. 2016. Changes in Ghanaian farming systems: Stagnation or a quiet transformation? IFPRI Discussion Paper 01504. International Food Policy Research Institute.

Jedwab, R. 2013. Urbanization without structural transformation: Evidence from consumption cities in Africa. George Washington University (mimeograph).

Kolavalli, S., E. Robinson, X. Diao, A. Apluerto, R. Folledo, M. Slavova, and F. Asante. 2012. Economic transformation in Ghana: Where will the path lead? IFPRI Discussion Paper 1161. Washington, DC, U.S.A.: International Food Policy Research Institute.

McMillan, M., and D. Rodrik. 2011. Globalization, structural change and productivity growth. NBER Working Paper 17,143.

Mellor, J. 1976. *New economics of growth.* Ithaca, NY, U.S.A.: Cornell University Press.

Ncube, M., and A. Shimeles. 2013. The making of middle-class in Africa: Evidence from DHS data. IZA DP No. 7352. Forschingsinstitut zur Zukunft der Arbeit—Institute for the Study of Labor.

Nin-Pratt, A., and L. McBride. 2014. Agricultural intensification in Ghana: Evaluating the optimist's case for a Green Revolution. *Food Policy* 48: 153–67.

Osei, R.D., and R. Jedwab. 2016. Structural change in a poor african country: New historical evidence from Ghana. In M. MacMillan, D. Rodrik, and C. Sepúlveda (eds.). 2016. *Structural Change, Fundamentals, And Growth: A Framework and Case Studies.* Washington DC: International Food Policy Research Institute, pp. 161–94.

Owusu, V., A. Abdulai, and S. Abdul-Rahman. 2011. Non-farm work and food security among farm households in Northern Ghana. *Food Policy* 36: 108–18.

Ravallion, M., S. Chen, and P. Sangraula. 2007. New evidence on the urbanization of global poverty. *Population and Development Review* 102 (1): 504–23.

Rosegrant, M., and P. Hazell. 2000. *Transforming the rural Asian economy: The unfinished revolution.* Oxford, U.K.: Oxford University Press.

Ruthenberg, H. 1980. *Farming systems in the tropics.* Oxford, U.K.: Oxford University Press.

Ruttan, V. W. 2002. Productivity growth in world agriculture: Sources and constraints. *Journal of Economic Perspectives* 16 (4): 161–84.

Timmer, C. P. 1988. The agricultural transformation. *Handbook of Development Economics* 1: 275–331.

Timmer, M. P., G. J. de Vries, and K. de Vries. 2015. Patterns of structural change in developing countries. In J. Weiss and M. Tribe (Eds.), *Handbook of Industry and Development*. (pp. 65–83). Routledge.

World Bank. 2016. PovcalNet: An online analysis tool for global poverty monitoring. The World Bank. http://iresearch.worldbank.org/PovcalNet/home.aspx.

8
Rural Nonfarm Enterprises in Tanzania's Economic Transformation
The Role of the Youth

Xinshen Diao, Eduardo Magalhaes, and Margaret McMillan[1]

8.1 Introduction

Since the beginning of the twenty-first century, Tanzania's economy has grown more rapidly than at any other point in recent history. Between 2000 and 2015 average annual GDP growth was 6.8 per cent and average annual labour productivity growth was more than 4 per cent. This is quite impressive when considering the 2.7–3.0 per cent annual population growth rate and a similar growth rate in the labour force during this period. Moreover, between 2002 and 2012 more than three quarters of this labour productivity growth was accounted for by structural change; the remainder of the growth is largely attributable to within sector productivity growth in agriculture. The growth attributable to structural change is almost entirely explained by a rapid decline in the agricultural employment share and an increase in the non-agricultural private sector employment share (Diao, Kweka, and McMillan 2017).

In spite of these changes, Tanzania remains heavily rural; between 2002 and 2012, the share of the population living in rural areas declined by only 6.5 percentage points from 76.9 to 70.4 per cent (Table 8.1). The share of youth living in rural areas undergoes a slightly greater decrease. However, as shown in Table 8.1, more than 60 per cent of youth still live in the rural areas in 2012. Living in rural areas is typically associated with farming, including for youth. But the statistics also show that between 2002 and 2012, the share of the rural population engaged in agricultural activities decreased by almost 10 percentage points (Table 8.1). This is also true for the youth cohort at the national level. While the absolute number of rural agricultural employment continues to increase, the growth rate of rural non-agricultural employment is much faster as shown in Table 8.1.

[1] We thank Hak Lim Lee and Peixun Fang for their contribution of the HBS data analysis in the chapter.

Xinshen Diao, Eduardo Magalhaes, and Margaret McMillan, *Rural Nonfarm Enterprises in Tanzania's Economic Transformation: The Role of the Youth* In: *Youth and Jobs in Rural Africa: Beyond Stylized Facts*. Edited by: Valerie Mueller and James Thurlow, Oxford University Press (2019). © International Food Policy Research Institute. DOI: 10.1093/oso/9780198848059.003.0008

In this chapter, we explore the nature of these rural nonfarm activities to better understand their contribution to the economic development and diversification of rural areas or 'rural transformation'. We pay particular attention to the youth in the analysis when the data allows.

The first part of our analysis uses data from Tanzania's 2012 Household Budget Survey to classify rural households based on their participation in the nonfarm economy. We identify the following three types of households: (1) households which do not participate in agriculture; (2) households which participate only in farming; and (3) mixed households, which both participate in the farm and nonfarm economy. We find that 11.2 per cent of households participate only in the nonfarm economy and that the heads of these households tend to be more educated. The share of households headed by youth that participate only in the nonfarm economy is higher, at 17.9 per cent (Table 8.3). We then explain the differences between households with and without rural nonfarm activities using a probit model. We find that being a youth-headed household increases the probability of specializing in rural nonfarm activities by 2–6 per cent, but they do not seem very different from other households when agriculture is still part of their household's livelihood. The most important determinant of whether a household engages in nonfarm activities is the education of the household head. For households whose heads have secondary or more education, the increase in the probability of engaging in nonfarm activities is between 8 and 38 per cent. This could be a major factor to explain a higher participation rate of nonfarm economy among youth-headed households.

The second part of our analysis uses data from Tanzania's first nationally representative survey of micro, small, and medium sized enterprises (MSMEs) to study the nature of rural businesses. This survey covers roughly 3 million businesses and 5 million people; around 75 per cent of these businesses are in rural areas. Diao, Kweka, and McMillan (2017) have shown that Tanzania's MSMEs are geographically disbursed throughout the country and that these enterprises generally operate in manufacturing and services. In rural areas, 20 per cent of these businesses are in the manufacturing sector while the remainder is in the services sector. The heart of our analysis begins with a description of the characteristics of the owners of these businesses in rural areas paying attention to young owners. Next, we examine the productivity of these businesses and show an enormous degree of productive heterogeneity in both rural and urban enterprises. We then examine employment growth among rural enterprises and find that only 10 per cent of rural enterprises experience any employment growth. Finally, we use the heterogeneity of the rural nonfarm enterprises to identify a group of firms with the potential to contribute to rural transformation. Using a probit analysis, we examine the characteristics of firms that make them more likely to fall into the category of 'high potential' firms in order to better understand the correlates of enterprise success in rural areas.

Our chapter contributes to the large and growing literature on the rural nonfarm economy in Africa. One strand of this literature focuses on farm/nonfarm linkages and the estimation of multipliers (see for example Haggblade, Hazell, and Brown 1989). This work is based on the idea that agricultural productivity growth can generate income and employment multipliers via production and consumption linkages. A second strand of this literature focuses on rural–urban linkages and stresses the importance of reducing barriers to the movement of labour and products from rural to urban areas. Research in this area tends to focus on migration and transportation costs. See for example de Brauw, Mueller, and Lee (2014) on migration and Gollin and Rogerson (2009) on transportation costs. A third strand of this literature studies the effects of farm/nonfarm linkages and rural/urban linkages simultaneously. A nice example of this type of work is the paper by Haggblade, Hazell, and Reardon (2010) that explores both internal processes of rural growth as well as the impact of globalization and urbanization on rural nonfarm activity.

To the best of our knowledge, none of the work on the rural nonfarm economy uses nationally representative firm level data to compare the characteristics of rural enterprises to those of urban enterprises.[2] Unlike most enterprise surveys conducted in Africa which are small in sample size (for example, most World Bank business environment surveys), the data we use is based on a nationally representative survey which covers roughly 5 million employees and 3 million small businesses in both rural and urban areas. Tanzania has one of the few comprehensive nationally representative surveys of small, micro, and medium sized enterprises (MSMEs) available in Sub-Saharan Africa.[3] More than 70 per cent of small businesses surveyed by MSME are in the rural areas and the rest are in urban areas (which in Tanzania are identified by local officials in consultation with the National Bureau of Statistics). This allows us to compare enterprises in rural and urban areas using the same dataset.[4]

The remainder of this chapter is organized as follows. In Section 8.2, we demonstrate the growing importance of rural nonfarm enterprises in the context of the Tanzanian economy. In Section 8.3, we describe the data and methods we use in our analyses. Section 8.4 describes our typology of households and examines the characteristics of households with and without rural nonfarm enterprises. In Section 8.5, we use the firm level survey to describe the characteristics of rural entrepreneurs and their businesses and identify a group of firms with the

---

[2] Jin and Deininger (2008) study rural nonfarm enterprises but not in comparison to urban enterprises.
[3] The government of Rwanda did carry out a survey of MSMEs recently but the survey does not include information on employment and productivity. Uganda has a similar nationally representative MSME survey in which the successfully interviewed firm number is less than 2,000 while Tanzania's survey interviewed more than 6,000 business owners.
[4] The survey used in Jin and Deininger (2008) covers only enterprises (1,239) and households (1,610) in Tanzanian rural areas.

potential to stimulate rural transformation; we call these firms the 'in-between' firms. In Section 8.6, we study the characteristics of the 'in-between' firms in order to better understand how policymakers might target these firms. Section 8.7 concludes with a summary of the main points and a brief discussion of policy implications.

8.2 The Role of Rural Nonfarm Enterprises in Tanzania's Economy

Three nationally representative surveys are used to describe the changes in shares of rural population and rural employment. These are the 2000–1 and 2011–12 rounds of the Household Budget Survey (HBS), the 2002 and 2012 Population Censuses, and the 2006 and 2014 Integrated Labour Force Surveys (ILFS). According to the two rounds of the census, which more accurately captures the change in population structure, the share of the population living in rural areas declined from 76.9 per cent in 2002 to 70.4 per cent in 2012, compared to 71.5 per cent in 2002 and 63.5 per cent in 2012 for youth (Table 8.1, first panel). Thus, Tanzania is urbanizing, but is still heavily rural.

The second panel of Table 8.1 contains agricultural employment shares from the three different surveys. While different surveys cannot be directly compared because of differences in the definition for agricultural employment, there is a clear trend of the share of agricultural employment declining more rapidly than the share of rural population.[5] Between the two rounds of the Census in the period of 10 years (2002–12), the agricultural share of employment declined by 15.3 percentage points overall and by 11 percentage points for youth, while between the two rounds of ILFS in 2006–14, the declines are 9.6 percentage points and 8.2 percentage points for the total population and youth, respectively. This trend holds also for rural total and youth employment, indicating the growth in rural nonfarm employment outpaced the growth in agricultural employment.

The third panel of Table 8.1 reports annualized employment growth rates in the recent 15 years computed from each two rounds of the three surveys. In general, employment in agriculture has been growing at a slower pace than total employment nationwide and in rural areas. In fact, according to the census data, the growth rate of agricultural employment is almost zero in 2000–12 for the rural total and negative for the rural youth. By contrast, non-agricultural employment has grown rapidly for the rural population and the rural youth, both with double-digit growth rates (see the bottom of Table 8.1).

---

[5] We noticed that the agricultural employment share did not fall between the two rounds of the HBS. We discussed possible data problems in the table's note, that is, the definition of agricultural employment for the early round of HBS seems to cause share of agriculture in total employment to be unrealistically low in 2000–1. This is further confirmed when the number from 2000–1 HBS is compared to the number of the 2002 Census.

Table 8.1. Rural population and agricultural employment shares and annual growth rates

	Rural total	Rural youth (15–34)	National	Total youth
Share of rural population (per cent)				
2002	76.9	71.5		
2012	70.4	63.5		
Agricultural employment shares (per cent)				
2000/01 (HBS)	86.3	87.1	76.7	76.1
2002 (Census)	93.2	93.4	81.1	74.2
2006 (ILFS)			76.5	74.4
2011–2012 (HBS)	89.0	87.6	74.8	72.2
2012 (Census)	79.5	81.4	65.8	63.2
2014 (ILFS)			66.9	66.2
Annualized growth rate (per cent)				
Population (2002–12, Census)	1.8	1.1	2.7	2.4
Total employment				
2000–11 (HBS)	1.2	0.9	2.2	1.9
2002–12 (Census)	1.6	0.2	2.5	1.6
2006–14 (ILFS)	0.3	0.4	2.4	1.9
Employment in agriculture				
2000–11 (HBS)	1.2	1.0	1.5	1.4
2002–12 (Census)	0.1	–1.2	0.4	0.0
2006–14 (ILFS)			0.7	0.4
Employment in non-agriculture				
2000–11 (HBS)	1.4	0.6	4.4	3.3
2002–12 (Census)	13.5	11.1	8.8	5.3
2006–14 (ILFS)			6.8	5.5

Notes: For the Census employment, data for current employees aged 10 years and above is used. Agricultural employment is based on the industry classification. For the Household Budget Survey (HBS), employees are for aged 15 years and above. Definition of agricultural employment differs between the two rounds of HBS. In HBS 2000–1, agricultural employees are defined as 'farming', while 'unpaid family helper' is considered as non-agricultural employment. In HBS 2011–12, agricultural employees are those 'working on farm'. Given that the number of 'non-agricultural unpaid family helper' in HBS 2000–1 is much larger than that in HBS 2011–12, agricultural employment in HBS 2000–1 is possibly underestimated, which leads to an unrealistically high growth rate in agricultural employment using HBS, as shown in the table. Employees in the Integrated Labour Force Survey (ILFS) are for age 15 years and above.

Sources: Most numbers are calculated by authors using the government official documents for Census 2002 and 2012, HBS 2000–1 and 2011–12, and ILFS 2006 and 2014 published by NBS (NBS 2006, 2011a, 2011b, 2014a, 2014b, and 2015). The numbers of Census 2002 agricultural employment share in rural total and rural youth and growth rates in agricultural and non-agricultural employment are calculated using the micro data downloaded from IPUMS (https://usa.ipums.org/usa/).

To help better understand the changing structure of Tanzania's employment, in Table 8.2 we compute net employment growth in detail among different economic sectors. While the agricultural sector still accounts for two-thirds of total employment in Tanzania, it has played a relatively minor role in net job increases

Table 8.2. Contribution to new employment by sector, formal and informal, 2002–2012

	Total		Formal		Informal	
	Number of	Share in total	Number of	Share in total	Number of	Share in total
	net increase	net increase	net increase	net increase	net increase	net increase
Agriculture	446,677	11.2	-3,865	-0.1	450,542	11.3
Mining	404,212	10.1	9,021	0.2	395,192	9.9
Manufacturing	313,882	7.8	103,049	2.6	210,833	5.3
Utilities	194,960	4.9	194,960	4.9	–	–
Construction	281,864	7.0	21,185	0.5	260,679	6.5
Trade services	966,807	24.2	1,304	0.0	965,503	24.1
Transport services	182,383	4.6	18,497	0.5	163,886	4.1
Business services	105,635	2.6	56,924	1.4	48,711	1.2
Public sector	224,579	5.6	224,579	5.6	–	–
Personal services	881,289	22.0	–	–	881,289	22.0
Total private non-agriculture	3,331,032	83.2	404,940	10.1	2,926,093	73.1
Total private economy	3,777,709	94.4	401,075	10.0	3,376,635	84.4
Total non-agriculture	3,555,611	88.8	629,519	15.7	2,926,093	73.1

Note: Employment is defined by the current employment status with age 10 or more years old.

Source: Authors calculation based on data from the Formal Employment and Earnings Survey and the Census 2002 and 2012 (NBS, 2006, 2007, 2014b, 2014c, 2014d, and 2014e).

as shown in Table 8.1. In fact, almost 90 percent of the net increase in jobs between the two census periods occurred in the non-agricultural sector. Considering that agricultural employment made up more than 80 per cent of total employment in 2002 (Table 8.1), this rapid non-agricultural employment growth is remarkable.

However, as is evident from Table 8.2, about 83 per cent of the increase in the private sector non-agricultural employment has taken place in the informal sector. We do not have access to detailed employment data at the sector level disaggregated by rural and urban. However, we know from Table 8.1 that nonfarm employment increased significantly in rural areas. If we assume that formal non-agricultural employment is more likely to take place in urban than in rural areas, then we can take the 88 per cent of growth in national informal employment as the lower bound for informal employment growth in rural areas. In the fourth section of this chapter, we will use the MSME data to further investigate the nature of this rural nonfarm employment.

Tanzania's rural economy is also evolving along another very important dimension. As shown in Figure 8.1, the gap between the share of agricultural employment and the share of agricultural GDP has started to narrow modestly in recent years (narrowing about 7.5 percentage points in 2001–11). This implies that not only has labour productivity in agriculture been growing but so too has its' productivity relative to other sectors of the economy. This is important because as shown by Diao, Kweka, and McMillan (2017), the declining agricultural employment share in Tanzania has contributed to economy-wide labour productivity growth

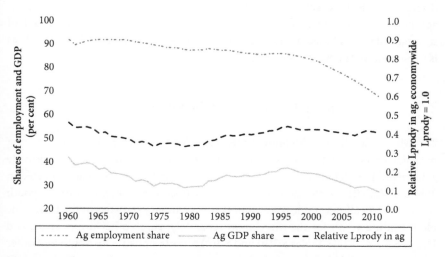

Figure 8.1. Shares of Tanzania's agriculture in labour force and GDP and relative labour productivity in agriculture

Note: Agricultural GDP share is measured in constant 2005 price.

Source: Authors, calculation using data of GGDC 2015 version.

through structural change. This is because measured labour productivity in agriculture has been lower than in many non-agricultural activities.

8.3 Data and Methods

We begin this section with a brief description of the two datasets used for the micro analysis in this chapter. We then describe the methodologies employed to analyse the characteristics of households which participate solely in the rural nonfarm economy compared to other types of households. Lastly we describe our methods for assessing the characteristics and potential of rural enterprises in comparison with those in urban areas.

8.3.1 Household Survey Data

The 2011–12 Household Budget Survey (HBS) is used for the micro analysis, which is discussed in detail in the Section 8.4. As we mentioned in the beginning of the chapter, HBS is a nationally representative survey, which is designed to provide estimates of household income and expenditure. However, it only covers mainland Tanzania and excludes Zanzibar. Like the MSME survey to be discussed below, the sampling framework used to conduct the HBS survey is based on the 2002 Census, which could possibly oversample rural households given that, as we discussed in the first section, the 2012 Census has shown a decline of 6.5 percentage points in the share of rural population from the 2002 Census. A set of summary statistics based on the 2011–12 HBS for the variables used in our analysis is presented in Appendix Table 8.A1.

8.3.2 Description of the MSME Data

The Micro, Small, and Medium Enterprise (MSME) survey is Tanzania's first nationally representative survey for small businesses. For this reason, we provide a description in detail based on a set of summary statistics of the data reported in Tables 8.3(a)–3(c) in this subsection. The discussion pays attention to the youth when the data allows. Table 8.3(a) reports the summary statistics of the total sample including youth for the three areas separately: rural, other urban areas, and Dar es Salaam, while Tables 8.3(b) and 8.3(c) reports statistics for youth and other adult owners of MSMEs respectively.

Among the 6,134 sampled firms, a total of 5,609 firms have all the information that we use in our analysis. Based on the information that is available, we have no reason to believe that the firms with missing information are 'select' in a particular manner. For example, they are dispersed across regions and firm size.

Table 8.3(a). Rural and urban MSME summary statistics

Names of variables	Value unit or range	Observations	Mean	S.D.	Observations	Mean	S.D.	Observations	Mean	S.D.
			Rural			Other urban			Dar es Salaam	
Business characteristics										
Number of employees per firm	Person	4,163	1.50	0.03	1,093	1.65	0.07	353	1.70	0.09
Number of full-time employees per firm	Person	4,163	1.28	0.02	1,093	1.41	0.06	353	1.48	0.07
Annual employment growth	[−.09, .25]	4,163	0.10	0.01	1,093	0.10	0.02	353	0.09	0.02
Per cent of firms registered with Brella	[0,1]	4,163	0.04	0.01	1,093	0.03	0.01	353	0.04	0.01
Per cent of firms with tax ID	[0,1]	4,163	0.03	0.00	1,093	0.08	0.01	353	0.08	0.02
Per cent of firms with business run out of home	[0,1]	4,163	0.49	0.01	1,093	0.45	0.02	353	0.52	0.03
Average monthly value added per firm	1,000 TZS	4,163	320	20.94	1,093	404	36.98	353	461	112.90
Average monthly sales per firm	1,000 TZS	4,163	557	71.64	1,093	722	133.12	353	686	123.05
Firm's age	Year	4,163	6.90	0.15	1,093	6.11	0.24	353	5.45	0.47
Per cent of firms with business as full-time	[0,1]	4,163	0.77	0.01	1,093	0.82	0.02	353	0.87	0.02
Keeps accounts in ledger	[0,1]	4,163	0.31	0.01	1,093	0.36	0.02	353	0.33	0.03
Hires paid workers	[0,1]	4,163	0.18	0.02	1,093	0.37	0.05	353	0.37	0.07
>20 customers per day	[0,1]	4,163	0.26	0.01	1,093	0.30	0.02	353	0.33	0.03
Firms powers business with electricity	[0,1]	4,163	0.08	0.01	1,093	0.30	0.02	353	0.39	0.03
Owner saves in formal bank account	[0,1]	4,163	0.04	0.00	1,093	0.13	0.01	353	0.12	0.02
Owner/household characteristics										
Age of owner	Year	4,163	36.97	0.25	1,093	35.96	0.43	353	35.90	0.77
Whether owner is female	[0,1]	4,163	0.48	0.01	1,093	0.68	0.02	353	0.64	0.03
Per cent of firms with business as main source of income	[0,1]	4,163	0.41	0.01	1,093	0.36	0.02	353	0.29	0.03

Continued

Table 8.3(a). Continued

Names of variables	Value unit or range	Observations	Mean	S.D.	Observations	Mean	S.D.	Observations	Mean	S.D.
Business characteristics		Rural			Other urban			Dar es Salaam		
Per cent of firms with farming as main source of income	[0,1]	4,163	0.26	0.01	1,093	0.06	0.01	353	0.00	0.00
Per cent of firms with business as only source of income	[0,1]	4,163	0.28	0.01	1,093	0.44	0.02	353	0.51	0.03
Per cent of firms' households that are not poor	[0,1]	4,163	0.45	0.01	1,093	0.54	0.02	353	0.62	0.03
Per cent of firms' households that are moderately poor	[0,1]	4,163	0.35	0.01	1,093	0.32	0.02	353	0.26	0.03
Per cent of firms' households that are very poor	[0,1]	4,163	0.20	0.01	1,093	0.14	0.01	353	0.12	0.02

Notes: Brella is Tanzania's Business Registration and Licensing Agency which opened in 1999. Household poverty was reported in the survey by an indicator variable equal to 0 if the household is not poor, 1 if the household is moderately poor and 2 if the household is very poor. The measure of poverty was computed using monthly household income as reported by survey respondents. TZS denote Tanzanian Shillings.

Source: Authors calculations using the MSME Survey 2010.

Names of variables	Value unit or range	Rural			Other urban			Dar es Salaam		
		Observations	Mean	S.D.	Observations	Mean	S.D.	Observations	Mean	S.D.
Business characteristics										
Number of employees per firm	Person	1,853	1.39	0.04	493	1.43	0.05	167	1.59	0.11
Number of full-time employees per firm	Person	1,853	1.23	0.03	493	1.28	0.06	167	1.39	0.06
Per cent of firms with tax ID	[0,1]	1,853	0.02	0.00	493	0.06	0.01	167	0.06	0.02
Per cent of firms with business run out of home	[0,1]	1,853	0.46	0.02	493	0.43	0.03	167	0.46	0.05
Firm's age	Year	1,853	4.67	0.13	492	4.11	0.22	166	4.04	0.32
Per cent of firms with business as full-time	[0,1]	1,853	0.77	0.02	493	0.84	0.02	167	0.91	0.02
Keeps accounts in ledger	[0,1]	1,853	0.30	0.02	493	0.37	0.03	167	0.29	0.04
Hires paid workers	[0,1]	1,853	0.14	0.04	493	0.23	0.05	167	0.23	0.07
>20 customers per day	[0,1]	1,853	0.28	0.01	493	0.29	0.03	167	0.38	0.05
Owner saves in formal bank account	[0,1]	1,853	0.04	0.01	493	0.08	0.01	167	0.11	0.03
Owner/household characteristics										
Age of owner	Year	1,853	27.92	0.15	493	27.29	0.26	167	27.77	0.43
Whether owner is female	[0,1]	1,853	0.50	0.02	493	0.66	0.03	167	0.55	0.05
Per cent of firms with business as main source of income	[0,1]	1,853	0.39	0.02	493	0.32	0.03	167	0.33	0.05
Per cent of firms with farming as main source of income	[0,1]	1,853	0.24	0.02	493	0.04	0.01	167	0.00	0.00
Per cent of firms with business as only source of income	[0,1]	1,853	0.31	0.02	493	0.51	0.03	167	0.56	0.05
Per cent of firms' households that are not poor	[0,1]	1,853	0.44	0.02	493	0.56	0.03	167	0.69	0.04
Per cent of firms' households that are very poor	[0,1]	1,853	0.20	0.01	493	0.11	0.02	167	0.07	0.02

Notes: Brella is Tanzania's Business Registration and Licensing Agency which opened in 1999. Household poverty was reported in the survey by an indicator variable equal to 0 if the household is not poor, 1 if the household is moderately poor and 2 if the household is very poor. The measure of poverty was computed using monthly household income as reported by survey respondents. TZS denote Tanzanian Shillings.

Source: Authors calculations using the MSME Survey 2010.

Table 8.3(c). Rural and urban MSME summary statistics: other adults

Names of variables	Value unit or range	Observations	Rural		Observations	Other urban		Observations	Dar es Salaam	
			Mean	S.D.		Mean	S.D.		Mean	S.D.
Business characteristics										
Number of employees per firm	Person	2,310	1.59	0.05	600	1.85	0.12	186	1.83	0.15
Number of full-time employees per firm	Person	2,310	1.33	0.02	600	1.54	0.10	186	1.58	0.14
Per cent of firms with tax ID	[0,1]	2,310	0.04	0.01	600	0.10	0.01	186	0.10	0.03
Per cent of firms with business run out of home	[0,1]	2,310	0.52	0.02	600	0.48	0.03	186	0.59	0.05
Firm's age	Year	2,310	8.77	0.23	600	8.07	0.39	186	7.10	0.90
Per cent of firms with business as full-time	[0,1]	2,310	0.76	0.01	600	0.80	0.02	186	0.82	0.03
Keeps accounts in ledger	[0,1]	2,310	0.32	0.01	600	0.34	0.02	186	0.39	0.05
Hires paid workers	[0,1]	2,310	0.22	0.03	600	0.49	0.10	186	0.54	0.13
>20 customers per day	[0,1]	2,310	0.25	0.01	600	0.31	0.03	186	0.26	0.04
Owner saves in formal bank account	[0,1]	2,310	0.05	0.01	600	0.17	0.02	186	0.13	0.03
Owner/household characteristics										
Age of owner	Year	2,310	44.47	0.27	600	44.29	0.41	186	45.32	0.71
Whether owner is female	[0,1]	2,310	0.47	0.02	600	0.70	0.02	186	0.74	0.04
Per cent of firms with business as main source of income	[0,1]	2,310	0.43	0.01	600	0.38	0.03	186	0.26	0.04
Per cent of firms with farming as main source of income	[0,1]	2,310	0.27	0.01	600	0.09	0.02	186	0.00	0.00
Per cent of firms with business as only source of income	[0,1]	2,310	0.26	0.01	600	0.37	0.03	186	0.46	0.05
Per cent of firms' households that are not poor	[0,1]	2,310	0.46	0.02	600	0.53	0.03	186	0.55	0.05
Per cent of firms' households that are very poor	[0,1]	2,310	0.20	0.01	600	0.17	0.02	186	0.18	0.04

Notes: Brella is Tanzania's Business Registration and Licensing Agency which opened in 1999. Household poverty was reported in the survey by an indicator variable equal to 0 if the household is not poor, 1 if the household is moderately poor and 2 if the household is very poor. The measure of poverty was computed using monthly household income as reported by survey respondents. TZS denote Tanzanian Shillings.

Source: Authors calculations using the MSME Survey 2010.

As shown in the first row of Table 8.3(a), most MSMEs are extremely small: mean employment is 1.5 in rural areas, 1.65 in urban areas outside Dar es Salaam, and 1.7 in Dar es Salaam. The very small size of MSMEs is at least in part due to a sample selection bias. The sampling framework is household-based rather than enterprise based which means that the survey probably under-sampled businesses outside households, particularly relatively large-sized firms.

Only 4 per cent of firms in rural areas are registered with Tanzania's Business Registration and Licensing Agency (BRELA), although this is similar to those in urban areas.[6] By contrast, more urban enterprises (8 per cent) have tax identification numbers than rural enterprises (3 per cent). While the MSME survey is a household-based survey, 49 per cent of rural firms report that their businesses are actually operating out of their homes and the number in urban areas is almost identical at 47 per cent. Therefore, the shares of nonfarm enterprises reported in Table 8.4 calculated from HBS 2011–12 data could significantly underestimate the importance of MSMEs in rural areas, given that HBS captures only home businesses.

Because there is no comprehensive registry of informal firms and because informal firms dominate the landscape in Tanzania, the sampling framework used to conduct the MSME survey is based on the 2002 Census. In addition, enumerators conducted interviews at the household level to identify enterprise owners. Thus, the sample is possibly skewed towards rural businesses. We report in Table 8.3(a) average monthly value-added and average monthly sales per firm. Value added is computed as the firm's average monthly sales minus the firms' average monthly costs of production. The mean value-added of rural firms is very close to the average monthly gross income of a formal employee in Tanzania, which is close to 337,000 Tanzanian Shillings according to Tanzania's Formal Employment and Earnings Survey (FEES) in 2010; the number is significantly higher for urban firms, especially for firms in Dar es Salaam. However, there is significant variation among surveyed firms in monthly value-added, indicated by the high value of the standard deviation (s.d.) in Table 8.3(a). This heterogeneity among small informal firms is a point to which we will return in detail later in the chapter.

Most MSME firms are young as indicated by the mean age of 6.9 years for rural firms, 6.1 years for urban firms outside Dar es Salaam, and 5.5 years for firms in Dar es Salaam. This is consistent with our findings in the first section that most nonfarm jobs created in Tanzania between 2002 and 2012 were created by small informal firms. Table 8.3(a) also indicates that 76 per cent of rural businesses operate full time, compared to 82 per cent in urban areas outside Dar es Salaam and 87 per cent in Dar es Salaam. More than 40 per cent of rural business

---

[6] BRELA is Tanzania's Business Registrations and Licensing Agency. It is a Government Executive Agency and was established on 28 October 1999. The aim of the agency is to ensure that businesses operate in accordance with regulations and to ensure that businesses follow 'sound principles'.

owners report that the business is the owner's main source of income with a significantly lower share of rural business owners (28 per cent) reporting that the business is the owner's *only* source of income. By contrast, 44 per cent and 51 per cent of urban business owners report that the enterprise is their only source of income. Not surprisingly, 26 per cent of rural business owners report that farming is their main source of income while only 6 per cent of urban business owners outside Dar es Salaam say that farming is their main source of income (none in Dar es Salaam).

Like their businesses, the owners of these small businesses are also relatively young. For the full sample the mean age of business owners is roughly 37 years in rural and 36 years in urban areas. Comparing the observation number in Table 8.3(a) for a full sample to that in Table 8.3(b) for young owners at age 15–34, it shows that more than 40 per cent of business owners are young, and the average age for the young owners is less than 28 years in both rural and urban areas.

Table 8.3(a) shows slightly under half of all business owners are women in rural areas and the number jumps to 68 per cent and 64 per cent in other urban areas and Dar es Salaam, respectively. Among the young owners reported in Table 8.3(b), the share of women owners is similar as the full sample in rural areas and in other urbans but is much lower (at 55 per cent) in Dar es Salaam.

Finally, we report at the bottom of Table 8.3(a) and Table 8.3(b) the three categories of income of the households in which the business owners reside for full samples and the young business owners, respectively. The measure of these three categories (very poor, modestly poor, and not poor[7]) was computed using monthly household income as reported by survey respondents. In general, households where the MSME owners reside are less poor: only 20 per cent of rural MSME owners live in households that can be described as very poor, and this is true also for the young owners. The proportions of MSME owners living in very poor urban households are lower than that in rural areas, 17 per cent for other urban and 18 per cent in in Dar es Salaam. The shares for young owners residing in the very poor urban households are even lower, 11 per cent for other urban and 7 per cent in Dar es Salaam.

We also report a set of summary of statistics for MSMEs whose owners are not young in Table 8.3(c). A t-test is conducted for all the variables reported in Table 8.3(a) between the young and other adult groups of MSMEs, and the six variables for which the t-test is insignificant are dropped from Tables 8.3(b) and 8.3(c). These six such variables include 'percentage of firms registered with BRELA', 'average monthly value added', and 'average monthly sales' per firm we discussed above.

---

[7] See the definition in the notes of Table 8.3(a).

We already know that most MSMEs are extremely small, while firms owned by younger owners are even smaller. As shown in Table 8.3(b), mean employment for such firms is 1.39 (instead of 1.59 for those owned by other adults) in rural areas, 1.43 (instead of 1.85) in urban areas outside Dar es Salaam, and 1.59 (instead of 1.83) in Dar es Salaam. Smaller size of MSMEs owned by youth could be due to relatively young firm age. The mean age for rural firms owned by youth is 4.67 years, three years younger than rural firms owned by other adults, with mean age of 8.77 years. The firm age gap is similar in urban areas between these two groups of firms: average age of urban firms owned by youth is 4.11 years outside Dar es Salaam and 4.04 years in Dar es Salaam, versus 8.07 and 7.10 years, respectively, for urban firms owned by other adults in these two locations.

Forty-three per cent of rural business owners who are not young report that the business is their main source of income with a significantly lower share (26 per cent) reporting that the business is the owners' only source of income. By contrast, among rural business owners who are young, only 39 per cent report that the business is their main source of income but 31 per cent report that the business is their only source of income. In the urban areas, there are more young owners, 51 per cent in other urban areas and 56 per cent in Dar es Salaam, who report that the enterprise is their only source of income, while for urban business owners who are not young the percentage is 37 per cent in other urban areas and 46 per cent in Dar es Salaam. The comparison between youth and other adult owners seems to indicate that young owners tend to be more likely to make MSMEs their only business both in rural and urban areas. As expected fewer MSME owners see farming as their main income source, and the percentage is even lower for young owners (24 per cent) than other adult owners (27 per cent).

8.3.3 Methodologies

The empirical strategy employed in this chapter aims to answer two questions: (1) What determines whether households participate in the nonfarm economy? (2) What determines whether nonfarm enterprises have the potential to grow and look more like formal firms and thus belong in what Lewis (1979) dubbed the in-between sector? Answers to these questions will contribute to a growing literature that recognizes the heterogeneity of nonfarm enterprises (see for example Bezu and Barrett 2012, Nagler and Naudé 2016). Both questions require the use of descriptive and econometric analyses.

Descriptive statistics for the HBS and MSME data provide a glimpse of the heterogeneity that is observed across households and firms. The means and standard errors presented in all the descriptive tables of this chapter were generated using the sampling design of the two surveys (HBS and MSME).

The econometric strategy employed in this chapter was motivated by the fact that we do not observe the levels of participation in the nonfarm economy, nor do we observe the potential of enterprises. We only observe whether these households and businesses fall within these categories. For the household data of HBS, we observe three types of households according to the engagements of household members' primary employment: nonfarm only, farm only, and mixed. The analysis thus focuses on the comparison of nonfarm households and the other types of households. For the firm data analysis using MSME survey, the high potential businesses are identified based on whether labour productivity is greater than the economy-wide productivity in the trade sector and we call small firms with high potential as 'in-between' firms following Lewis (1979).[8] In practice, this means that the left-hand side variable is binary in nature in the econometric analysis.

We use a probit model[9] for the two analyses using data from the HBS and MSME surveys. The probit model assumes that the actual y (left-hand side variable) is latent, that is, it is not observable but is inferred from variables that are observed. Equation (1) shows this relationship.

$$\Pr(y = 1|x) = \Pr(y^* > 0|x) \tag{1}$$

Where y is an indicator variable for whether a certain household or business meets the criteria described above and y^* is an unobserved variable that when greater than 0 causes y to be equal to 1 (for example, being a nonfarm only rural household in the HBS probit model or an in-between firm in the MSME model) and 0 otherwise.

The specifications of the probit models are provided in the Section 8.4 for the HBS survey and the Section 8.5 for the MSME survey. Marginal effects are reported. The marginal effects can be interpreted as the change in the predicted probability given a 1 unit change in the right-hand side in the case of continuous variables or a discrete change in the case of categorical variables. All estimations present robust standard errors in accordance to the sampling design. Since the survey was not in any way stratified and subnational units are not representative, we have not clustered the standard errors to any specific subnational location.

---

[8] Labour productivity is measured by value-added per worker at the firm level. We only consider firms to be in-between if their labour productivity is higher than the economy-wide productivity of the trade sector.

[9] Given the fact that the observed variable ranges between 0 and 1, traditional ordinary least squares regression analysis is not appropriate for two main reasons: First, some of the fitted values obtained from an OLS regression may and mostly likely will be outside the interval of 0 and 1 and hence yielding biased and non-valid inferences. Second, a probit model is more efficient if the error term follows a normal distribution.

8.4 Characteristics of Households with Rural Nonfarm Activities—An Analysis at the Household Level Using HBS data

We begin this section for an analysis at the rural household level using the data of HBS 2011–12. The analysis focuses on assessing the size of rural nonfarm economy by number (or share) of rural households that participate in such nonfarm economy and the differences between households with and without rural nonfarm participation.

8.4.1 How Large is the Rural Nonfarm Economy?

Using the HBS and according to the primary employment of households' members we first classify rural households into three types: (a) agriculture-only households without engagement of rural nonfarm activity; (b) households engaged in both agricultural and non-agricultural activities (mixed type); and (c) households with non-agricultural activity only without engagement in agriculture. For the last two types we further disaggregate them by with and without nonfarm home businesses (enterprises). Table 8.4 reports the distribution of the three types of households by shares of household, population, and employment. We also consider youth separately in this distribution either for youth as heads of households or as family members.

Table 8.4. Distribution of three types of rural households in Tanzania in 2012

		Agri. & non-agri. mixed		Non-agriculture only	
	Agri. only	With nonfarm enterprises	Without nonfarm enterprises	With nonfarm enterprises	Without nonfarm enterprises
Share by household numbers	61.4	22.1	5.4	5.8	5.4
Share by youth-headed households	56.9	20.5	4.7	8.7	9.2
Share by population	58.4	25.8	6.3	5.1	4.4
Share by employment	59.4	26.6	6.6	3.9	3.5
Share by youth employment	58.1	24.1	5.3	6.1	6.4

Notes: The HBS asked individual households whether they have a home business and an ISIC rev4 code is used for assigning sectors to the business. We consider ISIC non-agricultural sectors only as nonfarm enterprises. The employment of non-agriculture is defined by the current primary employment that is not in agriculture.

Source: Authors' calculations based on the data of HBS 2011–12 (NBS 2014a)

Like other low income countries in Africa, most regions in Tanzania are predominantly rural (Davis, Di Guiseppe, and Zezza 2014). Farming activity dominates rural Tanzania—more than 60 per cent of rural households engage only in agricultural activities in 2012 (Table 8.4), and less than 40 per cent engage in nonfarm in different ways. More youth-headed rural households engage in nonfarm activities than the rural average, but still the majority of such households engage only in agricultural activities (Table 8.4). For many rural households with nonfarm activities, these activities are part of their livelihood side-by-side with farming, that is, they are agricultural and non-agricultural mixed households accounting for 27.5 per cent total rural households and 25.2 per cent youth-headed rural households. Approximately 11 per cent of households specialized in rural nonfarm and the share is much higher (17.9 per cent) for youth-headed rural households. A small portion of rural households who participate in both farm and nonfarm economies have own nonfarm businesses, while about half of households who specialize in rural nonfarm have their own nonfarm business (and the other half are the employment participants of rural nonfarm, Table 8.4).

8.4.2 Characteristics of Households in the Rural Nonfarm Economy

We explain the differences between households with and without rural nonfarm activities using a probit model for a set of household characteristics and a set of community variables. The community variables were used to capture the presence of public goods. The equation below provides the specification of the model,

$$y_i{}^* = a + \beta_1\left(H_i\right) + \beta_2\left(C_j\right) + \beta_3\left(D_r\right) + \varepsilon_i$$

where H_i is a vector of households' characteristics, C_j is a vector of infrastructure or other community level factors, and D_r is a set of regional dummies. The variables in the vector H_i include a dummy for youth (age 15–34) as household heads, a dummy for female as heads of households, number of youth in households, dummies for the levels of education of the household heads (less than primary as comparable), dummies for farm size defined by cultivated areas that are categorized into four groups: no-land, farms with land less than 2 ha, farms with land 2–5 ha, and farms with land greater than 5 ha (farms with land less than 2 ha as comparable), and a dummy for households with paid loans to banks or family friends in the past 12 months. Vector C_j contains a set of variables related to access to infrastructure at the community level and other community level factors including daily public transformation to regional capital, electricity, mobile phone signal, internet, banks, informal finance, cooperatives, a major state employer (for example, a factory), and weekly market. ε_i is the iid error term.

	(1)	(2)	(3)	(4)	(5)
	HH with nonfarm compared with those without	Nonfarm HH only, compared with all others	HH with nonfarm enterprises, compared with all others	Nonfarm HH only, compared with the mixed	HH with nonfarm enterprises compared with HH with nonfarm job
Household variables					
Youth-headed households (with age 15–34)	−0.024 (0.021)	0.022* (0.009)	−0.017 (0.020)	0.056** (0.021)	0.008 (0.025)
Female-headed households	−0.026 (0.023)	0.019 (0.012)	−0.033 (0.020)	0.071** (0.025)	−0.027 (0.031)
Level of education (less than primary as the comparable)					
Primary	0.099*** (0.020)	0.056*** (0.014)	0.075*** (0.019)	0.081* (0.032)	−0.014 (0.030)
Secondary	0.378*** (0.039)	0.188*** (0.021)	0.084* (0.039)	0.286*** (0.038)	−0.217*** (0.040)
Number of youth (15–34) in household	0.037*** (0.008)	0.001 (0.004)	0.024** (0.008)	−0.021* (0.010)	−0.007 (0.010)
Cultivated land (with less than 2ha land as the comparable)					
No cultivated land	0.470*** (0.042)	0.236*** (0.018)	0.117*** (0.033)	0.360*** (0.028)	−0.160*** (0.031)
2-5ha	−0.002 (0.021)	−0.037** (0.013)	0.027 (0.021)	−0.082*** (0.023)	0.087** (0.034)
>5 ha	0.070 (0.037)	−0.028 (0.024)	0.062 (0.035)	−0.083 (0.056)	0.021 (0.047)
HH paid loans to bank or family friends in past 12mo	0.197** (0.066)	0.052* (0.023)	0.180** (0.064)	0.048 (0.047)	0.066 (0.073)

Continued

Table 8.5. Continued

	(1)	(2)	(3)	(4)	(5)
	HH with nonfarm compared with those without	Nonfarm HH only, compared with all others	HH with nonfarm enterprises, compared with all others	Nonfarm HH only, compared with the mixed	HH with nonfarm enterprises compared with HH with nonfarm job
Community variables					
Public transportation to regional HQ from EA	0.047	0.045*	0.041	0.077*	0.019
	(0.045)	(0.020)	(0.042)	(0.039)	(0.048)
Electricity in EA	-0.030	-0.009	-0.038	0.008	-0.032
	(0.048)	(0.019)	(0.044)	(0.036)	(0.040)
Mobile signal in EA	-0.058	0.035	-0.060	0.112**	-0.029
	(0.047)	(0.021)	(0.037)	(0.041)	(0.042)
Internet in the EA	0.018	0.004	0.025	-0.022	0.026
	(0.059)	(0.017)	(0.057)	(0.037)	(0.069)
Bank in the EA	0.124	0.003	0.099	-0.048	0.044
	(0.148)	(0.048)	(0.152)	(0.130)	(0.145)
Cooperative primary society in the EA	-0.137***	-0.044**	-0.107**	-0.031	-0.010
	(0.039)	(0.016)	(0.037)	(0.032)	(0.039)
Informal financial service in the EA	0.106**	-0.006	0.102**	-0.064*	0.043
	(0.041)	(0.014)	(0.037)	(0.032)	(0.037)
Major employer (that is, business or factory) in the EA	0.034	0.067***	-0.030	0.159***	-0.108*
	(0.047)	(0.017)	(0.043)	(0.037)	(0.048)
Weekly market in the EA	0.074	0.041**	0.048	0.064*	-0.028
	(0.039)	(0.014)	(0.035)	(0.031)	(0.034)
Obs	4,011	4,011	4,011	1,569	1,569

Note: Only rural households are included in the regressions. Number of the sample obs. is 4,130. Standard errors in parentheses. * p < 0.05; ** p < 0.01; *** p < 0.001.

Source: Probit regression results using 2012 Tanzania HBS data (NBS 2014a).

We report the marginal effects of the probit regression results in Table 8.5. Different columns of Table 8.5 report the results when rural households who have nonfarm activities are compared to different groups of other households. In column (1), the rural households with nonfarm (including those either specializing in nonfarm or in the mixed group) are compared to those specializing in farming ($y_i^* = 1$ for rural households with nonfarm). In column (2) rural households specializing in nonfarm (= 1) are compared to all others. In column (3) households with nonfarm enterprises (= 1) are compared to all others. In column (4) households specializing in nonfarm activities (= 1) are compared to agricultural/ non-agricultural mixed households. Finally, in column (5) households specializing in nonfarm with nonfarm enterprises (= 1) are compared to those specializing in nonfarm without nonfarm enterprises (that is, with only nonfarm jobs).

We start with the probit regression results associated with youth as household heads. The results of different regressions indicate that being a youth-headed household increases the probability of specializing in rural nonfarm activities by 2 and 6 per cent (columns (2) and (4)), but they do not seem very different from other households when agriculture is still part of their household's livelihood (columns (1) and (3)). Among households specializing in nonfarm activities, youth headed households with nonfarm enterprises are not different from other households only having nonfarm jobs (column (5)). In general, female-headed households in nonfarm households are not different from other households. Only when female headed households are compared to mixed households, do we observe a 7 per cent increase in the probability of specializing in nonfarm activities (column (4)). Households with more young family members have a greater probability to engage in nonfarm activity, ranging from 2 to 4 per cent (columns (1) and (3)) when agriculture is still part of the household's livelihood. However, when we focus on the households specializing in nonfarm, a higher number of young family members generate either no difference from other households (columns (2) and (5)) or decreased probability of specializing on nonfarm activities (by 2 per cent, column (4)). Households that have paid loans to banks or family friends in the past 12 months show an increase of 5 to 20 per cent in the likelihood of engaging in nonfarm activities depending on the comparison group. Thus, it may be because they specialize in nonfarm activities, they borrowed in the past and have to pay back (and columns (2) and (3) might be used to support this argument).[10, 11]

The probit regression results show that the most important determinant of whether a household engages in nonfarm activities is the education of the

---

[10] Given the cross-sectional nature of the data, we can rule out the possibility of simultaneity bias.
[11] On the other hand, it is possible that past borrowing has nothing to do with nonfarm businesses and paying back such debt forces households to engage in rural nonfarm activities in addition to farming to earn some cash income (and column (1) might be used to support this argument). The literature suggests that both stories are plausible.

household head. Households whose head has a primary education observe an increase of 5 to 10 per cent in the probability of engaging in nonfarm enterprises compared to without primary education (except for households with nonfarm jobs). For a household whose head has secondary or more education, the increase in the probability of engaging in nonfarm activities is between 8 and 38 per cent. However, we also note that more educated households are less likely to own their own businesses, which is consistent with the idea that higher levels of education are often the requirement for a regular nonfarm job in rural areas.

We also consider the relationship between participation in nonfarm activities, farm size, and whether a household has access to land. Households without farmland witness a greater increase in the probability of engaging in nonfarm businesses than households with farm land less than 2 hectares. Only when households specializing in nonfarm and having their own business are compared to households with nonfarm jobs, it shows that households without land are less likely to have their own business and more likely to have nonfarm jobs. Among the households with land, the impact of farm size is mixed. Households with farmland between 2 and 5 hectares often witness a decrease in the probability of engaging in nonfarm businesses than households with the smallest plots. This relationship disappears for households with more than 5 ha of land possibly because relatively few households have this much land.

In Table 8.5, we also explore whether community level variables such as public infrastructure, financial services, and market activity play a role in determining the prevalence of rural nonfarm activity. These variables are part of community questionnaires of HBS 2011–12. We use access to daily public transport to the regional capital as a proxy for road access. The result shows that households in communities with access to daily public transportation observe increases of 4–8 per cent in the probability of participating in nonfarm activities. While the use of electricity for doing business especially in the manufacturing sector is important, the variable is insignificant in all five specifications; this is also true for access to the internet. This may be because access to electricity and the internet access at the community level do not necessarily imply access at the household level. Alternatively, it could be a result of the fact that products produced in this manufacturing are not very demanding in terms of electricity.[12] Availability of a mobile phone signal increases the predicted probability of specializing in nonfarm activities by 11 per cent relative to mixed households, but is insignificant in the other regressions. We also find no significance of the presence of formal banks. On the other hand, access to informal finance increases the predicted probability of participating in nonfarm activities and engaging in nonfarm businesses, but reduces the probability of specializing in nonfarm activities. Results for the access to formal and informal finance at the community level seem to indicate informal financing is the main channel to borrow money.

---

[12] We thank our reviewer for pointing out this possibility.

The presence of cooperatives in communities reduces the likelihood of nonfarm activities by a range of 4 to 11 per cent. This is perhaps because communities with cooperatives are more heavily agricultural. On the other hand, the existence of a major state employer such as a business or a factory in the community increases the probability of specializing in rural nonfarm activities by 6 to 16 per cent depending on the comparison group but reduces the probability of running household businesses relative to working in nonfarm jobs (column (5))—probably because in communities with such state-run businesses, nonfarm jobs are more plentiful and attractive. Finally, the existence of a weekly market increases the probability of a household specializing in rural nonfarm activities relative to all other households and relative to mixed households. The mixed results regarding the role of infrastructure are puzzling. As noted, this may be because the community level variables are too 'rough' a proxy for access at the household level. However, the lack of significance of these variables may also be associated with the small scale of rural nonfarm enterprises. According to Tybout (2000), low levels of economic density and interaction may lead to small, diffuse pockets of demand, which in turn result in small, localized production and services. We revisit this issue in the Section 8.5 using the MSME data.

8.5 Characteristics of Rural Nonfarm Enterprises and Their Owners—An Analysis at the Firm Level using MSME Survey Data

A vibrant rural nonfarm sector can play an important role in rural transformation. To get at the extent to which the rural nonfarm sector can play a role in labour productivity growth and poverty reduction in rural areas, we use the MSME survey data to examine the motivations of business owners in the rural nonfarm sector as well as the characteristics of their businesses. In previous work (Diao, Kweka, and McMillan 2017) we identified a group of MSMEs that belong in what Arthur Lewis (1979) referred to as the in-between sector. According to Lewis (1979) these firms play an important role in the transformation process. In that work, we showed that rural enterprises are on average slightly less productive than their urban counterparts (and this is confirmed again in Table 8.3(a) of the Section 8.3 in this chapter) but we did not explore in detail the characteristics of rural enterprises or rural entrepreneurs. We also did not compare characteristics of rural entrepreneurs and enterprises across geographic locations due to the limited observations in many geographic locations.

We begin with a description of location and industrial composition of MSMEs. We follow this with an exploration of the extent to which rural entrepreneurs are in business solely for the purposes of survival, for example, 'reluctant entrepreneurs', or whether they are in business because they can make a good living this way. To get at these issues, we examine the following: (i) self-reported motivations for business ownership; (ii) the productive heterogeneity of MSMEs; and (iii) employment growth in MSMEs.

8.5.1 Locations and Industrial Composition of MSMEs

In Table 8.6, we report the distribution of employment and numbers of MSMEs by rural, other urban, and Dar es Salaam, and we also compare such distribution with the distribution of population. We also report the distributions for MSMEs owned by youth and by other adults separately. While more than 67 per cent of population live in rural areas, rural MSMEs account for 52 per cent of total MSME employment and number of firms. The percentages of employment and numbers of firms owned by youth in rural areas are slightly lower (49.8 per cent) than the MSMEs owned by other adults (52 per cent and 54 per cent respectively) in rural areas.

There seems to be a similar relationship between the distribution of MSME employment/firms and distribution of population in Dar es Salaam and in other urban areas. 15.8 per cent of MSME employment and 17.3 per cent of MSME firms are in Dar es Salaam, where 12.2 per cent of the national population resides. Likewise, 32.6 per cent of MSME employment and 30.7 per cent of MSME firms are in other urban areas, which contain 20.4 per cent of the population. The breakdown of MSMEs owned by youth and other adults also follows a similar proportion (Table 8.6).

In Table 8.7, we report the industrial distribution of MSMEs by rural, other urban, and Dar es Salaam. We further look at the distributions for the two subgroups: MSMEs owned by youth and by other adults in the table. Although the MSMEs operate in a wide range of activities, the bulk of these activities can be classified into trade services (80 per cent) and manufacturing (15 per cent). However, more rural firms (19.8 per cent) engage in manufacturing than the urban firms (10.1 per cent in other urban and 7.2 per cent in Dar es Salaam). This can also be seen from the second panel of Table 8.7, that is, 72 per cent of total manufacturing firms are in rural areas but 52 per cent of total trade service firms are in rural areas. This is an expected pattern, as manufacturing enterprises operate mainly in food processing, which has strong links to agriculture. Without further information, however, it is not possible to identify which ones and exactly how these linkages work. This is an important area for future research. Between the two urban locations, more trade service firms are in Dar es Salaam (87.6 per cent) than in other urban areas (83.0 per cent)—a clearly demand-driven pattern in small firms' establishment in urban areas.

Comparing youth owners to other adult owners, youth seem to engage more in trade services than other adults, who engage more in manufacturing. The exception is in other urban locations where more MSMEs owned by other adults are in trade business and youth engage more in either manufacturing or other businesses.

Table 8.6. Distribution of population and MSMEs (weighted, percentage)

	Population	MSME employment	Number of business
	All	All MSMEs	
Rural	67.4	51.6	52.1
Other urban	20.4	32.6	30.7
Dar Es Salaam	12.2	15.8	17.3
Total	100	100	100
	Youth	MSMEs owned by youth (15–34)	
Rural	65.0	49.8	49.8
Other urban	21.3	32.0	31.3
Dar Es Salaam	13.7	18.2	18.9
Total	100	100	100
	Other adults	MSMEs owned by other adults	
Rural	70.6	52.9	54.1
Other urban	19.2	33.1	30.0
Dar Es Salaam	10.3	14.0	15.9
Total	100	100	100

Source: Population is from HBS (2012) and MSME employment and number are from MSME survey (2010).

Table 8.7. Sectoral distribution of rural and urban MSME firms in the survey (weighted, percentage)

	Per cent of total in each location				Per cent of total in each sector		
	Rural	Other urban	Dar es Salaam	Total	Rural	Other urban	Dar es Salaam
Total	100.0	100.0	100.0	100.0	54.2	31.2	14.6
Manufacturing	19.8	10.1	7.2	14.9	71.9	21.1	7.1
Trade services	76.5	83.0	87.6	80.2	51.7	32.3	16.0
Others	3.8	6.9	5.2	4.9	41.1	43.5	15.4
Youth owners							
Youth total	100.0	100.0	100.0	100.0	53.0	29.9	17.1
Manufacturing	15.1	11.2	3.5	12.0	67.1	27.9	5.0
Trade services	81.7	77.2	93.3	82.4	52.6	28.1	19.4
Others	3.2	11.6	3.1	5.7	29.5	61.0	9.5
Other adult owners							
Other adult total	100.0	100.0	100.0	100.0	54.7	31.8	13.5
Manufacturing	21.8	9.6	9.3	16.2	73.5	18.8	7.8
Trade services	74.2	85.5	84.3	79.2	51.3	34.3	14.4
Others	4.0	4.9	6.4	4.6	47.6	33.7	18.7

Source: Authors calculations using the MSME Survey 2010.

8.5.2 Self-reported Motivations of Small Business Owners

The MSME survey includes three questions designed to elicit the reasons for opening a business. Responses to such self-reported motivations for a business could help us assess the extent to which rural entrepreneurs are in business solely for the purposes of survival, for example, 'reluctant entrepreneurs', or whether they are in business because they can make a good living this way. The responses to these questions are tabulated using sample weights in Tables 8.8–8.10. In these three tables, we also report responses separately for young and other adult owners in addition to the total samples. Again, in the youth and other adult panels of the tables, we only report variables that are statistically different between youth and other adults.

The first question is: What was your main occupation before you started this business? Responses to this question are reported in order of how often they were recorded in Table 8.8. The biggest difference between rural and urban entrepreneurs is that 56.5 per cent of rural entrepreneurs report that their main occupation prior to starting the business was farming; the share is only 19.3 per cent in urban areas outside Dar es Salaam. Very few respondents (4.8 per cent) in rural areas report that they were unemployed prior to starting the business; this is not true in urban areas where 11.3 and 9.7 per cent of MSME owners in other urban and Dar es Salaam report that they were unemployed before starting their business. Unlike in rural areas, urban business owners are much more likely to report that they were previously employed in a private company or running a similar sized business in another line of business. It is also much more common for urban business owners to report that they were previously a housewife or homemaker (26.6 per cent in other urban and 34.1 per cent in Dar es Salaam) than for rural respondents (12.3 per cent).

The second and third panels of Table 8.8 are the summaries of the responses from youth owners and other adult owners of MSMEs. The responses to many questions are not significantly different between these two subgroups of MSMEs, and therefore such responses are not included in the table. For many of the remaining responses in Table 8.8, the differences between youth and other adults are insignificant in rural areas, but significant in urban areas. For example, similar large shares (52.5 and 59.8 per cent) of rural young and other adult entrepreneurs report that their main occupation prior to starting the business was farming; but in other urban areas, the share is only 15.6 per cent for young respondents while it is 23.0 per cent of other adult respondents. In other urban areas 14.2 per cent of MSME young owners report that they were unemployed before starting their business, while the share is only 8.5 per cent for other adult owners. Interesting, 10.6 per cent of Dar es Salaam's non-youth entrepreneurs report that they used to be a government employee or a civil servant, compared to only 1.9 per cent of youth entrepreneurs (and similar small shares, 0.5 per cent and 3.7 per cent, for young and other adult owners in other urban areas). The fact that 11 per cent of

Table 8.8. Occupation prior to starting business of MSMEs (weighted, percentage)

	Rural	Other urban	Dar es Salaam	Total
All MSMEs				
Unemployed	4.8	11.3	9.7	7.6
Housewife (homemaker)	12.3	26.6	34.1	20.0
In education, at various levels	3.2	5.5	5.4	4.2
Employed in large private enterprise in similar business	0.4	1.7	2.9	1.2
Employed in large private enterprise in a different business	1.7	4.7	6.9	3.4
Employed in a similar sized private business in the same line of business	0.6	1.5	1.9	1.0
Employed in a similar sized private business in another line of business	0.6	0.8	3.0	1.0
Ran a similar sized business in the same line of business	0.9	2.0	1.9	1.4
Ran a similar sized enterprise in another line of business	9.5	16.4	20.0	13.2
Civil servant/employed by the government	1.8	2.1	6.0	2.5
I was employed by some individual	0.6	2.2	1.9	1.3
Rearing of cattle	0.5	0.4	0.2	0.4
Farming	56.5	19.3	0.7	36.7
I was selling food	0.6	1.4	1.1	0.9
Others	4.8	3.5	2.4	4.0
None	1.2	0.6	2.0	1.1
Youth owners				
Unemployed	5.3	14.2	9.8	8.9
In education, at various levels	5.4	9.5	8.7	7.2
Employed in large private enterprise in similar business	0.7	2.0	3.9	1.7
Employed in a similar sized private business in the same line of business	0.6	2.4	3.5	1.6
Employed in a similar sized private business in another line of business	0.7	0.1	3.3	0.9
Civil servant/employed by the government	0.4	0.5	1.9	0.7
Farming	52.5	15.6	0.5	32.1
Others	3.5	2.9	2.5	3.2
Other adult owners				
Unemployed	4.5	8.5	9.5	6.4
In education, at various levels	1.4	1.7	1.6	1.5
Employed in large private enterprise in similar business	0.2	1.3	1.8	0.8
Employed in a similar sized private business in the same line of business	0.6	0.6	–	0.5
Employed in a similar sized private business in another line of business	0.6	1.5	2.7	1.2
Civil servant/employed by the government	3.0	3.7	10.6	4.2

Continued

Table 8.8. Continued

	Rural	Other urban	Dar es Salaam	Total
Farming	59.8	23.0	1.0	41.0
Others	5.8	4.0	2.2	4.8

Note: This table is prepared based on the question 'what was your main occupation before you started this business?' in the MSME survey, and a unique answer is provided by individual MSME owners. Number of the full sample obs. is 4,163, and 1,853 for the MSMEs with youth as owners. The sum of each column in the first panel for all MSMEs is 100.

Source: Authors calculations using the MSME Survey 2010.

other adult owners of MSMEs in the country's largest city seem to give up a paid government job to open their own enterprises deserves more analysis to fully understand the motivation of small business entrepreneurs.

The second question is: for what reason did you choose your line of business? Responses to this question are reported in Table 8.9 by three broad sectors: manufacturing, trade services, and other services as well as by rural, other urban, and Dar es Salaam. Again, the responses that are statistically different between young and other adult owners are reported for these two subgroups separately in the table. In rural areas, half of all business owners say that the reason they chose their line of business is because they saw a market opportunity. This response is similar for manufacturing and trade services. The shares for the similar response are lower in other urban areas and in Dar es Salaam than in rural areas. The second most common reason for operating in a line of business in rural areas is that the owners' capital could only finance that line of business, which is more common in urban areas. This seems to indicate that capital constraint for small business development is more binding in urban than in rural areas. The third most common reason for picking a line of business in rural areas was prior experience in that line of business, but apportionment for this reason are much lower than the two previous ones. Among young and other owners, the order of these three reasons are similar, which tells us that when coming to decide what kind of business, the reasons are similar regardless of young and other adult entrepreneurs in either rural or urban areas.

The third question is: if you were offered a full-time salary-paying job, would you take it? Responses to this question are reported in Table 8.10 and indicate that only 46.6 per cent of all small business owners would leave their current business for a full-time salaried position, but the share is higher in rural areas and other urban areas (47.8 and 48.6 per cent respectively) than in Dar es Salaam (37.7 per cent). Young adults show a stronger preference for a full-time salary job (instead of being a business owner). In rural areas 54 per cent of young owners would prefer a full-time paying job, compared to 42 per cent for other adults. This is similar in urban

	Rural enterprise			Other urban enterprises			Enterprise in Dar es Salaam		
	Manufacturing	Trade services	Rural total	Manufacturing	Trade Services	Other urban total	Manufacturing	Trade services	Dar Es Salaam total
All MSMEs									
I had previous experience in this line	25.0	15.2	18.3	39.6	15.5	19.5	37.0	9.7	18.5
Friends/relatives are in this line	20.6	13.4	14.8	21.0	19.4	17.8	13.2	16.4	12.8
I saw a market opportunity	48.2	51.6	50.0	36.3	43.1	41.6	14.6	46.4	39.2
My capital could only finance this business	36.1	42.1	41.8	26.2	47.4	43.3	46.8	46.8	47.7
No apparent reason	2.9	6.0	4.5	4.3	2.9	4.2	3.2	5.2	4.7
I could start business gradually	0.0	0.1	0.1	0.0	0.1	0.5	0.0	1.0	0.6
Goods are easy to manufacture and sell	1.4	2.0	2.0	0.2	1.5	1.6	0.0	0.9	1.0
I just wanted to be near my house	0.8	1.0	0.9	0.0	1.8	1.2	0.0	0.0	0.4
I have been trained in it, I am an expert	1.6	0.4	0.6	6.2	0.1	1.1	9.4	0.4	0.9
Goods are available	0.3	0.4	0.5	0.0	0.4	0.2	0.0	2.7	1.4
I perceived it to be profitable	1.3	1.6	1.7	0.0	2.6	1.8	0.0	0.2	0.1
I liked it	0.7	1.0	1.3	3.5	1.5	1.6	1.8	1.1	1.1
Business does not have many problems	1.4	0.6	0.7	0.0	0.3	0.3	0.0	1.6	1.2
Other	1.0	2.5	2.2	5.7	2.4	3.1	1.3	3.2	2.4
None	0.3	1.3	0.8	2.0	0.9	1.2	1.3	0.0	1.1

Continued

Table 8.9. Continued

	Rural enterprise			Other urban enterprises			Enterprise in Dar es Salaam		
	Manufacturing	Trade services	Rural total	Manufacturing	Trade Services	Other urban total	Manufacturing	Trade services	Dar Es Salaam total
Youth owners									
I had previous experience in this line	22.9	13.9	17.6	42.7	12.5	18.5	30.8	11.1	19.2
Friends/relatives are in this line	22.3	14.9	15.0	26.8	25.2	22.1	2.2	21.4	15.4
I saw a market opportunity	52.1	51.7	50.9	37.7	43.3	40.4	2.2	43.0	36.2
My capital could only finance this business	37.7	44.5	43.6	15.4	45.3	39.9	74.3	48.6	50.0
No apparent reason	1.9	6.0	4.8	8.7	4.8	6.8	0.0	2.6	4.0
I just wanted to be near my house	0.0	1.2	0.7	0.0	0.5	0.6	0.0	0.0	0.0
I liked it	0.7	1.4	2.0	2.5	3.0	2.1	4.0	0.0	0.7
Other adult owners									
I had previous experience in this line	26.2	16.5	18.9	37.3	18.2	20.5	42.4	7.8	17.7
Friends/relatives are in this line	19.7	11.9	14.6	16.6	14.0	13.6	22.7	10.0	9.8
I saw a market opportunity	46.1	51.6	49.2	35.2	42.9	42.8	25.4	50.7	42.7
My capital could only finance this business	35.2	39.8	40.3	34.3	49.4	46.6	22.9	44.5	45.0
No apparent reason	3.5	6.0	4.3	0.9	1.2	1.7	5.9	8.5	5.4
I just wanted to be near my house	1.2	0.8	1.0	0.0	3.0	1.8	0.0	0.0	0.9
I liked it	0.8	0.7	0.7	4.3	0.2	1.2	0.0	2.4	1.6

Note: Number of the full sample obs. is 4,163, and 1,853 for the MSMEs with youth as owners. Multiple answers are allowed for individual MSME owners.

Table 8.10. Job satisfaction in MSME survey (weighted, percentage)

	Rural	Other urban	Dar es Salaam	Total
All MSMEs				
If you were offered a full-time salary paying job, would you take it?	47.8	48.6	37.7	46.6
Who would you rather work for?				
A large private company	17.9	27.4	43.1	24.0
Government	68.6	62.9	44.6	63.9
Someone else's business	10.5	6.2	10.8	9.1
Anywhere	3.0	3.4	1.5	3.0
And why do you say that?				
Better security of income	81.7	83.8	81.4	82.3
Shorter hours	5.1	5.7	3.5	5.1
Less risk	1.8	1.8	3.0	1.9
To get pension	1.5	1.6	–	1.4
I am less educated	2.2	0.9	1.9	1.8
They listen to the opinions of the employees	1.1	1.0	–	1.0
As long as I get a living	0.6	0.4	–	0.5
Job security	2.1	0.6	–	1.4
Others	2.2	2.3	9.9	3.1
None/Nothing	1.7	2.1	0.2	1.6
Youth owners				
If you were offered a full-time salary paying job, would you take it?	54.0	52.9	38.2	51.1
Who would you rather work for?				
A large private company	20.0	36.7	33.8	27.2
Government	65.4	54.8	49.6	59.9
Someone else's business	11.0	6.0	14.0	9.7
Anywhere	3.7	2.6	2.7	3.2
And why do you say that?				
Better security of income	81.5	86.2	80.4	82.9
Shorter hours	4.0	4.6	3.5	4.1
Less risk	2.2	2.7	5.5	2.8
To get pension	0.9	1.4	–	1.0
I am less educated	2.7	0.7	3.6	2.2
They listen to the opinions of the employees	0.9	0.4	–	0.6
As long as I get a living	0.8	0.2	–	0.5
Job security	2.5	0.4	–	1.5
Others	2.8	1.4	6.6	2.8
None/Nothing	1.6	1.9	0.4	1.6
Other adult owners				
If you were offered a full-time salary paying job, would you take it?	42.6	44.4	37.1	42.5
Who would you rather work for?				
A large private company	15.7	16.9	54.3	20.4
Government	72.0	72.2	38.7	68.3

Continued

Table 8.10. Continued

	Rural	Other urban	Dar es Salaam	Total
Someone else's business	9.9	6.5	7.0	8.5
Anywhere	2.4	4.3	–	2.7
And why do you say that?				
Better security of income	81.8	80.9	82.6	81.6
Shorter hours	6.2	6.9	3.5	6.1
Less risk	1.4	0.6	–	1.0
To get pension	2.1	1.9	–	1.8
I am less educated	1.7	1.1	–	1.4
They listen to the opinions of the employees	1.3	1.7	–	1.3
As long as I get a living	0.4	0.6	–	0.4
Job security	1.7	0.7	–	1.2
Others	1.5	3.3	13.8	3.5
None/Nothing	1.7	2.3	–	1.7

Note: This table is prepared based on three questions: (1) 'If you were offered a full-time salary paying job, would you take it?' (2) 'Who would you rather work for?' and (3) 'Why do you say that?' A unique answer is provided by individual MSME owners to each of the last two questions. Rural, urban, and national total MSMEs, MSMEs owned by youth, and MSMEs owned by other adults for the sum of these two questions are 100 respectively. Number of the full sample obs. is 4,163, and 1,853 for the MSMEs with youth as owners.

Source: Authors calculations using the MSME Survey 2010.

areas where 52.9 per cent of young adults prefer a full-time paying job compared to 44 per cent for other adults.

Approximately, 64 per cent all respondents who would prefer a full-time salaried job say they would like to work for the government, and the proportions are 68.6 and 62.9 per cent in rural and other urban areas but only 44.6 per cent in Dar es Salaam, where more government jobs are concentrated. The responses from rural and other urban MSME owners are consistent with results reported in Duflo and Banerjee's analysis of the economic lives of the poor (2007). Between youth and other adults, other adults seem to prefer a government job than youth in rural and other urban areas, but the opposite occurs in Dar es Salaam where youth prefer government jobs than other adults. Large private companies are more attractive to small business owners in Dar es Salaam than in other places particularly among other adults. The predominant reason for preferring a full-time salaried position is better security of income, which is consistent between youth and other adults and across different locations.

8.5.3 The Productive Heterogeneity of Rural Enterprises

We use kernel densities of the log of value added to examine the productive heterogeneity of MSMEs. Value added is computed as the firm's average monthly sales minus the firms' average monthly costs of production and is in nominal units of local currency. Firms in the MSME database report sales monthly and thus we can take seasonality into account. Our analysis of the productive heterogeneity of firms in the MSME sector reveals two important features of these firms.

First, there is a significant degree of productive heterogeneity among both rural and urban enterprises. This can be seen by examining the density of the log of value added per worker in Figure 8.2. Value added per worker is reported for both rural enterprises and urban enterprises, and urban enterprises are further disaggregated into other urban and Dar es Salaam. We also create a figure (Figure 8.3) for value added per worker for small businesses owned by youth and by other adults. In both Figures 8.2 and 8.3 the vertical lines represent average labour productivity in Tanzania's economy in 2010 in the agricultural sector (light gray), the trade services sector (middle gray) and the manufacturing sector (dark gray). Surprisingly, the distribution of the log of value added per worker or labour productivity for rural firms is almost identical to the distribution for

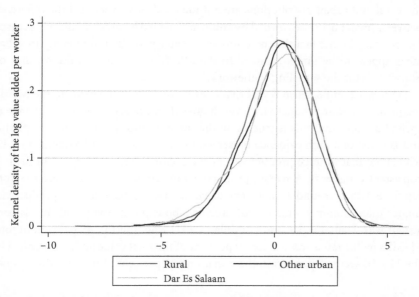

Figure 8.2. The distribution of the log of value added per worker among MSMEs in 2010 by location

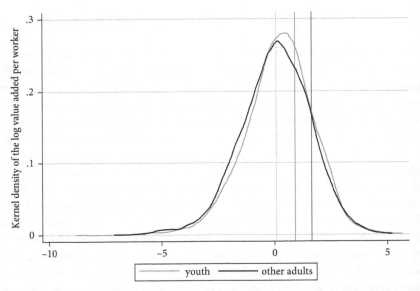

Figure 8.3. The distribution of the log of value added per worker among MSMEs in 2010 by young and other adult owners

urban firms. In fact, a test of stochastic dominance[13] rejects the hypothesis that the rural and urban distributions are not identical. Also, there is little difference between small businesses owned by youth and owned by other adults. One reason for this may be the fact that medium-sized enterprises that are mainly in urban areas appear to be under-sampled in the MSME survey due to the reliance on households for the sampling framework.

Figures 8.2 and 8.3 also reveal that a little over half of the firms in the MSME sector have labour productivity levels higher than the economy-wide average in agriculture and that this is true in all the three locations. This is not surprising and is consistent with evidence presented by Diao, Kweka, and McMillan (2017) who show that average productivity in the sectors dominated by small firms is consistently higher than average productivity in agriculture. We can also see from Figure 8.2 that around 15 per cent of rural MSMEs have labour productivity higher than economy-wide manufacturing labour productivity. This too is consistent with Diao, Kweka, and McMillan (2017) who find that 15 per cent of total MSMEs in Tanzania account for 70 per cent of the total value added generated by the MSME sector. By contrast, the remaining 85 per cent of the MSMEs account

---

[13] A stochastic dominance test compares the cumulative density function of the log of the value added in rural and urban areas. To establish whether the two curves originate from the same distribution, we have used the Komolgorov-Smirnov test of equality of distribution. We were not able to reject the null hypothesis that the distributions of urban and rural value added were the same (p-value=0.9).

for only 30 per cent of the value added generated by the MSME sector. These results underscore the productive heterogeneity of the MSMEs in both rural and urban areas.

8.6 Using the MSME Survey to Identify 'High Potential' Rural Enterprises

The main takeaway from the previous section is that *some* rural MSMEs have the potential to contribute significantly to rural transformation in Tanzania. To identify the characteristics of these firms, we separate the 'high potential' MSMEs from the rest using both qualitative information and performance-based measures of labour productivity. Following Lewis (1979), we call these groups of firms the 'in-between' firms. This terminology is meant to capture the idea that the characteristics of these firms place them somewhere in-between Tanzania's modern (most productive) and informal (least productive) firms. For example, the in-between firms may keep written accounts and be quite productive, but not be registered. For the purposes of this chapter, we include in the in-between group of firms only firms whose owners report that they would not quit their job for a salaried position, and in which labour productivity is greater than economy-wide labour productivity in trade service sector, represented by a vertical line in the middle of Figures 8.2 and 8.3 between the line for the economy-wide labour productivity of agriculture on the left and the line for the economy-wide labour productivity of manufacturing on the right. Using these criteria, we find that out of 5,609 sampled firms 944 firms that can be classified as belonging in the in-between sector, 45 per cent of which are rural firms, accounting for 10 per cent of total sampled rural firms.

To understand what distinguishes businesses with high potential, we have identified several explanatory variables that have been commonly used and tested in the relevant literature. These variables cover a host of business characteristics and are likely to provide a complete picture of the determinants of high potential businesses. Four categories of variables were identified: owner's personal characteristics, business characteristics, infrastructure and technology, and financial and other services. Using a probit model, we explored the characteristics of the most successful businesses considering these four categories of variables as explanatory variables in the regression. The dependent variable is 1 if a firm belongs to the in-between[14] category, the one we indicated in the fourth section as with high potential, and 0 otherwise. The regression shows that several

---

[14] As a reminder, for a firm to be considered in-between it must fulfil two conditions: First, its owner would not leave the business for a full-time salaried job, and second, labour productivity must be higher than the economy-wide trade productivity.

variables that we expected to be statistically significant were not. The absence of significance does not mean that these variables are irrelevant to the analysis. Rather, it is possible that this is a consequence of the cross-sectional nature of the data, which constrains to provide comparison points for both business and owner's characteristics. Nevertheless, we highlight a few main findings from the probit regressions focusing on the marginal effects in Tables 8.A4(a)–8.A4(c) in the Appendix.

Results for the owner's personal characteristics suggest that in-between firms are less likely to be headed by females on the order of 5 to 8 per cent depending on the location of the business. The two most important determinants of in-between firms are whether the owner is not poor and whether the owner views the business as growing. Both variables are highly significant and lead to non-negligible increases in the probability of being in the in-between category. Common sense confirms the feasibility of these results. Non-poor business owners are less likely to require loans and to have to sacrifice on labour or the quality of services provided due to lack of resources. Similarly, business owners who are optimistic about their firm's future and potential are also more likely to be driven to achieve success and to use resources in ways that are productive. Thus, none of the results described showed differences in the signs and presence of significance across the three locations (rural, other urban, and Dar es Salaam). The variable of 'seeing business as a market opportunity' shows significant results for national total and urban enterprises, a 3 and 4 per cent increase in the probability of being in the in-between category, respectively, but not for rural enterprises. 'Membership to a business association' also increases the probability of a firm falling in the in-between category. The absence of significance for young business owners is not surprising given that most business owners are young. Education, marital status, and whether the owner has taken expert advice are not significant. Education illustrates this point well. Evidence abounds about the positive effects of education on the performance of both businesses and individuals, but it needs panel data to verify it, as gains from education often are not immediately reflected in the performance of businesses. Similar logic can be applied to the owner receiving expert advice. Without more information about when individuals completed their education or how long has the owner received expert advice, it becomes difficult to gauge the true importance of these variables. The lack of significance of these variables may also reflect the lack of variability in the data.

A considerably more varied pattern of significance across geographies is found for business characteristics. Results for the variables under the business characteristic are not particularly surprising. For example, a one-unit increase in the number of employees reduces the probability of being an in-between firm by slightly over 2 per cent across locations. Businesses that run full-time, on the other hand, increase the probability of being in the in-between category by 6–7 per cent depending on location. Both signs fall within our expectations for two reasons.

First, the survey is designed to capture small businesses. Second, running a full-time business indicates that the business probably experiences some degree of success, or else owners would be inclined to find other sources of income. Less obvious, however, is the fact that holding written accounts is only significant in rural areas. Moreover, the coefficients for firms that have regional customers and whose number of daily customers exceeds 20 a day are positive and significant both nationally and in rural areas, which suggest that the national results were likely driven by rural areas. Changes in the predicted probabilities associated with having regional customers range from 3–5 per cent for all firms and for rural firms respectively. Firms with a daily number of customers higher than 20 are also more likely to be in the in-between category; the predicted probabilities range from 5.8 to 6.8 per cent nationally and in rural areas. The lack of significance of written accounts, regional customers, and number of daily customers in urban areas could be the result of lower variability among urban firms relative to rural areas, particularly because the survey has a much greater number of rural enterprises than urban. Non-significant variables such as market access, the nature of firms' suppliers (whether small traders or nationwide), and whether the firm has a licence may be a result of the fact that the average firm in the dataset is relatively young (about four years old). This, in turn, might suggest that not enough time has gone by for firms to be able to develop a consistent and systematic source of supply. A similar case could be argued for market access. As for whether firms have licences, the lack of significance might be a result of delays from regulatory agencies to provide licences without much red tape. In all cases, additional data about when firms started resorting to suppliers or gained access to markets (or time to receive a licence) would shed light on additional potential reasons for the absence of significance of these three variables.

The variables related to infrastructure and technology are also considered in the regressions. The gains in predicted probability obtained by using a mobile phone to conduct business range from 2.5 to nearly 8 per cent nationally and in urban areas respectively. Curiously, the fact that the owner owns a calculator is only significant at the national level with an associated change in the predicted probability of being in the in-between category of 4.2 per cent. The most important factor in the set of infrastructure and technology variables is 'whether the business uses electricity to light their businesses'. Increased predicted probabilities are observed across geographies, with gains ranging from nearly 7 per cent in rural areas to slightly over 8 per cent in urban areas. The absence of significance for variables such as 'whether the business has office equipment or a cooling facility' might also be related to the age of the firm and its ability to set up a complete and fully functional office structure. Here too, panel data would provide insights about the importance of these variables.

Variables related to the access of financial and other services do not show a systematic pattern of significance. Significant results are observed for firms that have received legal services and owners that use profits to invest in buildings and land in rural areas. The former is associated with a decrease in the probability of being in-between while the latter is associated with an increased probability of being in-between. None of the variables in these categories was significant at the national level. Businesses that use profits to reinvest in the business in urban areas observe a change in the predicted probabilities of being in-between of nearly 9 per cent. While patterns of significance are scattered for this category, the significant results fall within expectations. This last category is perhaps the category for which panel data would be the most helpful. The establishment of credit, and access to financial institutions and their services may require a considerable time, which in practice means that the effects of the variables in this category require a longer time-frame to be adequately measured.

8.7 Summary and Policy Implications

The results presented in this chapter may be summarized as follows. We have shown that although Tanzania remains heavily rural, the composition of economic activity in rural areas has changed significantly over the past decade and a half. Between 2002 and 2012, the share of the population living in rural areas dropped by only 6.5 percentage points and remains high at 70 per cent. However, the share of the rural population engaged in nonfarm activities almost tripled over this same period going from a very low level of 6.8 to 20.5 per cent. This increase is similar among rural youth. This increase provides the motivation for our investigation into the nature of rural nonfarm activities and whether rural youth differ from other adults in the remainder of the chapter.

We began our investigation by studying the distribution of rural nonfarm activity at the household level. To do this, we first created a typology of households in rural areas classifying them into three groups based on the work status of individuals living in the households. We find that 11.2 per cent of rural households participate only in the nonfarm economy and that the heads of these households tend to be more educated. The share of households headed by youth who participate only in the nonfarm economy is higher, at 17.9 per cent. We explain the differences between households with and without rural nonfarm activities using a probit model. We find that being a youth-headed household increases the probability of specializing in rural nonfarm activities by 2 to 6 per cent, but they do not seem very different from other households when agriculture is still part of their household's livelihood. The most important determinant of whether a household engages in nonfarm activities is the education of the household head. For households whose heads have secondary or more education, the increase in the probability of engaging in nonfarm activities is between 8 per cent and

38 per cent. This could be a major factor to explain a higher participation rate of nonfarm economy among youth-headed households.

Next, we used Tanzania's first nationally representative survey of micro-, small-, and medium-sized enterprises to investigate the businesses owned by the members of rural households. Again, we pay attention to the owners who are young. We found an enormous amount of heterogeneity among these businesses and youth as owners are often not a main factor to explain such heterogeneity. Roughly 20 per cent of these businesses in rural areas operate in the manufacturing sector, a share almost doubling that in urban areas; the rest of these businesses are in the services sector. Around half of rural business owners report that they wouldn't leave their business for a full-time salaried position, and slightly more than half of young owners prefer to leave for a full-time salaried job in answer to the same question. This is encouraging as it suggests that half of these businesses are owned by 'gung ho' entrepreneurs as opposed to 'reluctant' entrepreneurs. We also show a significant degree of heterogeneity in the labour productivity of these businesses, but the difference in labour productivity is unlikely to be related to rural and urban locations or owner's age. Using a probit specification we explored the characteristics of the most successful businesses. We found the following for rural businesses: (i) those owned by females are less productive; (ii) businesses that operate full-time are more productive; (iii) businesses operated by owners who live in households that are not poor are more productive; (iv) owners who see their businesses as growing are more productive; and (v) businesses with more customers and regional (vs local) customers are more productive.

We conclude that policies designed to stimulate rural transformation need to be sufficiently targeted in order to achieve results, but there is little evidence that policies should target youth and other adult owners differently. Large programmes designed for small businesses in general are likely to be disappointing because of the underlying heterogeneity in types of firms and their productivity. Instead, policymakers interested in stimulating nonfarm employment and productivity growth in rural areas will need to focus on the most productive small firms. To do this, policymakers will need to design products—financial and otherwise—that are attractive to firms with potential for growth that are not attractive to businesses that are unlikely to succeed.

Appendix

Table 8.A1. Summary statistics of main variables of 2012 HBS used in the regression: rural

Variable	Number of HHs or EAs	Means	SE	LL	UL
Youth-headed (between ages 15–34)	4,130	0.268	0.010	0.249	0.287
Female-headed	4,130	0.241	0.009	0.222	0.259
No primary education	4,130	0.270	0.013	0.243	0.296
Completed primary education	4,130	0.673	0.012	0.649	0.697
Completed secondary education or more	4,130	0.058	0.008	0.043	0.073
Number of youth (15–34)	4,130	1.577	0.051	1.477	1.677
No cultivated land	4,130	0.053	0.009	0.034	0.072
0–2 ha of cultivated land	4,130	0.565	0.019	0.528	0.602
2–5 ha of cultivated land	4,130	0.296	0.015	0.267	0.326
>5 ha of cultivated land	4,130	0.086	0.010	0.066	0.105
Household paid loans to bank or family friends in past year	4,130	0.023	0.005	0.013	0.032
Public transportation to regional HQ in EA	157	0.756	0.038	0.682	0.830
Electricity in the EA	157	0.238	0.037	0.165	0.311
Mobile signal in the EA	157	0.821	0.034	0.753	0.889
Internet in the EA	157	0.086	0.024	0.039	0.133
Bank in the EA	157	0.024	0.012	0.000	0.047
Cooperative primary society in the EA	157	0.381	0.042	0.298	0.464
Informal financial service in the EA	157	0.450	0.043	0.366	0.535
Major employer (that is, business, factory) in the EA	157	0.161	0.032	0.098	0.225
Weekly market in the EA	157	0.295	0.040	0.217	0.373

Note: The estimates account for survey sampling design.

Source: Authors calculation using data of 2012 HBS.

Table 8.A2. Summary statistics of main variables of 2012 HBS used in the regression: urban

Variable	Number of HHs or EAs	Means	SE	LL	UL
Youth-headed (between ages 15–34)	6,056	0.343	0.010	0.324	0.362
Female-headed	6,056	0.249	0.009	0.231	0.267
No primary education	6,056	0.084	0.007	0.071	0.098
Completed primary education	6,056	0.632	0.014	0.605	0.659
Completed secondary education or more	6,056	0.283	0.017	0.251	0.316
Number of youth (15–34)	6,056	1.747	0.042	1.663	1.831

No cultivated land	6,056	0.702	0.034	0.635	0.769
0–2 ha of cultivated land	6,056	0.217	0.024	0.170	0.265
2–5 ha of cultivated land	6,056	0.054	0.010	0.034	0.074
>5 ha of cultivated land	6,056	0.026	0.011	0.004	0.049
Household paid loans to bank or family friends in past year	6,056	0.039	0.006	0.027	0.052
Public transportation to regional HQ in EA	223	0.943	0.025	0.894	0.992
Electricity in the EA	223	0.852	0.044	0.764	0.939
Mobile signal in the EA	223	0.846	0.031	0.786	0.907
Internet in the EA	223	0.292	0.037	0.219	0.366
Bank in the EA	223	0.155	0.024	0.108	0.203
Cooperative primary society in the EA	223	0.188	0.033	0.124	0.252
Informal financial service in the EA	223	0.650	0.040	0.572	0.729
Major employer (that is, business, factory) in the EA	223	0.416	0.044	0.329	0.503
Weekly market in the EA	223	0.207	0.039	0.129	0.284

Note: The estimates account for survey sampling design.

Source: Authors calculation using data of 2012 HBS.

Table 8.A3. Summary statistics of main variables of 2012 HBS used in the regression, by types of rural households

Variables	Agri. only HH	Non-agri. only HH with nonfarm enterprises	Non-agri. only HH without nonfarm enterprises	Mixed HH with nonfarm enterprises	Mixed HH without nonfarm enterprises
Youth-headed (between ages 15–34)	0.249	0.401	0.459	0.246	0.232
Female-headed	0.265	0.269	0.215	0.178	0.227
No primary education	0.320	0.124	0.074	0.229	0.237
Completed primary education	0.660	0.700	0.567	0.726	0.665
Completed secondary education or more	0.020	0.177	0.359	0.045	0.099
Number of youth (15–34)	1.433	1.643	1.501	1.827	2.134
No cultivated land	0.010	0.291	0.427	0.017	0.042
0–2 ha of cultivated land	0.600	0.531	0.415	0.509	0.596
2–5 ha of cultivated land	0.314	0.148	0.114	0.348	0.232
>5 ha of cultivated land	0.075	0.030	0.044	0.126	0.130

Continued

Table 8.A3. Continued

Variables	Agri. only HH	Non-agri. only HH with nonfarm enterprises	Non-agri. only HH without nonfarm enterprises	Mixed HH with nonfarm enterprises	Mixed HH without nonfarm enterprises
Household paid loans to bank or family friends in past year	0.012	0.062	0.041	0.036	0.029
Public transportation to regional HQ in EA	0.736	0.899	0.850	0.749	0.764
Electricity in the EA	0.217	0.369	0.512	0.196	0.220
Mobile signal in the EA	0.844	0.830	0.871	0.759	0.763
Internet in the EA	0.069	0.181	0.110	0.087	0.139
Bank in the EA	0.019	0.006	0.045	0.037	0.012
Cooperative primary society in the EA	0.420	0.292	0.283	0.336	0.336
Informal financial service in the EA	0.406	0.479	0.497	0.537	0.504
Major employer (that is, business, factory) in the EA	0.131	0.328	0.439	0.123	0.193
Weekly market in the EA	0.255	0.429	0.406	0.322	0.369
No. of sample obs.	2,512	244	231	880	221

Note: The estimates account for survey sampling design, and the number of total rural household obs. is 4,130.

Source: Authors calculation using data of 2012 HBS.

Table 8.A4(a). Probit results for probability of being in-between rural and urban enterprises, marginal effect: owner's personal characteristics

	All	Urban	Rural
Education (completed secondary or higher)	−0.00555	0.00285	−0.0191
	−0.0253	−0.0386	−0.0255
Marital status	−0.0344	−0.0788	0.00685
	−0.0343	−0.0508	−0.0293
Female	−0.0561[***]	−0.0847[**]	−0.0496[***]
	−0.02	−0.0415	−0.0178
Head of household is young (15–34)	0.013	0.00119	0.0203
	−0.0167	−0.0276	−0.0201
Owner is not poor	0.0656[***]	0.0871[***]	0.0450[***]
	−0.0156	−0.0273	−0.0134

Owner is a member of a business association	0.0419	0.109*	−0.0433
	−0.0455	−0.0658	−0.0338
Owner has taken expert advice	0.0916	0.0284	0.135
	−0.0695	−0.0785	−0.0969
Saw business as a market opportunity	0.0280**	0.0481*	0.0148
	−0.014	−0.027	−0.0117
Views business as growing	0.0594***	0.0595**	0.0642***
	−0.013	−0.0241	−0.0124

Note: In Tables A4(a)–A4(c) dependent variable is a binary variable which takes the value of 1 if the firm is in the in-between category and 0 otherwise. Firms in the 'in-between' category satisfy the following two conditions: (i) owner wouldn't leave the firm for a full-time salaried job; and (ii) labour productivity is higher than economy-wide labour productivity in trade. Number of the full sample obs. is 4,163, and 2,310 for rural. *** p < 0.01, ** p < 0.05, * p < 0.1.

Source: Authors estimation using MSME data.

Table 8.A4(b). Probit results for probability of being in-between rural and urban enterprises, marginal effect: business characteristics

	All	Urban	Rural
Firm's age	0.00134	0.000915	0.00142
	−0.001	−0.00202	−0.00105
Firm size (number of employees)	−0.0241***	−0.0274**	−0.0215*
	−0.00899	−0.0117	−0.0111
Business runs full-time	0.0723***	0.0652**	0.0683***
	−0.0174	−0.0305	−0.0181
Firm has market access	0.00901	−0.00264	0.00115
	−0.0191	−0.0563	−0.0189
Firm keeps written accounts	0.0198	−0.0232	0.0544***
	−0.0176	−0.0303	−0.0165
Firm has licence	0.00994	0.0331	−0.00894
	−0.0201	−0.0372	−0.0143
Firm has regional customers	0.0343**	0.00709	0.0573**
	−0.0157	−0.0259	−0.0227
Number of daily customers is more than 20	0.0587***	0.0422	0.0687***
	−0.0139	−0.0262	−0.0165
Firm's suppliers are small traders	−0.0163	−0.0395	0.0099
	−0.0136	−0.0272	−0.0128
Firm's suppliers are nationwide	0.0496	0.0574	0.0176
	−0.0418	−0.058	−0.0567

Note: Number of full sample obs. is Number of the full sample obs. is 4,163, and 2,310 for rural. *** p < 0.01, ** p < 0.05, * p < 0.1.

Source: Authors estimation using MSME data.

Table 8.A4(c). Probit results for probability of being in-between rural and urban enterprises, marginal effect: infrastructure, technology, and financial services

	All	Urban	Rural
Infrastructure and technology			
Owner uses a mobile to conduct business	0.0450**	0.0779*	0.0143
	−0.0216	−0.0407	−0.0163
Firm owner has a calculator	0.0424**	0.0464	0.0372
	−0.021	−0.0327	−0.0258
Business has office equipment	0.0285	0.0407	0.0219
	−0.0265	−0.0435	−0.0205
Business owns a cooling facility	0.0202	−0.0106	0.11
	−0.0317	−0.0374	−0.072
Business uses electricity to light business	0.0802***	0.0837**	0.0692*
	−0.0252	−0.0326	−0.0392
Financial and other services			
Owner regularly sends and receives	0.0279	0.0249	0.0232
money for business	−0.0187	−0.0339	−0.0212
Firm has received legal services	0.0343	0.159	−0.0824**
	−0.0883	−0.133	−0.033
Firm has received technical services	−0.00217	−0.0268	0.0134
	−0.0493	−0.0668	−0.0493
Owner uses profit to expand business	0.0329	0.0892**	−0.00386
	−0.0228	−0.0387	−0.0207
Owner uses profits to buy stocks in advance	0.0149	0.0158	0.0114
	−0.0143	−0.0286	−0.014
Owner uses profits to invest in buildings	0.0458	0.0357	0.0566*
and land	−0.0314	−0.0482	−0.0339
Observations	5,551	5,590	5,570
Nsub	5,551	1,427	4,124
F	10.38	4.553	27.28
P-value	0	3.16E-08	0

Note: Number of the full sample obs. is 4,163, and 2,310 for rural. *** $p < 0.01$, ** $p < 0.05$, * $p < 0.1$.

Source: Authors estimation using MSME dataset.

References

Banerjee, A. V., and E. Duflo. 2007. The economic lives of the poor. *The Journal of Economic Perspectives* 21 (1): 141–67.

Bezu, S., and C. Barrett. 2012. Employment dynamics in the rural nonfarm sector in Ethiopia: Do the poor have time on their side? *Journal of Development Studies* 48 (9): 1223–40.

Davis, B., S. Di Giuseppe, and A. Zezza. 2014. *Income diversification patterns in rural sub-Saharan Africa: Reassessing the evidence*. Policy Research Working Paper 7108, the World Bank.

Diao, X., J. Kweka, and M. McMillan. 2017. *Economic transformation from the bottom up: Evidence from Tanzania.* IFPRI Discussion Paper 1603. Washington DC, U.S.A.: International Food Policy Research Institute.

De Brauw, A., V. Mueller, and H. L. Lee. 2014. The role of rural–urban migration in the structural transformation of sub-Saharan Africa. *World Development* 63 (2014): 33–42.

Gollin, D., and R. Rogerson. 2009. *The greatest of all improvements: Roads, agriculture, and economic development in Africa.* Department of Economics, Williams College, A mimeo.

Haggblade, S., P. Hazell, and J. Brown. 1989. Farm–nonfarm linkages in rural sub-Saharan Africa. *World Development* 1 (8): 1173–201.

Haggblade, S., P. Hazell, and T. Reardon. 2010. The rural nonfarm economy: Prospects for growth and poverty reduction. *World Development* 38 (1): 1429–41.

Jin, S., and K. Deininger. 2008. Key constraints for rural nonfarm activity in Tanzania: Combining investment climate and household surveys. *Journal of African Economies* 18 (2): 319–61.

Lewis, W. A. 1979. The dual economy revisited. *The Manchester School* 47 (3): 211–29.

Nagler, P., and W. Naudé. 2016. *Non-farm enterprises in rural Africa: New empirical evidence.* Policy Research Working Paper 7066. Washington, DC: U.S.A.: The World Bank Group.

Tanzania, NBS (National Bureau of Statistics). 2006. Tanzania 2002 Census: Analytic Report, Volume X. Dar es Salaam: National Bureau of Statistics, Ministry of Planning, Economy, and Empowerment.

Tanzania, NBS (National Bureau of Statistics). 2007. Analytic Report for Employment and Earnings Survey 2002. Dar es Salaam: National Bureau of Statistics, Ministry of Planning, Economy, and Empowerment.

Tanzania, NBS (National Bureau of Statistics). 2011a. National Household Budget Survey 2000–2001. Dar es Salaam: National Bureau of Statistics, Ministry of Finance.

Tanzania, NBS (National Bureau of Statistics). 2011b. Integrated Labour Force Survey 2014, Analytical Report. Dar es Salaam: National Bureau of Statistics, Ministry of Finance.

Tanzania, NBS (National Bureau of Statistics). 2014a. Household Budget Survey: Main Report, 2011/12. Dar es Salaam: National Bureau of Statistics, Ministry of Finance.

Tanzania, NBS (National Bureau of Statistics). 2014. Tanzania 2012 Census: Basic demographic and socio-economic profile. Dar es Salaam and Zanzibar: National Bureau of Statistics, Ministry of Finance, Office of Chief Government Statistician, Ministry of State, President's Office, State House and Good Governance.

Tanzania, NBS (National Bureau of Statistics). 2014c. National Accounts of Tanzania Mainland 2001–2013. Dar es Salaam: National Bureau of Statistics, Ministry of Finance.

Tanzania, NBS (National Bureau of Statistics). 2014d. Revised National Accounts Estimates for Tanzania Mainland, Base Year, 2007. Dar es Salaam: National Bureau of Statistics, Ministry of Finance.

Tanzania, NBS (National Bureau of Statistics). 2014e. Formal Sector Employment and Earnings Survey: Analytical Report 2013. Dar es Salaam National Bureau of Statistics, Ministry of Finance.

Tanzania, NBS (National Bureau of Statistics). 2015. Integrated Labour Force Survey 2014, Analytical Report. Dar es Salaam: National Bureau of Statistics, Ministry of Finance.

Tybout, J. R. 2000. Manufacturing firms in developing countries: How well do they do, and why? *Journal of Economic Literature* 38 (1): 11–44.

9

Youth Mobility and its Role in Structural Transformation in Senegal

*Elisenda Estruch, Lisa Van Dijck, David Schwebel,
and Josee Randriamamonjy*

9.1 Introduction

Senegal is a youthful country, with over 60 per cent of people below the age of 24 years and up to 77 per cent of the population below the age of 35 years. Over 100,000 new young job seekers (between 15 and 34 years old) join the labour market every year in Senegal (World Bank 2016).

Although the agricultural sector employs nationally almost half of the labour force, the sector accounts only for about 16 per cent of GDP (World Bank 2017). Low productivity growth in this sector combined with an unbalanced labour market has led to a wider economic stagnation of the rural economy. This creates major challenges for the rural youth to access productive and decent jobs and reach their work and life aspirations (Hathie et al. 2015). Whilst there is a growing body of empirical analysis on youth employment in Sub-Saharan Africa, important gaps remain and especially in relation to youth in rural areas in the Francophone countries of West Africa, such as Senegal.

This chapter aims to complement the existing literature on employment dynamics in Senegal, focusing in depth on rural youth in the context of structural transformation. First, a stocktaking of the state of the agricultural sector and the wider rural economy is provided and how this relates to youth employment dynamics in rural areas of Senegal. In Section 9.2, through a literature review, the context for rural youth employment is discussed by looking in detail at the agricultural sector, the rural-non farm economy and the challenges and opportunities characterizing the rural labour market. Section 9.3 analyses the transitions of youth, either to the rural non-farm economy (RNFE) or to urban areas and abroad and attempts to provide a better understanding of patterns, motivations, and constraints youth face when engaging in the RNFE or in migrant labour. To do so, we use descriptive statistics from the latest Household Data Surveys of 2001 (ESAM-II) and 2011

Elisenda Estruch, Lisa Van Dijck, David Schwebel, and Josee Randriamamonjy, *Youth Mobility and its Role in Structural Transformation in Senegal* In: *Youth and Jobs in Rural Africa: Beyond Stylized Facts.* Edited by: Valerie Mueller and James Thurlow, Oxford University Press (2019). © International Food Policy Research Institute. DOI: 10.1093/oso/9780198848059.003.0009

(ESPS II) and the Migration and Remittances Household Survey.[1] The findings suggest that there are limited rural employment opportunities for youth, leading to a slow pace of rural poverty reduction. Rural youth still work mainly in poor quality jobs in agriculture, although they increasingly try: (i) to diversify their and their family's income by engaging in rural nonfarm employment, or (ii) to look for options outside rural areas by migrating to urban areas or abroad. Section 9.4 follows with a brief review of the main policies and programmes that have been implemented in the same period as the analysed data in Senegal in order to identify their strengths, weaknesses, and areas for improvement. We conclude with a discussion around the key findings.

9.2 State of Agriculture and the Rural Labour Market

Senegal is a lower-middle income country with the fourth largest economy in West Africa. In 2015, Senegal had a GDP growth rate of 6.5 per cent, becoming the second fastest growing economy in West Africa (World Bank 2016). However, between 2000 and 2015, Senegal experienced a lower average economic growth, of 4.1 per cent, than the rest of Sub-Saharan Africa (SSA) with 6 per cent. This economic growth has not been large enough to match the high population growth, leading to an average GDP per capita growth of only 2.3 per cent in that period, half of that experienced in SSA (ibid).

In economic terms, the Senegalese economy is mainly dominated by the service sector, accounting for 60 per cent of GDP, followed by the industrial sector with 24 per cent of GDP (Figure 9.1). Although the agricultural sector employs nationally around half of the labour force, the sector accounts only for about 16 per cent

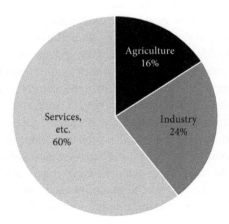

Figure 9.1. GDP contributions, Senegal, 2017

Source: World development indicators, World Bank.

---

[1] See description of the data in the annex.

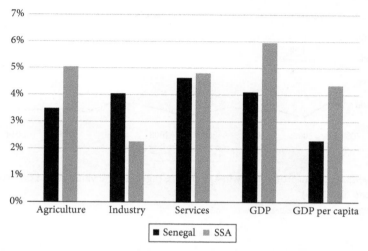

Figure 9.2. Drivers of economic growth, average growth, 2000–2015
Source: World development indicators, World Bank.

of GDP. With an annual growth rate of 3.5 per cent, the agricultural sector is growing slower than the service and industrial sectors. Compared to the rest of Sub-Saharan Africa, the agricultural sector is also growing at a slower pace (Figure 9.2). Growth levels fluctuate heavily as Senegal's agriculture is highly vulnerable to unpredictable weather; severe floods and droughts are common and only 1.3 per cent of agricultural land is equipped for irrigation.

9.2.1 Agricultural Sector

On a macroeconomic level, the agricultural sector in Senegal seems to be stagnant, as labour- and land-productivity have remained constant or have grown slowly over the past decade (Figure 9.3 and Figure 9.4). Senegal's low labour productivity is caused by an unchanged employment rate in agriculture coupled with low technological improvement (Seck 2016, Shaw 2014). The agricultural sector employs 46 per cent of the total employed population, composed by a male and female employment rate in the sector of respectively 49 and 44 per cent. Contrary to the Sub-Saharan African average, the employment rate has decreased only slightly, leading to a lower and stabilized agricultural value added per worker (ibid).

Similarly, land productivity, here projected by cereal yield, is around 20 per cent lower than the Sub-Saharan Africa average. Land and labour productivity are influenced by a low uptake of technology. For example, in 2014, per hectare of arable land only 7 kilogram of fertilizer was used in Senegal, compared to 16 kilogram on average in Sub-Saharan Africa (World Bank 2017).

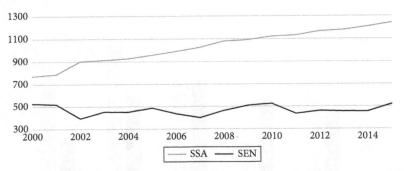

Figure 9.3. Labour productivity in agriculture (agricultural value added per worker, constant 2010 US$)

Source: World development indicators, World Bank.

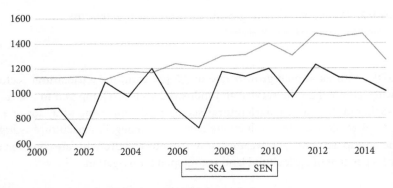

Figure 9.4. Land productivity (cereal yield, kg per ha)

Source: Food and Agriculture Organization (FAO).

According to the World Bank, agriculture is at fourth place in government spending after education, health, and nutrition, which represent the bulk of the state budget. The percentage of public spending on agriculture evolved in terms of GDP, rising from 9.8 to 10.9 per cent between 2005 and 2009 (World Bank 2014). The country would have thus achieved the Maputo objective, which requires that a minimum of 10 per cent of total public expenditure be directed at agriculture. However, at a time when the authorities declare their intention to prioritize agriculture in their strategy of accelerated growth, the growth in investment in the sector appears insufficient (Oya and Ba 2013). Out of the total budget for agriculture, subsidies for the distribution of agricultural inputs are the main component of expenditure with 46 per cent of resources. Much needed infrastructure works follow with 11 per cent. By contrast, the resources devoted to agricultural research (3.1 per cent) and training (0.5 per cent) are negligible. Intra-sector allocation of expenditure shows that agricultural public expenditure is concentrated on crop farming, receiving nearly 64 per cent of the total budget. Other sectors, such as livestock and fisheries, are hence left with little funds and support (World Bank 2014).

9.2.2 Rural Nonfarm Economy

The Senegalese rural nonfarm economy (RNFE) is dominated by manufacturing, and wholesale and retail trade, and is limited in size and employs only 23 per cent of the employed population (ANSD 2013). The RNFE is mainly composed of informal small-scale businesses and is characterized by a high level of self-employment. The main hindrances to formalization of businesses are the lack of entrepreneurial and technical education or skills as well as underinvestment in infrastructure and the weakness of regulation and taxation institutions. Youth have special difficulties in finding the resources to create or upgrade their own businesses (Ndione 2015).

Increasingly, more rural households are diversifying their incomes and engaging both in farm and nonfarm activities. In nearly a quarter of all rural households, both farm and nonfarm activities coexist (ANSD 2013). While nonfarm activities play an important role in household livelihood strategies in rural Senegal, they typically complement farm activities rather than constitute a viable farm exit strategy (Ndione 2015).

In order to reduce rural poverty effectively and develop a wider rural economy, it is important to enhance the RNFE and its linkages with farm economy. The effects emerge through backward and forward production linkages from agriculture to rural input suppliers and agro-processors, and through expenditure linkages as farm incomes are spent on locally produced goods and services or invested in nonfarm activities (Maertens 2009). Spillover effects from the nonfarm economy to the farm economy increase productivity and profitability in agriculture (Anríquez and Stamoulis 2007).

In Senegal, linkages between farm and nonfarm economic sectors, which are important in creating multiplier effects for growth and rural development, are weak. Small farmers are only to a limited extent involved in the value chain leading to low profitability and to a lack of employment opportunities and attractiveness for youth (Davis et al. 2002). Moreover, the agribusiness sector, which in many cases is more labour intensive and where added value along the agrifood value chain can be generated more easily, is small in Senegal compared to the Sub-Saharan Africa average (Schaffnit-Chatterjee 2014).

9.2.3 Rural Labour Market

The stagnant productivity in the agricultural sector is indicative of a wider, cross-sectoral problem of an unbalanced rural labour market, with a labour supply characterized by a large young workforce with limited education and access to productive resources, and a labour demand characterized by low rural investments, access to markets, and rural job creation (Hathie et al. 2015). Moreover, lack of access, especially for youth, to productive resources such as land, credit, and social capital, are restraining overall rural productivity levels in both agricultural and non-agricultural activities (ibid).

Data from ANSD 2004 and 2013 shows that indeed the Senegalese labour supply is characterized by a large share of poorly educated and low-skilled labour force. There are significant education limitations in the country, as the percentage of people over 25 years old having completed primary and secondary education is respectively 22 per cent and 6 per cent (ANSD 2013). Low levels of education characterize especially the rural and female population. The situation has however improved in the last decade as shown by the increase in the gross enrolment rate in secondary schooling between 2001 and 2011 from 16 to 40 per cent (ANSD 2004, 2013). National alphabetization rates have also grown from 38 to 52 per cent, and from 23 to 33 per cent in rural areas (ibid). Rural areas continue to lag behind in terms of educational attainment as shown by the fact that only 30 per cent of the rural population has benefited from any form of education compared to 51 per cent in urban areas. There also remains a 10 per cent gap between rural young men and women (ANSD 2013).

Moreover, in rural areas, few youth transition from primary to secondary education, due to high dropout rates and poor quality of education, which leads to low levels of literacy. Furthermore, the actual skills of the workforce are often not aligned with the labour market demand needs (Guarcello 2007). Skills acquired during higher education often do not match those required in the rural labour market. This indicates a deep structural shift that needs to take place in order to create more high-level jobs and utilize the increased human capital (ibid). At the same time, in line with the process of structural transformation, as agriculture moves away from subsistence farming and the RNFE increases in relevance, improving the skills of the rural workforce is key to facilitate the mobility of surplus labour within agriculture and towards other activities (ibid).

Labour supply is strongly influenced by the high population growth and subsequent youth bulge. The Senegalese population amounts to 14.3 million people and grew at an annual rate of 3.1 per cent between 2001 and 2011 (ANSD 2004, 2013). The country is demographically quite young with an average age of 22 years and with one-third of the population aged between 15 and 34 years. This means that a growing number of young people are entering the labour market every year, resulting in an excess of labour supply and subsequent pressures on the labour market to integrate them all. Between 2001 and 2011, the strongest growth in population was observed in older age groups, indicating the youth bulge is slowing down (ANSD 2013).

In rural labour markets, often the most decisive factors in improving the pay and working conditions of rural workers are a dynamic agricultural sector, increased public and private investment, and a tighter labour market (Oya 2010). In other words, besides improving the skills development and other supply-side policy interventions, demand-side interventions, such as investments targeting job creation, are critical (ILO 2008).

The formal labour demand is limited, as Senegal's rapid population growth was not matched by job creation in the formal sector at an equal rate and thus led to a booming of the informal sector. The latter is dominated by subsistence agriculture and small-scale informal (family-based) firms (Golub and Hayat 2014). Although wages in the formal sector are three times higher than those in the informal sector, the formal private sector employs just 6 per cent of the total population (ibid). Conversely, in the informal sector, registration and taxation are absent, formal contracts and social protection rare, wages inefficiently low, underemployment the norm, and labour rights weak (Roubaud and Torelli 2013). Furthermore, the small size of the operations of many rural enterprises poses also constraints in terms of job creation as they lack economies of scale. Ultimately, agricultural labour demand is limited and characterized by intra and inter-year variations, on account of weather conditions and the seasonal nature of agricultural labour, limiting the number of long-term formal contracts even further (Leavy and White 1999).

There are still more people living in rural areas than in urban areas, respectively 57 and 43 per cent of the population, although urbanization is occurring at remarkable pace: while the urban population increases at an annual rate of 3.9 per cent, the rural population grows annually by 2.6 per cent (World Bank 2017). Urbanization is also driven by significant internal migration: by 2009, almost 2 million Senegalese, or 14 per cent of the total population, had migrated within the country (IOM 2009). In the past, migration was essentially from rural to urban areas, generally from the semi-arid regions towards Dakar; or from rural to rural areas following a seasonal pattern (that is, those who migrate during the rainy season to provide additional support) (ibid). Today, the Dakar region, but more generally the urban axis or Dakar–Thiès–Touba (the second largest city in the country), polarizes 60 per cent of migration and represents 47 per cent of the country's population. The attractiveness of this urban axis largely determines the structure and dynamism of economic activities, including service provision to surrounding areas. It also determines the opportunity space for many rural youth (in particular from the Groundnut Basin). Nonetheless, there are also other secondary cities and towns to consider, such as M'bour, which is growing due to tourism and fishing activities, and Ourossogui and Louga, which are cities with a history of international migration that attract remittances and also an influx of (return) migrants (ibid).

The unbalance on the rural labour market affects youth in particular as shown by relatively high and growing youth unemployment and underemployment rates. In total, 11 per cent of rural youth (aged 15–34) are unemployed, with significant gender differences: 4.4 per cent of male youth and 15.4 per cent of female youth in rural areas (ANSD 2013). Compared to 14.7 per cent of male and 20 per cent of female youth in urban areas, unemployment is lower in rural areas. However, underemployment is more severe among rural youth, affecting 8.5 per cent of male youth and 29.3 per cent of female youth (ibid). Compared to urban areas, youth employment in rural areas is characterized by a lower labour income, higher levels of underemployment, and a stronger gender bias (Guarcello 2007).

The low agricultural productivity rate is causing incomes to remain low and poverty widespread in the rural space. Poverty affects 57 per cent of rural households compared to 33 per cent in urban households (ANSD 2013). Moreover, poverty reduction in rural areas is slower than in urban areas, with a decrease of respectively 12 and 20 per cent between 2001 and 2011 (ANSD 2004, 2013). Poverty is most severe among self-employed agricultural workers, among which, in rural areas 61 per cent remain poor, representing nearly 1.9 million people. Among other dependents, mainly contributing family members in rural areas, 64 per cent is poor representing nearly 1.4 million people (ANSD 2013).

9.3 Youth Transitions in the Rural Economy

9.3.1 Are Youth Leaving Agriculture?

The limited economic opportunities in the agricultural sector make the sector unattractive for youth and pushes them to seek employment opportunities in other sectors and locations.[2] As such, rural Senegal is characterized by a high degree of intergenerational mobility between farm and nonfarm employment: only one-third of farmers' children stayed in farming, indicating a high rate of exiting from farm activities (Lambert, Ravallion, and Van de Walle 2011).

Those who stay in agriculture increasingly engage in mixed-income activities, working in both farm and nonfarm activities (Alobo Loison and Bignebat 2017). Diversification may function as a household strategy to manage risk and overcome market failures, or represent specialization within the household. Therefore,

---

[2] The methodology used in this section is based on both data and policy analysis. The data analysis relies on two national household surveys of Senegal: ESAM-II (2001) and ESPS-II (2011), as well as a migration survey, MRHS (2009) (see description of the data in the annex).

diversification can be into both high and low-return sectors, and can represent a pathway out of poverty or a survival strategy (Davis, Di Giuseppe, and Zezza 2016). And so, young people and their families decide to diversify either because of a lack of agricultural economic opportunities or because they are pulled by other income generating activities.

The Senegalese working age population, the population above between 15- and 64-years- old, amounts to 8.3 million people. Of this working age population (above 15 years), only 57 per cent is active, being either employed or looking actively for employment (World Bank 2017). Between 2001 and 2011, the increase in the numbers of inactive people, in particular among youth, is striking (see Figure 9.5). The low activity rate can be partly explained as it includes students, people without remunerated activity (not including subsistence farmers), and retired people. The rise in the number of youth being inactive or unemployed also shows the lack of employment opportunities both in the urban and rural areas, which is demotivating people to enter the labour market. The activity rate is unevenly distributed among gender, with 68 per cent of working age men being active and 45 per cent of women. The lower activity rate for women can be related to social norms such that women often have more non-remunerated (household) tasks. Activity rates are higher in rural areas, 74 per cent for men and 50 per cent for women, than they are in urban areas (ESPS-II 2011).

Between 2001 and 2011, the share of employed people decreased in both rural and urban areas. However, the total number of people employed decreased in rural areas and increased in urban areas (Figure 9.5). The decline in total rural employment is mainly due to a fall in youth employment. Such fall is mirrored by, on the one hand, an increase in youth unemployment rates, from 2.5 per cent in 2001 to

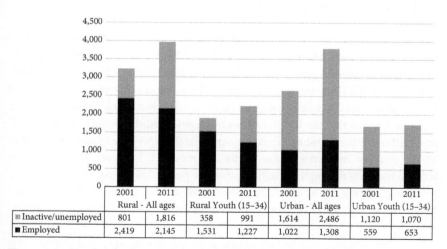

	2001	2011	2001	2011	2001	2011	2001	2011
	Rural - All ages		Rural Youth (15–34)		Urban - All ages		Urban Youth (15–34)	
Inactive/unemployed	801	1,816	358	991	1,614	2,486	1,120	1,070
Employed	2,419	2,145	1,531	1,227	1,022	1,308	559	653

Figure 9.5. Rural and urban working age population, by activity (per 1,000)

Source: Authors' calculations based on ESAM-II 2001 and ESPS-II 2011.

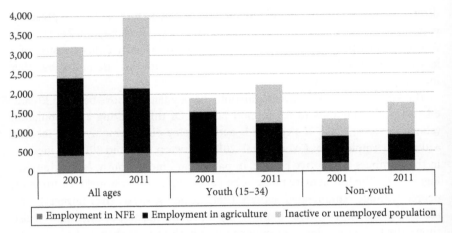

Figure 9.6. Rural working age population, by activity and age group (per 1,000)

Source: Authors' calculations based on ESAM-II 2011 and ESPS-II 2011.

9.6 per cent in 2011. In rural areas, unemployment is significantly more prevalent among female youth than male (15.4 per cent and 4.4 per cent respectively). And, on the other hand, labour participation of youth is lower because youth over the age of 15 stay longer in education.[3] The literacy rate of the rural population aged above 15 increased from 23 to 39 per cent in that period, indicating an increase in school attendance (ANSD 2004, 2013).

Looking into rural employment across sectors, agriculture is clearly the dominant sector of primary employment in rural Senegal. Examining the structure of agricultural employment reveals that most farmers are either self-employed or employed in the family farm, and that working for a wage remains a marginal activity.

Figure 9.6 and Table 9.1 show that, between 2001 and 2011, the number of people active in agriculture has decreased from 82 per cent of all employed people to 77 per cent (or a decrease of annually 0.6 per cent). Table 9.1 in particular indicates that such a decrease is mainly driven by a fall in self-employment, even if there is also a small increase in unpaid family work in household farms. Moreover, Figure 9.6 shows that the RNFE did not manage to absorb people leaving agriculture, although the number of people active in the RNFE has grown from 18 to 23 per cent (or an increase of annually 2.4 per cent). However, the increase in volume is clearly not high enough to offset the people leaving agriculture.

Disaggregating by age indicates that most of the decrease in agricultural employment is caused by changes in youth employment. Young agricultural

---

[3] Since 2001, education is compulsory and free in Senegal for children up to 16 years old. High school, which aims at students aged 16 to 19 is thus not compulsory.

Table 9.1. Employment in agriculture and the rural nonfarm economy

	2001			2011		
	Youth (15–34 yrs) N = 22,410	*Non-youth (>35 yrs) N = 14,264*	*All ages N = 36,674*	*Youth (15–34 yrs) N = 54,570*	*Non-youth (>35 yrs) N = 39,337*	*All ages N = 93,907*
Employment in agriculture	85%	76%	82%	81%	72%	77%
Of which working for wage in agriculture	2%	2%	2%	3%	2%	3%
Of which self-employed in own farm	31%	77%	47%	26%	71%	44%
Of which unpaid family worker in HH farm	67%	21%	51%	70%	26%	53%
Employment in nonfarm economy (NFE)	15%	24%	18%	19%	28%	23%
Of which working for wage in NFE	26%	19%	23%	25%	21%	23%
Of which self-employed in NFE	48%	77%	62%	40%	71%	56%
Of which unpaid family worker in NFE	25%	4%	15%	34%	8%	20%

Source: Authors' calculations based on ESAM-II, 2001 and ESPS-II, 2011.

workers are mostly unpaid family members and are unlikely to be self-employed. Between 2001 and 2011, the share of rural youth employment in the agricultural sector decreased annually at a 0.5 per cent, a similar pace observed for the non-youth mainly due to the decrease in self-employment. At the same time, the share of youth employment in the RNFE has increased annually faster than for the non-youth (2.2 and 1.7 per cent respectively), mainly driven by an increase in the number of non-paid family workers in the family enterprise. Youth are progressively working as unpaid family workers in the RNFE, suggesting they are being pushed out of agriculture rather than pulled by remunerative and decent employment opportunities.

Youth employed in the RNFE are on average slightly older, more often male and more educated when compared to youth employed in agriculture (for details on the individual characteristic of youth see Table 9.A1 in the Annex). The difference in years of education is remarkable. Youth employed in the RNFE have on average been enrolled in school twice as much time as those employed in agriculture. Looking at the households of youth employed in either agriculture or the RNFE, data show that the household heads of youth employed in the RNFE compared to the ones employed in agriculture, are on average younger, more often female, and more educated (for details on the characteristics of households of youth see Table 9.A2 in the Annex). The household itself is also smaller and with less dependents. Only one-third of the households of youth employed in the RNFE are found in the poorest tercile of rural households, compared to two-thirds for the households of youth employed in agriculture. Likewise, one-third of the households with youth employed in the RNFE are in the richest tercile (compared to only 10 per cent of households of youth employed in agriculture), making them on average wealthier and less prone to poverty than households of youth employed in agriculture. As expected, households of youth working in the RNFE have less land and their farms are smaller. Correlated to the remoteness of agricultural fields, youth working in agriculture live further away from markets and in smaller towns than youth employed in the RNFE.

As income generating activities are often decided at the household level, it is important to have a closer look at the sector of employment of the household. According to the ESPS-II, 43 per cent of all rural households are only farming, 23 per cent combine farm and nonfarm employment, and 26 per cent are nonfarm households. Households combining farm and nonfarm activities are similar to farming only households in terms of the characteristics of the household head (age, gender, marital status, farm size, access to land) but differ in years of schooling (1.29 years versus 0.81 years) and household size (13 members versus 10 members). Moreover, mixed households are on average wealthier than farming-only households (50 per cent versus 71 per cent of households in poorest tercile), as the income from nonfarm activities is an important source of household income. When comparing nonfarming households with those combining farm and nonfarm activities, households heads among the nonfarming are more often women (24 per cent versus 11 per cent) and higher educated (2.41 years versus 1.29 years of schooling). Their households are on average smaller (9 versus 13 members) and are wealthier (29 per cent versus 16 per cent in richest tercile).

In general, the RNFE engages higher educated people from wealthier families than the agricultural sector does, which indicates that creating more jobs in the RNFE will contribute to alleviate rural poverty, especially if associated with inclusive growth policies ensuring equal access to education. A large part of the rural population who remain in agriculture as a survival strategy could complement or substitute their income with nonfarm employment, if provided with employment opportunities in the RNFE. This would increase household's incomes and could contribute to improve agricultural productivity, through increased resources for productive investments.

9.3.2   Are Youth Leaving Rural Areas? Rural Youth Migration and Labour Market Transition

Another alternative of coping with low economic opportunities in rural areas is migrating. Senegal, like many developing countries, is marked by high levels of internal migration and particularly elevated levels of international migration (Herrera and Sahn 2013). Due to increasingly difficult living conditions within the country and the successful international migration experience of earlier migrants, many Senegalese, and in particular youth, decide to migrate abroad to the most developed African countries, as well as to Europe and the United States. The key destination countries are The Gambia, France, Italy, Mauritania, Germany, and Ghana (IOM 2009).

The decision to migrate is often taken at family or even village level and involves the strategic choice of sending its best offspring away with a view to diversify its risks, and to build a social network (Azam and Gubert 2006). Youth migrate mostly in search of a better job, especially those who are better skilled or educated, which leads to a brain drain (Dia 2005). Pursuing more advanced education as well as undertaking apprenticeships are also reasons for leaving, in particular to the region of Saint-Louis which hosts many universities and of the educational institutions. Macroeconomic push-factors inducing migration are the increasing number of Senegalese living in poverty, climate change, and the deterioration of the environment (progression of desertification and rainfall-related problems) which lead to a reduction in agricultural yields. For example, in the Groundnut Basin, the Delta, and Niayes regions, 51 per cent of young people who migrated to an urban area did not possess any resource (land or livestock) (Mercandalli and Losch 2017). Nonetheless, around one out of four international migrants returned to Senegal after five years abroad, indicating that circular or seasonal migration is a recurrent phenomenon (Flahaux, Mezger, and Sakho 2011).

An important effect of migration is the high volume of remittances sent by migrants to Senegal, which is one of the highest in Sub-Saharan Africa. Total remittances represent around 10 per cent of Senegalese GDP, exceeding foreign direct investment and official development aid. The money sent by international migrants increases per capita income in some regions by about 60 per cent compared with households not receiving remittances from abroad (Diagne and Diane 2008). Close to 50 per cent of remittances sent back to Senegal are used for current consumption, 25 per cent for precautionary savings, 20 per cent for real estate investments, and less than 5 per cent for productive investment (IOM 2009). The linkages between remittances and increased productivity in the household's farm are therefore most likely weak. Additionally, in some cases remittances from migrated family members has led to a decline in labour market participation and reduced incentive to create own business by members who stayed behind as they

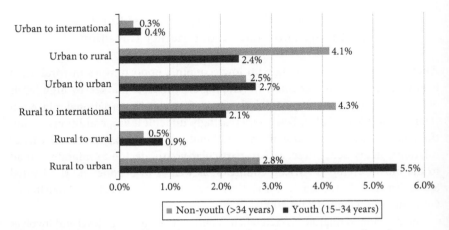

Figure 9.7 Migration by origin, destination and age (as a percentage of total population)

Source: Authors' calculations based on MRHS 2009 from the World Bank.

relied more on remittances to meet their needs (Ndiaye et al. 2015). Reduced labour participation can also entail a positive outcome of migration when the flow of income increases educational uptake or reduces hazardous work.

According to the stocktaking of migrants in 2009 (World Bank 2009b), Senegal counts over 1.2 million migrants, of which 75 per cent are internal migrants. Over half of all migrants come from rural areas and 60 per cent are young, aged 15 to 34 (ibid). Looking into migration flows, MRHS 2009 captures information from households that had internal or international migrants about the pre and post residence of former member (N=1278 for youth 15-34-year-old, and N=929 for non-youth 35-year-old and above). Figure 9.7 indicates that more people are leaving rural areas than arriving. Rural youth are more likely to migrate to the urban areas (5.5 per cent of all rural youth) while their older counterparts are more likely to move abroad (4.3 per cent of all rural non-youth). Youth are leaving rural areas more often than their older counterparts do (8.5 per cent of all rural youth versus 7.6 per cent of all rural non-youth), indicating that the rural exodus has a young face.

Remarkably, people who move internationally are more likely to come from rural areas, for all ages. The fact that many people, particularly older people, are moving from urban to rural areas might indicate they stay and work for a while in urban areas but return to their place of origin at a certain time.

The main reasons for internal migration in Senegal are family-related (63 per cent), for work (17 per cent), and for education (14 per cent). When only looking at the rural population, the importance of work increases considerably (to 73 per cent for internal migration and to 83 per cent for international). Work

Table 9.2. Migration patterns of youth leaving agriculture

Exit rural agriculture to	Rural	Urban	Abroad
Agriculture	3.40%	10.26%	
Self-employment	38.23%	17.14%	
Other (paid or unpaid family worker)	17.07%	7.01%	
Non-agriculture	2.75%	32.23%	
Self-employment	24.11%	65.56%	
Other (paid or unpaid family worker)	20.58%	10.30%	
Total N=665	6%	42%	51%

Source: Authors' calculations based on MRHS 2009 from the World Bank.

is equally the main reason to migrate for rural youth (58 per cent for those moving internally and 69 per cent for those moving abroad). The main reasons for people to move out of the rural space are the attraction of employment opportunities outside rural areas or the lack of employment opportunities in the rural space itself. Gender is also a key factor that distinguishes the reasons rural individuals migrate: women's number one reason to migrate is family-related (63 per cent) (ESPS-II).

The sector in which rural migrants were employed before moving varies by destination. Table 9.2 describes the migration patterns of youth active in agriculture before moving. Senegalese youth migrants leaving rural agriculture are most likely to move abroad, followed by moving to an urban area, whereas a low percentage migrate to another rural area. Those moving to an urban area are mainly self-employed outside the agricultural sector.

Looking at the characteristics of migrant youth and their households, based on labour transition data, it emerges that the youth who move out of agriculture but stay in rural areas to work in the RNFE are on average more frequently males, older, and less educated than youth undertaking a migration-induced labour transition (see Table 9.A3 in the Annex for details). Especially in terms of education, the difference is substantial (1.65 years versus 4.34 years). The households of the sub-group of youth who leave agriculture but remain rural are on average smaller, located in smaller communes, and poorer than households of youth undertaking a migration-induced labour transition. This indicates that the less-educated workers from poorer households are staying in rural areas while more educated workers from richer households are leaving the rural space altogether. The potential employment opportunities and the distance of migration influences the chosen destination. Less-educated workers might have more employment possibilities in rural areas, and poorer or disadvantaged households cannot always afford the elevated cost associated with long-distance migration.

9.3.3 Are Youth Driving Rural Transformation?

A gradual rural transformation is taking place in Senegal as shown by the decrease in agricultural employment and the increase in the RNFE, although the latter is still small and involves few people. The young population nevertheless leads this process of rural transformation.

However, when looking at the type of employment that this process entails, the increase in employment in the RNFE has been entirely associated with more unpaid family work, indicating that youth are being pushed more out of agriculture than attracted towards productive activities in the RNFE.

The RNFE is dominated by wholesale and retail trade, by repair of motor vehicles, motorcycles, and household goods, followed by manufacturing, real estate, and construction. Between 2001 and 2011 wholesale and retail trade increased from 7.8 per cent to 11.4 of rural youth total employment and manufacturing from 2.1 per cent to 4.5 per cent, increasing employment opportunities for youth in rural areas.

Comparing households receiving and not receiving remittances, data show that households with youth and receiving remittances are more likely to combine farm and nonfarm employment than households with youth not receiving remittances, indicating that the presence of youth influences the decision to use remittances to diversify the households' income. These income flows allow the recipient households to diversify into the non-agricultural sector by dedicating productive members, most often youth, to these activities (see Table 9.A4 in the Annex). Most of the households with youth receiving remittances are nonfarm households. This logic is twofold: on the one hand, nonfarm households are economically wealthier than other types of households so they have more resources to engage in migration; on the other hand, remittances sent back to these households strengthen their economic position which facilitates the transitions from agriculture to the RNFE.

9.4 Agricultural Policies Influencing Youth and Rural Transformation in Senegal

The employment outcomes of rural youth in Senegal are in part a consequence of the agricultural, employment, and rural development policies of the Senegalese government over the years. Policy interventions have an impact on rural labour markets as well as on agricultural productivity, shaping the challenges and opportunities rural youth face.

During the French colonization, the Senegalese agricultural sector was strongly state-guided. After the country's declaration of independence in 1960, the agricultural sector struggled to adapt, resulting in a deterioration of the sector and an elevated dependency on imported food (Oya and Ba 2013). After decades of weak performance in the agricultural sector, as of the year 2000, the sector regained national attention and a more active agricultural policy was put in place in order to economically revive the sector. As such, in the following years a set of large-scale policies were adopted, namely:

- the Agro-Sylvo-Pastoral Orientation Act (LOASP), which is the legal framework for the development of agriculture and the reduction of poverty in rural areas (2004);
- the Return to Agriculture plan (REVA) to promote youth employment in agriculture and avoid distress migration (2006);
- annual programs of structural adjustment in an attempt to reduce the dominance of the groundnut production and diversify agricultural production (2003–7); and
- the Great Push Forward for Agriculture, Food and Abundance programme (GOANA), aimed to increase domestic production of Senegal's main food and export crops (especially rice) and achieve self- sufficiency and food security by 2015 (2008).

In December 2013, the government launched the Emerging Senegal Plan (PSE) which has been the reference for economic and social policy in the medium and long term, with the aim of making Senegal an emerging economy by 2035. Job creation is a key priority for the PSE and the plan envisages increasing the decent work opportunities at the rate of 100,000 to 150,000 new jobs per year. In line with the PSE, new programmes and projects were initiated, including

- the Accelerated Programme for Agriculture in Senegal (PRACAS) which is the agricultural component of the PSE and the most important programme for agriculture (2014);
- the Programme to Promote Youth and Female Employment (PAPEJF), which aims to contribute to the creation of decent jobs for youth and women (2013); and
- the Project to Support the Promotion of Entrepreneurship of Youth in Rural Areas (PAJER) specifically targeting youth, entrepreneurship, and value chains (2015).

Acknowledging the specific lack of employment opportunities for youth, the National Agency for the Promotion of Youth Employment (ANPEJ) was created in 2014 to coordinate all youth-employment-related policies, envisaging policy coherence and efficient action. Moreover, a specific policy to promote youth employment in rural areas (PPEJMR, Politique de Promotion de l'Emploi des Jeunes en Milieu Rural) was under formulation in 2016 with the aim of addressing rural youth's lack of access to labour market information, productive resources, and entrepreneurial skills.

Between 2000 and 2012, many of the agricultural policies were ambitious and lacked policy coherence, which hampered the implementation. Moreover, there was more attention on agribusiness development, neglecting the needs of small-holders and rural youth (who often encounter obstacles in accessing land, credit, and so on). Also, migration policy was strongly focused on preventing rural migra-tion instead of efficiently managing the flows of migrants and the remittances to rural areas (Oya and Ba 2013, Antil 2010, Banque Mondiale 2006).

As shown in previous sections, the employment situation of rural youth did not improve significantly between 2000 and 2012. On the one hand, employment in agriculture decreased but this decrease was not offset by more productive jobs in the RNFE. The policies and programmes in place would have neither led to a diversification of agricultural production, nor did the country become self-sufficient in rice and other staple crops. On the other hand, poverty decreased in rural areas but farmers and households dependent on agriculture have less secure and more vulnerable employment and have a higher incidence of poverty than the rest of the population.

Since 2012, the new government has been implementing what appears to be a more coherent policy framework for the agricultural sector and rural development. The needs of rural youth and their employment challenges are specifically addressed in many programmes and projects such as the ones described above. As they are relatively recent, it will take some time to assess their actual implementation and impacts.

9.5 Conclusions

In Senegal, low agricultural productivity growth, fuelled by underinvestment in the sector and an unbalanced rural labour market, has led to a stagnant agricul-tural sector which has hampered the performance of the wider rural economy. Accordingly, rural economic development, in combination with a high population growth, has been too limited to enable significant results in reducing poverty in rural areas. This situation is creating major challenges for the rural population, in particular rural youth, to access productive and decent jobs.

The large majority of the rural population in Senegal is employed in agriculture, albeit there is a general downward trend in agricultural employment, particularly among rural youth. Data analysis shows that there has been a considerable reallo-cation of agricultural labour into urban areas and abroad, and to a lesser extent into the rural nonfarm sector. These patterns would indicate that a process of rural transformation is taking place in the country.

This gradual rural transformation is mainly brought forward by youth, who are entering the labour market, as their share of employment in the RNFE is growing faster than that of their older counterparts. However, some concerns emerge as the type of employment opportunities are being found in rural areas, as they are increasingly working as non-paid family workers in the RNFE, indicating that they are pushed out of agriculture rather than pulled by remunerative and decent employment opportunities in the nonfarm economy.

Rural youth and their families are increasingly diversifying incomes by engaging in the agricultural and the nonfarm sector. Education and wealth of the family are key factors driving such diversification at household level: more educated youth within wealthier families are more prone to engage in the RNFE than less educated youth from less wealthy families. Hence, complementing or substituting income with rural nonfarm employment is a livelihood strategy providing a pathway out of poverty.

Many Senegalese youth are leaving the rural areas altogether and migrating to urban areas or abroad. Once again, higher education and household wealth play a key role in determining who undertakes this pathway. Those who are more educated and wealthier are moving to urban areas or abroad, while the least educated youth from the poorest households are more likely to migrate to another rural area to find employment in the nonfarm economy. Youth who exit agriculture by migrating internally are most likely to find a job as self-employed in the nonfarm economy in urban areas.

In the past, the Senegalese government's actions to tackle structural problems and lift agricultural productivity in the rural economy have had insufficient results in terms of agricultural productivity and job creation, especially of youth. Conversely, a new generation of policies and programmes seems to be now in place, targeting rural youth's needs associated with financial support and a more supportive and stable policy environment. Developing the human capital of rural youth has become a priority for the government, although it is still necessary to further focus on enhancing the labour demand in rural areas.

To conclude, there remains a large untapped potential in the rural economy to boost opportunities for rural youth. Efforts to promote farmers' productivity and incomes would also be helpful, as the skills of the agricultural workforce, especially youth, are crucial to tap into this potential. Moreover, higher labour productivity reduces vulnerability and vice versa, and thus contributes to rural poverty reduction. At the same time, as young people may also exit agriculture, more jobs need to be created in off-farm agriculture-related activities. Development of midstream and downstream value chains promotes off-farm employment, providing opportunities for inclusive rural transformation.

The participation of young entrepreneurs should be ensured in this process of transformation, as well as the support for the development of agro-industry and infrastructure to better connect rural and urban areas. Improved connections between rural areas and nearby small urban centres can play a catalytic role in mediating the rural–urban nexus and providing small-scale producers with greater opportunities, as well as serving as hubs for a thriving nonfarm sector. It is therefore essential to support the dynamic development of employment opportunities.

Inclusive policies and more targeted investments in agricultural and rural development, leading to rural transformation, should be further strengthened to promote more and better opportunities for the younger generations, while at the same time helping to end rural poverty in Senegal.

Annex: Data Description

For the data analysis of youth employment in the rural nonfarm economy (RNFE), two nationally representative cross-sectional surveys were used: the second 'Senegal Household Survey' (ESAM-II), conducted in February–April 2001, and the 'Senegal Poverty Monitoring Survey' (ESPS-II), conducted in August–December 2011. Both surveys were implemented by the Senegalese National Agency for Statistics and Demography (ANSD) in cooperation with the World Bank and other UN agencies (United Nations Development Programme, World Food Programme, and ILO).

The surveys include questions on household composition, education, household welfare, labour characteristics, sources of income, and more specific farm features such as land and technology. ESAM-II pooled 6,624 households of which 3,240 were rural. ESPS-II surveyed in total 17,891 households of which 7,560 were rural.

To account for seasonal variation in agriculture, a 12-month recall period was used. Only a subsample (one-third) of the sampled households were administered the household consumption expenditure module that ESPS-II featured. Therefore, a separate household asset index that covered the entire sample was created to measure household wealth (following Sahn and Stifel 2003). The data used to create the 'commune size' variable was retracted from ANSD.

For the migration analysis, the 'Migration and Remittances Household Survey' (MRHS) implemented by the World Bank in 2009 was used (World Bank 2009a). The survey was conducted both at household and individual level and addresses labour market status, expenditure, motivation for migration, remittances, and so on. The MRHS surveyed a total of 17,878 individuals and 1,983 households, of which 36 per cent had no migrants, 30 per cent had internal migrants, and 34 per cent had international migrants.

For the purpose of this analysis, youth are defined as people between 15 and 34 years old and the working population is defined at 15–65 years old. All data allows controlling for rural/urban areas and sectors, as well as for main household and individual characteristics. All structure and growth figures reported are derived from weighted data.

Table 9.A1. Individual characteristics of rural youth employed according to sector of employment

2011 Rural areas (12-month reference)	Youth employed in agriculture (N = 10,021)		Youth employed in rural nonfarm economy (N = 2233)		T-test
	Mean	SE	Mean	SE	
Individual characteristics					
Age	23.05	0.06	25.39	0.11	
Female (%)	0.43	0.00	0.35	0.01	***
Married (%)	0.54	0.00	0.49	0.01	***
Years of schooling	1.70	0.03	3.11	0.09	
Household characteristics					
Age of HH head	52.13	0.15	50.39	0.33	***
Female HH head (%)	0.07	0.00	0.20	0.01	
Years of schooling of HH head	0.81	0.02	1.94	0.08	
HH size	14.38	0.08	12.54	0.14	***
Age dependency ratio	1.11	0.01	0.96	0.01	***
Wealth index (%)					
– Poorest tercile	0.65	0.00	0.36	0.01	***
– Middle tercile	0.25	0.00	0.35	0.01	
– Richest tercile	0.11	0.00	0.29	0.01	
Farm size (ha)	6.50	0.08	4.07	0.11	***
Land tenure (%)					
HH land owned	0.89	0.00	0.68	0.01	***
HH land rented in	0.07	0.00	0.04	0.00	***
HH land used for free	0.02	0.00	0.25	0.01	*
Distance to market (in km)	61.45	0.67	28.70	0.95	***
Community characteristics					
Population commune	6,2303	592.28	9,9709	3561.00	

Note: (a) Paired student t-test of youth employed in agriculture versus without youth employed in the rural nonfarm economy; (b) *** means statistical significance at 1% level, * means statistical significance at 10% level.

Source: Authors' calculations based on ESPS-II, 2011.

Table 9.A2. Households with youth characteristics according to sector of employment

Households with youth	Farming only HH (N = 3636) Mean	SE	Mixed farm—nonfarm HH (N=1961) Mean	SE	Nonfarm only HH (N=1602) Mean	SE	Paired t-test Farming-only versus mixed	Mixed versus nonfarm
Age of HH head	50.43	0.24	52.64	0.32	48.76	0.37		***
Female HH head	0.10	0.00	0.11	0.01	0.24	0.01		***
Married HH head	0.92	0.00	0.93	0.01	0.86	0.01		***
Years of schooling of HH head	0.81	0.04	1.29	0.07	2.41	0.11		
Household size	10.47	0.09	12.93	0.15	9.40	0.13		***
Age dependency ratio	1.27	0.01	1.15	0.01	1.14	0.02	***	
Wealth index								
– Poorest tercile	0.71	0.01	0.50	0.01	0.36	0.01	***	***
– Middle tercile	0.21	0.01	0.34	0.01	0.36	0.01		
– Richest tercile	0.07	0.00	0.16	0.01	0.29	0.01		
Farm size (ha)	4.81	0.09	4.81	0.13	3.28	0.10		***
Land tenure								
– HH land owned	0.86	0.01	0.83	0.01	0.58	0.02	***	***
– HH land rented in	0.05	0.00	0.06	0.01	0.02	0.00		***
– HH land sharecropped	0.01	0.00	0.02	0.00	0.01	0.00		
– HH land used for free	0.07	0.01	0.09	0.01	0.38	0.01		**
HH uses fertilizer	0.36	0.01	0.38	0.01			***	
HH uses agricultural equipment	0.49	0.01	0.45	0.01			***	
Distance to market (in km)	62	1.13	39	1.08	24	0.90	***	***
Population of commune	61,550	1,164	70,397	1,709	110,356	4,816	***	***

Note: (a) *** means statistical significance at 1% level, ** means statistical significance at 5% level.

Source: Authors' calculations based on ESPS-II, 2011.

Table 9.A3. Characteristics of migrated youth and their households according to labour transition

Youth (15–34 years old) migrants from rural areas	Agriculture to rural nonfarm economy N=70		Other transition from rural areas N=258		T-test
Individual characteristics of migrants before migration	*Mean*	*SE*	*Mean*	*SE*	
Female	0.03	0.02	0.23	0.03	***
Age of departure	22.27	0.65	20.33	0.39	**
Years of schooling before migration	1.65	0.35	4.34	0.38	***
Characteristics of former household of migrants					
Average household size	11.31	0.77	12.72	0.43	
Average monthly per capita expenditure	8,348	540	11,967	1,178	
Commune population	46,257	14,664	187,143	300,692	***

Notes: (a) Paired student t-test of youth labour transition agriculture to rural nonfarm economy versus youth other labour transition; (b) *** means statistical significance at 1% level, ** means statistical significance at 5% level.

Source: Authors' calculations based on MRHS 2009 from the World Bank.

Table 9.A4. Sector of employment of rural households by remittances status

HH with youth	Receiving remittances N=1187		Not receiving remittances N=651		T-test
	Mean	SE	Mean	SE	
Farming only HH	0.20	0.01	0.26	0.02	**
Mixed farm HH	**0.19**	0.01	**0.16**	0.01	
Nonfarm HH	0.51	0.02	0.56	0.02	***

Notes: (a) Paired student t-test of HH with 15–34 receiving remittances versus HH with 15–34 not receiving remittances; (b) *** means statistical significance at 1% level, ** means statistical significance at 5% level, * means statistical significance at 10% level.

Source: Authors' calculations based on MRHS 2009 from the World Bank.

References

Alobo Loison, S., and C. Bignebat. 2017. *Patterns and determinants of rural household income diversification in Senegal and Kenya.* Journal of Poverty Alleviation and International Development, 8 (1).

Anríquez, G., and K. Stamoulis. 2007. Rural development and poverty reduction: Is agriculture still the key. *Electronic Journal of Agricultural and Development Economics* 4 (1): 5–46.

ANSD. 2004. *Rapport de synthese de la deuxième Enquête Sénégalaise Auprès des Ménages (ESAM-II).* Dakar, Senegal: Agence nationale de la statistique et de la démographie.

ANSD. 2013. *Rapport définitif de la deuxième Enquête de Suivi de la Pauvreté au Sénégal (ESPS-II).* Dakar, Senegal: Agence nationale de la statistique et de la démographie.

Antil, A. 2010. *Les 'émeutes de la faim' au Senegel - Un puissant rélévateur d'une défaillance de gouvernance.* Paris, France: Institut Français des Relations Internationales.

Azam, J., and F. Gubert. 2006. Migrants' remittances and the household in Africa: A review of evidence. *Journal of African Economies* 15 (suppl_2): 426–62.

Banque Mondiale. 2006. *Développements récents et les sources de financement du budget de l'état. Revue des Dépenses Publiques.* Washington DC, U.S.A.: The World Bank.

Davis, B., S. Di Giuseppe, and A. Zezza. 2016. Are African households (not) leaving agriculture? Patterns of households' income sources in rural Sub-Saharan Africa. *Food Policy* 67: 153–74.

Davis, B., T. Reardon, K. Stamoulis, and P. Winters. 2002. *Promoting farm/nonfarm linkages for rural development: Case-studies from Africa and Latin-America.* Rome, Italy: FAO.

Dia, I. 2005. Déterminants, enjeux et perceptions des migrations scientifiques internationales africaines: Le cas du Sénégal. *Stichproben, Wiener Zeitschrift für kritische Afrikastudien* 8: 5.

Diagne, Y., and F. Diane. 2008. *Impact des transferts des migrants sur la pauvreté au Sénégal.* Document d'Etude N°07. Dakar, Sénégal: Ministère de l'Economie et des Finances du Sénégal, Direction de la Prévision et des Etudes Economiques.

ESAM-II. 2001. *La deuxième enquête sénégalaise auprès des ménages (ESAM II).* Dakar, Senegal: Agence nationale de la statistique et de la démographie.

ESPS-II. 2011. *Deuxieme enquête de Suivi de la Pauvreté au Sénégal (ESPS-II).* Dakar, Senegal: Agence nationale de la statistique et de la démographie.

Flahaux, M., C. Mezger, and P. Sakho. 2011. *La migration circulaire des Sénégalais.* CARIM Notes d'analyse et de synthèse 2011/62. San Domenico di Fiesole, Italy: Robert Schuman Centre for Advanced Studies, Institut universitaire européen.

Golub, S., and F. Hayat. 2014. Employment, unemployment, and underemployment in Africa. The Oxford Handbook of Africa and Economics (1): 136–153.

Guarcello, L. 2007. Understanding youth employment outcomes in Senegal. UCW Working Papers. Rome, Italy: University of Rome "Tor Vergata".

Hathie, I., I. Wade, S. Ba, M. Niang, X A. Niang. 2015. Emploi des jeunes et migration en Afrique de l'Ouest (EJMAO): Rapport final-Sénégal: IPAR.

Herrera, C., and D. Sahn. 2013. Determinants of internal migration among Senegalese youth. (No. 201308). CERDI.

ILO. 2008. *Promotion of rural employment for poverty reduction.* Report IV International Labour Conference, 97th Session, 2008, Genève, Suisse: International Labour Organization.

IOM. 2009. *Migrations au Sénégal: Profil national 2009.* Genève, Suisse: Organisation internationale des migrations.

Lambert, S., M. Ravallion, and D. Van de Walle. 2011. *Is it what you inherited or what you learnt? Intergenerational linkage and interpersonal inequality in Senegal.* Policy Research Working Paper No. 5658. Washington, DC., U.S.A.: The World Bank.

Leavy, J., and H. White. 1999. *Rural labour markets and poverty in Sub-Saharan Africa.* Brighton, U.K.: Institute of Development Studies, University of Sussex.

Maertens, M. 2009. Horticulture exports, agro-industrialization, and farm-nonfarm linkages with the smallholder farm sector: Evidence from Senegal. *Agricultural Economics* 40 (2): 219–29.

Mercandalli, S. and B. Losch, ed. 2017. *Rural Africa in motion: Dynamics and drivers of migration south of the Sahara.* Rome, Italy: FAO and Cirad.

Ndiaye, A., O. Niang, Y. Y. Ndione, and S. Dedehouanou. 2015. *Migration, remittances, labor market and human capital in Senegal.* (No. 2016-10). PEP-PMMA. Working Paper series 2016-10. Nairobi, Kenya: Partnership for Economic Policy (PEP).

Ndione, Y. C. 2015. *Senegalese rural households multiple livelihoods strategy: A potential solution for rural employment issues.* Dakar, Senegal: IPAR.

Oya, C. 2010. Rural labor markets in Africa: The unreported source of inequality and poverty. *CDPR Development Viewpoint* (57).

Oya, C., and C. Ba. 2013. *Les politiques agricoles 2000–2012: Entre volontarisme et incohérence.* Dakar, Senegal: IPAR.

Roubaud, F., and C. Torelli. 2013. *Employment, unemployment and working conditions in urban labor markets of Sub-Saharan Africa.* Washington, DC, U.S.A.: World Bank.

Sahn, D., and D. Stifel. 2003. Exploring alternative measures of welfare in the absence of expenditure data. *Review of income and wealth* 49 (4): 463–89.

Schaffnit-Chatterjee, C. 2014. *Agricultural value chains in Sub-Saharan Africa. From a development challenge to a business opportunity.* Frankfurt, Germany: Deutsche Bank Research.

Seck, A. 2016. Fertilizer subsidy and agricultural productivity in Senegal. *The World Economy*, 40 (9), 1989–2006.

Shaw, C. 2014. *Agricultural technology adoption in West Africa.* Doctoral dissertation, Texas A&M University.

World Bank. 2009a. *Migration and Remittances Household Survey (MRHS)*. World Bank Microdata Library. Washington, DC: World Bank. http://microdata.worldbank.org/index.php/catalog/534. Accessed 1 July 2016.

World Bank. 2009b. *Migration and Remittances Household Survey in Senegal*. World Bank Microdata Library. Washington, DC: World Bank. http://microdata.worldbank.org/index.php/catalog/534. Accessed 1 July 2016.

World Bank. 2014. *Situation Economique du Sénégal : apprendre du passé pour un avenir meilleur. Senegal economic update; no. 1*. Washington, DC; World Bank Group.

World Bank. 2016. *Country overview Senegal*. Washington, DC: World Bank. http://www.worldbank.org/en/country/senegal/overview. Accessed 1 July 2016.

World Bank. 2017. *World Development Indicators*. Washington, DC: World Bank. http://data.worldbank.org/data-catalog/world-development-indicators. Accessed 4 December 2017.

10

Conclusion

Valerie Mueller, Gracie Rosenbach, and James Thurlow

10.1 Overview

The prospect of widespread youth unemployment in Sub-Saharan Africa, and the social instability and political unrest that this could bring, is a major concern for governments, both in Africa and in developed countries. Most development strategies in Africa today emphasize the importance of creating more and better jobs for young people as the basis for achieving *inclusive* economic growth. Behind this focus on employment lies a sense of alarm or urgency, borne out of the view that Africa's 'youth bulge' is an unprecedented global challenge, and that African countries will struggle to absorb enough young job seekers over the coming decades. These concerns are perhaps most pronounced in *rural* Africa, where most of the world's poor population reside and where agriculture remains the primary income source for most households. The conventional view is that African youth do not aspire to work in agriculture, in part because the sector is characterized by low productivity and limited growth and is far from the dynamic lifestyles offered by cities. Yet employment prospects in urban areas are also limited and so most youth in Africa will inevitably need to find jobs somewhere in the rural economy.

Africa's youth bulge does present a challenge, but for many people it is also viewed as an opportunity to further rural development. A young and better-educated workforce could lead to greater use of more sophisticated farm technologies, commercial agricultural practices, and an expansion of rural nonfarm enterprises. These are crucial steps for accelerating agricultural transformation in Africa, and young men and women could be the 'agents of change' that the region so badly needs. The literature and debate around youth employment in Africa is therefore one of contrasts—between urgent concern on the one hand and cautious optimism on the other.

This book has questioned some of the stylized facts that underpin the prevailing narratives and policy debate about youth employment in rural Africa. Is Africa's youth bulge unprecedented? Are youth more likely to adopt modern farm technologies and practices? Are youth more likely to engage in rural nonfarm activities or migrate to urban centres? Are policymakers adequately responding to the youth employment challenge, and are rural youth themselves mobilizing and demanding policy reforms from their governments?

Valerie Mueller, Gracie Rosenbach, and James Thurlow, *Conclusion* In: *Youth and Jobs in Rural Africa: Beyond Stylized Facts*. Edited by: Valerie Mueller and James Thurlow, Oxford University Press (2019).
© International Food Policy Research Institute.
DOI: 10.1093/oso/9780198848059.003.0010

To address these questions, the book has presented a series of thematic and country case studies that analysed household and firm surveys across a range of country contexts. This approach differs from recent studies on youth employment in Africa, which have usually relied on country-level data and/or focus on regional trends. Our detailed country focus and use of survey data allowed us to better reflect the wide variations that are observed across and within African countries. The book's focus on *rural* Africa and the participation of youth in *agricultural* transformation also helps fill an important gap in the literature. This final chapter revisits the stylized facts and summarizes the authors' key findings.

10.2 Nuancing the Facts

10.2.1 Africa's Demographic Transition and Economic Trends are No Worse than Those of Other Developing Regions When They Experienced Their 'Youth Bulges' Three Decades Ago

Chapter 1 identified when developing regions experienced their peak youth bulges, as measured by the share of young people in the working age population. Africa's youth bulge peaked in the early-2000s, which was almost three decades later than in other regions. Population projections indicate that, by the middle of this century, Africa will be the only region contributing to growth in the global workforce. By then, Africa will need to create 30 million new jobs every year as its population expands. However, while the timing of Africa's youth bulge is unique, its scale is not. Youth were about a third of Sub-Saharan Africa's working age population in the early-2000s, which was close to what is was in other regions three decades ago. Thus, while the absolute size of Africa's youth bulge may be daunting from the view of smaller and more developed regions, it is more important to consider the youth bulge from the perspective of African countries themselves and ask whether they are able to absorb enough young job seekers.

Using historical data, including surveys and population censuses, Chapter 1 compared the economic conditions in Africa since the early-2000s to the conditions in other regions around the time of their youth bulges. Africa certainly faces different conditions today than other regions did in the past, including a more competitive global economy. However, there are areas where Africa's trends are no worse, and are sometimes better, than they were elsewhere. Africa in the early-2000s was at a similar stage of development as East Asia and South Asia were in the late-1970s and early-1980s. Although Africa has fallen short of emulating East Asia's pace and pattern of economic development, it has greatly exceeded the growth rates achieved in South Asia soon after its youth bulge peaked. Like Africa, South Asia experienced continued growth in its rural population, despite urbanization, but unlike Africa, agricultural growth in South Asia was almost nonexistent at that time, whereas agriculture has grown rapidly in Africa in recent years. Like other regions, Africa has significantly improved school enrolment, but not to the same extent as East Asia or Latin America, and the quality of schooling in Africa is of major concern. Overall, the authors concluded that Africa's youth bulge is not unprecedented, and that Africa may not have a 'youth problem' per se. Instead, Africa faces the broader challenge of creating better jobs for all of its working age population, both young and old alike. At the centre of this challenge is the need to transform African agriculture and the rural economy.

10.2.2 Evidence that Youth are More Likely to Adopt Improved Farm Technologies is Mixed, and Even Where It Exists, the Effect on Agricultural Productivity May Be Small

Raising agricultural productivity is the first step in transforming the agricultural sector, allowing farmers to, at a minimum, meet their own food needs. The prevailing view is that, because youth in Africa today are better educated and more familiar with information technology than adults, they are more likely to adopt advanced farm technologies and practices (e.g. use improved seeds and chemical fertilizers, or benefit from receiving extension services). Making agriculture attractive to youth also requires increasing farm *profitability*, which depends not only on agricultural intensification, but also commercialization. The question therefore is not whether youth are better educated than adults—they surely are— but whether youth are able to translate their education into more productive and commercial farming practices.

The five country case study chapters used nationally-representative surveys that spanned the post-2000 period and included information on farm input use and rural services. The authors found mixed evidence that young farmers use better technologies. **Chapter 5** on Ethiopia, for instance, found that youth-headed households were *less* likely to have received and used advice from extension officers, and more importantly, *less* likely to have used improved technologies, such as fertilizers, seeds, or row planting. That said, younger farmers in Ethiopia were found to be more likely than older farmers to use labour-saving technologies, such as tractors. Similarly, **Chapter 6** on Malawi found that young farmers (aged 15–24 years) use fewer modern inputs than older farmers, although input use was found to be higher when the more expansive definition of youth was used (ages 15–34 years). The authors concluded that it is only once youth become heads of their own households that they have a greater propensity than previous generations to seek out and use improved farming techniques. This underscores the importance of youth having access to farmland and thus being able to make decisions about farming practices. **Chapter 7** on Ghana found that it was education, rather than youth itself, that implied greater use of farm inputs. This is surprising, since younger farmers are often expected to be more open to new technologies and knowledge than older famers are, even when they have similar levels of schooling.

Overall, the new evidence presented in the country chapters suggests that it does not necessarily follow that having a younger population leads to greater adoption of improved farm technologies. Moreover, while education is strongly associated with the use of improved technologies, at least in our case study countries, the effect of input use on farm productivity may still be relatively small. This could explain why agricultural productivity growth in Africa has remained sluggish, despite substantial improvements in educational attainment.

10.2.3 Youth are More Likely to Engage in Rural Nonfarm Activities, but the Level of Off Farm Employment Remains Low and Most Youth Continue to Work in Agriculture

History suggests that higher agricultural productivity and commercialization leads to an expansion of the rural nonfarm economy, including the processing and trading of agriculture-related products, as well as other kinds of occupations that arise to serve nonfarm workers as they concentrate around rural markets. Thus, as agricultural transformation progresses, we expect to see more farm households diversify into nonfarm activities or even specialize in off-farm work. This process should create new job opportunities for rural youth, especially those without access to farm land. The prevailing view is that youth themselves, by being better educated and less inclined to work on the farm, may be well-positioned to establish rural businesses and drive this stage of agricultural transformation.

New evidence from our country case studies confirms that youth are generally more likely than adults to be employed in off-farm jobs. However, the extent to which this is true varies across countries, and its implications for rural trans-formation are unclear. **Chapter 5** on Ethiopia, for example, found that youth aged 25–34 years have a greater probability of working in nonfarm enterprises, but that the size of the nonfarm sector remains extremely small. While youth are driving growth in off-farm employment, the nonfarm sector itself is *not* a significant driver of rural transformation in Ethiopia. Similarly, **Chapter 6** on Malawi found little evidence of any significant process of rural transformation or of youth being in the vanguard of any changes in employment patterns. Malawian youth are more likely to extend their schooling than start new businesses in the rural non-farm economy, and once Malawian youth leave school, they are still more likely to work in agriculture.

Chapter 7 on Ghana is more supportive of the prevailing view. It found that youth are far more likely than adults to run nonfarm enterprises, especially in the less developed northern region of the country. However, Ghana is transforming rapidly and many households, irrespective of the age of their members, are leaving agriculture to work in the rural nonfarm economy. What is concerning, however, is that young Ghanaians are less likely than adults to find work in the formal sector, and instead engage in informal trading and other low-productivity occupations. Ghana's youth are participating in the country's structural change, but it is adults who are benefiting more from this process. As in Ethiopia and Malawi, the Senegalese case study in **Chapter 9** found that youth who leave agriculture are often pushed into unpaid family work in rural nonfarm enterprises, rather than being pulled into more remunerative and decent off-farm employment opportunities. Perhaps for this reason, most Senegalese youth who leave agriculture go in search of employment outside of the country.

Chapter 8 on Tanzania used firm-level data to examine the factors that determine the success of rural nonfarm enterprises. As in the other case studies, the authors found that youth are more likely than adults to engage, and even specialize, in rural nonfarm activities. However, amongst rural firms, those businesses that are run by adults are generally more productive than those run by youth. Overall, the five case study chapters reveal considerable differences across countries, but they all conclude that, even when youth are more likely to work in the rural nonfarm economy, they are also more likely to have low productivity jobs in the informal sector or run less successful nonfarm businesses. This limits the contributions of youth to rural transformation in these countries.

10.2.4 Education is Important for Rural Nonfarm Employment, but on Its Own it is not Enough to Ensure Success

A common finding across all five case study chapters is that people working in nonfarm jobs tend to have more years of schooling. This is often seen as one of the reasons why youth are more likely to work off the farm. **Chapter 8** on Tanzania, for example, found that households whose heads have at least secondary education are as much as 38 per cent more likely to engage in nonfarm activities. However, the returns to education may be lower for youth than for adults. As mentioned above, adults in Tanzania are far more likely to work in more productive sectors or run more successful nonfarm businesses. These households are also less likely to be poor.

Moreover, all the case studies identify factors other than education that are also important determinants for participation and success in off-farm work. **Chapter 7** on Ghana, for example, found that better access to markets, public transportation and electricity increase the likelihood of a rural household working in the non-agricultural sector, regardless of whether the household head is young or educated. **Chapter 6** on Malawi found that education alone is insufficient to enable youth to obtain nonfarm employment. The authors found that older Malawians are more likely to work in the nonfarm sector, and from this they concluded that capital accumulation, work experience, and the development of social and economic networks are more important than education in enabling individuals to find work outside of agriculture. **Chapter 5** on Ethiopia also found that younger youth (aged 15–24) are no more likely to engage in nonfarm work. The authors concluded from this that work experience and social networks may be important, beyond just education levels, which are higher for this age group.

Thus, while the higher education levels of youth are undoubtedly an asset, there is no guarantee that youth will lead or benefit from the rise in the rural nonfarm economy. Investing in education is therefore necessary but insufficient. Investments in infrastructure and market development are also important to ensure that youth (and adults) can participate in the process of agricultural transformation.

10.2.5 Participation in the Rural Nonfarm Economy Differs for Young Men and Women

Evidence on the roles of young men and women in the agricultural transformation process is mixed. On the one hand, **Chapter 6** found that males dominate off-farm employment in Malawi, whereas women are more likely to remain in agriculture. Interestingly, the authors find that women who recently gave birth are less likely to engage in nonfarm employment of any sort, whereas infant care does not appear to affect the extent to which women engage in farm work. **Chapter 9** also found that young men in Senegal are more likely than young women to be employed in the rural nonfarm economy, possibly reflecting the large education gap between men and women in this country. As in Malawi, Senegalese men were also found to be more likely than women to emigrate in search of work.

In contrast, **Chapter 7** found that being a female-headed rural household in Ghana increased the probability that the household engages in nonfarm activities, although this relationship weakens over time. Although **Chapter 8** found that men and women in Tanzania are almost equally likely to work in the rural nonfarm economy, the authors also found that women are less likely to run more productive or successful nonfarm enterprises. Female-run enterprises in Tanzania tend to be in lower-value manufacturing, such as food processing, rather than higher-value services. It should be noted, however, that these gender differences are less important than other factors, such as education, in explaining why some businesses are successful. One implication from this is that investing in women's education in Tanzania, and possibly elsewhere, should help close the gender gap by allowing young women to participate in and benefit more from agricultural transformation.

10.2.6   Youth are More Likely to Migrate, but not Always for Work Reasons or to Urban Areas

Agricultural transformation is initially driven by increases in agricultural prod-uctivity and then by deepening farm-nonfarm linkages as farmers commercialize and rural markets become more important. Eventually, however, the focus shifts to supplying urban consumers in fast-growing cities and towns. At this stage, workers in rural areas may decide to migrate in search of better job opportunities in urban areas. Agriculture continues to be the core of the rural economy, but the national economy is increasingly driven by urban development. The prevailing view is that, given land shortages in rural areas and higher returns to education in urban areas, youth are more likely than adults to migrate, and may therefore con-tribute more to economic growth and structural change.

Chapter 2 used household panel survey data to examine the pattern of migra-tion in four African countries, and to evaluate what determines youth decisions to migrate in two of these countries. The author found that younger people are more likely to migrate. However, most migration is between rural areas, rather than to cities and towns, and the main reasons for migrating are often not work-related. Rural–rural migration, for example, is higher amongst women and is often motiv-ated by marriage. Migration distances are also quite short. In contrast, workers who move to urban areas are not only more likely to claim moving for employ-ment reasons, but they also travel far greater distances. That said, there is consider-able variation across countries. In Ethiopia, for example, many young migrants to urban areas move to attend secondary schools that are unavailable in rural areas.

Migration generally leads to greater income diversification, but new migrants often work in agriculture before finding employment in the nonfarm sector. Chapter 2 found that, in Malawi and Tanzania, migration to urban destinations offered more employment opportunities for youth in the non-agricultural sector. However, while the probability of finding a job in a high-return activity is higher for youth who move to urban areas, this does come with greater risk of becoming unemployed. In contrast, intra-rural migration also promotes income diversifica-tion, but migrants are less likely to work exclusively in rural nonfarm jobs, and the income gains from migration are smaller.

The author of Chapter 2 concludes that rural–urban migration in Malawi and Tanzania facilitates the movement out of agriculture, usually into higher-return activities. However, only a small share of rural youth become rural–urban migrants. In contrast, far more youth are likely to migrate between rural areas and so this is the more formative mobility pattern in the transformation process. It is the main driver of income diversification amongst youth, although it rarely involves a shift into exclusive non-agricultural employment. This means that, while youth are more likely to urbanize than adults, the importance of this for youth and for structural change should not be overstated.

10.2.7   Rural Nonfarm Job Opportunities are Better Closer to Bigger Cities, but Jobs in the Food System may be More Important Closer to Smaller Towns

As mentioned above, the case studies found that access to urban markets is a major factor in determining the likelihood of youth working in the rural nonfarm sector. However, two of the case studies also found that it is important to differentiate between urban centres of different sizes. Chapter 6 on Malawi, for example, found that better access to *large* urban centres of 50,000 people or more is strongly associated with nonfarm employment, but that proximity to smaller urban centres had little influence on the employment choices of youth in surrounding rural areas. The authors concluded that smaller towns have less of a role to play in changing labour patterns and contributing to structural change in Malawi.

Chapter 7 on Ghana conducted more detailed analysis of how urbanization affects employment outcomes for youth and adults. The authors found that proximity to large cities in the south of the country greatly increased the likelihood of a household engaging exclusively in non-agricultural work. The authors also found that manufacturing is more dominant in areas that are less urbanized (i.e. closer to smaller towns than bigger cities). This is because informal manufacturing in these rural areas primarily consists of food processing for local markets, which can take place at the household level. In contrast, households living closer to big cities are more likely to have members employed in the service sector, including jobs in the formal sector and outside of the agriculture-food system. Unlike in Malawi, the authors conclude that smaller towns in Ghana are important for promoting youth employment in rural areas. The difference between the two countries may be that economic growth and urbanization are slower in Malawi and less of the country's rural population live in peri-urban areas. In fact, Malawi's rural population density is one of the highest in Africa. For these reasons, the linkages between small towns and rural areas in Malawi may be weaker, or less important, than they are in Ghana.

10.2.8   Youth are Only Slightly More Likely to Protest than Adults, but They are More Likely to be Driven by Concerns about Unemployment

Some of the concerns about youth employment in Africa stem from the view that underemployed youth are especially prone to anti-government behaviour, including public protests and violence. A contrasting view is youth are better educated today and so may place more demands on their governments to enact policy reforms that address employment issues. Chapter 4 examined the political participation of youth using historical data on local protests and household surveys from 16 African countries. The author asked whether youth are more likely to protest than adults, and if the issues that motivate youth have changed over time?

She found that youth are more likely to protest than adults, but that the gap is extremely small, suggesting that concerns about youth protest may be overstated. Protest activity is a form of mobilization used in almost equal measure by both age groups. For young and old, being better educated and/or poor are strong motivators for protest. However, the author found that young people are also more likely to protest if they are unemployed and if they lack trust in political institutions. If governments in Africa wish to avoid protests, then youth employment needs to be a high priority, and job creation projects need to match young people's skills and aspirations. Governments need to generate greater trust that youth policies and initiatives are aimed at enhancing youth's *long-term* economic prospects rather than simply mobilizing their short-term political support.

10.2.9 Youth Employment is Now a Major Policy Goal, but the Means of Achieving this Goal are not Well Represented in Current Policies

Creating more and better jobs for youth is a major policy priority for most African countries today. This differs from the early-2000s, when policies often focused on poverty reduction rather than job creation (i.e. on 'pro-poor' rather than 'inclusive' growth). However, making youth employment a policy goal does not necessarily mean that national policies include the kinds of interventions needed to promote youth employment. **Chapter 3** developed a framework for systematically classifying policies based on whether they adequately address key constraints to youth employment in rural areas. The authors applied the framework to 47 national, rural and agricultural policies in 13 African countries.

They found that policies tend to be strongest on labour supply issues, such as self-employment and skills development. Most national policies, for example, emphasize rural education as a means of improving the prospects of young job seekers. Policies are much weaker on labour demand issues, such as how to stimulate private sector job creation in the agriculture-food system beyond the farm—an area that the country case study chapters identified as being particularly important for rural youth. Industrial policies, for example, rarely identify concrete interventions for private sector development or discuss how demand for young rural workers will be incentivized. As the case study chapters found, rural youth are far less likely than adults to be employed in the private sector, and so national policies should explicitly support informal businesses in rural and peri-urban areas.

The authors found that social and policy dialogue is the weakest area in the design of national policies. A lack of participation by rural youth in the policy process means that their specific needs are given insufficient attention. For example, policies rarely identify *rural* youth as a target group, but instead focus on youth in general, often implicitly giving greater weight to the needs of urban youth. This is alluded to in **Chapter 4** on the political participation of youth, which discussed the commonly-held view that rural youth are less likely than urban youth to use protest to demand policy reforms from their governments. Governments need to promote institutional channels that enable youth to participate in decision-making, such as cooperatives, producers' organizations, and youth associations.

10.3 Way Forward

There is clear need to strike a better balance between alarm and optimism when it comes to Africa's youth bulge. Addressing youth employment in Africa is a global challenge, but it is one that was overcome by other developing regions when they experienced a similar demographic transition three decades ago. The pressure to create jobs in rural areas is particularly acute, given that Africa's rural population is growing, and its rural economy is still underdeveloped. Yet even in rural areas there is cause for optimism. Evidence suggests that agriculture is transforming in many African countries, albeit slowly, and that youth are often participating in this process. More needs to be done by governments to help young farmers adopt better technologies and run successful rural businesses. To do this, however, we need a better understanding of the constraints facing African youth. This book provided new evidence that allowed us to revisit some of the stylized facts that shape the policy dialogue around youth employment in rural Africa. Further research is needed:

First, global and regional studies have helped position youth employment as a major policy objective within the global development community. However, the insights from our case studies confirm that more detailed analysis is needed at country and subnational levels. Country case studies are more likely to reveal the unique characteristics of national employment dynamics and structural change and provide a firmer basis for decision-making. More importantly, our findings revealed major variations within countries, such as between peri-urban areas outside small towns versus big cities, or between young men versus women. Studies that rely on national and cross-country data cannot provide the information needed to design policies that address the specific needs of different geographies and population groups.

Secondly, more and better survey data is needed on employment, migration, and businesses in rural areas. The case studies showed how many rural workers are engaged in multiple farm and nonfarm activities, yet data on secondary employment and part-time work is often quite limited. More information is needed on migrant and emigrant workers, including the economic relationships they have with households in home countries and rural areas. Finally, more data is needed on rural firms. Household surveys are crucial for understanding workers' constraints, but many businesses in rural Africa are not household enterprises and so are not captured by household surveys. It is difficult to design policies to promote private sector development in the rural nonfarm economy without information on what makes some businesses successful and others not.

Finally, national policies need to be evaluated based on their contributions to achieving employment goals, including youth employment in rural areas. Chapter 3 in this book showed how current policies often fall short of addressing the constraints facing young job seekers. However, policies should be evaluated, not just on their design, but on their implementation and outcomes. Understanding the gap between design and implementation, for example, requires multidisciplinary approaches that consider both political and economic constraints in the policy process. While the scale of policy reforms and actions needed to address Africa's youth bulge is daunting, there is fortunately an increasing alignment of interests and incentives: African governments have made youth employment a policy priority, and African youth are demanding policies that improve their job prospects. This creates promising opportunities to enact policies that effectively address rural youth employment—policies that are grounded in local evidence rather than stylized facts.

Index